New Perspectives on Gender and Migration

Routledge/UNRISD Research in Gender and Development

1. New Perspectives on Gender and Migration
Livelihood, Rights and Entitlements
Edited by Nicola Piper

United Nations Research Institute for Social Development

UNRISD is an autonomous agency engaging in multidisciplinary research on the social dimensions of contemporary problems affecting development. Its work is guided by the conviction that, for effective development policies to be formulated, an understanding of the social and political context is crucial. The Institute attempts to provide governments, development agencies, grassroots organizations and scholars with a better understanding of how development policies and processes of economic, social and environmental change affect different social groups. Working through an extensive network of national research centres, UNRISD aims to promote original research and strengthen research capacity in developing countries.

Current research programmes include: Civil Society and Social Movements; Democracy, Governance and Well-Being; Gender and Development; Identities, Conflict and Cohesion; Markets, Business and Regulation; and Social Policy and Development. For further information on UNRISD work, visit www.unrisd.org.

New Perspectives on Gender and Migration

Livelihood, Rights and Entitlements

Edited by
Nicola Piper

Routledge
Taylor & Francis Group
New York London

Routledge
Taylor & Francis Group
270 Madison Ave,
New York NY 10016

Routledge
Taylor & Francis Group
2 Park Square, Milton Park,
Abingdon, Oxon, OX14 4RN

© 2008 by United Nations Research Institute for Social Development (UNRISD)
Routledge is an imprint of Taylor & Francis Group, an Informa business

Transferred to Digital Printing 2009

International Standard Book Number-13: 978-0-415-95649-9 (Hardcover)

Except as permitted under U.S. Copyright Law, no part of this book may be reprinted, reproduced, transmitted, or utilized in any form by any electronic, mechanical, or other means, now known or hereafter invented, including photocopying, microfilming, and recording, or in any information storage or retrieval system, without written permission from the publishers.

Trademark Notice: Product or corporate names may be trademarks or registered trademarks, and are used only for identification and explanation without intent to infringe.

Library of Congress Cataloging-in-Publication Data

New perspectives on gender and migration : livelihood, rights and entitlements / edited by Nicola Piper.
    p. cm. -- (UNRISD research on gender inequality in an unequal world ; 1)
Includes bibliographical references and index.
ISBN 978-0-415-95649-9 (hardback : alk. paper)
    1. Women immigrants. 2. Women alien labor. 3. Women's rights. 4. Social stratification. I. Piper, Nicola.

JV6347.N48 2007
305.48'96912--dc22
                                2007007138

ISBN10: 0-415-95649-8 (hbk)
ISBN10: 0-415-87449-1 (pbk)

ISBN13: 978-0-415-95649-9 (hbk)
ISBN13: 978-0-415-87449-6 (pbk)

Visit the Taylor & Francis Web site at
http://www.taylorandfrancis.com

and the Routledge Web site at
http://www.routledge.com

Contents

Figures vii
Tables ix
Foreword xi
Acknowledgements xiii

1 International Migration and Gendered Axes of Stratification: Introduction 1
   NICOLA PIPER

2 Finding a Place in Stratified Structures: Migrant Women in North America 19
   MONICA BOYD AND DEANNA PIKKOV

3 Gendered Migrations, Livelihoods and Entitlements in European Welfare Regimes 59
   ELEONORE KOFMAN

4 Gendered Migration in Oceania: Trends, Policies and Outcomes 101
   SIEW-EAN KHOO, ELSIE HO AND CARMEN VOIGT-GRAF

5 Gender, Migration and Livelihoods: Migrant Women in Southern Africa 137
   BELINDA DODSON

6 Feminised Migration in East and Southeast Asia and the Securing of Livelihoods 159
   NICOLA PIPER AND KEIKO YAMANAKA

7 Gendered Migrations in the Americas: Mexico as Country of
   Origin, Destination and Transit   189
   MARTHA LUZ ROJAS WIESNER AND HUGO ÁNGELES CRUZ

8. Political Participation and Empowerment of Foreign Workers:
   Gendered Advocacy and Migrant Labour Organising in
   Southeast and East Asia   247
   NICOLA PIPER

9. Using Human Rights Law to Empower Migrant Domestic
   Workers in the Inter-American System   275
   MARGARET L. SATTERTHWAITE

Contributors   323
Index   327

Figures

2.1 Categories of admission for immigrants admitted to Canada 1990–2000 (January 1–December 31)   24
2.2 Categories of admission for immigrants admitted to the United States, 1990–2000 (April 1–March 31)   25
2.3 Percentage female in annual admission of permanent residents, Canada and the United States, 1990–2000   26
2.4 Percent in the labour force, foreign born and native born population age 25–64, by sex, Canada (2001) and the United States (2000)   38
3.1 International migration by category of entry, selected OECD countries, 2004, harmonised data   63
4.1 Percentage of female settler arrivals to Australia by migration category, 1991–2005   107
4.2 Percentage of female settler arrivals (primary migrants and accompanying spouses) by visa category, Australia, 1993–2005 and 1999–2000   107
4.3 Percentage of female temporary migrants and accompanying family members, Australia 1996–1997 and 2000–2001   109
7.1 Mexico. Temporary work-related migrants residing in Mexico, by sex, according to the time period of their most recent trip to the United States   200
7.2 Chiapas. Entry of documented Guatemalan agricultural workers 1995–2003   219

Tables

2.1 Percent distribution of immigrants by source area, Canada and the United States, 2001 — 23
2.2 Percentage of total admission of immigrants in the family and economic categories who are females, 1990–2000 — 27
2.3 Percentage of total admissions of immigrants on the basis of humanitarian criteria who are females, 1990–2000 — 29
3.1 Percentage of women in the immigrant population in selected European countries — 64
3.2 Female employment by sector and birth status — 65
3.3 Percentage of women in highly skilled occupations — 71
3.4 Female employment rates 1995–2004, homestate women 15–64 years — 84
3.5 Typology of welfare regimes, migration and female employment — 86
3.6 Employment of women by nationality in selected countries — 89
3.7 Employment of foreign-born by sector, 2003–2004 average — 90
4.1 Settler arrivals to Australia by migration category, 1991–2005 — 105
4.2 Employment rates, labour force participation rates and unemployment rates for women and men born in Asia and the Pacific Islands, and total overseas born, aged 25–54 years, by duration of residence in New Zealand, and New Zealand-born aged 25–54 years, 2001 — 117
4.3 Occupational classifications of labour market tested work permit holders in New Zealand by gender, 2003–04 — 120
4.4 Occupational categories of emigrants from Fiji by gender, 1990–2002 — 122
5.1 Maximum number of people to be admitted in quota work permit categories (Republic of South Africa, 2003) — 152

Tables

6.1	Number of unskilled female migrant workers by sending country and proportion of females in total outflows, 1979–1996	164
6.2	Occupation, immigration status, country of origin, and number of unskilled female migrant workers by receiving country/economy and percentage of total number in the early 2000s	166
7.1	Mexico. Index and degree of migratory intensity by state, 2000	198
7.2	Mexico. Temporary work-related migrants residing in Mexico, by sex and various sociodemographic characteristics, according to the time period of their most recent trip to the United States	201
7.3	Mexico. Percentage distribution of temporary migrant women who return from the United States, according to various characteristics, 1993–1997 and 1998–2000	203
7.4	Mexico. Mexican agricultural workers working in Canada, by sex, 1974–2002	208
7.5	Mexico. Cases of 'aseguramiento' [holding] of foreigners, according to regional INM office, 2001–2003	223
7.6	Chiapas. Total cases of 'aseguramiento' [holding] and holding of foreign women, by region of origin, 2001 and 2004	225
7.7	Chiapas. Cases of 'aseguramiento' [holding], according to principal country of origin, by sex, 2001 and 2004	226

Foreword

Over the past two decades, international migration has resurfaced as a prominent feature of contemporary social and economic life. This is reflected in current political and scholarly debates in countries across the world. In this context both researchers and policy actors are paying increasing attention to a variety of problems, both economic and social, that are linked to migration, as well as the opportunities that such flows are creating for the countries, communities and migrants involved. Migration is less and less a definitive movement; it involves instead a constant flux of people, resources and ideas within and between countries. It also involves new trends such as feminization, illegality, temporary and circular, and South-South movements.

This book examines recent theoretical and empirical developments in international migration from a gender perspective. Its main objective is to analyse the diversification and stratification of gendered migratory streams to highlight the key axes of differentiation among male and female migrants with regard to skill level, legal status, country of origin, and mode of entry. In turn a migrant's position in relation to these axes influences access to entitlements and rights and the securing of livelihoods in the countries of origin and destination alike. Unlike previous works, the global outlook of this book highlights the significance of intra-regional migration and allows for comparison across regions.

Many of the chapters that appear in this volume were commissioned as background papers for the 2005 UNRISD report, *Gender Equality: Striving for Justice in an Unequal World*. UNRISD would like to thank the European Union, the Department for Research Co-operation of the Swedish International Development Agency (Sida/SAREC), the International Development Research Centre (IDRC, Ottawa, Canada) and the government of the Netherlands for their financial support for making this work possible.

Thandika Mkandawire
Director
UN Research Institute for Social Development

Acknowledgements

I owe a great deal of gratitude to a number of individuals and institutions that have contributed to this volume. This publication project was conceived while I was working at the UN Research Institute for Social Development (UNRISD) as a Consultant in 2004. I would like to thank Dr. Shahra Razavi (research coordinator, Gender Programme) for inviting me to spend six months in Geneva assisting with the preparation of UNRISD's flagship report *"Gender Equality – Striving for Justice in an Unequal World"* (2005) which was an invaluable experience for me and a wonderful environment to work in. Dr. Razavi did a great job coordinating not only the compilation of the UNRISD report but also the subsequent publication of the series of five volumes of which this anthology is part.

I would like to acknowledge the input of various colleagues who generously took the time to read some chapters and make constructive comments. In particular I am indebted to Professor Eleonore Kofman, Dr. Parvati Raghuram, and Deanna Pikkov.

No anthology can be produced without willing contributors and I thank all of the individual authors for their initial interest, their original and high-quality research work which has fed into this volume, and the great spirit with which they helped shape this book. Three of the chapters in this book were originally commissioned as background papers for the above mentioned UNRISD report. I would like to thank those authors for their revisions and up-dates, and the newly recruited authors for providing the missing material and discussions which give this book a truly global outlook. And many thanks to those individuals who may have provided editorial and other assistance to the individual authors but whose input I am not aware of.

I am indebted to the following individuals for technical and other assistance: Paul Keller for his great job translating the chapter by Rojas Wiesner and Ángeles Cruz which was originally written in Spanish; Manjit Kaur and Laavanya Kathiravelu (both research assistants at the Asia Research Institute, National University of Singapore) for their editorial and formatting assistance as well as psychological support during the final weeks of this project; and last but not least Routledge's editor Benjamin Holtzman.

During the final stage of preparing this manuscript, I was invited to spend one month at the Centre for East and South-East Asian Studies, University of Lund, as Visiting Fellow. I would like to thank Professor Roger Greatrex and Dr. Kristina Joensson for making this happen, in order to provide me the much needed 'quiet' space to give this book its final touch.

Nicola Piper
Singapore

1 International Migration and Gendered Axes of Stratification
Introduction

Nicola Piper

Major advances have been made over the last few decades in migration research resulting in an abundant theoretical and data rich literature on gendered aspects of cross-border movements. It is now well established that gender is a crucial factor in our understanding of the causes and consequences of international migrations and it has been amply shown that gender is relevant to most, if not all, aspects of migration (Carling 2005; Piper 2005a; Donato et al. 2006). Political change or policies may affect men and women differently, resulting in gendered patterns of migration; laws regarding both emigration and immigration often have gendered outcomes; and policies that affect the integration, or re-integration, of migrants into societies may also affect men and women differently. This has implications for male and female migrants' livelihoods, rights and entitlements. In turn, the ways in which migrants engage as civic and political actors in the process of migration are also often mediated by gendered norms, expectations, and opportunities for agency.

Gender intersects with other social relations, such as class and/or caste, migration status, ethnicity and/or race, generational cleavages, etc. Taken together, a complex map of stratification emerges with its own dynamics of exclusion/inclusion and power relations. It is important to highlight these dynamics in both destination and origin countries to emphasize that migrants *leave and enter* gendered and stratified societies (with qualitative and quantitative differences depending on specific context). This book, in fact, examines the various axes of stratification and the implications on gender with regard to contemporary forms of international migration from a cross-regional comparative perspective.

From a broad perspective, the chapters in this volume are concerned with outlining recent trends and shifts in migration patterns and policies from a gender perspective. Furthermore, the discussions of these changes within gendered migrations also highlight the *regional* nature of some of these movements and the (policy, legal) responses to them (see Dodson, Piper and Yamanaka, Rojas Wiesner and Ángeles Cruz, Satterthwaite, all this volume). 'Regional', here, refers to flows within, for instance, Asia or Africa. From an empirical viewpoint, these constitute vast areas, and in fact most of the individual chapters which are based on qualitative data discuss sub-regional flows (such as East and South East Asia, Southern Africa, Central America). Such regional outlook allows for a cross-regional comparison, a rare aspect that is missing from many existing volumes on gendered migration which have tended to focus on one region only (such as Kofman et al. 2000; Andall 2003; Tastsoglou & Dobrowolsky 2006).

It is a fairly common phenomenon for scholars on women in migration to focus on one specific type of migrant worker or type of employment/sector. Domestic work in particular has been given much attention (e.g. Huang et al. 2005; Ehrenreich & Hochschild 2002) to the neglect of other types of work or mode of entry. The contributions by Boyd and Pikkov, Kofman, and Khoo et al. (this volume) investigate migrant women's labour market position vis-à-vis home-state women, and most chapters discuss the socio-economic and legal differences between various types of migrant women, as well as migrant women in relation to migrant men.[1] In this sense, a gender analysis and a focus on women go hand in hand and this is what the notion of 'gendered axes of stratification' is trying to capture.

SHIFTS IN GLOBAL MIGRATION FLOWS AND POLICY

Globally, the landscape of international migration has become increasingly diversified as a result of broader changes in the global economy and geopolitics in addition to policy shifts in recent years. An increasing propensity for people to move between countries during and after working life can be witnessed in all regions of this world. International migration has become a global phenomenon leaving few countries unaffected by international flows (UN 2004). It has, thus, become an established feature of contemporary social and economic life globally, indicative of the continuing salience of migration in its two major manifestations: economic migration (work) and forced migration owing to persecuting (asylum). It is not surprising that cross-border mobility has, in general, attracted a great deal of international policy attention in recent years (ILO 2004; GCIM 2005; UNFPA 2006). Academic studies on contemporary flows of migration have since the 1980s increasingly acknowledged and highlighted a wide range of issues related to one of the key features of contemporary migration flows today: its feminisation. This specific aspect has also been highlighted by United Nation (UN) agencies and the policy-making community (UNFPA 2006; UNRISD 2005; UN 2004; ILO 2004). The feminisation of migration is connected to at least four phenomena: (1) improved statistical visibility, partly related to a changed perception of women-dominated migration as 'work migration' in its own right (see Rojas Wiesner & Ángeles Cruz, this volume); (2) the increasing participation of women in most, if not all, migration streams; (3) the increasing inability of men to find full-time employment in the origin countries; and (4) the growing demand for feminized jobs in destination countries.

Global estimates by sex confirm that for more than 40 years since 1960, female migrants reached almost the same numbers as male migrants. By 1960, female migrants accounted for nearly 47 out of every 100 migrants living outside their countries of birth. Since then, the share of female emigrants among all international migrants has been rising steadily, to reach 48 per cent in 1990 and nearly 49 per cent in 2000. By 2000, female migrants constituted nearly 51 per cent of all migrants in the developed world and about 46 per cent of all migrants in the developing countries (ILO 2003: 9). Just as women's economic contribution to their families and communities has become increasingly significant, so too has women's presence in migration flows. This is reflected in the increasing percentages of women in migration flows to all world regions.

In 2002, the proportion of legal migrants to the United States (US) was 54 per cent. In Southeast and East Asian countries that admit migrants exclusively for temporary labour purposes, the share of independent women in the labour migration flows has been increasing sharply since the late 1970s (ILO 2003: 9), and in some cases, women clearly dominate over their male counterparts. The Philippines have now surpassed Mexico as the world's largest labour exporting country. South Asia is mainly a labour exporting sub-region where women's (official) mobility is subject to serious restrictions (with the notable exception of Sri Lanka). Hence, countries such as Bangladesh and Nepal predominantly send male migrants, with the fewer numbers of women migrating being largely confined to the skilled categories or to the use of unofficial channels (Siddiqui 2001; Dannecker 2005).

Research on gendered migration from a regional perspective is still in its infancy in much of Africa and Latin America which is partly related to the unavailability, or patchy nature, of statistical data (Dodson, this volume; Rojas Wiesner & Ángeles Cruz, this volume). Feminisation is particularly evident in flows from both Central and South America to Southern Europe. In Africa, high levels of poverty, disease and male unemployment explain the steady increase in female migrants at a rate that is faster than the global average (UNFPA 2006: 23). With regard to intra-regional migration, in both Africa and Latin America, women seem to dominate short-range migration streams involving immediate border crossings for trading or service-sector related jobs, rather than longer-range migration to destinations far afield. Although women's participation in the latter has been on the increase, it appears that men still dominate this stream (see also Kofman, this volume, who points to women constituting a minority among migratory streams from Africa to Europe). Sub-Saharan African women are highly represented among migrating health workers, especially nurses, many of whom migrate across regions (Dovlo 2006; Buchan & Calman 2004). Out-migration of health workers is a well studied phenomenon and a controversial component of the debate on the migration-development nexus.

These global trends indicate new developments in terms of the scale of international migration and entry of women into migration streams that used to be dominated by men (i.e. women as independent economic migrants and main income earners) (UN General Assembly 2004). The demand in feminised sectors has become so strong that there is some evidence of male migrants attempting to enter feminised streams (especially nursing) because of the legal channels and breadth of destinations 'on offer'.[2] More research, however, is required on this issue.

On the whole, statistics on international migration by gender that make it possible to identify the characteristics of migrants is still uneven across countries (see e.g. Rojas Wiesner & Ángeles Cruz; Dodson, this volume). Moreover, much of the available data refers to stocks rather than flows. Inevitably, most surveys also underestimate those entering in an irregular manner and the undocumented as well as the extent of transient circulation (Morokvasic 2003; Asis 2005). The high presence of women in informal and unregulated types of jobs, restrictions on their right to work, and involvement in activities that are deemed to be criminal offences or against public order (e.g. prostitution) mean that a higher proportion of women are statistically invisible. Gender analysis, however, should not be limited to statistics broken down by sex alone. Rather, it ought to raise awareness about broader social factors that influence women's and men's roles, and their access to resources, facilities, and services. The analysis of the role of gender in migration should, therefore, be mainstreamed into social policy agendas by governments in the destination as well as origin countries (UNRISD 2005).

On the national level, international migration has also attracted a great deal of policy attention. The reasons stem in part from xenophobic political considerations in destination countries, but also from the process of ageing under way in most industrialized countries posing new challenges to the care economy. There are also concerns about brain and skills drain from the perspective of developing countries. Countries of origin have also begun to show increasing interest in their nationals residing overseas[3] and the benefits of their remittances or investments. Within and beyond these considerations, there are gendered ramifications of migratory processes.

With regard to patterns and nature of today's migration flows, major policy concerns relating to international migration that have been highlighted in the existing literature or policy documents can be summarized as follows: (1) rising numbers of irregular/undocumented migration; (2) increasing shift toward temporary and circular migration as opposed to permanent settlement (involving the skilled and less skilled); (3) related increasing 'bifurcation' between skilled and less skilled migration in the ease of migration between countries; (4) increased deterioration of human security and human displacement; and (5) the impact of migration on economic and social development. All of these issue areas have gender implications.

One of the main aspects this book deals with is the trend toward increasing diversification and polarization, resulting in highly stratified migratory movements. The notion of 'polarization' highlights the differences between skilled and less skilled. 'Diversification' refers to intra-group differences (e.g. as demonstrated by Rojas Wiesner & Ángeles Cruz, this volume; Mexicans in the US today are more diverse in terms of skill, place of origin, modes of entry etc.; 'Asians' in Australia constitute a highly diverse group, see Khoo et al., this volume) as well as inter-group differences (more nationalities have appeared on the migration 'scene' than before; the number of destination countries has increased with more countries having shifted from being a purely 'sending' to becoming simultaneously destination countries; there is also more diversity with regard to the temporal component: migrants of a specific nationality might migrate either on a long-term or short-term basis to the same destination). Hence a statement such as "49% of Filipino migrants are male and 52% female" actually says very little.

As demonstrated in the chapters by Khoo et al. and Boyd and Pikkov (this volume), diversification has also become part of the traditional 'settler' countries' experience. There are more temporary migrants today than before, and in addition, there is also more out-migration of 'native' citizens from 'settler' countries, as recent work on the Australian diaspora, for instance, has shown (Hugo et al. 2003). This raises the issue of replacement migration (which to date is probably best studied in the context of health worker migration). All of this renders the separation of countries into categories of 'senders' and 'receivers' meaningless.

Last but not least, 'stratification' emphasizes the combined effects of gender, ethnicity, legal status, skill level, and mode of entry or exit. This is also played out geographically: migrants with high socio-economic status tend to go to higher income and more developed countries (i.e. the US, Canada, Europe, Hong Kong, Singapore) as the fees charged and the skills demanded are higher. Religion, and social norms associated with it, also plays a certain role with some Muslim countries giving preference, and being preferred, by migrants of the same faith (e.g. Indonesian domestic workers going in larger numbers to West Asia than elsewhere). Asian women migrating within Asia tend to be less qualified and belong to no higher than lower-middle class, hence many of them migrate to closer destinations within the region (Oishi 2005: 111). The gendered and geographic stratification of migration has implications on labour market experience, entitlements and rights.

THE ROLE OF GENDER IN STRATIFIED AND POLARIZED MODES OF ENTRY

Migrants leave and enter already gender segregated labour markets in the origin and destination countries. This is related to gendered social norms as reflected, among others, in gendered access to education in their country of origin and different access to skill training at the destination which results in gendered human capital accumulation. Migrants are subject to gendered dimensions of state regulation 'at home' and 'abroad'. The feminisation of migration from certain countries is often an indicator for rising male un- or under-employment (Sassen 2003). In addition, it is also a signifier of the social acceptance of women's presence in the workforce, due to certain historical processes such as women's pull into plantation work under colonialism or as part of specific economic development processes, such as export-led industrialization and/or focus on investment in the tourism industry (Oishi 2005; Piper 2002).

Increasing female migration is not always a signifier of their increased freedom of movement or increased independence (Erel et al. 2003). As temporary contract workers on legal work permits, both male and female migrants are often tied to one specific employer in one specific line of work — and when this is a job classified as 'unskilled' and is linked to the informal sector of the economy, this results in limited wage earning power and has thus implications for sustaining family members back home — i.e. for the livelihood of migrants. This is compounded by the emergence of a complex 'migration industry' with the involvement of brokers and recruiters who charge various types of fees, often exceeding 'legal' ceilings (Verité 2005). Furthermore, labour laws are often not enforced, the freedom of association is widely violated, and undocumented migration is tacitly approved and legal status denied by many receiving states. While two of the male-dominated sectors are classified as the most dangerous types of work — construction and agriculture — domestic work has also been recognized as one of the most vulnerable types of employment with high levels of isolation and widespread occurrence of abusive practices (ILO 2004). As women in lower skilled jobs often end up in (certain) reproductive spheres of the labour market (as domestic workers, sex workers), they work in jobs that are socio-legally not recognized as 'proper' work.

At the same time, more women today are among the professional and skilled category of migrants but often within feminised sectors such as health and education (Khoo et al., Boyd & Pikkov, Kofman, all this volume). It is, in fact, the increasing significance of employment in health which has been subject to a number of global studies (e.g. Kingma 2005, Buchan & Calman 2004) as well as in relation to gendered welfare states and the crisis of care (Kofman, this volume). As welfare and social professionals, migrant women are often compelled to accept subordinate and less secure employment. They are often not provided with the same quality of benefits that other white-collar workers might expect when working abroad such as housing, transportation and family relocation (Van Eyck 2004). Although classified as skilled workers, this does not necessarily come with a permanent residence permit. Many jobs in the health and education sectors are contracted and highly dependent on the labour market situation, as exemplified in the recent changes in the United Kingdom (UK)'s hiring procedure. This makes, among others, family reunification a difficult, if not impossible, decision.

What this indicates is that the migration landscape is constantly changing with increasing levels of complexity — and so are the gender issues involved. A complex system of inequalities has emerged not only between countries located in the North and South, but also within the South itself (Oishi 2005; Dodson, this volume; Piper & Yamanaka, this volume) as well as within the North as exemplified by migration from EU Accession countries to the more established European Union (EU) member states (Morokvasic et al. 2003; Kofman, this volume). Hence, migration has to be placed in a broader context — analytically and empirically — than often done to capture the complex picture of gendered axes of stratification.

In the chapters by Khoo et al., Boyd and Pikkov, Kofman, and Piper and Yamanaka (this volume), the category of 'female migrant' is broken down to show the differences between skilled migrant women and the lesser skilled, refugee or trafficked women and migrating wives. As a result, in each category, migrant women tend to face more obstacles and sources of discrimination than the average male migrant based on modes of entry open to them and the types of jobs they perform. This has implications for their access to citizenship, rights and entitlements.

National policies toward regulation and practices governing the entry and residence of migrants have changed to some extent in recent years. Industrialized countries in Europe, North America and Oceania still admit permanent residents on the basis of three long-established principles: family reunification, economic considerations and humanitarian concerns. However, there has been an increasing move towards a dilution of 'settlement' principles in ways that favour the needs of the labor market. Policy makers are increasingly urged to tailor migration selection to meet these demographic and economic needs. As a result, 'guest worker' type of regimes are re-emerging (ILO, 2004). Although present in all types of migrant categories, the majority of migrant women still enter via family reunification schemes in the 'North' (Kofman, this volume; Boyd & Pikkov, this volume; Khoo et al., this volume), most women migrate as independent contract workers or as irregular workers in much of the 'South' (Piper & Yamanaka, this volume; Dodson, this volume).

The increasing shift toward temporary and circular migration as opposed to permanent settlement in the highly developed destination countries is differently experienced by migrants according to skill, gender, and ethnicity. The increasing bifurcation between skilled and less skilled migration in the ease of cross-border movement between countries is accompanied by a clear gender bias, with most highly skilled migrants being male (intra-company transfers, Information Technology [IT] workers, etc.) (Kofman, this volume; Boyd & Pikkov, this volume). With women dominating certain sectors (household, sex/entertainment, sweatshop), they are also prominent in this category of migrants. Official policy, however, largely neglects this group of migrants and, as a result, the numbers of undocumented migrants are high.

It has to be noted that the categorisation into skilled and less skilled type of workers requires closer examination through a gender lens. Ironically, many skilled women become less skilled migrant workers purely because of the lack of demand in the jobs they are qualified for — a phenomenon referred to as 'de-skilling' (Kofman, this volume). This has in particular been noticed in regard to two highly feminised jobs: nursing and domestic work. Despite their classification (by immigration policies) as skilled migrants, de-skilling has been highlighted by existing studies as a common phenomenon experienced by foreign nurses. With domestic work constituting the major legal channel available to women in most regions of this world, including West and Southeast Asia[4], it is not rare to find fairly well educated women taking on this type of job categorised as 'unskilled'. At the same time, there are less skilled women who are turned into skilled migrant workers because of the otherwise controversial nature of their jobs or of their physical mobility. For instance, in the Philippines, the government classifies women departing to Japan, Korea and Taiwan on the entertainer visa as 'professional overseas performing artists'. A recent study by the International Organisation for Migration (IOM) (2003: 65) describes the classification of entertainers as professional or skilled as an "anachronism" because most of the women are rarely trained as professional entertainers or performing artists. At the same time this raises a feminist concern about 'reproductive' or 'care work' often not being considered as requiring skills. In a similar vein, Dodson (this volume) highlights the narrow interpretation of skills in South Africa's new Immigration Act characterized by "hard-nosed economic imperatives" which clearly favour men. Another example is provided by the case of Bangladesh: as the out-migration of less skilled Bangladeshi women is banned by the government, female factory workers in Malaysia are classified as skilled to allow them to migrate legally.[5] Thus, the official categories of 'skilled' and 'unskilled' need deconstructing to expose their social embeddedness, as argued by Dodson (this volume). Commonly used classifications do not always reflect or recognize the actual level of skill or professionalism but are rooted in the economic and gender disparities that exist between origin and destination countries as well as within societies.

One of the key subjects of debate in Europe as well as North America and Australia regarding refugee women, is the extent to which women have access as asylum seekers and are subsequently able to gain recognition either as Geneva Convention refugees, a secondary status or even less secure humanitarian protection. It is clear that women are less able to reach western countries as principle applicants due to their lesser resources. The potential and actual under-representation of women in various humanitarian-based modes of entry reflects the gendered nature of the definition of a refugee associated with the UN 1951 Convention (Boyd 1998; Boyd & Pikkov, Kofman, Khoo et al., all this volume). National policies have rarely addressed these gender issues with the notable exception of Canada and Australia (Boyd & Pikkov; Khoo et al., this volume).

LIVELIHOODS, ENTITLEMENTS, AND RIGHTS

Migrants leave and enter societies via a variety of channels or migration schemes. What we can increasingly observe globally is a tendency toward 'bifurcation' between skilled and less skilled migration in the ease of migration between countries, with the skilled typically being offered 'better deals' with regard to entitlements and rights. The supply and demand structures of specific types of migrants follow gender stereotypes and roles, and the rights and entitlements that are attached to, or the result of, specific modes of entry are, therefore, also gendered. When a gender dimension is incorporated into the analysis, it brings to the fore the *social* dimensions of the issues under investigation. In the specific context of migration, this is to remind us of the daily reality of migration and the actual situation of migrants who are in need of employment, health care, housing, security and education. Access to entitlements is determined by formal and informal sets of rules and regulations defined by law, social norms and conventions. An analysis of differentiated access to systems of rights or entitlements and the issue of how access in turn impacts on welfare, well-being and agency of individual migrants could shed light on social inequality based on gender (cf. Truong 1997).

The concept of 'entitlements' has been adopted by First World writers and needs to be distinguished from 'rights'. 'Entitlements' refer to "actually existing (rather than only moral and legal) claims that people can make on a range of resources in order to meet culturally defined standards of a good life".[6] Following Sen's definition, Lister (2006) argues that entitlements are not just a matter of legal rights but also of social rules and norms. She also notes that the distinction between rights and entitlements is not always clear. In some respects, the issue of what constitutes rights and entitlements corresponds to the distinction between de facto and substantive rights in the migration literature which is derived from the context of migration of the highly developed North (Kofman 2006; Piper, 1998). The relevance of this Northern debate on entitlements for migrants in high income countries in the developing world is a matter for further discussion. The chapters by Boyd and Pikkov and Kofman (this volume) place the discussion of entitlements not only within the framework of gendered migration but also in the context of the overall erosion of entitlements. In this sense, the notions of entitlements and rights might move even closer together (see below).

The concept of livelihoods is used in this book to refer to capabilities, assets and strategies that people use to make a living.[7] Although conventionally used by development scholars to refer to means and strategies for maintaining and sustaining life in the context of underdevelopment, livelihoods is used here more broadly as a synonym for jobs or incomes in the context of constrained circumstances or 'tenuousness of existence'[8] (as exemplified in the chapters by Boyd & Pikkov, and Kofman, this volume). In the context of gender, the term originally emerged from writings about women in the Third World, but it is argued here that 'livelihoods' can be appropriately applied to the situation of migrants in the developed destination countries where we can observe a wide range of different migrant configurations. The point, thus, made is that it is misleading to divide the world of work conceptually in a way that suggests that mixtures of formal and informal work do not exist in rich countries. As shown above, migrants, and more so migrant women, are predominantly not in full-time secure employment but over-represented in care services, home-based informal service provisioning and small- or medium-sized businesses of various kinds. By discussing migrant women in their multiple and stratified roles or categories, the notion of 'livelihoods' allows us to go beyond employment and incorporate different forms of living and acquiring incomes and resources, e.g. paid and unpaid caring, social transfers etc.[9]

From the perspective of origin countries — many of which fall under the category of lesser or low developed countries — access to, and the ability to remain in, paid overseas work constitutes an ever more important means to secure livelihoods (Briones 2006). Existing studies have shown that it is in particular single and married women who increasingly carry the burden of their households' survival (Olwig & Nyberg-Sørensen 2002; Oishi 2005; Sassen 2003). Emigration is thereby an important strategy used by women to do so.

The increasing presence of women in migration streams are largely the result of men's inability to find employment on the one hand, and employers' needs and market demands in feminised sectors on the other. In addition, as noted by Dodson (this volume), women's securing of livelihoods can also be connected to the urge of wanting to escape patriarchal control and gender-based discrimination or abuse.

In a highly political environment of restrictive immigration controls which constrain migration as a livelihood strategy for many, coupled with oppressive development policies which have obliterated livelihood access in countries of origin, seriously undermine the beneficial outcomes of migration (Briones 2006). By focusing on the issues of livelihoods, entitlements and rights, this book's central objective is to unravel the complexities of gendered migrations with the aim to bridge the social, political and economic spheres of migration and migrants' lives from the perspective of the destination and origin countries.

THE RIGHTS OF MIGRANTS

Much of the debate on the rights of migrants has focused on the legalistic aspects revolving around the existing international law framework for the protection of migrants (Cholewinski 1997; Aleinikoff & Chetail 2003; Satterthwaite 2005) or on more specific rights, such as political rights (Layton-Henry 1990), and this has typically occurred in the context of liberal states' role as countries of immigration (Joppke 1998). Another angle taken by existing scholarship is (formal) citizenship, with the starting point being again the perspective of 'proper' immigration, where settlement and family reunification is an option. This does not, however, reflect the situation of increasing numbers of temporary migrant workers or the undocumented (Piper 2006). It has also been argued that demanding citizenship rights could actually be detrimental for migrant women's ability to access work abroad in a non-western, non-liberal context (Bell & Piper 2005).

As shown above, emerging policies by destination governments result in increasingly stratified rights and entitlements. Citizenship is becoming less important for the skilled who obtain most rights via permanent residency status. At the same time, changing citizenship is becoming easier for the privileged and the toleration of dual citizenship is increasing (Dauvergne, forthcoming). For the lesser skilled, citizenship is of less immediate importance than accessing overseas employment in general (Briones 2006). International migration of both, the skilled and lesser skilled, is set up increasingly as circulatory and, therefore, not closely in tune with citizenship. The skilled, however, enjoy overall a greater range of benefits and choices to do with unequal access to the permanent residency (PR) status and the opportunity to settle (as in the US, Canada, Australia and New Zealand in particular) which is largely denied to the lesser skilled, although it has been noted that even the permanence of PR is being affected by pressures of globalization (Dauvergne, forthcoming).

Rights as a concept easily conjure up the image of a legalistic approach focusing "on what the law says" by downplaying the dynamic aspects of the political processes at play (VeneKlasen et al. 2004). The chapters by Piper and Satterthwaite (this volume) address the limitations of traditional rights approaches that place the content of international law at the core of rights work instead of noting the importance of starting with an understanding of rights as a political process and the notion of "rights as a work in progress" (VeneKlasen et al. 2004). When rights exist on paper, the challenge lies in guaranteeing their implementation and institutional avenues for claiming them. When rights are not recognized by governments, efforts to advance and expand rights not yet enshrined in law are highly important (Piper 2006; VeneKlasen et al. 2004).

By introducing a social movement or activist perspective into the academic debate on the human rights of migrants, Piper (this volume) follows Johnston (2001) by taking a social scientific perspective on rights. This means that rights first appear not when governments recognize them, but when people begin demanding and exercising them.[10] It is through meaningful organisations that such an enabling environment can be created leading to the empowerment of workers through education, knowledge provision and collective action. But political organizing of migrants is also gendered. "The gendered nature of organisational structures involved in the political struggle for the recognition of migrants' rights does not only reflect gender segregated labour markets but also the gendered nature of law" (Piper, this volume, chapter 8; see also Satterthwaite, this volume).

The subject of migrants' rights thus clearly emerges as an issue broader than national citizenship[11] and typically relates to debates on international human rights. What we can broadly observe regarding the legal situation of migrants is that there are serious protection gaps largely to do with changing migration patterns and the dominance of certain types of migrants who have emerged as particularly vulnerable, especially migrant women (Piper & Satterthwaite, 2007). It is in particular foreign workers' rights which have been described as among, if not *the,* least clear and enforced group of human rights targeting marginalized groups such as refugees, women, and children.[12] The lack of recognition of migrants' rights in practice means migrants have little real access to rights which is largely related to political and cultural bias against foreign workers (Gosh 2003). Migrants' rights are in fact a highly contested subject as is also reflected in the low ratification rate of migrant specific human rights instruments. Another major reason, however, is the absence of a social movement capable of supporting the rights of all migrants, legal and undocumented, and the lack of advocacy in the field of migration policy (Thouez 2005). There are, however, interesting developments in this regard in several parts of this world (Piper 2005b).

Reflecting the increasing participation of women in economic migration streams, gender perspectives have more recently been introduced into the debate on the human rights of migrants. It has been argued that the protective capacity of existing human rights law is inadequate in the case of certain jobs that are predominantly carried out by women (Piper & Satterthwaite, forthcoming). Also, the intersecting forms of discrimination based upon multiple identities of women rather then race or migrant status alone has led to legal scholars arguing for a comprehensive approach to the otherwise scattered nature of international legal instruments which typically address just one such identity at a time (Satterthwaite, 2005 and this volume). The 1990 UN Convention on the Rights of All Migrant Workers and their Families (CRMW) might in fact not be the most suitable international human rights document for advocating and ensuring migrants and migrant women's rights. This is similar with regard to the International Labour Organization's (ILO) migrant specific instruments and the ILO's principles of equality and non-discrimination. Ensuring equity with native workers under the ILO conventions and the UN Convention may not be sufficient, particularly for women working in sectors where there is no protection for native workers either. In this context, creative advocacy is crucial in bridging the fragmented nature of international human rights instruments, as argued by Satterthwaite (this volume).

Moreover, it is, in fact, on the regional level that we can observe promising developments with regard to acknowledgement and promotion of migrant workers' rights (Satterthwaite, this volume). Regional human rights bodies play an important role in consolidating a rights-based approach to migration. The most progressive example here is the Inter-American Human Rights System and the creation of its own Rapporteurship on migrant workers. It could, therefore, be argued that it is at the regional rather than global level where substantial progress can be made with regard to migrants' rights. Multilateral binding instruments are often perceived by states as open-ended undertakings which compromise their sovereignty in the migration area. Therefore, regional agreements could be seen as less threatening.

A further angle which complicates the discussion of the human rights of migrants is provided by Rojas Wiesner and Ángeles Cruz (this volume) by highlighting the role of Mexico not only as migrant origin but also as a transit and destination country. The rights of incoming migrants have not been as much politicized as the rights of Mexicans in the United States. For cases such as Mexico, which are State Parties to the CRMW and which have shifted from being a sole migrant origin to becoming also a destination country, this raises a number of important issues with regard to human rights obligations. The post-apartheid challenges faced by South Africa which is eagerly attempting to remove race- and gender-based forms of discrimination for its citizens can easily result in the producing of a new non-South African 'other with lesser rights (Dodson, this volume).

SITUATING THIS BOOK CONCEPTUALLY AND EMPIRICALLY — CONCLUDING REMARKS

This book's main objective is to analyze the diversification and stratification of gendered migratory streams to highlight the key axes of differentiation among male and female migrants with regard to skill level, legal status, country of origin, and mode of entry. In turn, a migrant's position in relation to these axes influences access to entitlements and rights and the securing of livelihoods in the country of origin and destination alike. Unlike previous works, the global outlook of this book highlights the significance of intra-regional migration and allows for comparison across regions.

Furthermore, the global perspective provided by the chapters in this volume shows that on the macro level, migration policies show a certain degree of convergence with regard to two major trends: (1) the intensified hunt for the highly skilled; and (2) the crack-down on irregular or undocumented migrants, many of whom are represented in lower or unskilled types of jobs. The two broad streams of the skilled and less skilled (regardless of legal status) are both comprised of male and female migrants but with qualitative and quantitative differences between and among them, some of which more subtle than others. The concern with "skill" (in a narrow definition) and "economic competitiveness" on the part of destination countries might exacerbate the already existing hierarchy of rights and entitlements. Further questioning of the social construction of 'skill' is required to address the female deficit among existing populations of skilled migrant workers. This would also be of relevance to the current debate on the developmental impact of migration on origin countries (UN 2006).

Apart from macro level convergences, the chapters in this book also demonstrate the existence of a 'multiple unevenness' with regard to gendered migrations — uneven in terms of research/data on gender (less on Africa and Latin America than on North America, Europe and Asia; uneven in that certain types of migrants are better researched than others); uneven in terms of rights and entitlements across the various groups of migrants with women highly represented among the worst off; and uneven political activism by and on behalf of migrants.

NOTES

1. The chapters do not discuss men-to-men relations.
2. There is some evidence of men taking up feminised professions in order to migrate (Manalansan IV, 2006). In the Philippines, for instance, cases of medical doctors have emerged who retrain as nurses in order to access the international labour market (personal communication, Dr. Maruja M.B. Asis, Scalabrini Migration Center, Manila).
3. In the literature, these are often referred to as "diasporas" or "transnational communities" which are two contested concepts in terms of their usage within social sciences (as opposed to history).
4. Domestic work is the single most important job category in the Gulf States mostly taken up by Indonesians, Sri Lankans and Filipinas. There are 250,000 Foreign Domestic Workers (FDWs) in Hong Kong, and of 500,000 foreign workers in total, 150,000 in Singapore are FDWs.
5. Personal e-mail communication with Dr. Petra Dannecker, November 10, 2005.
6. This refers to the definition given by UNRISD in an unpublished background paper.
7. See also Oxfam (www.oxfam.org.uk/what_we_do/issues/livelihoods/introduction.htm; downloaded on 07/18/2006).

8. I owe this last expression to Parvati Raghuram, email communication, 20 June 2006.
9. I owe this point to Eleonore Kofman, personal communication from 11 September 2006.
10. Johnston relates this to his discussion of citizenship and I extend this here to a broader human rights discussion.
11. Citizenship as a concept is, however, not irrelevant but it takes on a different meaning in the context of transnational political activism (see Ball and Piper 2002 and Rodriquez 2002).
12. As in the 1951 Geneva Refugee Convention, the Convention on the Elimination of All Forms of Discrimination against Women (CEDAW) and the Convention on the Rights of the Child (CRC).

REFERENCES

Aleinikoff, T.A. and V. Chetail (eds.) (2003), *Migration and International Legal Norms*, The Hague: T.M.C. Asser Press.

Andall, J (ed.) (2003) *Gender and Ethnicity in Contemporary Europe*, Oxford: Berg.

Asis, M.M.B (2005) 'Recent Trends in International migration in Asia and the Pacific', in: *Asia-Pacific Population Journal*, vol. 20(3): 15–38.

Ball, R.E. and N. Piper (2002) 'Globalisation and Regulation of Citizenship — Filipino Migrant Workers in Japan', in *Political Geography* (special issue), vol. 21(8): 1013–1034.

Bell, D. and N. Piper (2005) 'Justice for Migrant Workers? The Case of Foreign Domestic Workers in East Asia', in: Will Kymlicka and Baogang Ye (eds.), *Asian Minorities and Western Liberalism*, Oxford University Press, 2005, pp. 196–222.

Boyd, M. (1998) 'Gender, Refugee Status and Permanent Settlement', *Gender Issues* vol. 16(4), pp. 5–21.

Briones, L. (2006) 'Beyond agency and rights: capability, migration and livelihood in Filipina experiences of domestic work in Paris and Hong Kong', Unpublished PhD Thesis, Centre for Development Studies, Flinders University of South Australia.

Buchan, J, and L. Calman (2004) *The Global Shortage of Registered Nurses: An Overview of Issues and Actions*, Geneva: International Council of Nurses.

Carling, J. (2005) 'Gender dimensions of international migration', *Global Migration Perspectives No. 35*, Geneva: GCIM. (http://www.gcim.org/mm/File/GMP%20No%2035.pdf)

Cholewinski, R. (1997) *Migrant Workers in International Human Rights Law — Their Protection in Countries of Employment*. Oxford; Clarendon Press.

Dannecker, P. (2005) 'Transnational Migration and the Transformation of Gender Relations: the Case of Bangladeshi Labour Migrants', in: *Current Sociology*, vol. 53(4): 655–674.

Dauvergne, C. (forthcoming) 'Migration Law-Citizenship Law Dichotomy', in: Seyla Benhabib and Judith Resnick (eds.), *Citizenship, Gender and Borders*, New York: New York University Press.

Donato, K., D. Gabaccia, J. Holdaway, M. Manalansan IV, Patricia Pessar (2006) 'A Glass Half Full? Gender in Migration Studies', *International Migration Review*.

Dovlo, D. (2006) 'Ghanaian Health Worker on the Causes and Consequences of Migration', in: K. Tamas and J. Palme (eds.), *Globalizing Migration Regimes*, Aldershot: Ashgate, pp. 118–130.

Ehrenreich, B. and A. R. Hochschild (eds.) (2002) *Global Woman: Nannies, Maids and Sex Workers in the New Economy*. New York: Metropolitan Books.

Erel, U., M. Morokvasic, K. Shinozaki (2003) 'Introduction. Bringing gender into migration', in: M. Morokvasic-Mueller, Umut Erel and Kyoko Shinozaki (eds.), *Crossing Borders and Shifting Boundaries, Vol. I: Gender on the Move*, Opladen: Leske + Bude, pp. 9–22.

Global Commission on International Migration (2005) *Migration in an Interconnected World: New Directions for Action'*, Geneva: GCIM.

Gosh, B. (2003) 'A Road Strewn with Stones: Migrants' Access to Human Rights', *Paper prepared for the International Meeting on Access to Human Rights*, Guadalajara, January 17–18, 2003, Geneva: International Council on Human Rights Policy

Huang, S., B.S.A. Yeoh and N. Abdul Rahman (eds.) (2005) *Asian Women as Transnational Domestic Workers*, Singapore: Marshall Cavendish.

Hugo, G., D. Rudd and K. Harris (2003) *Australia's Diaspora: Its Size, Nature and Policy Implications*. CEDA Information Paper No 80. Melbourne: Committee for the Economic Development of Australia.

ILO (2003) *Preventing Discrimination, Exploitation and Abuse of Women Migrant Workers: An Information Guide — Booklet 1: Why the Focus on Women International Migrant Workers*. Geneva: ILO.

ILO (2004) *Towards a Fair Deal for Migrant Workers in the Global Economy*. Geneva: ILO.

ILO Socio-Economic Security Programme (2004) *Economic Security for a Better World*, Geneva: ILO

International Organisation for Migration (IOM) (2003) *World Migration Report*, IOM: Geneva

Johnston, P. (2001) 'Organize for What? The Resurgence of Labor as Citizenship Movement', in H. Katz and L. Turner (eds.), *Rekindling the Movement: Labor's Quest for Relevance in the 20th Century*, Ithaca: Cornell University Press

Joppke, C. (1998) 'Why Liberal States Accept Unwanted Migration', *World Politics*, vol. 50(2): 266–93.

Kingma, M. (2005) *Nurses on the Move — Migration and the Global Health Care Economy*, Ithaca: Cornell University Press.

Kofman, E. (2006) 'Migration, Ethnicity and Entitlements in European Welfare Regimes', in: A. Guichon, C. van den Anker and I. Novikova (eds.), *Women's Social Rights and Entitlements*, Basingstoke: Palgrave, pp. 130–54..

Kofman, E., A. Phizacklea, P. Raghuram and R. Sales (2000) *Gender and International Migration in Europe*, Routledge, London.

Lister, R. (2006) 'Gendered Social Entitlements: Building blocks of women's citizenship', in: A. Guichon, C. van den Anker and I. Novikova (eds.), *Women's Social Rights and Entitlements*, Basingstoke: Palgrave, pp. 8–18.

Manalansan IV, M. F. (2006) 'Queer Intersections: Sexuality and Gender in Migration Studies', in: *International Migration Review*, vol. 40(1): 224–249.

Morokvasic, M. (2003) 'Transnational Mobility and Gender: A View from Postwall Europe', in: M. Morokvasic-Mueller, Umut Erel and Kyoko Shinozaki (eds.), *Crossing Borders and Shifting Boundaries, Vol. I: Gender on the Move*, Opladen: Leske + Bude, pp. 101–136.

Morokvasic-Mueller, M., U. Erel and K. Shinozaki (eds.) *Crossing Borders and Shifting Boundaries, Vol. I: Gender on the Move*, Opladen: Leske + Bude.

Oishi, N. (2005) *Women in Motion — Globalization, State Policies, and Labor Migration in Asia*, Stanford: Stanford University Press.

Olwig, K.F. and N. Nyberg-Sørensen (eds.) (2002) *Work and Migration: Life and Livelihoods in a Globalizing World*, London: Routledge.

Piper, N. (2006) 'Economic Migration and the Transnationalisation of the Rights of Foreign Workers — A Concept Note', *ARI Working Paper Series No. 58*, February 2006, ARI: Singapore (http://www.nus.ari.edu.sg/pub/wps.htm)

Piper, N. (2005a) 'Gender and Migration', commissioned background paper for the Global Commission on International Migration', Geneva: GCIM (http://www.gcim.org/en/ir_experts.html)

Piper, N. (2005b) 'Rights of Foreign Domestic Workers — Emerging of Transnational and Transragional solidarity?, in: *Asian and Pacific Migration Journal*, vol. 14(1-2): 97–120.

Piper, N. (2002) 'Global labour markets and national responses: legal regimes governing female migrant workers in Japan', in: Gills, D.-S. & Piper, N. (eds.), *Women and Work in Globalising Asia*, London: Routledge, pp. 188–208.

Piper, N. (1998) *Racism, Nationalism and Citizenship: the Situation of Ethnic Minorities in Germany and Britain*, Aldershot: Ashgate.

Piper, N. and M. Satterthwaite (2007) 'Migrant Women', in: R. Cholewinski, R. Perruchoud and E. Macdonald (eds.), *International Migration Law: Developing Paradigms and Key Challenges*, The Hague: T.M.C. Asser Press.

Rodriguez, R. M. (2002) Migrant Heroes: Nationalism, Citizenship and the Politics of Filipino Migrant Labor," *Citizenship Studies*, 6(3): 341–356.

Sassen, S. (2003) 'The feminization of survival: alternative global circuits', in: M. Morokvasic-Mueller, Umut Erel and Kyoko Shinozaki (eds.), *Crossing Borders and Shifting Boudnaries, Vol. I: Gender on the Move*, Opladen: Leske + Bude, pp. 59–78.

Satterthwaite, M. (2005) 'Crossing Borders, Claiming Rights: Using Human Rights Law to Empower Women Migrant Workers', *Yale Human Rights and Development Law Journal*, no. 8, pp. 1–66. (also on: http://papers.ssrn.com/abstract=680181).

Siddiqui, T. (2001) *Transcending Boundaries: Labour Migration of Women from Bangladesh*, Dhaka, The University Press.

Tastsoglou, E. and A. Dobrowolsky (eds.) (2006) Women, Migration and Citizenship: Making Local, National and Transnational Connections, Avebury: Ashgate.

Thouez, C. (2005) 'Convergence and divergence in migration policy: the role of regional consultative processes', *Global Migration Perspectives No. 20*, Geneva: GCIM (http://www.gcim.org).

Truong, T.-D. (1996) 'Gender, international migration, and social reproduction: Implications for theory, policy, research and networking', in: *Asian and Pacific Migration Journal*, vol. 5(1): 27–52.

UNFPA (2006) *A Passage to Hope — Women and International Migration*, New York: UNFPA.

United Nations (2006) *International Migration and Development — Report of the Secretary General*, New York: United Nations.

United Nations (2004) *Women and International Migration, World Survey on the role of women in development — Report of the Secretary-General*, New York: United Nations.

UNRISD (2005) *Gender Equality — Striving for Justice in an Unequal World*. Geneva: UNRISD.

Van Eyck, K. (2004) *Women and International Migration in the Health Sector*, Ferney-Voltaire Cedex: Public Services International.

VeneKlasen, L., V. Miller, C. Clark and M. Reilly (2004) 'Rights-based approaches and beyond:challenges of linking rights and participation', *IDS Working Paper no. 235*, Brighton: Institute of Development Studies.

Verité (2005) 'Protecting Overseas Workers — Research Findings and Strategic Perspectives on Labor Protections for Foreign Contract Workers in Asia and the Middle East', *Research Paper*, December 2005, Amherst, MA: Verité.

Yamanaka, K. and N. Piper (2006) 'Feminised Migration in East and Southeast Asia: Policies, Actions and Empowerment', *UNRISD Occasional Paper no. 11*, Geneva: UNRISD.

2 Finding a Place in Stratified Structures
Migrant Women in North America

Monica Boyd and Deanna Pikkov

INTRODUCTION

In less-developed nations, structural adjustment programs are shrinking opportunities for male employment and traditional forms of profit making, contributing to declining government revenues, and stimulating international migration (Sassen 1988). At the same time, growing insecurities cause states, households, and individuals to increasingly rely on women's labour, in what is often called a "feminization of survival" (Migration Policy Institute 2003; Sassen 2000). A direct consequence is the increasing percentage of working women in migration flows to all world regions, including North America (Zlotnik 2003). Unfortunately, even in North America, migrant women are often disadvantaged relative to men.

Despite the efforts of the women's movement of the 1970s and 1980s, and the subsequent enactment of affirmative action legislation, gender stratification, defined as asymmetrical relations of power and access to resources that privilege men, persists in both Canada and the United States. Consequently, the modes of entry into North America are gendered: men and women often enter under different categories of admission. Migrant women often enter as wives and dependents of men who sponsor their admission, and they are usually less likely to enter on humanitarian or economic grounds. Once they arrive, immigrant women face a gender stratified labour market where they are frequently employed in female-typed occupations: "women's jobs." Overall, the negative impacts of gender combine with those of being an immigrant, causing immigrant women to be "doubly disadvantaged," and likely to be over-represented in marginal, unregulated, and poorly-paid jobs.

For the most part, Canada and the United States have undergone similar developments in their immigration policies. From the start, both countries sought migrants as permanent residents. Then, beginning in the 1960s, both dismantled their earlier immigration policies which permitted migration only for those of European, and thus white, origins. One result of the new immigration legislation has been a dramatic shift in the origin, and color composition, of permanent residents. Canadian and US cities now present a vibrant mix of ethnic and racial groups and individuals from every corner of the globe. Despite the opportunities that immigration provides newcomers, and despite the remarkable accomplishments of immigrants over time, outcomes and opportunities are not evenly distributed as regards employment, especially with respect to women. For example, there is now a very real potential for immigrant women to be triply disadvantaged in the labour market by virtue of being female, foreign-born, and phenotypically non-white.

However, such stratification systems and immigration policies evolve, and are applied within certain historical, political, and ideological contexts. In a historical context, the shared US-Mexico land border has set the stage for state-regulated migration on a temporary basis. For example, the Bracero program permitted the legal and temporary entry of Mexicans to work for American farmers. Another important legacy of the shared Mexico-US border is the sustained flow of migrants who enter the US illegally. As a result, temporary workers and illegal migrants are key items in any discussion of female migration into the United States. In Canada, less attention is paid to these two categories of migrants, partly because the land border is shared with the United States rather than with a newly-developed country.

The political systems of the two countries also contain differences which shape the lives of migrants. At both the federal and provincial levels, the Canadian system is a parliamentary one, in which party leaders typically maintain strong control over their party's elected members of parliament. At the federal level, two governing bodies exist, an elected parliament and an appointed senate, with appointments terminated either by resignation or retirement at age 75. Federal-provincial relations are codified and on-going, achieved by Premier meetings, and by federal-provincial meetings between representatives of departments. Such a system is not run by regulations enshrined in legislation, but rather, by guiding principles. As a result, alterations in immigrant admissions policies can occur with little visibility via bureaucratic guidelines. As such, government departments have some discretion to fine tune guidelines, for example with respect to refugee women facing gender-related persecution.

In contrast, the United States system is congressional, consisting of an elected House of Representatives and an elected Senate. Party control over elected members is more precarious, and energetic politicians can be highly entrepreneurial, sometimes even contradicting party platforms. Accompanying the implicit system of checks and balances found in the governing structure (the Congress and the Senate; the Executive and the Judiciary) is the development of a powerful lobbying system comprised of fiercely-engaged interest groups. These features of governance affect development of American immigration policies. For one thing, immigration legislation is highly visible and subject to capture and contest by interested parties. For another, difficulties in obtaining consensus over the diverse issues contained in a comprehensive immigration bill mean that immigration legislation has been piecemeal, with separate acts or laws focussing solely on refugees, or on temporary workers, or on other issues, such as amnesties. Within this context, specific acts combine to produce competing results, and some issues are subject to continual revisiting: debates and legislation on temporary workers and amnesties are recurring events.

In the realm of social service provision, Canada and the United States show some differences as well. Despite on-going devolution of responsibilities to the provinces, the Canadian federal government remains more engaged in the policy and social support arenas than does the US, and this ongoing engagement may reflect fundamental differences in values as well as different political histories, including a greater influence of social democratic governments in Canada. Individualism is emphasized in the United States and collectivism in Canada, each rooted in the initial principles of nation-statehood of "life, liberty and the pursuit of happiness" for the US, and "peace, order and good government" for Canada (Lipset 1990). Whatever the role of values and political histories, distinct differences are seen in the two countries' health care systems, with privatized, user pay in the US versus federally-funded, provincially-supplied and universal health care coverage in Canada. These differences naturally affect immigrant access to health care.

Although differences exist in governance, in policy engagement, and possibly in values, the countries are similar ideologically. First, both are liberal welfare states, in which safety nets are extended to members on the basis of their attachments to paid work. Second, in both, ideological, political and policy climates have shifted over the 1980s and 1990s to include neo-liberal principals that emphasize the importance of an unfettered economy, and a minimally-engaged government with respect to regulating the market and providing benefits.

Such neo-liberal principles and accompanying policy climates have three implications in the field of immigration generally and for immigrant women in particular. First, rules and regulations that make up migration regimes bear the imprint of neo-liberal discourse. This is seen in debates over whom to admit, which increasingly emphasize the entry of those who can contribute to the market and enhance global competitiveness. It also is evident in the encouragement of growing numbers of temporary workers, as well as in increased user-fees and administrative surcharges. Second, in both countries, the pull toward free-market policies is consistent with lax enforcement of wage and workplace regulations, the persistence of stratified labour markets in which immigrant women often find themselves in the bottom strata, and listless affirmative action/employment equity legislation, which also negatively affects immigrant women. Third, in both countries, residents receive diminished social entitlements in the wake of a general erosion and privatization of social provision. These changes, which are consistent with neo-liberal commitments, unduly affect the poor, and especially poor immigrants with educational or language deficits, among whom women are disproportionately present.

Immigrant disadvantage, then, occurs mainly within the erosion of entitlements available to all residents. Furthermore, as an additional strategy to avoid the high costs of immigrant integration, hierarchical citizenship statuses may increasingly appear on the North American policy horizons. Signs exist in the growing numbers of temporary workers and in recent proposals in the US and Canada to augment this group by converting irregular migrants into temporary workers. Immigration reform and specifically whether temporary (and illegal) workers will be granted a path to full legal citizenship is a key domestic political issue in the US in this first decade of the 21st century.

Taken together, the migration of women and their livelihoods and entitlements in Canada and the US reflects the forces of globalization, as well as individual country similarities and differences in principles of stratification, economic structures, systems of governance, and adherence to neo-liberal principles. The chapter begins with a look at changes in migration patterns, and gives an analysis of new migration regimes and their effects on women. The next area of concern is gendered work environments and how these are tied to recent government decisions. Finally, the chapter examines immigrant entitlements, showing where government actions regarding social programs affect all immigrants generally, and immigrant women specifically.

CHANGED MIGRATION REGIMES: WHAT CAN WE EXPECT?

Overview

The broad distinctions between "settler," "guest-worker," and "colonial" migration regimes still apply in the main "settler" countries (Australia, New Zealand, Canada, and the US), which continue to welcome large-scale immigration, and where access to both labour markets and citizenship remains easy in comparison with Europe. While significant convergence among settler, guest-worker, and colonial regimes has occurred, differences still exist, and some European regimes remain influenced by the original guest-worker assumptions of migrant return. Consistent with this, most immigrants to Europe must make lengthy adjustments in status from temporary to permanent residence before becoming eligible for citizenship. In North America, the overwhelming majority of legal immigrants achieve permanent residence automatically upon entry, and are eligible for legal citizenship within three to five years. Exceptions include visitors, students, and temporary workers.

This relatively generous treatment of immigrants is reflected in Canada's refusal to ratify the International Convention on the Protection of the Rights of All Migrant Workers and Members of their Families, which entered into force on 1 July 2003, with 27 signatory nations. Canadian officials argued that "[t]he vast majority of persons who would be considered as migrant workers under the definition of the Convention enter Canada as permanent residents...[and]...enjoy legal rights and social benefits as Canadian citizens."[1] The government found that the Convention did not fit the Canadian case, and despite supporting the policy's aims, declined to be party to it (Verma 2003).[2]

Nonetheless, the recent ascendancy of neo-liberal discourse has been accompanied by a shift in how immigrants are viewed in North America. Specifically, economic rationalization of immigration policy has led to efforts to recruit highly-skilled workers, to reduce obligations to lower-skilled workers, and to reduce the numbers of "expensive" asylum-seekers. Such trends, examined in detail below, foreshadow changes that could threaten the reputation for generosity toward immigrants that North American regimes have historically enjoyed.

Who gets in — Family and economic migration

Historically, Canada and the United States received migrants primarily from Europe. Country-origin criteria for immigrant suitability were eliminated in Canada and the US in the 1960s, thereby removing overtly racist approaches to the selection of migrants for settlement. Added to this, the growing prosperity of Western and Southern European countries reduced residents' incentives to migrate. As a result, the origins of migrants to North America dramatically altered. By the beginning of the 21st century, migrants from Asia were well represented, if not dominant, in the annual flows of permanent residents to Canada and the US, and migrants from Latin and South America entered the US in large numbers (see Table 2.1).

Table 2.1 Percent distribution of immigrants by source area, Canada and the United States, 2001

Region	Canada[a]	United States[b]
Total	100.0	100.0
Europe and the United Kingdom	17.3	16.7
US (Canada)	2.4	2.8
South and Central America	8.0	41.6
Africa and the Middle East	19.2	6.3
Asia and Pacific	53.0	30.9
Not stated	0.1	1.7

Source: Canada, 2002a: Citizenship and Immigration, p. 8. United States, 2003a. Department of Homeland Security. Table 2. (a) Calendar year, January 1–December 31. (b) Fiscal year, April 1–March 31.

However, neo-liberal notions of efficiency and competitiveness are increasingly employed to recommend a new kind of discrimination — against those who lack education and language skills. This is motivated by a desire to obtain the immediate benefit of skilled workers, fuelled by the belief that such workers will integrate more easily, while uneducated immigrants are hard on the public purse. Consequently, policy-makers are urged to tailor immigrant selection to reflect those human-capital characteristics considered most likely to ensure net national advantage.

This discourse occurs within the context of existing principles of admissibility. Starting with legislative changes in the 1960s, and entrenched in subsequent legislation in the last quarter of the twentieth century, both Canadian and American immigration policies admit permanent residents on the basis of three principles: family reunification, economic contribution, and humanitarian concerns. The trend towards targeting young, highly-skilled entrants for permanent residence is most evident in Canada, while Latin American migration to the US demonstrates the lesser importance in that country of skill-based admissions (Antecol, Cobb-Clark & Trejo 2003). A series of Canadian regulatory changes in the 1980s and 1990s quietly restricted immigration based on family reunification, and emphasized the intake of those who would make economic contributions. By the end of the 1990s, the majority of new immigrants to Canada consisted of "economic immigrants" and their immediate families (Figure 2.1). In the US, meanwhile, despite calls from economists and policy-makers to implement changes that would result in a better "quality" of immigrant (Lowell 2001), a majority of legal entrants still enter as relatives of legal

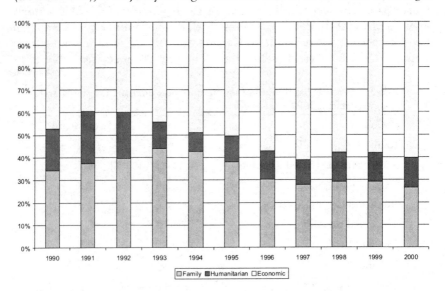

Figure 2.1 Categories of admission for immigrants admitted to Canada 1990–2000 (January 1–December 31).

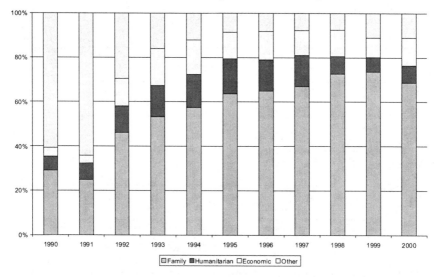

Figure 2.2 Categories of admission for immigrants admitted to the United States, 1990–2000 (April 1–March 31).

residents (Figure 2.2).[3] A variety of political and administrative factors militate against the adoption of more skill-selective entrance requirements in the United States, including: backlogs of applications; the bypassing of quotas and queues by sponsors with legal citizenship; and the politicized nature of the debate in the US, at a time when the electoral importance of the huge Hispanic population is taken very seriously by both Democrats and Republicans.

Women and modes of entry

From the end of World War II, the number of females in annual immigration flows to Canada and the United States has closely resembled the number of males (Boyd 1992). In the early 1990s, the female share of total migration briefly dropped in the US with the legalization of workers under the Immigration Reform and Control Act (Figure 2.3), as many of these workers were men. Since then, the percentage of females has climbed to over 50 percent of the total flow of permanent residents in both countries, with the somewhat higher percentages for the US being consistent with higher levels of migration for purposes of family reunification (see Figure 2.2).

In principle, women who seek permanent resident status in Canada and the US enter in ways similar to men. They may be admitted on the basis of their family ties, their economic contributions or on humanitarian-based concerns. Within each of these categories of "admissibility," they may enter as independent or autonomous "principal applicants," or they may enter

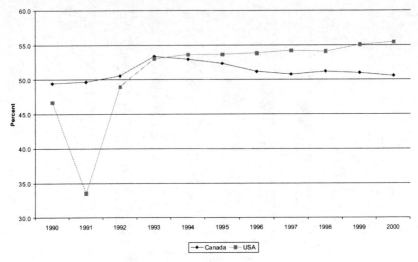

Figure 2.3 Percentage female in annual admissions of permanent residents, Canada and the United States, 1990–2000.

as "tied movers" who are members of a migrating family or household unit. But gender, defined here as those social and cultural ideals, practices and displays of masculinity and femininity that constitute gender roles, relations and hierarchies (Hondagneu-Sotelo 1994), determines the modal category. In both countries, females predominate among migrants entering on the basis of family reunification criteria, but represent less than half of those entering on the basis of economic criteria (Table 2.2). Not surprisingly, only where labour flows are destined for female-typed jobs, such as nurses or domestics, do women predominate as economic migrants. For example, women constituted 84 percent of workers in the 2001 statistics for the Canadian Live-In Caregiver program, discussed later in this chapter (Citizenship and Immigration Canada 2002a). Thus, the mode of entry for women would seem to reflect their stereotypical roles as wives, daughters, and caregivers.

Gender stratification influences how women migrants are admitted into North America in other ways. One example is in the high fees associated with immigration. In Canada, a family of four entering as skilled worker or family class immigrants will pay 2305 ($Cdn) for processing and permanent residence fees, while in the US the same family of four would pay 1240 ($US) or, if the principal applicant enters first, up to 1790 ($US) if petitioning fees are included.[4] It might be argued the high fees, if not explicitly designed for, at least have the unintended consequence of dampening the ardour of persons seeking migration on the basis of family ties, especially those from countries with low standards of living. By extension, the fees specifically deter women from initiating migration attempts. Since gender hierarchies in source countries usually are associated with low earnings

Table 2.2 Percentage of total admission of immigrants on the family and economic categories who are females[a], 1990–2000

Year	Canada[b]		United States[c]	
	Family	Economic	Family	Economic
1990	54.9	49.2	54.2	50.9
1991	56.0	50.2	54.8	50.3
1992	57.1	50.1	56.5	48.6
1993	58.0	51.6	56.4	47.7
1994	57.5	50.7	56.6	49.0
1995	58.3	49.5	56.9	49.5
1996	58.8	48.3	57.1	49.9
1997	59.8	47.8	57.6	49.2
1998	60.9	47.5	56.8	48.1
1999	61.2	47.1	57.4	49.5
2000	61.6	46.7	58.5	49.4

Notes: (a) For example, of all persons admitted to Canada in 1990 as immigrants (permanent residents) on the basis of family ties, 54.9 were female. (b) Calendar year, January 1–December 31. (b) Fiscal year, April 1–March 31.

of women compared to men, women who seek to immigrate as principal applicants or as autonomous migrants bear a higher relative financial burden than their male counterparts.

Government policies to minimize social spending can dampen the extent to which women, once admitted as permanent residents, facilitate subsequent migration under the principles of family reunification. In both Canada and the US, family members are admissible if they meet health and security criteria and are "sponsored." Sponsors are relatives who agree to provide a family-based safety net to ensure that persons admitted under the auspices of family reunification do not make demands on government social assistance programs for a number of years. Proof regarding the financial capacity to undertake sponsorship obligations are required. Although incomes from spouses and common law partners may be pooled (the US allows pooling of earnings from some other relatives as well), gender differences in earnings dictate that a female who is the sole sponsor has a higher risk of being rejected than her male counterpart.

Gender biases in immigration regulations can be minimized by the implementation of gender based analysis. As developed over the years, and articulated in Canada's Federal Plan for Gender Equality presented to the United Nations Conference of Women, gender based analysis is consistent with the mainstreaming of a gender perspective in all policies and programs (Status of Women Canada 2000) Critics observe that the impact of gender based analysis can be minimized by limited leadership capacity, neo-liberal policies accompanied by the absence of resources (Burt & Hardman 2001; Grace 1997; Teghtsoonian 2004), and by its narrow focus on gender alone (Grace 1997; Hankivshy 2004). Nevertheless, following the representation of several non-governmental organization (NGO) women's groups (Walton-Roberts 2004) gender based analysis provided a framework for gender sensitive changes in several sections of Canada's Immigration and Refugee Protection Act (IRPA), effective June 2002 (Citizenship and Immigration Canada 2002). And in the US, starting in 1995, a President's Interagency Council on Women was mandated to encourage gender mainstreaming; this agency was replaced in 2001 with the Office of International Women's Issues. Despite these administrative structures, critics charge that the concept of gender mainstreaming lacks visibility and impact in the United States (Hankivsky 2004).

Gendering refugees

In addition to admissions for permanent residence which are based on family reunification and economic criteria, humanitarian-based admissions occupy a significant place in policies in both Canada and the United States and have been incorporated into post-1960s legislation. But while gender neutral in wording and appearance, laws and procedures for admitting persons on humanitarian principles cannot be equated with gender parity in outcomes.

In the past, the equal representation of women in refugee settlement programs has been of concern (Keely 1992). Statistics for United Nations Human Rights Council (UNHRC)-assisted refugee populations show that women age 18–59 equal or outnumber their male counterparts (UNHRC 2001, 2002), yet throughout the 1990s, females of all ages represented less than half of refugee and asylum seekers admissions in the United States, and of Canadian admissions in the refugee class (Table 2.3). The gender gap in admissions is larger when using data on principal applicants, since such data exclude spouses and dependents: in 2000, 33 percent of the principal applicants in the refugee class admissions in Canada were women (Citizenship and Immigration Canada 2002a).

The potential and actual under-representation of women in various humanitarian-based modes of entry reflects the gendered nature of criteria associated with resettlement and the definition of a refugee associated with the UN 1951 convention (Boyd 1998). In order for resettlement to occur, a person usually must be defined as a refugee and in this way have claims of persecution validated through the refugee determination process. However, industrial countries that agree to resettle refugees often add admissibility criteria designed in part to weed out people who are likely to require long term social assistance, to the basic eligibility criteria. For the most part, eligibility is a necessary, but not sufficient, criterion of admissibility;

Table 2.3 Percentage of total admissions of immigrants on the basis of humanitarian criteria who are females[a], 1990–2000

Year of admission	Canada[b]	United States[c]
1990	40.3	46.7
1991	38.5	48.1
1992	38.7	48.2
1993	42.6	49.0
1994	43.7	49.1
1995	43.1	48.5
1996	45.7	47.6
1997	44.6	46.8
1998	46.0	46.6
1999	45.9	48.7
2000	46.4	48.0

Notes: (a) For example, of all persons admitted to Canada in 1990 as immigrants (permanent residents) on the basis of humantrian concerns, 40.3 were female. (b) Calendar year, January 1–December 31. (b) Fiscal year, April 1–March 31.

assessments of education, job skills and income potentials must be made as well.

Gender stratification and gender hierarchies heighten the probability that women will not meet the refugee admissibility criteria necessary for permanent settlement in an industrial country. For one thing, gendered hierarchies in refugee camps can result in refugee men occupying important mediating positions that, in turn, increase their chances of selection for settlement elsewhere (Martin 1991). Gender stratification in most societies, particularly less industrialized ones, also means that women often have less education than men, and exhibit different or non-existent labour market skills and experiences, suggesting that women are likely to experience greater difficulty in meeting self-sufficiency criteria invoked by an industrial country for admission. In addition, many women have children and other dependents for whom they are responsible. As a result of all these concerns over self-sufficiency, selection procedures may favour the overseas selection of men for permanent settlement (Boyd 1998).

Yet it is widely acknowledged that women are extremely vulnerable to the violence and abuse that occurs both in flight and in temporary settlement areas, including camps, in areas near to the countries of origin. Women who are single heads of family, or whose adult male relatives are unable to support them, are at risk of expulsion, refoulement (forcible return), sexual harassment, rape, torture, prostitution and other forms of exploitation. Sadly, such vulnerabilities frequently co-exist with low chances for permanent settlement, since these women also are likely to be assessed by potential settlement countries as requiring a great deal of assistance.

Starting in 1987, the United Nations High Commissioner for Refugees (UNHCR) requested assistance in protecting such vulnerable women through permanent settlement. In response, the Canadian department in charge of immigration developed a Woman at Risk program, which was followed by similar initiatives in Australia and New Zealand. "Women at Risk" lack the normal protection of a family unit, and find themselves in situations where the local authorities cannot assure their protection (Citizenship and Immigration Canada 2004b). They do not have to have the same potential for settlement as do other refugees or humanitarian based cases. Although the program is premised on principles of gender-based justice, admission numbers are small, with only about 2,250 women and their dependents settled since admissions began in 1988. The numbers reflect the extended time required for economic integration, if any such integration occurs, and the high cost of caring for these individuals from private and state funds.

The United States does not have a formal "women at risk" program. Rather, its first priorities are compelling protection cases or refugees for whom no other durable solution exists, and who are referred for US resettlement either by the UNHCR or by a US Embassy. Although women are included within the P-1 category, non-governmental organizations question if such inclusion properly identifies women in need of protection. Moreover, they ask whether it provides full access to the resettlement system, and if women receive appropriate services once settled (Refugee Council USA, 2004; Lawyers Committee for Human Rights 2002).

By and large, women may be more handicapped than men in having their claims for refugee status recognized if they enter Canada or the United States first and then seek admissibility as refugee claimants. Disadvantages arise in part because the definition of a refugee, which should be gender neutral, is in fact androcentric (Boyd 1998; Lawyers Committee for Human Rights 2002). According to Article 1 of the 1951 United Nations Convention Relating to the Status of Refugees, a refugee is a person who "owing to well founded fear of being persecuted for reasons of race, religion, nationality, membership of a particular social group or political opinion, is outside the country of his nationality and is unable, or owing to such fear, is unwilling to avail himself of the protection of that country." The UN definition of a refugee, which emerged in the aftermath of World War II and the Cold War, drew attention to violations committed by the state against individuals (Connors 1997). Critics observe that the focus on the actions of the state and the violation of civil and political rights privileges the public side of the public/private divide.

Building on these arguments, a central concern of feminist writings is that the UN Convention definition privileges the recognition of refugee status for men. Embedded in this concern are two core themes. First, in most societies, gender roles and gender stratification prescribe that men are the key participants in the public arena while women are restricted to the private sphere. As a result, the forms of persecution experienced by women in more private settings are less likely to be recognized as grounds for persecution. Second, the indirect role of the state in generating and/or sustaining harmful acts is not likely to be acknowledged. Moreover, the emphasis on the violation of civil and political rights both deflects attention away from the affirmative duty of the state to ensure rights and ignores the existence of society-wide discrimination against women (Connors 1997).

On International Women's Day, 1993, the Chairperson of the Immigration and Refugee Board of Canada released guidelines for women refugee claimants who feared gender-related persecution. These were the first guidelines drafted by any country to specifically address gender-related persecution. Since then, guidelines have also been adopted by the United States (Scialabba 1997). Despite their differences (Macklin 1999), both American and Canadian guidelines note the need to be gender sensitive when considering the grounds for persecution, as well as the need to make special efforts for women claimants during the refugee determination process (such as having female interviewers). However, both stop short of declaring gender a social group and an explicit basis for persecution.

TEMPORARY WORKERS

Temporary migrants include students, refugee claimants or asylum seekers whose appeals for permanent residence are awaiting adjudication, and those admitted for the purpose of short term employment. In recent years, the number of temporary workers has increased substantially in both Canada and the United States, in somewhat different ways. On the one hand, immigration experts in Canada enthusiastically promote fine-tuned "management and monitoring of the increasingly lucrative flow of temporary entrants" (Rekai 2002). On the other hand, in the United States, the growing "backdoor" permanent immigration via the temporary system has increased skill levels among permanent immigrants (Lowell 2001).

The term "temporary worker" refers to disparate categories of entrants, with different prospects under immigration rules. Temporary worker categories address labour shortages in "skilled" (desirable and well-paid) sectors and "lower skilled" (undesirable and poorly-paid) sectors. In Canada, the first subgroup includes managerial and professional workers coming in under the auspices of the North American Free Trade Agreement (NAFTA), and workers admitted under IT programs. Most of the highly skilled workers come to Canada from the US and Europe. The second group includes Live-in Caregivers, Seasonal Agricultural Workers, and others. Most of the women in this group are from the Philippines, and most of the men are from Mexico and the Caribbean.

In Canada, the temporary-worker category has doubled since the 1980s (Citizenship and Immigration Canada 2002b). The total number of foreign worker temporary entries to Canada in 2000 was 89,000, which is about 0.03 percent of the Canadian population (Rekai 2002). Women account for a little less than 30 percent of this total, but show small, steady gains (Citizenship and Immigration Canada 2002b). The top country of origin for women temporary workers in 2002 was the US, with the Philippines coming second. Large numbers of women also came from Japan, Australia, the UK, and France, with smaller numbers coming from Germany, Mexico, China, Ireland, and India (Citizenship and Immigration Canada 2002b). Albeit limited, evidence indicates that women temporary migrants are more likely than men to be in low-skill work (Ruddick, n.d.).

In general, temporary workers in Canada face entry barriers in obtaining permanent residency. When applying under the current "point system," they receive credit for employment and connections in Canada, but these are generally insufficient if the applicant lacks higher education and good language skills. Such disadvantage underlies on-going revisions to Canadian programs admitting women as live-in domestic workers during the last thirty years. There is a longer history associated with the recruitment of women as domestics, and whether they were admitted as permanent migrants and whether they were required to live-in. However, program changes in 1973 mandated a live-in requirement and temporary status. Subsequent political pressure applied by a number of groups resulted in revisions in 1981 that allowed live-in domestic workers to apply for permanent resident status. However additional criteria to those used initially to admit live-in caregivers were imposed. In 1992, initial admissibility requirements were increased, emphasizing education, training and language skills, but subsequent requirements upon application for permanent residence were discontinued. Caregivers, most of whom are women, may now apply for permanent residency for themselves and their immediate families living abroad after successfully fulfilling a two year contract (Arat-Koc 1997; Macklin 1992; Stasiulis & Bakan 2003). The on-going political pressure by NGO groups on this issue demonstrates a degree of resistance within Canada to the idea of second-class citizenship.

In the US, the total number of temporary worker entries in 2002 was 1,200,000 which, at 0.04 percent of the US population, is comparable to the Canadian percentage (Rekai 2002). Large increases followed after 1992, when the Immigration Act of 1990 came into effect. This Act, which attempted to increase the number of high-skilled immigrants to the US, nearly tripled the number of employment-based admissions in the permanent stream and expanded the number of visas for temporary workers (Lowell 2001). Most of the recruitment of temporary workers in the US is in high skill categories, with only about 8 percent admitted in low skill categories, as labour shortages in lower-skilled sectors are filled by the large pool of irregular immigrants, making specific provision unnecessary. The

H-1B visa is the largest category of entry for temporary high skill workers. These workers are professionals and other highly-skilled individuals, who usually hold a baccalaureate or higher degree. Computer-related and engineering occupations account for 70 percent of these visas.

Detailed breakdowns of the composition of these flows are difficult to locate. However, in 2000, almost half of the H-1B petitions approved by the United States were granted to persons born in India. It would appear that women are most likely to predominate in the H-1A (expired in 1995) and H-1C visa categories, which target nurses (Jachimowicz & Meyers 2002). While not synonymous with temporary visas, census data for the US indicate that Asians are over-represented as engineers, scientists, and health care professionals. While men dominate in most of these fields, women are also well represented. In 1990, 5 percent of female college graduates in the US workforce were Asian women, but they accounted for 10–15 percent of female engineers, architects, computer scientists, and researchers. Similarly, nearly 25 percent of health care workers in public hospitals in large US cities are Asian, and 90 percent of Asian American nurses are foreign born (Espiritu 2003).

Irregular migrants

The terms "irregular", "non-status", "undocumented" and "illegal" are all used in research and popular documents to refer to migrants who enter a country: (1) legally with valid documentation but who violate the terms of their admissions (for example, those on visitors' visas); (2) legally but with fraudulent documentation; or (3) illegally, that is without undergoing formal admission. The irregular population in the US is estimated at about 11 or 12 million, representing over one-quarter of all foreign-born in the country. Backlogs are thought to be responsible for a good part of this population, as family members, a majority of whom are women and children, can wait for as long as 10 years for a visa (McKay 2003). Women are estimated to comprise about 41 percent of this group. Undocumented immigrants who work are estimated to be 6 million, and they account for 5 percent of the work force. They earn less than other workers, with two-thirds making less than twice the minimum wage. Ninety-six percent of undocumented men are in the work force, and an estimated 62 percent of women from this population participated in the labour market, despite the fact that they were more likely than US citizens to have children (Passel, Capps & Fix 2004). In sum, the International Monetary Fund (IMF) reports that work performed by undocumented workers accounts for 10 percent of the US economy (Jimenez 2003a).

Employers and other advocates point out that many sectors of the US economy (and many US households) have come to rely on a ready supply of cheaper, undocumented workers to maintain profitability and competitiveness. The "nannygate" scandal in 1993, when Zoe Baird withdrew herself from consideration for US Attorney General after she was found to have illegally employed an undocumented Peruvian woman as a housekeeper, highlighted the widespread middle-class employment of non-status women as domestic workers. Raids on retail giant Wal-Mart resulted in the arrest and deportation of 300 undocumented workers in 2003. And about half of all farm workers are reported to have irregular status. In other words, strong demand for immigrant workers exists, and this demand is met in part through aggressive formal and informal recruitment by employers. That legal channels are inadequate to meet this demand is illustrated by the fact that the annual cap for low skill temporary workers in the US for 2004 was reached three months into that year (Krissman 2005). This has led some to argue that the United States has a de-facto guest-worker regime based on irregular migrants, although such an analysis assumes an identity of interest between government and low-wage employers that is at least questionable.

The years 2005 and 2006 marked a sustained effort on the part of the White House to push through an overhaul of immigration law as substantial as that of 1986. As we go to press, most commentators see the prospects for a deal in 2006, with November elections looming, as slim. If no reconciliation of the separate bills that were passed by the House and Senate occurs by the end of the year, the process begins all over again. Nonetheless, it is instructive to look at the bills and their respective strategies to tackle the issues of labour demand and irregular migration. The Senate passed its Comprehensive Immigration Reform Bill (S.2611) with bipartisan, and presidential, support. The bill promises an enlarged legal temporary workforce consistent with President Bush's 2004 immigrant policy reform proposal (although the suggested number of annual entrants under the program was dramatically reduced to 200,000 in negotiations). The bill would also grant illegal immigrants a conditional amnesty that would make up to ten million irregular migrants (those who had been in the country for more than two years) eligible for legalization. The plan involves waiting periods of various lengths depending on period of residence, and a fine of around US$2000. The bill also authorizes increases in border security, and a new system of employer verification of employee legality.

The contrast with the bill passed in the House of Representatives on immigration earlier in the year (H.R.4437) is dramatic, most notably in that the House bill makes absolutely no provision for legalization of the undocumented or for a guest worker program. On the contrary, it makes illegal residence or its aid subject to federal criminal penalties, while increasing border security. The crucial question of whether a guest worker program would include a path to citizenship has been largely eclipsed by the controversy over amnesty. At the moment it appears that the Senate bill confirms a path to citizenship, in the stated right of temporary workers to self-petition for permanent status after four years. However, the fact that this right was stripped in one amendment and then reinstated in another during Senate deliberations demonstrates its vulnerability. Given the enormous gulf that exists between supporters of the House and Senate bills, the prospects for this right remaining intact are highly uncertain, even if a comprehensive bill were to be signed into law. Without a path to citizenship, the temporary worker program would bear a striking resemblance to European guest worker programs. Critics charge that President Bush's 2004 proposal, upon which S.2611 is partly based, would result in institutionalizing a large class of legal residents with second-class status.

Implications for women migrants include the fact that the informal and flexible nature of much of undocumented women's employment will make their participation in any amnesty less likely, further stratifying mixed-status households, and increasing women's dependence on male family members. Indeed, researchers have found this kind of gender bias in the 2.7 million legalizations that occurred under the Immigration Reform and Control Act (IRCA) in 1986, which were easier to obtain for men (Powers, Seltzer, & Jing Shi 1998). And on a practical level, the reality of mixed-status families, where US-born children have full citizenship, complicates any requirement that workers return to countries of origin. Currently, it is estimated that there are over 3 million US-citizen children whose parents have irregular status (Passel et al. 2004).

In Canada, meanwhile, the issue of irregular immigrants has recently surfaced after two decades of neglect following the amnesty-based federal "Long Term Illegal Program" between August 1983 and July 1985. Statistics for those who had resided in Canada illegally for five years and sought admission reveal that women represented about half the total number of applicants, with percentages rising to 70 percent for applicants from the Caribbean. Nearly two-thirds worked as domestics (Boyd 1989). Current estimates of undocumented immigrants range to 200,000, and little is known except what has been reported in small case studies. It is clear, though, that women have a strong presence among irregular status residents. Most achieve their irregular status as a result of failing to leave the country after a rejected application for refugee status, or as a result of overstaying tourist or student visas. Little is known about livelihoods, or countries of origin, though Latin Americans are well-represented.[5]

One specific sector, the Canadian construction industry, has been actively lobbying for an enlarged temporary worker program to regularize the status of what they claim are 76,000 undocumented workers within the Ontario construction industry alone. Federal Immigration Officials plans to introduce a pilot project within this industry, which would have seen two year visas granted to participants based on labour market demand, language and job skills, were cancelled by the new Conservative federal government in 2006. Again, given that a majority of undocumented women are thought to be engaged in domestic work, they are unlikely to have been reached by such initiatives, although there was talk of eventually extending the program to textile and service industry workers.

Finally, no discussion of the presence of women among the irregular population would be complete without acknowledging trafficked workers.

The vulnerability of women to trafficking is attributed variously to individual circumstances, such as living in dysfunctional families, to systems of gender discrimination and gender practices, to displacement processes resulting from natural and human instigated catastrophes, and to the disruptive effects of development processes. In particular, the existence of a supply of women to be trafficked for sex work is associated with the feminization of survival which derives from the disruptive and unstable economic conditions associated with development, and linked to international neo-liberal monetary policies (Sassen 2000).

Although trafficking in women can refer to the movement of women as domestic workers, as "mail order" brides, and as sex workers, the latter commands the most attention. The epicenter of trafficking women for sex work is within Asia, and fans out from Asia and the former USSR countries to Europe. Precise numbers are impossible to obtain (Hughes 2000), but annual estimates on the total numbers trafficked for both sexes and for a variety of work range from 18,000 to 20,000 in the United States (United States 2003). In Canada, annual estimates range from 8,000 to 16,000, and include some who may eventually enter the US. During the mid to late 1990s, over 1,000 temporary work authorizations a year were issued for exotic dancers, but these figures are not a reliable indication of the number of women transported across national boundaries into Canada for sex work for two reasons: the correspondence between exotic dancers and sex workers is not exact; and many women in the sex trade enter in other ways, either as family members, as visitors who overstay their visas, or as irregular migrants (McDonald, Moore, & Timoshkina 2000).

A harsh reality for undocumented immigrants is that they are vulnerable to deportation at any time for any infraction of the law. While this has grave implications for trafficked women, undocumented immigrant women who suffer physical abuse at the hands of their spouses are also vulnerable. In response to this susceptibility, battered women's advocates pressured the US Congress to create a provision in the 1994 Violence Against Women Act, or VAWA, which reserves green cards for undocumented immigrant women who have been physically abused (though the abuse must be suffered at the hands of a citizen or lawful permanent resident spouse), and allows them to petition for permanent residency without the knowledge or support of their husbands.[6] By 2001 17,907 women had applied under the provision (Keneya 2002).

GENDERED LIVELIHOODS

Overview

The impacts of neo-liberal economic regimes are seen in the recent restructuring processes of many countries. Strategies meant to enhance competitiveness and efficiency, and encourage foreign investment include the privatization of public enterprises and institutions, deregulation of labour markets, and reductions in social spending. Reductions in funding allocated to health and care work have not only re-emphasized women as the providers of care, but re-directed, wherever possible, the site of care activities out of the public arena and into private settings. As well, neo-liberal strategies often intensify pre-existing markers of gender, racial and immigrant stratification.

Inequalities in the labour market

Opportunities within North American labour markets have recently been transformed by the growth of the service economy. While this growth has occurred across the developed world, nowhere is the trend more marked than in Canada and the United States, where by the end of the 1990s, nearly 75 percent of total *formal* employment was in service industries. Women are disproportionately present in this service economy, filling half of all positions within producer and distributive service subsectors, and more than twice as many women as men are employed in personal and social services (OECD 2000). Moreover, women's participation rates have risen in all Organization for Economic Co-operation and Development (OECD) labour markets, while rates for men have declined (Hobson, Lewis, & Seem 2002). While men still have higher rates of labour market participation than women in all countries, the gap continues to narrow.

These shifts in participation rates by gender and economic activities are partially explained by a decline in traditionally male extraction and manufacturing industries. The use of a 'flexibilized' female labour force to break the monopoly of male unions is also important (Sassen 2000). And while much of service sector growth is fuelled by growing use of information technology within the 'knowledge economy', the concept of care provides another key to understanding structural change (Hobson 2002; Leira & Saraceno 2002). A care deficit, which occurs when women are incorporated into the labour market on the male model, creates a need for social services (Hochschild 1995). In North America, high and ever-increasing numbers of working women, their choices conditioned by increasing freedoms and declining real household incomes, have fuelled this demand. Unfortunately, the sectors of the service economy in which the majority of jobs are created are prime generators of insecure and low-waged employment, especially within the context of government privatization of social services. In essence, the domestic and political social contracts on which capital accumulation and growth are premised are being rewritten in North America, and new contracts appear to maintain immigrant women's more marginal location in the work force.

With respect to economic livelihood, the term "doubly disadvantaged" highlights the labour market marginality that results from the combined liabilities of being both immigrant and female. Indicators of such marginality

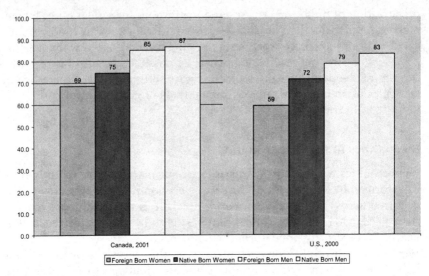

Figure 2.4 Percent in the labour force, foreign born and native born population age 25–64, by sex, Canada (2001) and the United States (2000).

include lower labour force participation, low status occupations and jobs, poor working conditions, and low earnings. Foreign-born women were the least likely of all groups, defined by birth-place and gender, to be in the formal labour force in North America in the 1990s (Figure 2.4; Bean & Stevens 2003; Schoeni 1998). While some of the disparity between groups may be explained by such factors as greater numbers of children in immigrant families and culturally-conditioned choices with regard to female employment outside the home, these rates are also partly reflective both of difficulties in finding employment among recently arrived women, and the quality of employment on offer.

In the US and Canada, structural change to labour markets has reinforced gendered occupational hierarchies in which immigrant women hold disadvantaged places. While immigrant women, including those from the developing world, are present among highly skilled workers, they are also disproportionately visible at the bottom rungs of stratified service, retail and manufacturing sectors. Variations exist by ethnicity or race, with African, Latin American, or Hispanic groups the most likely to be in low skill jobs (Boyd 2001; Shumway & Cooke 1998; Wright & Ellis 2000).

Similar patterns are evident with respect to unemployment, underemployment, working conditions, and earnings. Along with poor non-immigrant women, many migrant women hold non-unionized, contract and part-time jobs with low wages and few benefits in the "new economy" (Neysmith & Chen 2000). Undocumented migrant women appear to be the most vulnerable to employment in unsafe working conditions, and because of their status, they are limited in their ability to organize or denounce workplace abuses (Schoeni 1998; Gammage 2003; De Anda 2000).

Irregular migrants, livelihood and protection

As discussed previously, little research exists with respect to irregular workers in Canada. In the United States, labour market participation is overwhelmingly in the following sectors: manufacturing, wholesale and retail trade (including restaurants), services provided to private households and businesses, agriculture, and construction. There is a marked occupational segregation by gender, with nearly half of newly-arrived undocumented men finding work as agricultural labourers, in food preparation or food service occupations, as gardeners, or as janitors, while 37 percent of newly-arrived undocumented women work in private households, and another 8 percent work as textile machine operators (Powers et al. 1998).

The employment of non-status workers in the United States became illegal in 1986, though enforcement is close to non-existent. Indeed, until recently, undocumented workers managed to hold onto many formal labour relations entitlements despite their illegal status. In 2002, however, the Supreme Court denied back pay and reinstatement to an undocumented worker, despite wrongful dismissal for union organizing, on the grounds that awarding such rights trivialized immigration laws and encouraged future violations. This ruling called into question other rights won by undocumented workers over the years, such as the right to remedy for discrimination on the basis of national origin, and the right to worker's compensation in the case of accidents (Mailman & Yale-Loehr 2002; Rosenfield 2002). These threats to legal rights are symbolically important, and undercut the efforts of non-status workers to organize and demand rights.

On a substantive level, the enforcement of labour protections in the US has experienced a steep decline that began during the Reagan presidency and which, although temporarily reversed during the Clinton years, continues. President Bush has made major cuts to agencies that implement and enforce National Labour Relations Act laws and guidelines, and the staffing of the National Labour Relations Board with anti-union Bush appointees will almost certainly see reversals of recent board decisions, such as one made in 2000 that made unionization of temporary workers easier (Robbins 2001). This steady deregulation of labour markets has given rise to many questions regarding whether granting temporary workers "the same protections American workers enjoy" is worth the risk of deportation once temporary visas expire. Difficulties in conducting research among the undocumented population mean studies that look at this group's labour force experience have been small and inconclusive. Still, while many studies find that being undocumented has significant costs, others report that legalization makes little difference to labour market advancement.

One such study (Powers et al. 1998) was conducted on over 4,000 previously undocumented immigrants legalized under IRCA. Respondents were surveyed for labour force participation and occupational status upon their arrival in the US, then again later when they were experienced, undocumented immigrants, and a final time, after they received documentation.

The study found that increases in occupational status or upward mobility were greatest in the undocumented period and more modest thereafter. In other words, length of residence in the US was more important than legal status, suggesting that undocumented workers have labour force experiences similar to those of other immigrants. Gender differences were marked, with women experiencing less and slower upward mobility. While some of this might have been the result of the lesser amounts of labour force experience of the women, a more powerful explanation is found in the concentration of women in household work that offers no chance of upward mobility and isolates workers, discouraging the development of informal networks that might help with the search for better jobs. Interestingly, there was some evidence that legalization might benefit women more than men. The authors hypothesized that greater access after legalization to occupations that require some kind of licensing or certification, such as nursing, teaching or using medical equipment, may be significant.

Regulating inequalities

The work profile of migrant women in Canada and the US suggests that they are disproportionately in jobs which, because they involve part-time, contract, or home-work, are less well protected. A wide variety of labour laws (such as those governing minimum wages, hours and overtime provisions, union recognition, and pay equity) limit coverage to full-time, well-paid, or unionized workers. And even these latter workers experience uneven protection, as evidenced by recent union actions. On the one hand, construction unions in Canada have demanded that any construction workers entering the country on temporary visas would receive the same wage as native workers. On the other hand, compliant private sector unions have accepted crippling pay cuts to workers when taking over from public sector unions, as nursing homes and other sections of the public health care system are privatized (Hasselriis, 2004).

Not all foreign-born women are employed in jobs that are low skill or represent non-standard forms of employment, defined as work that is part-time, temporary, or own account self employment (Townson 2003). In fact, the recruitment of nurses from outside North America may be seen as explicit recruitment of high skilled labour. Moreover, in Canada, some of the women entering for a two year temporary period under the Live-in Caregiver Program received training as nurses (Pratt 1999). As well, marital homogeny in which partners are of similar educational backgrounds means that many women whose partners enter as skilled workers also have valuable labour market skills.

However, the entry of highly skilled women is not necessarily synonymous with their employment in high skill work, or with equality in the workplace. Immigrant nurses are a case in point. In response to domestic shortages, both Canada and the United States encourage the migration of nurses in their immigration laws and regulations. In Canada, nurses enter under the skilled worker provisions found in various immigration acts. They also may enter on a temporary basis if Human Resources Development Canada determines that the jobs offered will not have a negative economic effect on the Canadian labour market. In the United States efforts to recruit nurses have been very explicit. Congress passed the Nursing Relief Act of 1989 that provided for the adjustment from non-immigrant to immigrant status of nurses who met certain conditions. Slightly over 7,200 women entered between 1990 and 1994 as principal applicants under this act.[7] Subsequently, Congress passed the Nursing Relief for Disadvantaged Areas Act of 1999 which established a new non-immigrant class of admission (H-1C) for temporary admission of up to 500 nurses a year for four years as a means of producing a short term solution for nursing shortages in under-served areas (United States 2003).

Although foreign trained nurses may receive higher salaries in Canada and the United States than they would in their countries of origin, the potential for exploitation is great (Kline 2003). Numerous case studies indicate that nurses may be employed as nurse's aides rather than as registered nurses; they may experience discrimination on the job in the form of lower pay, fewer promotions; and they may be readily fired (Stasiulis & Bakan 2003; Calliste 2000; Das Gupta 1996; Espiritu 1999). Hospitals in the United States with a shortage of nursing personnel that heavily recruit foreign born nurses are municipally run and located in inner city areas (Brus 1995). Also, immigrant nurses faced the same conditions as American-born nurses during the 1990s: deteriorating wages and health care restructuring that generates negative views regarding the climate for patient care (Clark, Clark, Day & Shea 2001; Schumacher 2001).

In Canada, meanwhile, during the1990s, conservative provincial governments reduced or stabilized financial transfers to hospitals for health care (Burke 2000) and precipitated work conditions that included substituting medical technology or other workers for tasks previously done by nurses, and intensifying managerial control (Stasiulis & Bakan 2003; Flynn 1998). A recent review of the use of temporary migrant nurses in Canada noted that temporary status reduced the capacity to move freely in the labour market, to receive competitive wages, and that such workers were frequently assigned to high stress units (Stasiulis & Bakan 2003). Furthermore, in Canada, shifting countries of origin, different modes of entry, deteriorating conditions of work and workplace practices routinely handicapped immigrant nurses of color. Throughout the 1990s and beyond, racially-based discrimination meant that Black women from the Caribbean were highly vulnerable to differential and unequal treatment: case studies indicate that much of the discrimination was intentional (Das Gupta 1996; Stasiulis & Bakan 2003).

Two other factors affect all highly-trained immigrant workers in Canada, including nurses: the devaluation of educational credentials received abroad and licensing and re-certification requirements of professionals. Regulated occupations, such as those in certain trades, law, engineering, and health areas, require certification and/or licensing, primarily through professional associations, often based on government statutes. While the purpose of licensing and certification is to assure public health and safety (Mata 1999; McDade 1988), these practices also are the defining characteristics of occupational internal labour markets which create monopolies on products and/or services by controlling labour supply. In Canada, certification requirements are often described as a form of systemic discrimination, in that criteria are created which are applied to the Canadian-born and foreign-born alike, but which disproportionately restrict the access of the foreign-born to trades or professions (McDade 1988; Singh Bolaria 1992). Devaluation of education credentials becomes part of this systemic discrimination when professional associations do not recognize foreign degrees as equivalent to those obtained within the country.

It appears that in the United States, deregulation has worked to the advantage of immigrant professionals, who are less hobbled by industry and professional association restrictions (Rekai 2002). However, the accreditation of immigrant professionals is of growing concern in Canada, stimulated in part by the growing share of skilled workers in the total intake of permanent migrants. Recent developments include: (1) the creation of several provincial task forces on the recognition of credentials obtained outside of Canada (Ontario government of 1989); (2) the generation of reports by policy institutes and federal government departments on the under-recognition of foreign credentials (McDade 1988; Mata 1999; Wright & McDade 1992); (3) the establishment in 1992 of a federal interdepartmental group; (4) a major conference in October 1999 in Toronto; and (5) a federal budget allocation of 13 million over two years to address the issue of foreign credential recognition, highlighted in the Governor General's Speech from the Throne at the opening of parliament (Guy, 1995).[8] Nonetheless, foreign-trained professionals must still make their way through a quagmire of specific professional association requirements, and the topic of immigrant women is virtually absent from these discussions.

A more general concern with discrimination based on race and sex underlies anti-discrimination legislation passed in Canada and in the United States. In both countries, legislation targets unintentional discrimination, seeking to remedy race and sex-neutral conventions and workplace practices that disadvantage persons of color and women. Yet an exhaustive review of US legislation reveals few significant results, partly because of the lack of funding during the neo-liberal political regimes of the 1980s and 1990s (Reskin 2001). Similarly, Canadian legislation passed in 1986, and replaced in 1995, has had limited results, particularly for women of color (Agocs 2002; Lum 1995). In seeking to explain the 1995 Canadian legislative reconfirmation of a progressive policy in the context of a growing neo-liberal political agenda, one study described the new legislation as "more teeth, less bite," noting the small or nonexistent monetary penalties, the latitude granted employers over goal setting, and equity exemptions for seniority and collective bargaining agreements under downsizing (Lum & Williams 1995). Most pertinent for migrant women, in both countries, affirmative-equity legislation covers limited sites of employment, such as federal contractors and the public service, and although it targets discriminatory outcomes by race and sex, it excludes outcomes based on foreign birth or immigrant status.

ALTERED ENTITLEMENTS

Overview

Immigrant experiences in the labour market are also affected by government policies relating to immigrant settlement policies, as well as by legislatively or administratively set rules and regulations, most often governing eligibility to mainstream social programs, but also those specifically targeted at immigrants and creating the potential for stratified citizenship (Fix & Zimmermann 1994).

As T.H. Marshall conceptualized it, citizenship refers to the set of civil, political and social rights that are bestowed upon members of a nation-state (Marshall 1981). The concept of full social citizenship implies that all members of a society have rights, unrestricted access to the labour market, to social investments such as education and language training, and to contributory and non-contributory social benefits, including publicly-provided health care and welfare benefits. The underlying premise of universality contrasts with neo-liberal agendas, which seek to reduce the social and economic obligations of states to their citizens by differentiating among its members as to who shall receive specific entitlements.

Migrants may be the most prone to reductions and elimination of entitlements. The large numbers, diverse phenotypical, social and economic characteristics, along with manifold entry and legal statuses of migrants today elicit questions of who belongs, and who shall hold membership in the nation-state.

Settling in: Implications for immigrant women

North American governments have never shouldered a comprehensive responsibility for settlement. Immigration policies of the 1960s and beyond incorporated the view that legal immigrants entering as family members or as workers should not be the responsibility of the state. But there have always been acknowledgments of the need to offer some assistance to refugees, and other migrants. Major areas of assistance typically include host country language(s) acquisition, employment related services, orientation services, and naturalization-related initiatives. Current descriptions imply an extensive and generous package of entitlements in both countries (Citizenship and Immigration Canada 2004c; Homeland Security, Citizenship, and Immigration 2003b). Yet by the mid-1990s, both American and Canadian governments had disengaged themselves from providing well-funded settlement assistance. Analyses of federal immigrant settlement policies in the United States report limited numbers of programs, reduced funding, and limited out-reach, accompanied by devolving federal authority and responsibility to individual states (Fix & Zimmerman 1994). A similar pattern of devolving federal responsibility occurred in Canada. In the 1994 budget, the Canadian federal government indicated that it was no longer prepared to be in the business of managing immigrant settlement policies and programs, including direct funding for language training. Following a pattern of decentralization found in other policy domains, the goal now is to "partner" with agencies that include provincial, territorial and municipal governments, businesses, not-for-profit groups, community groups, educational institutions, and individuals (Treasury Board of Canada 2004). Under various agreements, the provinces of Quebec, British Columbia and Manitoba now assume direct responsibility for the design, administration and delivery of services to newcomers settling in those provinces. Most notable in this change is the stability of funding during a time of high immigration: settlement funding for language training, immigrant settlement, adaptation and mentoring programs outside Quebec has remained constant since 1996–1997 (Citizenship and Immigration Canada 2003a).

These changes in *modus operandus* and in levels of funding obviously affect both women and men, but the impact of devolving services and funding levels may have a greater impact on women because of gender differences in need. Language training in Canada illustrates the potential for inequity. It is well understood that reduced language skills usually have negative consequences for immigrants, as language proficiency in the host country language(s) is an important resource in the integration process. Women who are not proficient in official languages have reduced labour force participation, higher rates of unemployment, and greater employment in production and processing occupations, in low skill occupations, and in the goods-producing sector of the economy. These correlates of low language proficiency are more severely felt by foreign-born women of color (Boyd 1999).

Compared to males, females are less likely to know English and/or French, Canada's two official languages upon arrival in Canada, thus increasing the likelihood of integration difficulties. During the 1980s in Canada, language training was provided to enhance the eligibility of immigrants for citizenship and to maximize economic productivity. Such programs, developed on labour market principles, risked excluding certain groups, notably women not destined for the labour force or not considered to need English or French in their paid work.

During the late 1980s and 1990s, there were two important policy developments. First, language knowledge increased in importance within the bundle of admissions criteria for skilled workers, thereby deflecting the cost of language training to other nations. Second, inside Canada, a new woman-friendly language program was introduced that allowed full- or part-time, self-assisted and distance learning, in both community contexts, with child minding provided on site. However funds have stabilized, and with inflation and large numbers of new immigrants, the per capita allotment has actually declined. There is a real risk that the immigrant women outnumber the existing slots (Boyd 1999), and the program is free only for newcomers, leaving uncertain the participation of women who have lived in Canada for longer than three to five years and who are not proficient in English or French.

Entry status and partial entitlements

In principle, both Canada and the United States readily extend civic and social citizenship rights to legal immigrants. However, in both countries, modes of entry as well as time spent in the host country may restrict immigrant access to societal resources and entitlements. Migrant women can be disadvantaged both if they perform care work in an employer's home, and if they enter the country later in life.

Canada and the United States are considered examples of welfare regimes in which entitlements are closely linked to economic "productive" activities rather than to care-oriented tasks in the home. Furthermore, many migrant women who perform care work in an employer's home operate in the invisible, or informal, economy. Paid in cash with no employer-paid benefits, they are vulnerable to abuse, as they can claim neither worker protection rights nor government work related benefits, such as unemployment insurance and pension benefits. There are no reliable estimates of the number of women employed in such circumstances, but as has been noted, for some origin groups, and for those who are in the country illegally, numbers are suspected to be high (Hondagneu-Sotelo 2001; Parreñas 2001; Repak 1994).

Canada's Live-In Caregiver Program (LCP) retains three elements of programs in place from 1973 on: the temporary authorization to be in Canada, the requirement that workers live in the homes of their employers, and the option of applying for permanent resident status after working as a live-in domestic worker for two out of three years while in Canada. One consequence is that workers, mostly women, who enter Canada under the LCP do not have the same rights of changing employers as do other residents. Although changing employers is permitted, women care givers often are reluctant to do so except in exceptional cases of abuse, since they are dependent on employers for documentation of weeks worked. Taken together, these difficulties in changing employers and the requirement that workers stay in live-in domestic employment for two out of three years while in Canada on a temporary work permit are considered to be indicators of stratified citizenship (Stasiulis & Bakan 2003). As well, although the Canadian government under LCP now requires a contract between employer and the LCP employee, it indicates that it has no legal authority to enforce it, and that workers must rely on provincial labour protection regulations. In many instances, these provincial regulations are substandard (Arat-Koc 1997; Stasiulis & Bakan 1997, 2003; Citizenship and Immigration Canada 2004).

Stratified citizenship entitlements for workers in the LCP program are a migrant women's issue, because at least 95 percent of these workers are women. The same is true for partial entitlements extended to elderly immigrant women in the form of pension benefits and access to income security programs. In both Canada and the US, financial support of the elderly rests on three pillars. The first is government income security programs which include flat rate benefits and income subsidies for impoverished elderly, as well government pension benefits such as the Canada/Quebec Pension Plan and Social Security (US) that are work related. The second pillar consists of private occupational plans, to which employers as well as employees may contribute. The third pillar rests on personal retirement actions that personal savings, wealth accumulation, and personal retirement savings plans.

Elderly immigrants, particularly recent arrivals, are most at risk of diminished or non-existent benefits from those government income programs which rest on work-related contributions. This risk occurs because both the Canada and the United States prorate pension benefits according to the length of time that benefits have been paid. In the US, all employed persons are required to pay Social Security premiums, although this requirement is most likely to be enforced in the formal economy. In order to be eligible for Social Security benefits, payments must be at or above a minimum level, and payments must have been made over 10 years, although they need not be consecutive years.

The major pension system in Canada consists of three federal programs to which are added various provincial supplements. Like other Canadian residents, immigrants who are in Canada legally may receive income from three federal programs: the Canada/Quebec Pension Plan; the Old Age Security Program (OAS); and the Guaranteed Income Supplement (GIS). But benefits may be reduced or even denied to immigrants who have fewer than 10 years of residence in Canada. The only exception to this ten year residency requirement is for those elderly immigrants from countries who have signed an International Social Security Agreement with Canada. Most signatories are developed countries, and no agreements exist between Canada and Asian countries, from which close to two thirds of all immigrants now come (Boyd 1991; Human Resources and Development Canada 2004).

Reflecting the longer life expectancies of women, elderly immigrants in the US and in Canada are disproportionately women. Some have aged in North America, and if they have paid benefits or have spouses with paid benefits, they may not be hampered by rules and regulations governing access to benefits. But of those who immigrated later in life, many will not meet the conditions for receiving benefits, relying instead on the safety net provided by the families that sponsored them. Such partial or non-existent entitlements have the potential to create dependency and elder abuse, and demonstrate the disadvantages associated with neo-liberal welfare regimes in which entitlements are closely linked to economic "productive" activities rather than care-oriented tasks.

Diminished entitlements

It is in health care and social assistance or welfare that the most dramatic changes to immigrant entitlements have occurred, particularly in the US. The welfare states of both countries operate mainly on a residualist, or means-tested, model of delivery. The most significant difference between the two countries is in their health-care systems — a large proportion of poor people are medically uninsured in the US, paying cash for expensive services or reliant on means-tested Medicaid benefits, while public health insurance is almost universally available to legal Canadian residents, after three months of residence. Exceptions to universal coverage in Canada include some classes of temporary foreign workers, visitors, foreign students, and irregular immigrants (Goldring & Berinstein 2003). Consistent with neo-liberal precepts, there has been both a steady reduction in, and restrictions on, cash welfare benefits in both countries, and an exhortation towards a renewed work ethic, seen most dramatically in the welfare-to-work strategies pursued aggressively in the US and some provinces in Canada. Under US reforms, child-care by single mothers has been completely removed as a legitimate basis for laying claim to support, replaced by tax credits granted to poor working parents (Orloff 2001).

Studies show that in the United States, poor Hispanic women, many of whom are migrants, and their children receive far less than optimal health care. Surveys conducted of service use in community clinics open to low-income and irregular status residents show, for instance, that undocumented migrant women receive fewer months of care during pregnancy (Norton, Kenney, & Ellwood 1996), and that Medicaid enrolment of children of irregular migrants (despite eligibility) is very low, with only 40 percent of eligible children receiving continuous coverage since birth (Halfon, Wood, Valdez, Pereyra, & Duan 1997). Nevertheless, fears of escalating and uncontrolled social service costs kindled California's infamous ideologically-motivated "tax revolt" of 1994, in which a decisive majority of Californians, including quite a few Latinos (Newton 2000), voted in favour of Proposition 187. The proposition sought to cut off health and social services, including access to public education, to undocumented migrants and their children.

The Proposition 187 initiative, though barred by the federal court, triggered a national debate that set the stage for the passing by Congress of a major welfare reform in 1996. The Personal Responsibility and Work Opportunity Reconciliation Act (PRWORA) was a thorough reform of all aspects of the US welfare system, and contained important changes that applied to everyone, such as a five-year maximum lifetime entitlement to welfare. However, many of its provisions were aimed squarely at the foreign-born population. The most dramatic was an unprecedented differentiation of legal permanent residents according to whether they were naturalized. Legal non-citizens are barred from public assistance, though eligibility is reinstated upon naturalization. This stratification of entitlements among legal residents has been identified as a watershed by critics, who point out that it is a departure from not only substantive, but also formal equality among legal immigrants with regard to entitlements.

Entitlements for irregular migrants were even more dramatically targeted in the Personal Responsibility and Work Opportunity Reconciliation Act (PRWORA). Although the right to public education guaranteed in a 1982 Supreme Court decision was upheld, the 1996 legislation barred access to all non-emergency health and welfare programs for irregular migrants and "aliens" paroled into the US for one year (Fragomen 1997). The only health care authorized at community clinics for those without legal documents of permanent residency is treatment of communicable disease, services for abused children and women, and immunization. In practice, only San Diego country, bordering with Mexico, has followed the federal law. In other jurisdictions with large immigrant populations, health care providers have quietly ignored it. Nonetheless, the provision of all other services is now discretionary, and thus vulnerable to legal and political challenge (Landa 2004), and there is some evidence of the reduced use of clinics post-1994 (Fenton, Catalano & Hargreaves 1996).

While a great deal has been written about consequences for migrants of the United States 1990s reforms (Bean & Stevens 2003; Fix, & Passel 1999; Fix & Passel 2002; Espenshade 1998; Zimmermann & Tumlin 1999), scant attention has been paid to the specific impacts on immigrant women of these reforms. Much of the impact undoubtedly is indirect, occurring when households or family members no longer are eligible for welfare and/or health care services, or choose not to claim benefits and utilize services as a result of fear that they will be turned away. This "chilling effect" is thought to be responsible for reductions in welfare use (Fix & Passel 1999; 2002; Borjas 2003; Kretsedemas 2003). Additional indirect outcomes have arisen from increases in deportations and family separations, and loss of services to US-born children of non-citizen parents (Hagan et al. 2003).

CONCLUSION

Concurrent with the increasing presence of women in international migration in the latter decades of the twentieth century are two developments affecting migrant women. First, as demand for entry has risen, governments in North America, as elsewhere, have attempted to stabilize or reduce the numbers of migrants, and to impose increasingly demanding criteria to determine who gets in. The resulting alterations in migration policy have changed who is legally admitted; they have stimulated the entry of irregular and temporary migrants; and in Canada they have enlarged the share of highly skilled migrants during the 1990s.

Second, coinciding, if not underlying these migratory changes, is a North American neo-liberal agenda which emphasizes an extensive deregulation of the labour market, a downsizing, decentralizing and erosion of the welfare state, and privatization of services. Together, these measures create the potential for a post-Marshallian citizenship in which social provision no longer seriously seeks to bridge the chasm between formal rights and substantive access to resources among the poor. In Europe, scholars note that proliferating legal citizenship statuses, which correspond with stratified entitlements, are a dominant government strategy to limit costs, while at the same time preserving the welfare state for a core constituency of full-status citizens (Kofman, 2002). Such formal stratifications are present in North America, as evidenced in Canada's Live-in Caregiver Program, in growing numbers of temporary workers in both countries, and in US welfare reform restricting entitlement for new immigrants. However, despite this, formally sanctioned exclusionary, or stratified, citizenship statuses have not been as extensively adopted in North America as in Europe. Erosion of social services and assistance as part of an attempt to reduce government responsibility for poverty among both native- and foreign-born, the growing income inequality that follows from the adoption of labour market deregulation as a principal strategy to fight unemployment, non-recognition of foreign credentials (especially in Canada) and persisting systems of gender and racial stratification that affect all citizens are more central in understanding migrant women's disadvantages with respect to livelihoods and entitlements in these two countries.

The future of North America's foreign-born residents, especially women, is uncertain. On the one hand, scholars point optimistically to an admirable record of socio-economic mobility and success of most immigrant groups over time and into the second generation. Gender awareness, if not sensitivity, also exists as seen in the development of gender related persecution guidelines and in a more limited context in Canada, with respect to language training programs. On the other hand, growing labour market inequality, deteriorating social provision, and fraying safety nets appear to threaten a continuation of this historic pattern for the majority of today's newcomers. Of particular concern is the trend toward a growing reliance on temporary categories of entry and residence, as well as increasing inequality in social provision. Such trends have the potential of maintaining and enlarging the struggles of migrant women to find permanent and legal residency and to keep a secure foothold in the North American post-industrial economies.

NOTES

1. See http://www.december18.net/web/general/page.php?pageID=84&menuID=36&lang=EN, accessed 15 May, 2005.
2. Critics counter that Canada imports temporary migrants for its Seasonal Agricultural Worker Program, and that some aspects of this (admittedly small) program appear to be in contravention of convention guidelines.
3. Economic migrants in Figure 2.2 refer to the category used by the United States Office of Immigration Statistics in compiling their statistics plus those admitted under the Nursing Relief Act of 1989.
4. Citizenship and Immigration Canada, Fee Schedule for Citizenship and immigrations Services (May 2006), http://www.cic.gc.ca/EnGlish/applications/fees.html.Accessed on 7 June 2006.; U.S. Citizenship and Immigration Services, G-1055 Fee Schedule (December 2005a), http://www.uscis.gov/graphics/formsfee/forms/files/g-1055.pdf. Accessed on 7 June 2006.
5. Luin Goldring, email, 3 February 2004.
6. See www.azcadv.org/HTML/batteredimmigrants.html, accessed 4 February 2004.
7. Personal communication with Linda Gordon, US Department of Homeland Security, 12 February, 2004.
8. The governor general is the representative of the (British) crown whose role is to ensure, under a parliamentary system, that Canada always has a prime minister and thus a political executive. The Speech from the Throne is given at the opening a session of Parliament and outlines the government's legislative plans.

REFERENCES

Agocs, C. (2002) "Canada's Employment Equity Legislation and Policy — the Gap between Policy and Practice", in: *International Journal of Manpower* vol. 23(3): 256–276.

Aleinikoff, T. A. and D. Klusmeyer (2002) *Citizenship Policies for an Age of Migration*, Washington, DC: Brookings Institution.

Antecol, H., D. A. Cobb-Clark, and S. J. Trejo (2003) "Human Capital and Earnings of Female Immigrants to Australia, Canada, and the United States", in J.G. Reitz (ed), *Host Societies and the Reception of Immigrants*, San Diego: University of California.

Arat-Koc, S. "'Mothers of the Nation' to Migrant Workers", in: A. B. Bakan and D. Stasiulis (eds), *Not One of the Family: Foreign Domestic Workers in Canada*. Toronto: University of Toronto Press, 1997.

Bean, F. D., and G. Stevens (2003) *America's Newcomers and the Dynamics of Diversity*. New York: Russell Sage.

Bolaria, B. S. (1992) "From Immigrant Settlers to Migrant Transients: Foreign Professionals in Canada", in V. Seasick (ed), *Deconstructing a Nation: Immigration, Multiculturalism and Racism in 90's Canada*, Halifax: Firewood.

Borjas, G. J.(2003) "Welfare Reforms and Immigrant Participation in Welfare Programs", in: J. G. Reitz (ed), *Host Societies and the Reception of Immigrants*, San Diego: University of California.

Boyd, M. (1989) *Migrant Women in Canada: Profiles and Policies*, Report prepared for Monitoring Panel on Migrant Women, Organization for Economic Co-operation and Development, Directorate for Social Affairs, Manpower and Education (1987), Ottawa: Employment and Immigration Canada, Public Affairs Inquiries and Distribution.

———. (1991) "Immigration and Living Arrangements: Elderly Women in Canada", in: *International Migration Review* 25 (spring): 4–27.

———. (1992) "Gender Issues in Immigration Trends and Language Fluency: Canada and the United States", in B. R. Chiswick (ed) *Immigration Language and Ethnic Issues: Public Policy in Canada and the United States*, Washington, DC: American Enterprise Institute.

———.(1997) "Migration Policy, Family Membership and Female Dependency: Canada and Germany", in: P. Evans, T. McCormack, and G. Wekerle (eds), *Remaking the Welfare State*, Toronto: University of Toronto Press.

———. (1998) "Gender, Refugee Status and Permanent Settlement", in: *Gender Issues* vol. 16(4): 5–21.

———. (1999) "Integrating Gender, Language and Visible Minority Groups", in: S. Hallos and L. Dredger (eds), *Immigrant Canada: Demographic, Economic and Social Challenges*, edited by Toronto: University of Toronto Press.

———. (2001) "Gender Inequality: Economic and Political Aspects," in: R. J. Brym (ed), *New Society: Sociology for the 21st Century*, 3rd ed., Toronto: Harcourt.

Brus, B.L. (1995) "The Rockefeller Agenda for American Philippines Nursing Relations", in: *Western Journal of Nursing Research* vol. 17(5): 540–555.

Burke, M. (2000) "Efficiency and the Erosion of Health Care in Canada", in: M. Burke, C. Mooers, and J. Shields (eds), *Restructuring and Resistance: Canadian Public Policy in an Age of Global Capitalism*, Halifax: Firewood.

Burt, Sandra, and S.L. Hardman (2001) "The Case of Disappearing Targets: The Liberals and Gender Equality", in: Leslie Pal (ed), *How Ottawa Spends 2001–2002: Power in Transition*, Don Mills: Oxford University Press.

Calliste, A. (2000) "Resisting Professional Exclusion and Marginality in Nursing: Women of Color in Ontario", in: M. A. Kalbach and W. E. Kalbach (eds) *Perspectives on Ethnicity in Canada: A Reader,*. Toronto: Harcourt.

Canada, Citizenship and Immigration (2002a) *Facts and Figures, 2001: Immigration Overview*, Ottawa: Minister of Public works and Government Services Canada.

———. (2002b) *Facts and Figures, 2001: Statistical Overview of the Temporary Resident and Refugee Claimant Population*. Ottawa: Citizenship and Immigration Canada.

———. (2002c) *Immigration and Refugee Protection Regulations, Gender-Based Analysis Chart*. Ottawa: Citizenship and Immigration Canada, http://www.cic.gc.ca/english/irpa/gender-irpa.html, accessed 28 March 2005.

———. (2003a) *Government Response to the Report of the Standing Committee on Citizenship and Immigration*. Ottawa: Citizenship and Immigration Canada. http://www.cic.gc.ca/english/pub/response-settlement.html, accessed 7 March 2004.

———. (2003b) *Immigrating as Parents, Grandparents, Adopted Children or Other Relatives*. Ottawa: Citizenship and Immigration Canada. http://www.cic.gc.ca/english/pdf/kits/guides/3998E.PDF, accessed 26 February 2004.

———. (2004a) *Application for Permanent Residence: Federal Skilled Worker Class*. Ottawa: Citizenship and Immigration Canada, http://www.cic.gc.ca/english/pdf/kits/guides/EG7.pdf, accessed 26 February 2004.

———. (2004b) "Overseas Selection and Processing of Convention Refugees Abroad Class and Members of the Humanitarian-protected Persons Abroad Classes", in *Overseas Processing Manual OP5*. Ottawa: Citizenship and Immigration Canada. http://www.cic.gc.ca/manuals-guides/english/op/op05e.pdf, accessed 13 February, 2004.

———. (2004c) *Sponsoring Parents, Grandparents, Children and other Relatives*. Ottawa: Citizenship and Immigration Canada, http://www.cic.gc.ca/english/pdf/kits/guides/5196E.PDF, accessed 26 February 2004.

———. (2004d) *The Live-in Care giver Program for Employers and Care givers Abroad*. Ottawa: Citizenship and Immigration Canada. http://www.cic.gc.ca/english/pub/caregiver/caregiver/index.html, accessed 7 March 2004.

———. (2004e) *Settlement Programs and Services*. Ottawa: Citizenship and Immigration Canada, http://www.cic.gc.ca/english/pub/you%2Dasked/section%2D14.html, accessed 2 March 2004.

Canada, Human Resources and Development (2004) *Infosheets on Social Security Agreements*. Ottawa: Human Resources and Development Canada, http://www.hrdc-drhc.gc.ca/isp/pub/interpub_e.shtml#a, accessed 8 March 2004. Note: Human Resources and Development Canada was split into two departments, and this is the "transition" web address.

Canada, Treasury Board Secretariat (2004) *Immigrant Settlement and Adaptation Program (ISAP)*, Ottawa: Treasury Board of Canada http;//www.tbs-sct.gc.ca/rma/eppi-ibdrp/hrdb-rhbd/h017_e.asp, accessed 4 March 2004.

Clark, P. F., D. A. Clark, D. V. Day, and D. G. Shea (2001) "Healthcare Reform and the Workplace Experience of Nurses: Implications for Patient Care and Union Organizing", in *Industrial Relations Review* vol. 55(1): 133–48.

Connors, J. (1997) "Legal Aspects of Women as a Particular Social Group", in: *International Journal of Refugees* 9 (Autumn): 114–28.

Das-Gupta, T. (1996) *Racism and Paid Work*, Toronto: Garamond Press.

De Anda, R.M.(2000) "Mexican-Origin Women's Employment Instability", in: *Sociological Perspectives* 43(3): 421–37.

Espenshade, T. J. (1998) "US Immigration and the New Welfare State", in: D. Jacobson (ed) *The Immigration Reader: American in a Multidisciplinary Perspective*, Malden: Blackwell, 1998.

Espiritu, Y. L. (1999) "Gender and Labour in Asian Immigrant Families", in: *The American Behavioral Scientist* 42(4): 628–47.

———. (2003) "Gender and Labour in Asian Immigrant Families", in P. Hondagneu-Sotelo (ed), *Gender and US Immigration: Contemporary Trends*, Berkeley; Los Angeles; London: University of California Press.

Ewing, W. (2004) "A New Bracero Program for the 21st Century", http://www.crlaf.org/coha1814.htm, accessed 6 February 2004.

Fenton, J.J., R. Catalano, and W.A. Hargreaves (1996) "Effect of Proposition 187 on Mental Health Service Use in California: A Case Study", in: *Health Affairs*, vol. 15(1): 182–90.

Fix, M. and W. Zimmermann (1994) "After Arrival: An Overview of Federal Immigrant Policy in the United States", in: B. Edmonston and J. S. Passel (eds), *Immigration and Ethnicity: The Integration of America's Newest Arrivals*, Washington, DC: Urban Institute.

Fix, M., and J. S. Passel (1999) *Trends in Noncitizens' and Citizens' Use of Public Benefits following Welfare Reform: 1994-97*, Washington, DC: Urban Institute.

———. (2002) *The Scope and Impact of Welfare Reform's Immigrant Provisions*, Washington, DC: Urban Institute.

Flynn, K. (1998) "Proletarianization, Professionalization and Caribbean Immigrant Nurses." *Canadian Woman Studies*, vol. 18(1): 57–60.

Fragomen, A. T. (1997) "The Illegal Immigration Reform and Immigrant Responsibility Act of 1996: An Overview", in: *International Migration Review* 31(2): 438–60.

Gammage, S. (2003) "Women Immigrants in the US Labour Market: Second Rate Jobs in the First World", in: *Women Immigrants in the United States*, Washington, DC: Woodrow Wilson International Center for Scholars.

Goldring, L., and C.Berinstein (2003) "More and Less Status: Critical Perspectives on Legal Status and Rights in Canada", Presentation for *Migration and Integration in the Americas*, 19–20 September 2003, CERLAC, York University, Toronto.

Grace, J. (1997) "Sending Mixed Messages: Gender-based Analysis and the 'Status of Women'", In: *Canadian Public Administration*, vol. 40(4): 582–598.

Guy, J. J. (1995) *How We are Governed: the basics of Canadian politics and government*, Toronto: Harcourt Brace.

Halfon, N., D.L. Wood, R.B. Valdez, M. Pereyra, and N.H. Duan (1997) "Medicaid Enrollment and Health Services Accessed by Latino Children in Innercity Los Angeles", in: *Journal of the American Medical Association*, vol. 277 (8): 636–641.

Hankivsky, O. (2004) "Gender Mainstreaming vs Diversity Mainstreaming: A Preliminary Examination of the Role and Transformative Potential of Feminist Theory", Paper presented at the Canadian Political Science Association annual meeting, 2004, http://www.cpsa-acsp.ca/papers-2004/Hankivshy.pdf, accessed 28 March 2005 (Permission to cite granted. Revised version *Canadian Journal of Political Science*, 2005, vol 38(4): 977–1001.

Hasselriis, K. (2004) "Health care workers in British Columbia face privatization, sweetheart contract." *Labour notes*, January 2004. http;//www.labournotes.org/archives/2004/01articles/b.html, accessed 12 February 2004.

Hobson, B., J. Lewis, and B. Seem (eds) (2002) *Contested Concepts in Gender and Social Politics*. Cheltenham; Northampton: Edward Elgar.

Hochschild, A. (1995) "The Culture of Politics: Traditional, Post-modern, Coldmodern and Warm-modern Ideals of Care", in: *Social Politics*, vol. 2(3): 331–46.

———. (2000) "The Nanny Chain." *The American Prospect* 3, January, pp. 32–36.

Hondagneu-Sotelo, P. (1994) *Gendered Transitions: Mexican Experiences of Immigration*. Berkeley: University of California Press.

———. (2001) *Doméstica: Immigrant Workers Cleaning and Caring in the Shadows of Affluence*. Berkeley: University of California Press.

———, (ed.) (2003) *Gender and US Immigration: Contemporary Trends*. Berkeley: University of California Press.

Hughes, D. M. (2000) "The 'Natasha' Trade: The Transnational Shadow Market of Trafficking in Women", in: *Journal of International Affairs*, vol.53(2): 625–51.

Jachimowicz, M. (2004) "Bush Proposes New Temporary Worker Program", *Migration Information Source*, http://www.migrationinformation.org/USfocus/display.cfm?ID=202, accessed 4 February 2004.

Jachimowicz, M., and S. Margon (2004) "Bush Boosts Immigration Enforcement in FY2005 Budget", Migration Information Source, http://www.migrationinformation.org/USfocus/print.cfm?ID=207, accessed 27 March 2004.

Jachimowicz, M., and R. McKay (2003) "Ashcroft: Undocumented Immigrants Subject to Indefinite Detention", Migration Information Source, http://www.migrationinformation.org/Feature/print.cfm?ID=123, accessed 4 February 2004.

Jachimowicz, M., and D.W. Meyers (2002) "Temporary High-Skilled Migration", *Migration Information Source*, http://www.migrationinformation.org/USfocus/print.cfm?ID69, accessed 12 February 2004.

Jimenez, M. (2003a) "US Starting to Embrace Illegal Workers", *Globe and Mail*. 17 November, A6.

———. (2003b) "Ottawa Aims to give Status to Illegal Foreign Workers." *Globe and Mail*, 14 November, http://www.globeandmail.com/servlet/story/RTGAM.20031114.wfore1114/BNPrint/National, accessed 10 February, 2004.

Kaneya, R. (2002) "At any Price: Marriage and Battered Immigrant Women." *The Chicago Reporter*, March 2002, http://www.findarticles.com/cf_dls/mOJAS/3_31/84184220/print.jhtml, accessed 4 February 2004.

Keely, C. B. (1992) "The Resettlement of Women and Children Refugees", *Migration World* vol. 20(4): 14–18.

Kline, D.S. (2003) "Push and Pull Factors in International Nurse Migration", in: *Journal of Nursing Scholarship*, vol. 35(2): 107–11.

Kofman, E. (2002) "Contemporary European Migration: Civic stratification and citizenship", in: *Political Geography*, vol. 21, pp. 1035–54.

Kretsedemas, P. (2003) "Immigrant Households and Hardships after Welfare Reform: A Case Study of the Miami-Dade Haitian Community", in: *International Journal of Social Welfare*, vol.12, pp. 314–25.

Landa, A.S. (2001) "Illegal Care? Treating Undocumented Immigrants in Texas", http://www.ama-assn.org/amednews/2001/10/01/gvsa1001.htm, accessed 4 February 2004.

Lawyers Committee for Human Rights (2002) *Refugee Women at Risk*. New York: New York Lawyers Committee for Human Rights, http://www.lchr.org/refugees/reports/refugee_women.pdf, accessed 13 February 2004.

Leira, A., and C. Saraceno (2002) "Care: Actors, Relationships and Contexts. The Multidimensional Caring Puzzle", in: B. Hobson, J. Lewis, and B. Siim (eds) *Contested Concepts in Gender and Social Politics*, Cheltenham; Northampton: Edward Elgar.

Lipset, S. M. (1990) *Continental Divide: The Values and Institutions of the United States and Canada*. New York: Routledge.

Lowell, L. B. (2001) "Skilled Temporary and Permanent Immigrants in the United States", in: *Population Research and Policy Review*, vol. 20(1): 33–58.

Lum, J. M. (1995) "The Federal Employment Equity Act: Goals vs. Implementation", in: *Journal of Administrative Sciences*, vol. 13(3): 207–15.

Lum, J. M., and A. P.Williams (2000) "Out of Sync with a 'Shrinking State'? Making Sense of the Employment Equity Act", in: M. Burke, C. Mooers, and J. Shields (eds), *Restructuring and Resistance: Canadian Public Policy in an Age of Global Capitalism*, Halifax: Fernwood.

Macklin, A. (1992) "Foreign Domestic Workers: Surrogate Housewives or Imported Servants?" in: *McGill Law Journal*, vol. 37, pp. 681–760.

———. (1999) "Comparative Approaches to Gender Based Persecution: Canada, US and Australia," in: Doreen Indra (ed), *Engendering Forced Migration*, Providence: Berghahn.

Mailman, S., and S. Yale-Loehr (2002) "Supreme Court Denies Back Pay to Fired Undocumented Immigrants", in: *New York Law Journal*, vol. 22 (April 2002), http://www.twmlaw.com/resources/backpay.html, accessed 4 February 2004.

Marshall, T. H. (1981) *The Right to Welfare and Other Essays*. London: Heinemann.

Martin, Susan Forbes (1991) *Refugee Women*, London: ZED Books.

Mata, F. (1999) "The Non-accreditation of Immigrant Professionals in Canada: Societal Dimensions of the Problem", Paper presented at the conference on *Shaping the Future: Qualifications Recognition in the 21st Century*, Toronto, Ontario, 1999.

McDade, K. (1988) *Barriers to the recognition of the credentials of immigrants in Canada*, Ottawa: Institute for Research on Public Policy.

McDonald, L., B. Moore, and N. Timoshkina (2000) *Migrant Sex Workers from Eastern Europe and the Former Soviet Union: The Canadian Case*, Ottawa: Status of Women Canada, http://www.swc-cfc.gc.ca/pubs/pubsalpha_e.html, accessed 23 January 2004.

McKay, R. (2003) "Family Reunification", *Migration Policy Institute*, May 2003, http://www.migrationinformation.org/USfocus/display.cfm?ID=122, accessed 4 February 2004.

Migration Policy Institute (2003) "Event Summaries: The Feminization of International Migration: Issues of Labour, Health, and Family Coping Strategies", Migration Policy Institute, http://www.migrationpolicy.org/events/030702_sum.html, accessed 2 March 2004.

Neysmith, S. and X.Chen (2002) "Understanding how globalization and restructuring affects women's lives: Implications for comparative policy analysis, in: *International Journal of Social Welfare*, vol, 11, pp. 243–53.

Newton, L.Y. (2000) "Why some Latinos Supported Proposition 187: Resting Economic Threat and Cultural Identity Hypothesis", in: *Social Science Quarterly*, vol. 81(1): 180–93.

Norton, S.A., G.M. Kenney, and M.R. Ellwood (1996) "Medicaid Coverage of Maternity Care for Aliens in California", in: *Family Planning and Perspectives*, vol. 28(3): 108–12.

OECD (2000) Chapter Three, in: *Employment Outlook 2000*, June 2000, http://www.oecd.org/dataoecd/10/48/2079561.pdf, accessed 5 March 2004.

Orloff, A. S. (2001) "Farewell to Maternalism: Welfare Reform, Ending Entitlement for Poor Single Mothers, and Expanding the Claims for Poor Employed Parents", Paper presented at Harvard seminar on Inequality and Social Policy, 26 February 2001, http://www.ksg.harvard.edu/inequality/Seminar/Papers/Orloff.PDF, accessed 16 February 2004.

Parreñas, R. S. (2001) *Servants of Globalization: Women, Migration and Domestic Work*. Stanford: Stanford University Press.

Passel, J. S., R. Capps, and M. E. Fix (2004) "Undocumented Immigrants: Facts and Figures", Urban Institute, January 2004, http://www.urban.org/urlprint.cfm?ID=8685, accessed 23 February 2004.

Power, J. (2003) "Europe's Fake Crisis over Immigration and Aging", in: *International Herald Tribune*, 31 July 2003, http://www.iht.com/cgi-bin/generic.cgi?template-=articleprint.tmplh&ArticleId=104649, accessed 19 February 2004.

Powers, M. G., W. Seltzer, and J. Shi (1998) "Gender Differences in the Occupational Status of Undocumented Immigrants in the United States: Experience Before and After Legalization", in: *International Migration Review*, vol. 32 (4): 1015–46.

Pratt, G. (1999) "From Registered Nurse to Registered Nanny: Discursive Geographics of Filipina Domestic Workers in Vancouver, BC.", in: *Economic Geography*, vol. 75(3): 215–36.

Refugee Council USA (2004) *US Refugee Admissions Program for the Fiscal Year 2004: Recommendations of the Refugee Council USA*, USA: Refugee Council, http://www.refugeecouncilusa.org/rcusa2004doc.pdf, accessed 13 February 2004

Rekai, P. (2002) *US and Canadian Immigration Policies: Marching Together to Different Tunes*, Toronto: CD Howe Institute, http://www.cdhowe.org/pdf/Rekai.pdf, accessed 12 February 2004.

Repak, T.A.(1994) "Labour Market Incorporation of Central-American Immigrants in Washington, DC", in: *Social Problems* vol. 41(1): 114–28.

Reskin, B. (2001) "Employment Discrimination and Its Remedies", in: I. Berg and A. L. Kalleberg (eds), *Sourcebook of Labour Markets: Evolving Structures and Processes*, New York: Kluwer/Plenum.

Robbins, T. (2001) "Unfriendly Relations: Bush Supporters take aim at Pro-labour Board", in: *The Village Voice*, 24–30 January 2001, http://www.labourers.org/Village_Bush_NLRB_1-15-01.htm, accessed 8 February 2004.

Romero, M. (2002) *Maid in the USA*, 10th anniversary ed., New York: Routledge.

Rosenfield, A.F. (2002) "Procedures and Remedies for Discriminatees Who may be Undocumented Aliens after Hoffman Plastic Compounds, Inc." , Memorandum GC 02-06, Office of the General Counsel, July 19, 2002, http://www.lawmemo.com/emp/nlrb/gc02-06.htm, accessed 8 February 2004.

Ruddick, E. (n.d) *Trends in International Labour Flows to Canada*, Ottawa: Citizenship and Immigration Canada, nd. http://www.cic.gc.ca/english/srr/pdf/res3di.pdf, accessed 24 February 2004.

Sassen, S. (1988) *The Mobility of Labour and Capital: A Study in International Investment and Labour Flow*, Cambridge: Cambridge University Press.

——. (2000) "Women's Burden: Counter-geographies of Globalization and the Feminization of Survival", in: *Journal of International Affairs*, vol. 53(2): 503–24.

Schoeni, R. F. (1998) "Labour Market Outcomes of Immigrant Women in the United States: 1970 to 1990", in: *International Migration Review*, vol. 32(1): 57–78.

Schumacher, E. J. (2001) "The Earnings and Employment of Nurses in an Era of Cost Containment", in: *Industrial Relations Review*, vol. 55(1): 116–32.

Scialabba, L. L. (1997) "The Immigration and Naturalization Service Considerations for Asylum Officers Adjudicating Asylum Claims from Women", in: *International Journal of Refugees* , vol. 9 (autumn 1997), pp. 174–81.

Shumway, J. M., and T. J. Cooke (1998) "Gender and Ethnic Concentration and Employment Prospects for Mexican-American Migrants", in: *Growth and Change*, vol. 29(1): 23–54.

Stasiulis, D. and A. B. Bakan (1997) "Regulation and Resistance: Strategies of Migrant Domestic Workers in Canada and Internationally", in: *Asian and Pacific Migration Journal* vol. 6(1): 31–57.

——. (2003) *Negotiating Citizenship: Migrant Women in Canada and the Global System*. New York: Palgrave Macmillan.

Status of Women Canada. *Canadian Experience in Gender Mainstreaming, April 2000* (2003) Ottawa: Status of Women, http://www.sws-cfc.gc.ca/pubs/cegm2000/cegm2000_1_e.html, accessed 28 March 2005.

Teghtsoonian, K. (2004) "Neoliberalism and Gender Analysis: Mainstreaming in Aotearoa/New Zealand", in: *Australian Journal of Political Science*, vol. 39(2): 267–84.

Townson, M (2003) *Women in Non-Standard Jobs: the Public Policy Challenge.* Ottawa: Status of Women.

UNHRC (2002) *2002 UNHRC Population Statistics (Provisional)*, Geneva: UNHRC, http://www.unhcr.ch/cgi-bin/texis/vtx/home/opendoc.pdf?tbl=STATISTICS&id=3f3769672&page=statistics, accessed 13 February 2004.

———. (2001) *Women, Children and Older Refugees: The Sex and Age Distribution of Refugee Populations with a Special Emphasis on UNHCR Policy Priorities*, Geneva: UNHRC, http://www.unhcr.ch/cgi-bin/texis/vtx/home/opendoc.pdf?tbl=STATISTICS&id=3b9378e518&page=statistics, accessed 13 February 2004

United States, Department of Homeland Security, Office of Immigration Statistics (2003a) *2002 Yearbook of Immigration Statistics*, Washington, DC: Superintendent of Documents.

———. (2003b) *The Triennial Comprehensive Report on Immigration.* (3rd report). Washington, DC: Homeland Security, Citizenship, and Immigration, http://uscis.gov/graphics/aboutus/repsstudies/addition.htm, accessed 2 March 2004.

———. (2004) *I-864 package, Affidavit of Support Package (Forms I-864, I-864A, I-864P, I-865).* Washington, DC: Homeland Security, Citizenship, and Immigration, http://uscis.gov/graphics/formsfee/forms/files/i-864pkg.pdf, accessed 26 February 2004.

United States, Department of Justice, Immigration and Naturalization Service (1995) *Memorandum: Considerations for Asylum Officers Adjudicating Asylum Claims from Women*, May 26, Washington, DC: Department of Justice.

———. (1991) *An Immigrant Nation: United States Regulation of Immigration, 1798–1991*, Washington, DC: Department of Justice.

Verma, V. (2003) *The Mexican and Caribbean Seasonal Agricultural Workers Program: Regulatory and Policy Framework, Farm Industry Level Employment Practices, and the Future of the Program under Unionization*, Report prepared for the North South Institute, 2003.

Walton-Roberts, M. (2004) "Rescaling Citizenship: Gendering Canadian Immigration Policy", in: *Political Geography*, vol. 23, pp. 265–81.

Wright, R. and M. Ellis (2000) "The Ethnic and Gender Division of Labour Compared Among Immigrants to Los Angeles", in: *International Journal of Urban and Regional Research*, vol. 24(3): 583–600.

Wright, R. E., and K. McDade (1992) *Barriers to the Recognition of the Credentials of Immigrants in Canada: An Analysis using Census Data*, Ottawa: Secretary of State and Health and Welfare Canada.

Zimmermann, W., and K. C. Tumli (1999) "Patchwork Policies: State Assistance for Immigrants under Welfare Reform", Occasional Paper Number 24, Washington, DC: Urban Institute.

Zlotnik, H. (2003) "The Global Dimension of Female Migration", Migration Information Source, http://www.migrationinformation.org/Feature/display.cfm?ID=109

DATA SOURCES FOR FIGURES 2.1-2.3 AND TABLES 2.2 AND 2.3:

Canada, Citizenship and Immigration. *Facts and Figures, 2000: Immigration Overview.* Ottawa: Minister of Public works and Government Services Canada, 2001. http://www.cic.gc.ca/english/pdf/pub/facts2000.pdf, accessed 12 April 2004.

Canada, Citizenship and Immigration. *Facts and Figures, 1999: Immigration Overview.* Ottawa: Minister of Public works and Government Services Canada, 2000. http://www.cic.gc.ca/english/pdf/pub/facts1999.pdf, accessed 12 April 2004.
Canada, Citizenship and Immigration. *Facts and Figures, 1998: Immigration Overview.* Ottawa: Minister of Public works and Government Services Canada, 1999. http://www.cic.gc.ca/english/pdf/pub/facts1998.pdf, accessed 12 April 2004.
Canada, Citizenship and Immigration. *Citizenship and Immigration Statistics 1996.* Ottawa: Minister of Public works and Government Services Canada, 1998a. http://www.cic.gc.ca/english/pdf/pub/1996stats.pdf, accessed 12 April 2004.
Canada, Citizenship and Immigration. *Citizenship and Immigration Statistics 1995.* Ottawa: Minister of Public works and Government Services Canada, 1998b. http;//www.cic.gc.ca/english/pdf/pub/1995stats.pdf, accessed 12 April 2004.
Canada, Citizenship and Immigration. *Citizenship and Immigration Statistics 1994.* Ottawa: Minister of Public works and Government Services Canada, 1997. http://www.cic.gc.ca/english/pdf/pub/1994stats.pdf, accessed 12 April 2004.
Canada, Citizenship and Immigration. *Citizenship and Immigration Statistics 1993.* Ottawa: Minister of Supply and Services Canada, 1996. http://www.cic.gc.ca/english/pdf/pub/1993stats.pdf, accessed 12 April 2004.
Canada, Citizenship and Immigration. *Immigration Statistics 1992.* Ottawa: Public Works and Government Services Canada, 1994. http://www.cic.gc.ca/english/pdf/pub/1992stats.pdf, accessed 12 April 2004.
Canada, Employment and Immigration. *Immigration Statistics 1991.* Ottawa: Minister of Supply and Services Canada, 1992. http://www.cic.gc.ca/english/pdf/pub/1991stats.pdf, accessed 12 April 2004.
Canada, Employment and Immigration. *Immigration Statistics 1990.* Ottawa: Minister of Supply and Services Canada, 1991. http://www.cic.gc.ca/english/pdf/pub/1990stats.pdf, accessed 12 April 2004.
United States. Unpublished tabulations 1990–2000. Washington, DC: Department of Homeland Security, Office of Immigration Statistics, 2003a. Released to first author, January, 2004.

DATA SOURCES: CHART 2.4

Statistics Canada. 2001 Census Public Use Microdata File of Individuals. Analysis conducted especially for this paper by first author.
United States Census Bureau. 2000 1% Census PUMS. *Integrated Public Use Microdata Series: Version 3.0* [Machine-readable database]. Minneapolis, MN: Minnesota Population Center [producer and distributor], 2004. http://www.ipums.umn.edu. Obtained from Steven Ruggles, Matthew Sobek, Trent Alexander, Catherine A. Fitch, Ronald Goeken, Patricia Kelly Hall, Miriam King, and Chad Ronnander. Analysis conducted especially

3 Gendered Migrations, Livelihoods and Entitlements in European Welfare Regimes

Eleonore Kofman

Although unwilling to acknowledge the significance of immigration and the contribution of migrants, European societies and states have a long history of immigration, both from neighbouring areas as well as from far-flung colonies throughout the world. In the initial post-war period until the stoppage of mass labour migration, distinct migratory regimes (colonial, hybrid, guest worker), defined in terms of the mode of entry, rights of residence and status of migrants, were characteristic of European countries (Kofman et al. 2000: 46–56). The more expansive colonial regime, as in the UK, not only brought in workers but also whole families. Though attenuated, colonial links have left their imprint on migratory regimes in a number of European states, including those which, in the earlier period, had been countries of emigration, such as Portugal and Spain. Entry and/or access to citizenship may be facilitated for individuals with direct links to the country of origin or from former colonies. Historical and cultural attachments continue to attract students and skilled migrants from erstwhile colonies. Other states too have had privileged links and favoured access to the labour market for some migrants. The Nordic countries, and in particular Sweden as the largest economy, have since the 1950s operated as a regional unit. Germany too, though pursuing a guest worker regime premised on the rotation of single migrants unencumbered by family responsibilities, has since the end of the 1980s, received large numbers of ethnic Germans who had immediate access to German citizenship.

However, just as the role of immigration in European societies has been marginalized, so too has an historical amnesia befallen female immigration. Yet as Hania Zlotnik (2003) points out, the percentage of female migrants in Europe (as in other developed regions) was already high (48.5%) in 1960. Indeed, amongst migrants from the Caribbean and the European periphery (Ireland and Southern Europe), many women migrated on their own or as workers with their spouses, often leaving their children behind. As with traditional societies of immigration, Europe states permitted family reunification from the 1970s, whilst entire families from former colonies also settled in states such as the UK, France, Netherlands, Belgium and Portugal.

Since 1989 the spaces of immigration have been modified as the European Union has expanded its borders and deepened integration. Those from the former periphery (Greece, Portugal and Spain) became part of the European Union in the 1980s, thereby enjoying the benefits of mobility and entitlements conferred upon EU citizens. However, as Louise Ackers (1998) has forcefully highlighted, intra-European migration remains profoundly gendered given its assumption of a male breadwinner model and derivative social rights[1]. Entitlements of family members, including the spouse, are channelled through those accorded to the worker. Furthermore, the low levels of intra-European migration may well partly reflect the continuing difficulty of transferring social entitlements, such as pensions.

Another round of enlargement of eight countries in Eastern Europe and two Mediterranean islands (Cyprus and Malta) took place in May 2004[2]. Immigration from Eastern and Central Europe has been a contentious issue so that only three countries opened up labour migration routes in 2004 — Ireland, Sweden and the UK. In the latter country, 427,095 workers registered between May 2004 and June 2006, of whom 62 percent were Polish and under 42 percent were women (Home Office 2006). Elsewhere a transitional period of up to seven years for full mobility has been imposed although Finland, Greece, Portugal and Spain withdrew restrictions on 1 May 2006[3]. Even without the right to reside permanently or work, many migrants from Eastern Europe had developed strategies to accumulate resources from short-term and rotational stays in what Mirjana Morokvasic (2003) depicts as a pattern of 'settled in mobility".

During the past decade, patterns of migration (countries of origin, types of migration, duration) have become more diversified and stratified in line with the general globalization of migration (Castles & Miller 2003). Diversification and accrued stratification emerged most forcefully in Europe at the beginning of the 1990s, with continuing and new geopolitical conflicts in neighbouring regions in Eastern Europe, Middle East and Africa. States responded to increasing numbers of asylum seekers by generating a range of statuses, each with attendant rights (Kofman 2002; Morris 2003). From the end of the decade, some states, and especially the UK and Ireland, selectively opened up their economic routes of entry, whilst further enacting highly restrictive legislation against asylum seekers. Labour migrants too encountered differential rights and entitlements according to their utility to the economy, social esteem and supposed ability to assimilate. Hence whilst IT workers and domestics were both in short supply, the former enjoyed the rights attached to the skilled unlike those working in low status employment in the household.

And throughout Europe as elsewhere, migrant women underpin the globalisation of care and social reproduction (Kofman & Raghuram 2006; Parrenas 2001; Yeates 2004b), yet except for the most skilled in the education and health sectors, their role is undervalued. An increasing proportion of female migrants are engaged in biological and social reproduction in the household, the community, the private sector and the state. The over-representation of Third country women (i.e. those with a citizenship from a state outside the European Union in devalued sectors of the economy), both as legal and undocumented migrants, has profound consequences for their entitlements compared to homestate women.

Many formal rights and entitlements are taken for granted by citizens of the European Union but for migrants, rights may be legally withheld and be subject to conditionality and discretion. Their relationship to entitlements, defined as access to resources, and covering material, social and symbolic dimensions, is more problematic and constrained by lack of rights. It is therefore not just a matter of the inability to exercise rights but also involves formal exclusion, which is sanctioned by immigration, residence and employment regulations.

Some of the key areas differentiating citizens and migrants are: the right to enter, conditions of residence and unlawful presence in the territory, security from deportation, the rights and conditions of family life, employment, including access to the public sector, self-employment and the liberal professions; access to citizenship and the ability to make the transition from one legal, residence and employment status to another. Formal dependency may be sanctioned through immigration legislation, a situation which particularly affects migrant women. They are bound as family members by a probationary period in most European states except if they can prove domestic violence.

For an increasing number of migrants, their lives are constrained in the present and in the future by their tenuous status and limited claims to welfare entitlements. Skill, nationality, legal status and channels of entry determine migrant women's rights, entitlements and obligations. The impoverishment of women's entitlements, their disproportionate presence in under-valued and criminalised sectors, such as prostitution, and the lack of protection within the workplace, especially within the confines of the home, limit a number of the key capabilities outlined by Martha Nussbaum (2003) — bodily integrity, control over one's environment, practical reason enabling one to plan one's life, and affiliation[4]. The various axes of stratification (skilled/unskilled; EU/non-EU; documented/irregular) and migratory channels express the status accorded to different migrants and determine the ability to exercise the above capabilities. These will be illustrated in relation to the different gendered immigration channels, notably that of labour, family and asylum.

This chapter focuses on the livelihoods and entitlements of Third country women, who enter on their own for work and education, as family migrants or as asylum seekers and refugees. It primarily focuses on first generation migrants, that is, those who were born in another country[5]. There is growing interest in the stratified rights and entitlements generated by immigration policies but as yet little on its gender dimensions. In particular we need to consider how immigration policies reflect a differential valuation of sectors and skills, forms of immigration, and the relationship of immigration, racialised exclusion and national identity, all of which are profoundly gendered. The distinction between statuses and their attendant entitlements has become increasingly formalised and clear-cut, especially in relation to the skilled and the less skilled in particular for those from non-EU, and in some cases non-OECD (Organization for Economic and Cultural Developement) countries, and between refugees and asylum seekers.

Whilst immigration policies categorise migrants according to status, economic utility and entitlements, the nature of the welfare regime is also important in generating migrant livelihoods in particular sectors. These in turn facilitate or constrain access to entitlements and the possibility of shifting from one set of entitlements to another. Although the relationship between migratory and welfare regimes is complex, we can see that in Southern European states, the lack of voluntary sector and public care services means that there is high dependence on labour hired by and working within the household. The nature of this labour often makes it difficult to be regularized (Moreno-Fontes Chammartin 2004), a procedure that has commonly been used in recent years in Southern European states. In Northern European states, both liberal and social democratic, household labour is contractually more complex, less visible and statistically difficult to capture. Nonetheless in all European states the globalisation of social reproduction has led to the migration and employment of women from the South to the North and between developed countries.

My intention in this chapter is to outline how we might combine an analysis of migratory patterns and systems in relation to different European welfare regimes which are at the same time being restructured and increasingly dependent on female labour through different migratory channels. Family members, asylum seekers, refugees, students all contribute to the formal and informal labour force. It is however not possible to explore in detail how gendered migratory and welfare regimes intersect (but see Sciortino 2004 on Italy). In this chapter I will confine my discussion to outlining some of the most significant relationships in a selection of welfare regimes.

The chapter is divided into three sections. The first section outlines the gendered characteristics of different categories of immigration (labour, family, asylum), associated entitlements and obligations, and the key axes of stratification, especially between skilled and less skilled, documented and irregular. Whilst the combination of immigration and labour markets stratify migrants, they do so in specific ways in different welfare regimes. Welfare states themselves generate particular openings for migrants. Thus the second section examines in more depth the ways in which employment relating to care, a core element of social reproduction, has developed within different welfare regimes, and in particular reference to five states — Sweden, Spain, France, Germany and the UK.

GENDER AND IMMIGRATION CATEGORIES

Migrant women have entered the European Union under different immigration categories and for different purposes. Until the stoppage of mass labour migration in the mid-1970s (earlier in the UK), female migrants constituted a significant minority of labour migrants but often entered without children. In many instances, their participation rate in the labour market was higher than homestate women at a time when many of the latter did not work. For example, in Germany migrant women, including those from Turkey, were sought after to work in manufacturing (Erdem & Mattes 2003). Following the halt to mass labour migration, family reunion became the main route of legal entry into the European Union and was predominantly female. Ever more restrictive measures have meant that a growing number of migrants in the European Union fall into the category of the undocumented. The European Union estimates that 500,000 migrants enter illegally every year whilst many more enter legally but become undocumented. By the 1990s, refugee flows with variable gender balances began to increase.

From the 1980s Southern European countries clearly shifted from being countries of emigration to countries of immigration, including a strong demand for female labour. Family reunification, initiated by female and male migrants, has also become more important. Since the 1990s, the opening up of Eastern Europe and its economic transformation resulted in loss of employment for women and the search for new possibilities in European Union countries. In particular new forms of transient labour migration, often based on a rotational system, have enabled women to undertake

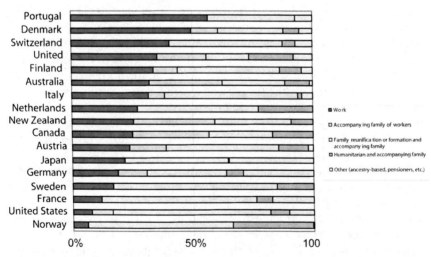

Figure 3.1 International migration by category of entry, selected OECD countries, 2004, harmonised data. Percentation of total inflows. For details on sources, please refer to http://www.oecd.org/els/migration/imo2006.

Table 3.1 Percentage of women in the immigrant population in aelected European countries

Countries	1994	2004
Italy	51.9	55.6
Portugal	52.4	54.4
Denmark	52.2	53.1
United Kingdom	52.9	53.0
Belgium	51.9	52.0
Spain	54.5	51.4
France	50.9	51.3
Ireland	51.4	51.1
Netherlands	49.8	50.9
Luxembourg	50.0	50.4

Source: European Community European Labour Force Survey

domestic work, care, cleaning and trading whilst maintaining familial responsibilities in their home countries (Morokvasic 1996). Others have gone into prostitution, of whom a number have been trafficked.

Though already high by the mid-1990s, women's presence has increased so that they now form the majority of the immigrant population in European countries (see Table 3.1). In particular, over half of migrant women have been in the European Union for less than five years, especially in Poland and Italy.

Overall, women predominate in migratory flows, including labour migrations, from Eastern Europe, Latin America and the Philippines. A very different gender composition with female minorities typifies migrations from the Middle East, Africa and China. At the same time, the proportion of women in a particular nationality may differ significantly between different states depending on the timing and type of flows. For example, in the early to mid-1990s, the proportion of Moroccan women in France, Belgium and the Netherlands, countries with a long history of family immigration, was around 45 percent compared to 11.5 percent in Italy and 26.0 percent in Germany (Ouali 2003).

The rest of this section deals with the different forms of gendered immigrations — labour, family and asylum and refugee. Each of these forms of entry engenders specific issues and policies. For example, labour migration is characterised by increasing formalisation of differences and stratified rights and entitlements between the skilled and the less skilled, the documented and irregular. Ever more states are welcoming the skilled but refusing to acknowledge the need for less skilled labour beyond the expanded EU. Family migration is characterised by more restrictive entry policies

Gendered Migrations, Livelihoods and Entitlements in Europe 65

and obligations in a number of countries, especially targeted at those from Muslim countries. In relation to asylum, although women do not fare worse amongst those who are attributed refugee status, fewer asylum seekers are obtaining a secure status and are thus the most severely disentitled from the basic capabilities in determining the course of their lives.

LABOUR MIGRATION

Migrant women are generally over-represented in those sectors in which homestate women are also over-represented (see Table 3.2), that is hotels and restaurants, education, health and households. Nevertheless foreign-born are particularly concentrated in hotels and restaurants and households.

Table 3.2 Female employment by sector and birth status women aged 15–64, 2003–2004, data pooled over EU countries

	Foreign-born		Native-born	
	Share of total employment of foreign-born women	Over-represented	Share of total employment of native-born women	Over-represented
Agriculture and fishing	1.1	No	3.3	No
Mining, manufacturing and energy	12.1	No	12.8	No
Construction	1.0	No	1.5	No
Wholesale and retail trade	12.6	Ind.	15.6	Yes
Hotels and restaurants	8.1	Yes	4.4	Yes
Education	8.1	Yes	11.2	Yes
Health and other community services	17.0	Yes	16.5	Yes
Households	6.2	Yes	1.6	Yes
Administration and ETO	4.7	No	7.5	Ind.
Other services	23.2	Ind.	21.2	Ind.

Note: Overrepresentation occurs when the share of foreign- or native-born women in one particular sector is more important than their share in total employment. Sectoral over-representation is supposed to be undetermined (Ind.) if the share of foreign-or native-born women in the employment divided by their share in total employment is higher than 0.9 and lower than 1.1.

Sources: European Community Labour Force Survey (data provided by Eurostat).Note: Columns do not sum to 100 because not all employed women indicate their sector of activity.

Most research on female migrant employment is even more concentrated in its concern with two sectors: the domestic sphere (cleaning and care), which has risen sharply in the 1990s, especially in Southern Europe but also in Northern countries (Cox 2006), and the sex industry where it is estimated that 80 percent of those trafficked are involved in sex work. The increase of sex trafficking in the 1990s, especially from Eastern and South Eastern Europe, which has to a great extent replaced flows from Latin America and Asia, is related to the globalization of the sex trade, which has become a lucrative business (Salt 2001), fuelled by the growing demand in destination countries for foreign and exotic prostitutes (IOM 1996). It is estimated that between 200,000 and 500,000 are working illegally as sex workers within the European Union, many of them having been trafficked.

Little research has been undertaken into female migrant presence in other areas such as industrial cleaning, retailing, hotel and catering and tourism, even though these employ large numbers of migrant women. The hospitality sector has traditionally depended on female labour but it has increasingly turned to migrant labour. Migrant women (8.1%) were employed in hotels and restaurant sectors in Europe; the number is especially high in Austria and Spain. Such employment may be particularly significant in tourist areas and large cities. It was estimated that 70 percent of catering jobs in London were carried out by migrants (Anderson et al. 2006).

Women too have used their skills to develop a niche in the community and inter-cultural sector in advocacy, mediation, translation and general community tasks. Some have sought autonomy and greater satisfaction through self-employment. Finally, a significant and growing number of migrant women from First and Third World countries are filling severe shortages in skilled sectors such as health, especially nursing, and education. They are contributing to the social reproduction of individuals, families and groups in different sectors and sites (Kofman & Raghuram 2006).

Yet writing on gendered migrations treats women's lowly occupations "as exotic, subservient or victimised, or relegated to playing supporting roles" (Pratt & Yeoh 2003) as homemakers. Such a perspective precludes a more accurate analysis of the implications of diversification and gendered stratification (Kofman 2002, 2004b). The focus on the domestic and sex work sectors arises in part from the development and interest in new and alternative global gendered circuits of servicing (Sassen 2001) and care (Ehrenreich & Hochschild 2003) to explain the transfer of female labour from poorer to richer countries. Men and women circulate differently in the new global economy. Men occupy an elite space of flows (Castells 1996) in a masculinised high-tech world of global finance, production and technology, the commanding heights of the knowledge economy, while women provide the services largely associated with a wife's traditional role — care of children and the elderly, homemaking and sex (Ehrenreich & Hochschild 2003). For Sassen (2001) migrant women fill the devalued, marginalized and flexible sectors of production and services in increasingly polarised global cities. On the other hand, Ehrenreich and Hochschild (2003) emphasise the production of care in its material and emotional dimensions, enabling the economic expansion in the First World to take place under neo-liberal conditions of welfare restrictions and flexible labour. Globalisation has led to the marketization of various services, including care, which is now brought into global care chains. These are defined (Hochschild 2000: 131) 'as a series of personal links between people across the globe based on the paid or unpaid work of caring'. The chains may vary in their number and connective strength, combining internal and international caring links. It also encompasses skilled work outside the household, such as nursing (Yeates 2004a, 2004b).

Employment opportunities have therefore opened up well beyond the narrower preoccupation with social reproduction within the household. Reproduction encompasses the whole array of biological and social activities and relationships involved in maintaining people, whether it be undertaken by the market, the community, the state or the household or combination of them (Kofman & Raghuram 2006). It should also be noted that migrants do not only provide material and emotional care for homestate populations but also for other migrants in their own families as well as through community organisations.

In the rest of this section I shall discuss in greater detail some of the key livelihoods linked with care and welfare and which have provided much of the sources of growth in female employment within the context of the globalisation of global chains of care and social reproduction.

Domestic work

Traditionally, domestic service was the major employer of women until after the Second World War (Sarti forthcoming) and this historical process is partially being recreated (Aguilar 2003) through the resurgence of domestic work, especially in Southern Europe where it is the main source of employment for migrant women. Nevertheless, throughout Europe, there has been an increase in paid employment in households (Cancedda 2001). In Spain 70 percent of working migrant women are to be found in this sector (Escrivà 2000). In Italy, there were 88,887 female domestic workers in 1999 from non-EU countries (Caritas 2001: 311), and on average 46.3 percent of domestic labour, rising to over 70 percent in the major cities in 1996, was performed by migrant women (Andall 2003). The participation of homestate women in the labour force is both dependent upon and creates demand for domestic work which is heavily supplied by women of migrant origin, though in some countries by established migrants and homestate labour as in France, the UK (Anderson 2000) and Germany (Hillmann 2005). Amongst established migrant women, the importance of this sector varies substantially so for example in France only 10 percent of Turkish women compared to 23 percent of Moroccans and 40 percent of Portuguese were employed in it (Borrel & Boeldieu 2001).

Though patterns of employment, especially the significance of live-in-domestics, are different between Southern and Northern countries, there are also common issues and problems relating to the nature of this work. The most widespread problems are the low pay and long working hours. Their inferior position and the highly personalised relationship with their employers make it difficult for domestic workers to receive their agreed pay or get time off. Employers regularly demand unpaid overtime. The health and safety situation in the home is not satisfactory, and if domestic workers are ill, they do not get paid and may even lose their jobs. Psychological, physical and sexual abuses are common.

Domestic work is naturalised as being particularly suited to women who are deemed to innately possess the requisite skills, transferred from one private space to another. At the same time, it is considered work of low social esteem, unworthy of work permits. Together with the racialization of migrant women, this reifies them in an inferior position which devalues their skills and portrays them as unskilled and only fit for domestic work. Yet so many studies of domestic work (Andall 2003; Zontini 2001) highlight the severe degree of deskilling and disqualification that many migrant women with full high school education and even university degrees experience. This applies particularly to Filipinas, Latin Americans and Eastern Europeans. The previous closure of European labour markets to Third country migrants with professional qualifications (with a few exceptions mainly in the health sector) meant that for many women the only way of gaining access as a labour migrant was either in the domestic sector or other low level service jobs. Many entered as tourists, or in some cases as students, and became overstayers. Hence the boundaries between the legal and the illegal are often blurred. Many are working irregularly and not covered by social security. In Spain, for example, 46.9 percent of those (176,000) covered by social security in 2002 were from Third countries, but of course a much larger number estimated at about 180,000 were irregular and with no coverage (Moreno-Fontes Chammartin 2004). In Italy, though 350,000 domestic workers were regularised in the 2002 amnesty[6], it does not mean that their working conditions change enormously or that they are able to move out of the sector and meet other aspirations. Ethnicised and racialised stereotypes may restrict them to migrant niches (Sarti forthcoming).

There are, of course, differences between countries and nationalities. Southern European countries recognise the domestic sector as an area of employment. Spain, which recognised it as salaried work in 1985, establishes an annual quota. Each round of regularization has drawn in larger numbers with the last one in Italy in 2002 receiving 700,000 of whom 350,000 whose from those in domestic work (SOPEMI 2004). In some Northern countries, for example Germany, it has become possible since

February 2002 for citizens of accession countries to work legally for up to three years in households that are taking care of a relative i.e. elderly care and are receiving benefits from the statutory long-term care insurance system (European Industrial Relations Observatory 2003; Menz 2002). Though legally employed and paid at German rates, the state has in effect sanctioned deskilling in stipulating that these carers cannot compete against German-trained nurses and home care employees and must be given a household assistant work permit so that 'untrained foreign workers' do not put those they care for at risk. This represents a somewhat different resolution of labour shortages compared to IT workers who are to be employed at the same grades as Germans. In the UK domestic workers quotas were phased out in 1979 and only retained as a concession to foreign employers; workers did not have their own permit or the right to change employers. Over the years numerous cases of abuse and exploitation were reported, and after years of campaigning by Kalayaan, led to a change in immigration regulations in 1997 and the special right of regularisation for those who remained in the country undocumented (Anderson 2000). However the UK Government announced on 10 March 2006 that it was intending to change the conditions of their presence in the UK and restrict migrant domestic workers to a 6 months business visa without any right to change employers. It will represent a totally retrograde step encouraging exploitation[7].

Stratification by nationality, religion, race and language skills, leads to different conditions and pay. Filipinas are generally viewed as the most valuable domestic workers, being Christian, English-speaking and well educated. On the other hand, Albanians in Greece or Moroccans in Spain are considered less valuable and have less negotiating power with their employers, often doing less rewarding work and receiving lower wages (Anthias & Lazardis 2000). Since the 1990s Eastern European women have joined the stock of domestic workers, especially in Austria and Germany. They have been predominantly pendular migrants (Morokvasic 1996; Ungerson 2005), often rotating a job between several people. In Germany they have rights of residence for up to 3 months, while others from Latin America and South East Asia are likely to be undocumented. What seems to be also emerging is a differential valuation between tasks which can be seen in the way that the care of the elderly is more likely to result in work permits (Germany) and regularisation (Italy) than for child care.

Au pairs, treated in official discourse as cultural exchange, started as a scheme between European countries (1969) that has been extended since 2003 to more Eastern European countries and those in the former Soviet Union. Though guidelines about remuneration and hours of work exist, the representation of au pairs as 'members of the family' makes it difficult to enforce. Thus it has actually become a form of hidden and cheap live-in domestic labour, often making up for the shortfalls in childcare provision (Cox 2006; Hesse & Pukhaber 2004). The contracts last between a year

(Germany) and two years (UK). Au pairs from other EU countries may move freely and reside in the country beyond the period of their contract while those from beyond the EU are more restricted. The opening up of labour markets to the accession countries is likely to mean a fall in au pairs from these countries (Anderson et al. 2006). Many from Eastern Europe have managed to prolong their stay using tourist visas and the contracts they made whilst au-pairs, as has been the case in Germany (Hesse & Pukhaber 2004).

Community and Inter-cultural

Encompassing a range of activities such as advocacy, mediation, interpreting and general community work, this is an area which has enabled migrant women to break out of manufacturing and low level service employment and deploy other skills. There is no systematic study of employment across this sector which is often providing welfare for other migrants and refugees, settled and new. Mediation between individuals and families of migrant origin and public authorities and agencies, especially welfare and legal services, has become common in European states (Kofman et al. 2000). Initially, migrant women did it on a voluntary basis and were not salaried. Nowadays, many women migrants and refugees, who are unable to work in the area of their qualification, have found employment in this sector, though this is not to say that voluntary work has disappeared (Institute of Working Lives 2005). One of the demands has been the recognition of mediators and inter-cultural specialists as a career (Delacroix 1997) and accreditation of training. Accreditation is after all applied to employment in caring services in France (Ungerson 2005). This could also facilitate movement into the public and paid voluntary sectors and offer a stepping stone into relevant professions. Whilst this sector could potentially open up more rewarding employment, it might, at the same time, leave migrants trapped in services for migrants, as has been noted in social work and teaching in Germany and the Netherlands (Lutz 1993). The expansion of integration programmes in the future may well only generate fixed-term and insecure employment dependent on funding for specific projects, as has happened in Sweden and the UK.

There has been interest in utilising the inter-cultural, defined as communication between cultures, as a resource that could be translated into professional competence in a range of fields such as trading, tourism, IT and media, and not exclusively in mediation and advocacy for migrant communities (Federal Institute for Vocational Training 2000). As with mediation, it should be viewed as a professional qualification and not just a personal feature of female migrants or something they are predisposed to. There is also potential for employment in the creation and management of cultural diversity and tourism for women in professional and entrepreneurial positions, and interfacing with the growth of the knowledge economy, rather than the precarious and seasonal employment usually associated with leisure and tourism.

Skilled labour in feminized sectors

Whilst the majority of female migrants fill less skilled jobs upon entry, they are not absent from the ranks of the skilled (see Table 3.3) (Erel and Kofman 2003). Skilled migration is heterogeneous (Iredale 2001) in its gender divisions, occupations and conditions of work. Men overwhelmingly form the mass of those moving within transnational corporations and in the Information Technology and Scientific sectors (HRST), upon which the notion of the highly skilled and the knowledge society has been constructed (Mahroum 2001; OECD 2002), and for whom movement was facilitated until the IT bubble burst. Within national workforces fewer women have been entering IT sectors but for migrant women, work problems are often compounded by the demand for constant physical mobility and flexibility between different places amongst software specialists (Raghuram 2004). 88 percent of the Green card permits in Germany in 2000 were taken up

Table 3.3 Percentage of women in highly skilled occupations; native- and foreign-born, aged 15–64, 2004

	Native-born	*Foreign-born*	*Foreign-born non-OECD*
Austria	38.2	25.3	18.6
Belgium	42.9	41.6	42.5
Denmark	43.3	38.6	33.9
Finland	42.8	32.5	21.9
France	37.7	30.5	31.1
Germany	46.0	30.5	–
Greece	36.6	13.5	6.8
Hungary	40.8	42.7	40.8
Ireland	40.0	47.9	–
Italy	43.9	29.2	20.4
Luxembourg	51.3	38.5	26.3
Norway	42.2	38.9	23.8
Portugal	25.7	33.6	31.3
Spain	36.2	21.6	12.3
Sweden	45.4	38.3	25.7
Switzerland	44.1	38.0	29.2
United Kingdom	36.2	43.7	39.8

Source: Table I.15. SOPEMI 2006

by men (SOPEMI 2001). The vast majority of scientists from Eastern European in the early 1990s were men, reflecting an uneven gender distribution in Germany rather than an imbalance in the sending countries (Morokvasic 2003).

Women, in contrast, have tended to go into what can be broadly classified as the welfare and social professions (education, health, social work), the public face of the global chain of care (Yeates 2004a, 2004b) and social reproduction (Kofman & Raghuram 2006). Until recently, these sectors have been largely closed (with the partial exception of the UK) to migrant labour (Kofman 2000) which, at best, was forced to accept subordinate and less secure employment. In the UK, for the period January 2004 to August 2005, 47 percent of work permits were for healthcare with 24.4 percent for nurses and 4.6 percent for doctors and 4.6 percent for teachers (Institute for Public Policy Research 2005).

Recourse to foreign nurses in response to the crisis in nursing has constituted a truly global labour market, especially in the UK and Ireland (Yeates 2004a). Other countries have recruited primarily in neighbouring regions (Buchan et al. 2003; Kingma 2001). Global patterns may change rapidly. For example the UK has in 2006 taken off nurses, except those in certain for specialist areas, from the list of shortage areas able to apply for a work permit[8]. Above all, it is the Philippines which supplies the overwhelming number but large numbers have been recruited from India, South Africa and other African countries. Though qualified nurses were recruited, a study of international nurse recruits in the UK, mainly from Europe, Australia, Africa and Philippines (Allan & Aggergaard Larsen 2003) found that many felt that their skills were not appreciated or respected and that they confronted racism and xenophobia. They also experienced a considerable degree of downgrading. Furthermore experiences varied considerably between the National Health Service, judged in more positive terms, and the private independent sector where they were frequently used as care assistants.

Whilst the most publicised, nurses are not the only area of shortages. Overseas doctors (non European Economic Area [EEA] qualified) form a large percentage of the UK medical labour market; in 2000 they constituted 26 percent of the hospital medical workforce. Most women had come to obtain further qualifications and training, and were, as with male doctors, in the lower and middle grades. In an increasingly feminised occupation, women form a significant proportion of migrant doctors with over half of those seeking registration with the General Medical Council in 1998 being female (Raghuram & Kofman 2002)[9].

Home language instruction, which local authorities have had to provide since the 1970s, has also presented women with more professional opportunities and has, for example in Sweden, put teaching tenth on the list of jobs done by migrant women (Knocke 1999). Teaching languages, both privately and in language schools has been a major source of employment, especially for educated women. A survey[10] by TOWER (Thessaloniki Organisation of Women's Employment and Resources) in Greece, largely representing repatriates and women from economically advantaged countries found that many had earned income from private English-language classes (Lukey-Coutsocostas cited in Rosewarne & Groutsis 2003). One of the major problems encountered by a number of women, many of whom had settled as a result of marriage or cohabitation, has been the recognition of foreign credentials. This issue will be taken up more fully in the section on family migration.

Care

This is a category (for a discussion of the concept see section on Welfare regimes, livelihoods and migration), though receiving considerable attention in recent years in the discussion of the transfer of labour from South to North, is very difficult to pin down and capture statistically. Care can be located within different sectors in official statistics, encompassing both households and health and social services; in the list of occupations, it may be placed in professional categories as well as personal services. It can require very different formal skill levels from nurses to nursing assistants, care assistant or to those who have the aptitude as women. It can occur in a variety of sites in public and private spaces, and with different employment contracts and degrees of regulation and commodification (Ungerson 2005). Nordic countries have relatively high levels of care workers, for example 9 percent in Sweden, compared to 5 percent in the UK and only 3 percent in Spain (Lethbirdge 2005). Care labour can be filled by established as well as new migrants, and those entering as labour migrants, through family migrations and asylum. There is evidence that some of the new forms of payment, such as direct cash for care and especially when it is not monitored or regulated, encourages the employment of undocumented women without residence status in Italy and rotational labour from Eastern Europe in Austria (Ungerson 2005). The interplay of these aspects vary by welfare regimes and lead, as we shall see, to very different recognition of its significance in immigration policies. I will discuss it more fully in a subsequent section on livelihoods, entitlements and welfare regimes.

Immigration status and entitlements

Some of the crucial axes demarcating the bundle of entitlements are those related to the valuation of human capital and skills in the labour market which are in turn assumed to be correlated with propensity to assimilate. As the previous discussion of specific sectors has highlighted, these skills have a strong gender dimension. The key dichotomies are between the skilled and the lesser skilled, and the legal compared to the undocumented. The two are connected since the lesser skilled are far more likely to enter illegally and become undocumented. In turn a migrant's position in relation to these axes influences access to the entitlement of family reunification, which though in principle stems from the right to family life, is in reality limited by a series of conditionalities.

The pattern that has generally emerged in European states is, on the one hand, an improvement of entitlements for the legally settled, in exchange for the acceptance of obligations and responsibilities, and, on the other hand, the withdrawal of basic economic and social rights for the most precarious, that is asylum seekers and the undocumented, who are more than ever at risk of deportation.

Skilled migrants are welcomed; they are represented as unproblematic, easily assimilated and, of course, beneficial to the economy. So in order to attract them, many countries have offered easier entry, the right to be accompanied by one's family and for them to work; permanent residence permit and eventual citizenship (Kofman 2002; Morris 2002). For example, the new German Immigration Law, in force since 2005 only grants immediate permanent residence to skilled migrants. The main shortages they are seeking to fill are in IT and engineering, both very masculine sectors. The UK eased entry for the skilled in September 2000. The Highly Skilled Migrants Programme (January 2002), based on points whose criteria of income, status in employment, educational level, is likely to favour men (Kofman et al. 2005)[11].

A distinguishing characteristic of skilled migration is its possibility of settlement and family reunification. Nurses in the UK are able to decide whether they want to bring in family members or not (Allan & Aggergaard Larsen 2003). Many do not because work commitments preclude it. It may also be easier for the skilled to bring in family members other than spouses or dependent children such as parents which is largely discretionary. Furthermore, female spouses of the skilled migrants are allowed to work, though not in sectors reserved for nationals or EU-citizens.

Even if many do not intend settling, skilled labour migrants have the possibility of renewing their contracts, of settling and eventually acquiring citizenship and bringing their families, entitlements that are not available to the lesser skilled. So although fewer in numbers than the less skilled, the expansion of skilled opportunities for female migrants highlights the diversity of migratory circuits, potential entitlements and the ability to exercise significant capabilities, such as ability to control one's environment, practical reason in defining one's life (Nussbaum 2003).

The lesser skilled generally enter as contract labour, or a revived guest worker system, without the possibility of transition to a more secure settlement status or the right to bring in family members. Gender of course structures the entry of the lesser skilled for although, as we have seen in the section on labour migration, opportunities for female labour have expanded throughout Europe, it is in sectors that are socially devalued and often unrecognised for purposes of official work permits. Even where quotas for domestic labour have been agreed, they are insufficient to meet the demand and are forcing female migrants to reside as undocumented migrants.

Being undocumented not only leaves one without access to basic entitlements (education, health), a right of citizens incorporated in many constitutions, but also renders eventual acquisition of citizenship difficult. Acquiring resident permits through regularization programmes, and hence being able to return to one's home country, become eligible for family reunification, and access welfare services and benefits, have often proved more difficult for women than men. The frequent regularisation exercises in Southern European states too may be more difficult for those in informal work and domestic labour who have to supply proof of employment (Anderson 2000). It is virtually impossible for those in the sex trade (Lazaridis 2001).

Family-linked migration

The 'family' in the context of family migration into the European Union is defined by the state; migrants cannot determine for themselves the persons who constitute their family. For those from outside the EU, it includes spouses and dependent children usually under the age of 18 years. Though ways of living together have altered radically in European states, migrants must still conform to traditional marriage patterns as the basis of entry into most European states. Only a few countries, for example in Scandinavia, the Netherlands, and more recently the UK, allow the entry of cohabiting or same-sex couples if they form 'relationships akin to a family' in the receiving society (Simmons 2004). The 'family of choice' is still some way off (Weeks et al. 2001). Parents are generally only permitted to join their families if they are dependent (Denmark, Spain and over 65 years in the UK), for humanitarian reasons (Germany), or if they are in serious difficulties (Netherlands). Thus the generally limited conceptualisation of the family leaves little consideration for problems generated by caring at a distance (Ackers 1998; Baldassar & Baldock 2000), cultural differences in familial relationships, and the role of grandparents or other collateral relations in providing nurturing and support for different members of the family.

Separated families are not a new phenomenon. In the earlier decades of post-war European immigrant, many couples, especially amongst the Portuguese, Spanish and Yugoslavs, left their children behind with kin in the country of origin (Charbit & Bertrand 1985). Today, the survival of the household in the country of origin increasingly depends on the livelihood of migrant women (Sassen 2000) who are creating a nexus between the formal and the informal sectors in circuits of counter-globalisation. Separated families, transnational mothering and parenting, and care at a distance, have once again become more important due to the nature of employment that is available for female migrants, often in personal services and initially without a residence permit. Women migrating from Eastern and Central

Europe within a rotational system (Morokvasic 2003) and those moving independently, for example from the Philippines, often leave their families behind for many years, sometimes leading to difficult long distance intimate relations (Parrenas 2005). At the same time, family members in the receiving countries may not be permitted recourse to public expenditure at least for the first few years.

In effect family migration encompasses a wide range of situations, each with a different gender composition. The classic family reunification of primary migrants is only one form; marriage migration of second and subsequent generations who bring in partners from their homeland, international marriages by citizens and non-citizens due to tourism, education and business and professional activities, and finally the movement of entire families, all add to the complexity (Kofman 2004). Family-linked migration remains the main source of permanent migration (estimated at about 65 percent of permanent immigration in the European Union), and has been particularly dominant in France and Sweden, which have low levels of labour migration (see Figure 3.1). In France, adding together family reunification and formation and the private and family life visa entries introduced in 1998, 73.3 percent of long-term entries (140, 142) were for family reasons (Regnard 2006). Only a quarter of family migration is from the traditional family reunification route, far more significant entry is of those joining French citizens, who are frequently the children of migrants. Whilst women dominate the various forms of family migrations, the percentage varies between 64 percent for family reunification to just over 50 percent involving a French citizen. In countries with large-scale labour migrants, many of whom have the right to be accompanied by their family, there is a substantial flow of accompanying members, for example 94,690 workers were accompanied by 52,520 family members in the UK (SOPEMI 2006). In Southern European states, family reunification immigration is on the increase. In Italy, for example, 26.4 percent or 366,122 of residence permits in 2000 were for family reunification (Caritas 2001). By 2004, 55.4 percent of Italian immigration was generated by family reunification and formation (SOPEMI 2006).

Yet despite the significance of this form of migration in Europe, it receives little attention but see European Migration Network 20007, International Centre for Migration Policy Development, 200?. In part this is due to its association with female migration and dependency rather than work and autonomy. The assumption is that (female) family migrants do not enter the labour force or are not concerned about employment (Kofman et al. 2000); it is merely a secondary issue. Virtually nothing is known of the professional aspirations of female family migrants, whether they enter under family reunification and formation regulations or as partners of skilled spouses. However, with the expansion in skilled migration and marriage migration (Ackers 1998; Riano 2003), there are an increasing number of educated women who are blocked in their career paths. Though immigration and employment regulations have been increasingly relaxed for spouses of skilled migrants, skilled women entering through marriage often still encounter immense difficulties in getting their qualifications recognised in regulated professions. This blockage is compounded in corporatist states with highly protectionist legislation circumscribing public sector employment, such as Germany and Switzerland. A study of Latin American women, who had married Swiss men and were living in Switzerland (Riano 2003), revealed three situations: no professional integration where women who had worked in their home countries had become inactive; professional integration below their qualifications where two-thirds worked in occupations such as language teachers or work in areas where they have been trained but at a lower level e.g. as an assistant; equivalent professional integration which was achieved by two women whose qualifications (PhD) had been obtained in North America and so were able to escape the de-qualification of many women from the Third World. The spouses of personnel in transnational corporations (TNCs) may also face difficult conditions and have little control over their professional life as trailing spouses constantly on the move (Hardill & MacDonald 1998).

Family migration, though underpinned by human rights conventions enshrining the right to family life, has in reality been closely regulated by a set of criteria based on resources (income, housing, ability to maintain members without recourse to public funds). However, success in applying for family reunification may be lower for migrant women due to their labour market position, difficulty in obtaining work permits as domestic workers, and ability to accumulate the necessary resources (income and access to housing). Their work as live-in domestics in Southern European countries presents an obstacle for female migrants to bring in male spouses and children. So what offers advantages for women in the beginning may present obstacles once they are more established. Becoming regularised and obtaining citizenship enables family reunification to become a reality (Escriva 2005). And of course for the skilled, it is much easier to meet the requirements for bringing in family members, whether spouses or parents.

The dependency and autonomy of spouses (Kofman et al. 2000), whose residence permits are linked to those of the primary migrant and the continuation of their marriage, are particular concerns. Although some countries have reduced the probatonary period, as in Germany where it was decreased from four to two years in 2001, others have lengthened it from one to two years in the UK, on grounds of the need to deter marriages of convenience, and in France from two to three years. Women marrying men from Third World countries are often viewed with suspicion (de Hart 1999). There have been some improvements in the interpretation of the probationary period in that domestic violence, if reported to public authorities, has increasingly been taken into account in deciding the right of the spouse to retain a residence permit in the event of a marriage breakdown.

The conditionality has been applied not just to the right to live a family life in the receiving country but also the obligations that new members must comply with in a number of European states, especially those with high proportions of family reunification migrants, compulsory integration programmes have also been implemented (Denmark, France, Germany). Failure to comply with such schemes, which are directed not just at those applying for citizenship but also long-term residence permits, may have serious consequences. Success may be rewarded with a reduction in years required for naturalisation, as in Denmark (European Industrial Relations Observatory 2003).

Entitlements may be tied to obligations of linguistic knowledge, shared values and general good behaviour i.e. the deserving migrant. As with entitlements, so too are obligations gendered as can be seen in the new 'integration contracts'. There is evidence that ability to participate and complete them successfully varies according to gender. In France, the percentage of women signing it has been lower by men, especially amongst those with little knowledge of French. Unsurprisingly some of the reasons women gave for not signing, such as spouses or community's refusal and child care, applied far more to them than men (Haut Conseil à l'Intégration 2006: 256–9). A French study of refusal rates for citizenship also found that two-thirds of those rejected on grounds of insufficient linguistic knowledge were women (FASILD 2003).

The assumptions behind these contracts have often been constructed on the basis of a gendered representation of problematic immigrant communities, composed of unruly young men and traditional females (generally Muslim), brought in from distant countries and unfamiliar with prevailing social and cultural values of the country in question. Hence the exhortation by Jack Straw, the British Home Office Minister, that marriage, if they be arranged, should be concluded with people close by rather than afar (Home office 2002).

In the context of crises over national identity and hostility over increased levels of immigration, family migrations have been targeted. As a result, the conditions of entry and residence have been tightened and the obligation to integrate made mandatory amidst concerns over belonging, cultural values and threats to national identity.

ASYLUM SEEKERS AND REFUGEES

Although men remain in the majority amongst asylum seekers, the gender balance has become more equitable since 1990. It is often difficult to obtain information on the demographic characteristics of asylum seekers. The Home Office in the UK has only published statistics on gender, age and nationality since 2001. 30 percent of principal applicants and 53 percent of dependants in 2004 were women (ICAR 2006). Gender ratios vary also according to different categories. In Norway for example, in terms of principal applicants in 2000, women formed 34 percent of asylum seekers, 38 percent of resettlement refugees pre-selected from camps, and 50 percent of those from the war zones of former Yugoslavia (Hauge Byberg 2002).

One of the key subjects of debate is the extent to which women have access as asylum seekers to West European countries and are subsequently able to gain recognition either as Geneva Convention refugees, a secondary status or even less secure humanitarian protection. In relation to access it is clear that women are less able to reach European countries as principal applicants due to their lesser resources. In the UK, the vast majority of asylum applicants able to make claims were men (78 percent) in 2002 but in 2003 this had dropped to 71.6 percent.

However, recognition as a refugee raises quite complex issues concerning whether their political activities and specific forms of gender persecution, such as sexual violence or behaviour and dress in public, are recognised in the asylum determination process (Wetten et al. 2001). Some argue that women's political activities, which are often located in the private sphere or involve sustaining dissidents, do not conform to the prototypical male refugee (Crawley 2001); others contend that women do not fare worse in the determination process (Bhabha 2002). In the UK more women (9%) obtained refugee status compared to men (5%) in 2003 (Home Office Asylum Statistics).Although Dutch analysis of the asylum determination process was not conclusive about gender bias, few of the asylum applications by women in the Netherlands were based on gender persecution grounds. Some European states (Denmark, Germany, Ireland, Norway, Sweden and the UK) have developed guidelines for gender persecution in their asylum determination process, along the lines implemented in Australia, Canada and the USA (Crawley 2001). Resettlement schemes to take the most vulnerable in the UK, as occurs in Norway and Sweden, may help women since they do not have to find the resources to travel, and selection criteria may include vulnerability rather than the narrower grounds of political persecution, interpreted in male terms.

Another set of problems relating to settlement and integration confront those granted some degree of protection. Though shared by other migrant women, refugee women face particularly severe problems in accessing entitlements to training, employment and language classes, especially those with children (Kofman, Lloyd & Sales 2002). Refugee women find it particularly difficult to enter the labour market as Norwegian data shows and fewer women participate in labour market schemes than men (Hauge Byberg 2002). In many countries asylum seekers are barred from employment until they acquire a recognised status (humanitarian or refugee). Being the non-principal asylum applicant for asylum can also make it more difficult to obtain the right to work. In general, refugees confront enormous cultural and language barriers, racism, prejudice and lack of recognition of qualifications (Westin & Dingu-Kyrklund 2000), but women refugees have additional burdens of child care and gender stereotyping in terms of suitable jobs, as well as for some, opposition from men to their participation in the labour markets (ECRE 2001; Sargeant et al. 1999). Refugee women with childcare responsibilities find it almost impossible to work. Qualified refugees in the UK are beginning to receive greater support to retrain, especially those with health qualifications.

Thus some of the most severe disentitlements (employment, welfare, family reunification, security) occur amongst asylum seekers and refugees. Increasingly asylum seekers have been criminalized, withdrawn from mainstream society and entitlements and deprived of the right to work. Nor do they have the right to choose where they live for many states impose policies of dispersal. Failed asylum seekers or those who have exhausted their ration of welfare, and do not officially have the right to work[12], can be compared to the diminishing number of Geneva Convention refugees who have full rights[13]. Only Convention refugees are able to bring their families in immediately without meeting the usual criteria of income and housing.

The analysis so far has focused on entitlements related to different forms of immigration flows and policies. An understanding of stratified rights needs to take account of more than formal entitlements based on entry and residence and legal statuses. Actual access to rights and the exercise of them are deeply affected by processes of racialisation and differential representation of groups. September 11, 2001 served to reinforce suspicion of Muslim populations depicted as inimical to Western values, especially in their views of gender relations and oppressive treatment of women. The current targeting of Muslim women raises a number of human rights challenges. Anti-discrimination legislation will have to counter the heightened racism against Muslims since September 11. 2001 and the various bombings in European cities, especially against those who visibly affirm their religious affiliation, as with veiled women in the workplace and in schools (Ahmad 2003). France, for example, has banned, since September 2004, the wearing of religious symbols in state public spaces, especially in schools (Freeman 2004). In Germany, several right-wing states have prohibited the employment of Muslim women wearing headscarves as teachers in schools. Thus the strengthening of Islamophobia (Runnymede Trust 1997) and emphasis on cultural practices (head scarf, arranged marriages, honour killings) associated with Islam focuses attention more than ever on Muslim women oppressed by patriarchal systems (Dietz & El-Shohoumi 2002). Even before the Gulf War, the link of Islam with terrorism and the oppression and expulsion of women from the public sphere in Afghanistan and the headscarf affair in France in 1989 had propelled Muslim girls into the limelight (Dayan-Herzbrun 2000). Apart from the veiling of Muslim women in public places, two extreme practices, that of forced marriages and honour killings, have captured much media attention which has often portrayed Muslim women as unrelentingly oppressed by dogma and without any religious autonomy.

WELFARE REGIMES, LIVELIHOODS AND MIGRATION

There is a growing literature on migrants and welfare states, relating to welfare rights (Bommes & Geddes 2000; Sainsbury 2004), civic stratification (Kofman 2002; Morris 2003) and racialised exclusion (Schierup et al. 2006), defined as a social hierarchy or stratification based on a combination of racialised ethnicity, gender and class. However there is little sustained or comparative analysis of migrants as providers of welfare, rather than as recipients of welfare entitlements. As noted in the discussion of labour migration, the livelihoods available to female migrants in Europe vary between welfare regimes. Yet, there has been little examination of gender, livelihoods and welfare regimes with the exception of domestic labour (Hillmann 2005; Schierup et al. 2006; Sciortino 2004; Williams 2005).

During the 1990s, Esping-Andersen's (1990) influential work on comparative welfare regimes generated a copious literature on its conceptualisation and classification into social democratic, conservative and liberal regimes. His model highlighted de-commodification, employment and stratification generated by the welfare state. The concept of decommodification commanded the most attention. It refers to 'the degree to which, individuals or families, can uphold a socially acceptable standard of living independently of market participation' (Esping-Andersen 1990: 37) which the transfer of social security and benefits (pensions, sickness, unemployment) enables[14] Although his typology has been criticised by feminists for its emphasis on cash transfers, it provides a useful framework with which to examine how immigration policies and welfare regimes interact, as long as we recognise that the regimes have changed. In the rest of this section I briefly explore the relationships between welfare regimes, degree of participation of homestate women in the labour market, demand and supply of caring labour and the use of female migrant labour. I do this through five different welfare regimes and immigration systems.

- Sweden has a social democratic welfare regime where the benefit system is based on universalism and a high degree of decommodification and socialization of family responsibilities with well-developed and publicly funded facilities. Though still with a high level of universal coverage and decommodification, more liberal economic and social measures have been implemented since the early 1990s (Schierup et al. 2006) Model Family migrants and large numbers of asylum seekers have dominated immigration flows since the stoppage of labour migration in 1972. Whilst getting refugee status has become much more difficult in the past few years, Sweden opened up to labour migration from the new accession countries in 2004.
- Germany is a conservative corporatist welfare regime with high levels of benefits and stratified earnings-related systems. It promotes family

values and a strict differentiation between men as breadwinners and women as wives and mothers. Care is provided by the family and the Church. It originally drew its migrants from the Mediterranean area as guest workers based on an ethnic and exclusionary model of incorporation. Following the end of the bipolar world, its migrants have increasingly come from Eastern Europe while the numbers applying for asylum have been high

- France, though also classified as a conservative corporatist welfare regime, does not follow a strong breadwinner model. The state has had responsibility for social care, especially child care (Fagnani & Letablier 2005). Women participate to a high degree in the labour market and have access to child care. The country has a long history of waves of immigration, both from neighbouring states and its former colonies in North and West Africa and South East Asia. Since the 1970s family migrations has dominated and in recent years asylum demands have risen sharply. Its limited official labour migration may be set to change as it seeks to move towards selective migration of the skilled and relaxes some of the restrictions against labour migration from accession countries.
- Spain has also been classified as a conservative of the Southern rim variety with stratified benefits, protected public sector employment and strong familialism. Its immigration history is more recent and diversified than countries in Northern Europe. Colonial links, too, play a part in migratory patterns, though its proximity to North Africa and the opening up of Eastern Europe have shaped its recent migratory patterns.
- The UK is usually typified as a liberal welfare regime, based on means-testing and welfare payments only adequate to maintain very modest living standards. Esping-Andersen considered it a combination of social democratic and liberal elements for the post-war period until the 1980s, but in the past 20 years it has been the vanguard of liberalising welfare states. Its migratory patterns and policies have been profoundly marked by its colonial ties. The implementation of neo-liberal policies in the 1980s contributed to the reduction of investment in professional training, eventually resulting in severe shortages, not just in information technology but also in many social and welfare occupations. Additionally, the UK sees itself positioned as a global player eager to compete in the market for skilled labour (speech by Barbara Roche, the Minister for Immigration on 11 September 2000). Its deregulated labour markets have fostered the employment of migrant labour.

In the past decade a wide-ranging analysis (Daly & Lewis 2000; Sainsbury 1999; Koninklijke Nerderlandse Akademie van Wetenschappen 2001) on care and shifting welfare regimes across gender and generations has taken place. Daly and Lewis (2000: 285) defined social care "as the activities and relations involved in meeting the physical and emotional requirements of dependent adults and children, and the normative, economic and social frameworks within which these are assigned and carried out. In analysing the changing context (demographic, economic, and social) of care in different welfare states, they raise issues of the division and infrastructure (cash, services) of care between state, market, family and community and the trajectories of change between them. The boundaries between sectors of care and individuals and families have shifted as welfare states have experienced crises of care arising from decreasing supply and increasing demand. They point out that much existing work on care has concentrated on the complexity of the everyday and neglected its role in the dynamic political economy of the welfare state.

The discussion about gendered welfare states and the crisis of care seems to have almost entirely ignored migrant women, despite the crucial role they have played in providing services and maintaining welfare states. Part of the reason is that the analysis of the globalisation of social reproduction (Anderson 2000; Maher 2004) has been conducted separately from studies of comparative welfare states. Similarly the social reproduction literature tends to assume that transnationalism is primarily due to the combination of women's formal employment and relatively unchanging gender relations in the household. Within this framework, market forces bring First and Third World women together. Only a few authors (Kofman et al. 2000; Williams 2003, 2005) have considered the extent to which migrant women have supplied the care underpinning welfare provision in the home, the community, the private sector and the state. Not only are migrant women "partial citizens" (Parrenas 2001), but through their labour they enable citizen women to access child and elderly care, both in and outside the home, to combine care and work, participate more fully in the labour force, and have time for other activities. And in addition, migrant labour leaves undisturbed prevailing gender norms in the household (Williams 2003). Of course the dependence of particular welfare configurations on migrant women's employment varies substantially between states. It is a complex issue which will be explored in relation to a number of developments: homestate women's employment, the relationship between the state, market, community and family in the provision of services, and the extent to which migrant labour is being used in care.

The increased *labour force participation* of homestate women in the past decade has characterised all EU countries except for Finland and Sweden where it has decreased and in Denmark a very slight increase (see Table 3.4. The breadwinner model has been replaced with an adult worker model where both partners work. In Scandinavian countries and in France female participation is very high or high with medium to low levels of part-time work. What distinguishes this group is the high full-time participation rate of women with young children, reflecting the provision of services either

Table 3.4 Female employment rates 1995–2004 homestate women aged 15–64 years

State	1995	2004	% Part-time 2004
Austria	59.4	61.4	41.9
Belgium	45.9	54.9	41.2
Denmark	69.5	73.5	33.9
Finland	58.4	66.8	17.5
France	53.6	58.1	29.6
Germany	–	60.5	40.6
Greece	37.8	45.3	8.0
Ireland	41.3	56.0	31.9
Italy	35.6	45.0	23.9
Netherlands	54.9	68.1	75.7
Portugal	54.5	61.5	13.1
Spain	31.1	47.3	17.5
Sweden	74.2	72.9	36.1
UK	62.3	66.9	44.5

Source: EUROSTAT Table I..A.1.2

through the public sector, as in Sweden, or a combination of public and household (registered child minders) services as in France. The market plays a much bigger role in the provision of care for the elderly. Intensified domestication of these caring services has led to the employment of migrant women in France, particularly of more recent arrivals. In a second group of countries, female employment, though substantially expanded in the past two decades, has occurred through women working part-time, often for a relatively short number of hours. In the absence of public or affordable market services a low percentage of women with young children are able to work full-time. This applies both to the continental corporate countries such as Germany as well as the more liberal system in the UK. The high percentage of part-time employment means that the use of migrant women (established and recent) for care remained low but is rising. The third grouping covers the southern rim, with the exception of Portugal, where the employment rate of women, including part-time, is low, as too is the proportion of women with young children working full-time. Thus in Southern countries the proportion of migrants employed in households to make good the deficiencies of public, community or market services is high and represents the major source of employment for female migrants.

The second aspect to be considered is the *relationship between the state, the market and the family in the provision of care and the reconfiguration of welfare delivery*. This needs to take account of services for children, the elderly and the disabled. Whilst feminists addressed the patchwork quilt of caring, particularly of child care in the early 1990s, they devoted less attention to care for the elderly and those with special needs, where public intervention had been much more limited in most European states. Trends in child care across European Union states are more coherent than for the elderly and are moving towards the acceptance of public subsidization of private (parental) caring (Daly & Lewis 2000: 293). For the elderly, changes are particularly complex and shaped by different sources and forms of privatization (Trydegard 2003). Deinstitutionalization, application of management and market principles (separation of the purchaser and provider and the creation of internal markets), de-professionalisation and more systematic targeting of recipients of care have all played their part in shaping a more privatized, managerial and informalized economy of care.

Leira's typology (2001), based on provision of services for young children under three and the elderly is useful, but was developed before the implications of the reconfiguration of welfare services (Daly & Lewis 2000: 286) during the latter half of the 1990s had become apparent. Hence to apply it to the current provision of service one has to include the shift from the direct provision by states as well as the application of market principles to public provision. We also have to take into account the blurring of the division between formal and informal work and the recent development of informal work which encompasses new forms of informal care work and inclusion based on care work (Geissler & Pfau-Effinger 2005). These processes have resulted firstly in semi-formal family-based care work where caring tasks undertaken by families and social networks are paid for, and secondly, informal care employment, based on the employment of paid workers (nearly all women) in the household, and in which the household acts as the employer.

It is clear that these economic and social changes have implications for the involvement of migrant labour in the provision of care within and beyond the household. The initial discussion of care provision outlines the level of provision for children and elderly in different welfare regimes before drawing out implications for the use of female migrant labour. Due to the absence of comparative studies of care and social reproductive labour which includes more skilled work, the analysis is limited to the less skilled sectors of migrant employment.

ABUNDANT SERVICES FOR BOTH YOUNG AND OLD (SWEDEN)

Universal coverage for publicly funded municipal child care for all working parents and students remains an objective in these countries (see Table 3.5). Nonetheless, in Sweden 40 percent of municipalities withdraw places

Table 3.5 Typology of welfare regimes, migration and female employment

Country	Welfare regime	Service provision	Homestate women employment+	Migrant women employment*
Sweden	Social Democratic	Abundant child and elderly	Very high employment, Medium p/t, High children	Insignificant domestic High social
Germany	Conservative Northern	Limited young and old	High employment High p/t Low child	Low domestic Low social
France	Conservative	Abundant child Limited old	High employment Medium p/t High child	Medium domestic Low social
Spain	Conservative Southern	Limited young and old	All low	High domestic Low social
UK	Liberal with social demoratic	Poor young and abundant old	High employment High p/t Low child	Low domestic High social

+The three indicators refer to rate of employment, part-time employment and full-time employment of women with children under 10 years.
*Domestic refers to employment in households and social to employment in education, health and other community services (see Tables 3.3 and Table 3.4).

where at least one parent has lost their employment (Letablier 2003). Although Swedish policy for the elderly (publicly financed and supplied according to need and not ability to pay) seems to remain constant in general terms, it has undergone considerable change in practice. The impact of market principles on public policy has been particularly marked in Sweden. To meet the expansion of the elderly population and demand for services, municipalities have evaluated needs more strictly, prioritising medical and social above household (cleaning, washing, and shopping). These services are largely provided by profit-making companies, for the most part large international ones. The four largest ones held 50 percent of the contracts. Private Swedish recruitment agencies are also supplying low-wage cleaning and domestic labour. Employment of carers has increased by 13 percent in the second half of the 1990s, especially those employed by the private sector (Trydegard 2003). These developments have created a gendered and racialised informal and casualised labour force using Eastern European, undocumented migrants, who are on the increase, and non-EU migrants (Schierup et al. 2006). And in targeting the frail elderly and reducing basic household services, social stratification has been deepened such that the better educated buy the deficit from the market while the lesser educated have turned to family and neighbours for care which is usually undertaken by older married and single women (Theobald 2005).

Abundant services for children but limited for the elderly (France)

The state has not necessarily sought to reduce expenditure but to change the way in which services are provided i.e. privatised and in the home. In France, although there are a large number of publicly financed crèches, there has been a shift in the 1990s to private forms of care supported by the state such as allowances for registered childminders and tax deductions for families who hire an employee to take care of a small child (Tobio 2001)[15]. Unlike childcare, legislation to help the dependent elderly in France (1994, 1996) was slow to develop. About 6 percent of the population over 65 years of age in 1996 lived in institutions, and the new policies were attuned to employment objectives encouraging the employment of home help or even unemployed relatives.

Abundant services for elderly but poor public provision for young children (UK)

Childcare has been expanded with the help of state subsidies to the private and associational sectors as part of a general strategy of shifting from welfare to workfare by increasing female participation in the labour force. In the UK, the National Childcare Strategy fits well into what some have called the social investment state where social expenditure is to provide an investment that sustains the nation's ability to compete in the global economy (Lister 2003). For the elderly, the restructuring of public services since 1980s can be seen clearly in the current dominance of the voluntary sector and private companies — 64 percent of contact hours in 2002 compared to only 2 percent in 1992. At the same time, fewer households were eligible for care to help them function independently due to the threshold at which people become eligible for care (Deol 2004), thus forcing more of the population to purchase services from the market.

Limited services for young and old (Germany, Spain)

The privatization of services means very different things in Germany compared to the Southern Rim countries. In Germany there is a relatively large voluntary, quasi-statutory welfare sector funded by the state which provides a range of services for children and the elderly (Daly & Lewis 2000). Young children are still seen as the responsibility of the mother but since the late 1990s, there is a legal right to kindergarten provision for children between three and six years. For the elderly considerable change has ensued from the implementation of home-based (1995) and institutional care (1996) allowances which have resulted in an expansion of private home-based care agencies (Behning 2005).

In the southern rim countries, the state contributes little to support family life with Spain spending the lowest percentage on childcare and the family in Europe (Tobio 2001) though there is increasing state intervention in social care (Leon 2005). Thus, working women with children call upon family members, while 6 percent of those employed used paid domestic help (survey conducted in 1998). Making family and employment compatible has begun to appear on the political agenda (Law for the Reconciliation of Work and Family Life 1999) and some initiatives for public child care have been taken at a regional level as in Catalunya. However, the norm for care of the dependent elderly remains a family issue; the proportion of the elderly living in institutions is low, 3 percent compared to the European average of 5 percent. Complementary services, such as home help, meals on wheels, and day centres, which are just beginning to appear (Tobio 2001).

Employment of migrant labour

Whilst the employment of female migrants in states with low levels of subsidy for family and care may be clear and shows up statistically (see Table 3.6), there are a whole series of changes which are likely to make the presence of migrant women in the household more significant as a result of the new mixed economy of care in other welfare regimes. In a highly labour intensive sector, this shift to a more diversified supply in effect produces an intensification of the domestic economy in which services are supplied by a plurality of providers: international and national companies, the voluntary sector (secular and religious), local authorities, national agencies, and individuals hired by households. The attempt by the state to balance demand and supply and by companies to work within low profit margins encourages the expansion of low paid, part-time and flexible employment (Lethbridge 2005). In addition, the introduction of cash for care policies, as in elder care in a number of countries, such as the Netherlands, Italy, France, UK and Austria, has commodified to varying degrees, previously informal and unpaid care arrangements with which households are able to employ domestic workers (migrant and a member of their own family) privately (Yeandle & Ungerson 2002).

The extent of domestification is not picked up statistically through the category of household services since those employed by companies will not be treated as employees of the private household. Hence in Sweden, the percentage of migrants employed in the household is insignificant. Yet at the same time, the number of migrants employed in the health and other community sector (covering all skill levels) is substantial and at 18.6 percent in 2003–2004 and is the highest in Europe after Norway (see Table 3.7). Furthermore, the focus on the domestic sector by many researchers misses out the substantial use of new and established migrant labour in

Table 3.6 Employment of women by nationality in selected counties

	Percentage			
	1994		2004	
	Foreigners	Nationals	Foreigners	Nationals
Household services				
Spain	27.1	6.9	36.0	4.6
France	14.7	3.5	21.1	3.8
Greece	35.0	1.5	42.4	1.3
Italy	10.3	2.3	27.9	1.6
UK	3.7	1.1	3.1	0.8
Hotel and Restaurants				
Germany	10.8	3.2	11.5	3.8
Spain	24.4	7.1	19.0	7.5
France	8.5	3.8	6.0	3.4
Greece	12.2	6.4	16.3	7.4
UK	6.5	5.7	7.6	5.2
Health and Social Services				
Belgium	14.5	19.3	15.9	22.4
Germany	11.9	11.7	15.7	19.6
Denmark	37.6	26.9	27.4	32.6
France	10.5	16.9	12.1	20.3
UK	21.0	18.8	25.0	20.6
Education				
Belgium	6.8	15.3	7.5	14.8
Germany	3.4	7.9	5.7	8.8
Spain	9.5	9.8	3.8	10.2
France	4.8	11.3	6.8	10.5
Italy	16.1	14.8	4.2	14.0
UK	12.5	11.4	11.4	14.4
Information Technology				
UK			1.5	0.8

Source: European Community Labour Force Survey

social reproduction in other sites such as schools, hospitals, and residential homes.

It is only recently that research on care has begun to take up the issue of employment as opposed to the gendered redistributive implications of

Table 3.7 Employment of foreign-born by sector, 2003–2004 average

Country	Percentage of foreign-born employment					
	HR	E	HC	H	A &ETO	Other
France	5.9	6.0	9.7	5.8	6.8	27.2
Germany	7.6	3.9	10.1	0.7	3.3	21.9
Greece	9.2	2.7	2.4	13.4	1.4	9.7
Ireland	13.2	6.4	12.5	–	2.9	25.4
Netherlands	8.2	5.4	12.2	–	6.6	28.2
Norway	8.6	8.0	20.7	–	3.7	27.0
Spain	12.0	3.6	3.7	12.2	2.0	18.5
Sweden	6.6	10.8	18.6	–	3.9	27.5
Switzerland	7.3	6.1	13.4	1.3	3.4	24.1
UK	9.0	8.4	14.5	1.0	5.2	31.9

Notes: HR = Hotel and Restaurants; E = Education, HC =Health and other community services, H = Households, A &ETO = Administration and ETO, Other = Other services. The numbers in bold indicates the sectors where foreign-born are over-represented i.e. the share in the sector is larger than the foreign-born in total employment
Source: SOPEMI 2006; Statlink: http://dx.doi.org.10.1787/636251543631

welfare regimes (Cameron 2003; European Foundation for the Improvement of Living and Working Conditions 2003; Ungerson and Yeandle 2002; Lethbridge 2005). However, this is not the only key dimension impacting on gendered welfare regimes that has been under-researched. The stratification generated by welfare regime is also of considerable relevance for understanding employment patterns. Conservative regimes have been defined in terms of their stratified rights, especially the secure tenure and generous benefits enjoyed by civil servants. This partly explains the exclusion of non-nationals from public employment, but which has since the mid-1990s been permitted for EU citizens. Furthermore, the boundaries of the civil service are drawn very broadly to include professions such as teachers. Liberal professions too operate in an exclusionary corporatist manner. Hence in France it has been estimated that one-third of public employment and a wide range of liberal professions (doctors, lawyers, vets) are barred to non-EU citizens (CERC 1999). Non-EU citizens are more likely to be employed in these occupations as assistants on less secure and generous contracts. On the other hand, liberal/social democratic states tend to have much lower barriers to public employment, usually demanding legal residence as the pre-requisite for employment in most areas. In addition, in these regimes the older regional and colonial links continue to influence the sources of skilled labour. In Sweden, three out of the four main female nationalities in the labour market are from the Nordic region (Finland, Norway, Denmark), constituting in total 42 percent of the stock of foreign labour (SOPEMI 2004:370). In the UK, female Commonwealth citizens are prominent in professions of social reproduction, both as permanent and temporary labour. At the skilled end, employment is eased through the recognition of professional training as in medical diplomas (Raghuram & Kofman 2002).

Thus the Scandinavian countries and the UK have the highest percentages of migrant women employed in social and welfare sectors of education and health (see Table 3.3). In Sweden these two sectors accounted for 29.4 percent of migrant employment in 2003–2004 and in the UK 22.9 percent. In continental corporate regimes, especially those in Southern rim, the percentages are far lower — 8.3 percent in France, 9.7 percent in Germany 5.1 percent in Spain.

CONCLUSION

The proliferation and polarisation of statuses affects both men and women migrants and refugees but its impact on women is different to that of men due to the channels through which they enter and the gendered division of labour. One of the key divisions is that between the skilled and the lesser skilled. Fewer women are to be found in the more privileged groups (skilled migrants, Geneva Convention refugees). Amongst skilled migrants, whose entry, rights and access to citizenship is being facilitated the areas of shortage still operate in men's favour. Caring, healing and educating people are undertaken by highly regulated professions (doctors, nurses, teachers, social workers) unlike IT, a new and far less regulated occupation. A points-based system, even if it does not privilege certain occupations, operates on criteria favouring men, for example, high level salaries or positions. And for skilled female spouses, the barriers to professional integration remain very strong due to problems of accreditation, lack of local experience and closure of public sector employment to non-citizens. The latter hits women hardest since the feminized professions in many European countries fall under the umbrella of civil service employment. National variations in the size of the civil service public sector are considerable e.g. between the low levels of the UK and the high levels in France. Conservative welfare regimes are thus likely to present the most difficult barriers to entry. As a result, many women, who have entered as family migrants, or who marry after entering as students or tourists, find their careers and professional aspirations blocked. The control over their environment and right to seek employment on an equal basis is thus severely compromised.

At the less skilled end of the employment spectrum, women face great difficulties in maintaining a legal status. Failure to acknowledge the economic and social value of women's work means that although their labour is in demand, it is not matched by official recognition in the form of work permits and proper employment contracts. Both women who enter as labour migrants and family members are thus more likely to be forced into the informal sector and undertake poorly paid and undervalued work with little social protection. Whilst domestic labour has captured much of the attention, numerous other sectors employ less skilled labour on flexible contracts or informally — industrial cleaning, hospitality and tourism, care outside the home.

As the analysis of different welfare regimes demonstrates, the opportunities for migrant women vary according to the nature of the regime and the stratification they create, especially through the closure around certain occupations. Absence of detailed studies of migrant women and men in key sectors of the welfare state, and the difficulty of statistically capturing what are often complex and contested notions of care, mean that we cannot ascertain more clearly the nature of migrant stratification in different regimes and the interplay between migration system and welfare regimes. One of the differences between regimes is the differential presence of migrant women in the public, voluntary, private and household domains. It is clear that Southern European familial welfare regimes generate employment in the household and that migrant women are stereotyped as being suitable for such employment. This is then reinforced by immigration policies which creates quotas for them in this sector. Escaping from this sector and pursuing other aspirations becomes very difficult. Yet elsewhere, including in social democratic regimes, there has also been shift in provision of and payment for care which is leading to the creation of employment for migrant women in public and private spaces with a variety of contracts and employers (public, welfare agencies, voluntary organizations, private firms and individual households. It has been argued that in Sweden many of these new forms of employment have generated a racialised casualisation of the labour market and reinforced an ethnicised class stratification (Schierup et al. 2006). And at the same time, opportunities for skilled female migrants have expanded in several countries (Ireland, UK), especially in sectors of social reproduction. In studying gendered migrations in Europe, we need to examine the complex interplay of migratory policy and changing welfare regimes and acknowledge the role that migrant women play in sustaining welfare provision.

NOTES

1. Recent legislation has sought to facilitate the movement of non-workers, such as students, spouses. Directive on Rights of Residence of Community Citizens.
2. Following an agreement in 2002 with the EU, Switzerland too has been incorporated into the EU migratory space although various economic and social rights will only fully come into force for r EU nationals in Switzerland by 2014.

3. Austria, Denmark and Germany have stated they will maintain restrictions for the full transitional period of seven years whilst Belgium, France, Italy and Luxembourg have relaxed their restrictions.
 4. Four of them seem to be particularly appropriate in charting degrees of autonomy and dependency experienced by migrant women:

    Bodily Integrity which refers to the ability to move freely from place to place; to be secure against violent assault and domestic violence; having opportunities for sexual satisfaction and choice in matters of reproduction; *Control over One's Environment* which includes having the right to seek employment on an equal basis with others.; having the freedom from unwarranted search and seizure. In work, it means being able to work as a human being, exercising practical reason and entering into meaningful relationships of mutual recognition with other workers; *Practical reason* which involves being able to form a conception of the good life and to engage in critical reflection about the planning of one's life; *Affiliation* has two elements. Firstly, that of being able to live with and toward others and to engage in various forms of social interaction. Secondly, having the social bases of self-respect and to be treated as a dignified person whose worth is equal to others.
 5. In many European countries the term migrant is both narrower and more extensive. Narrower in the sense that too often a 'migrant' is someone from a Third World country with value systems different to prevailing European norms, ignoring those who migrate from culturally or economically similar societies. Frequently, the migrant woman, and especially if Muslim, quintessentially exemplifies the weight of tradition. At the same time, 'migrant' may, in states such as Austria, Germany and Switzerland, be applied to all non-nationals, many of whom have been born and educated in the country. In this case it is difficult distinguishing those of migrant origin from recent arrivals.
 6. They were seen to be less threatening and of strategic importace for the Italian economy (Fasano and Zucchini, 2002)
 7. Migrant domestic workers who enter the UK accompanying their employer can leave that employer if they are abused or exploited and receive basic protection under UK employment law, and they are entitled to the national minimum wage, statutory holiday pay and a notice period. As a worker, their visa is renewed annually, and renewal is dependent on the migrant domestic worker being in full-time employment as a domestic worker in a private household. There is also a right to apply for settlement and for family reunification. In the new proposals they will loose rights to settlement and will not have the time or the ability to appeal against non-fulfilment of rights or abuse. This is all being done on grounds that UK should obtain all its less skilled labour from within the EU
 8. Financial problems in the National Health and the inability of new British-trained nurses to find a job, have led to the severe restrictions on the recruitment of overseas nurses. However it is very likely that trained burses will be recruited into the care sector, possibly as care assistants rather than as nurses.
 9. As with nurses major changes have occurred in relation to overseas doctors whose postgraduate training scheme has been ended, due in part to the expansion of British-trained doctors, the availability of EU doctors and the financial crisis in the NHS.
 10. Of the 116 women surveyed, 61 percent had come from EU countries with 45 percent having a Greek spouse or life partner. 78 percent had a university

degree of which a third were at a post-graduate level. About 10 percent were repatriates who had been born in Greece and had returned after a period of study or work abroad and had encountered problems in reintegrating.
11. Data obtained from Work Permits UK show that about 29 percent of applicants from 2002 to September 2004 were female. A large number of points in the UK system come from having a PhD or a high status position in an organisation. It is difficult as yet to make any comparisons since Canada only dispensed with an occupational grid in 2002, while Australia's retains a strong occupational element. Both UK and Canada lowered their level of points for entry, in the UK from 75 to 65 in November 2003. A new system of managed migration integrating the Highly Skilled category as tier 1 is gradually being implemented.
12. France had already withdrawn the right to work in 1991 but in the UK it was permitted for the principal applicant after six months but discretionary for other members. Inevitably the outcome was unfavourable to women. However since July 2003 this right has been withdrawn for everyone in an attempt to further dissuade asylum seekers.
13. In the UK even the status of Convention refugees has been made precarious since they will not be given an automatic right to settlement for five and can therefore still be sent back if within the first years the situation of the country of origin is deemed to have sufficiently improved (Home Office, 2005: 22).
14. Feminists pointed out the inadequacy of his theorisation of familial relations and the conceptualisation of de-commodification in terms of income maintenance (pensions, sickness, unemployment) which enables the individual to be less dependent on market forces. Instead Lewis (1993) proposed an alternative male breadwinner typology (high, medium, low) based on the extent to which social policy maintains women's dependence on men.
15. This system exists for those who are legally employed and registered which means they have rights like any other employee. Many do not use it because it involves employers and employees in high rates of social security payments.

REFERENCES

Ackers, L. (1998) *Shifting Spaces. Women, migration and citizenship within the European Union*. Policy Press, Bristol.
Aguilar, F. (2003) 'Global migrations, old forms of labor and new transborder class relations', in *Southeast Asian Studies* vol. 41, no. 2, pp. 137–61.
Ahmad, F. (2003) 'Still 'In progress?' — methodological dilemmas, tensions and contradictions in theorizing South Asian Muslim women', in N. Puwar and Parvati Raghuram (eds.), *South Asian Women in the Diaspora*. Routledge, London.
Ahmad, F. and S. Sheriff (1999) 'Muslim women of Europe: welfare needs and responses', in *Social Work in Europe*, vol. 8, no, 1, pp.2–10.
Allan, H. and J. Aggergaard Larsen (2003) '"We Need Respect": experiences of internationally recruited nurses in the UK* Royal College of Nurses, London.
Andall, J. (ed) (2003) Gender and ethnicity in contemporary Europe. Oxford: Berg.
Anderson, B. (2000) *Doing the Dirty Work*. Zed Press, London.
Anderson, B., M. Ruhs, B. Rogaly, and S. Spencer (2006) Fair Enough? Central and Eastern migrants in low-wage employment in the UK, available at http://www.compas.oc.ac.uk/changing status

Anthias, F. and G. Lazaridis (eds.). (2000) *Gender and Migration in Southern Europe. Women on the Move.* Berg, Oxford.
Baldassar, L. and C. Baldock (2000) 'Linking migration and family studies: transnational migrants and the care of aging parents', in B. Agozino (ed.), *Theoretical and Methodological Issues in Migration Research.* Ashgate, Aldershot.
Behning, U. (2005) 'Changing long-term care regimes: a six country comparison of directions and effects', in B. Pfau-Effinger and B. Geissler *Care and Social Integration in European Societies,* Policy Press, Bristol.
Bhabha, J. (2002) *More or less vulnerable? Women, children and the asylum paradox.* Paper presented at 43rd Annual Studies Association Convention, International Studies Association, New Orleans, 23–27 March.
Bommes, M. and H. Geddes (2000) Immigration and welfare: challenging the borders of the welfare state. London.
Borrel, C. and J. Boeldieu (2001) 'De plus en plus de femmes immigrés sur le marché du travail', *INSEE Première,* No. 791.
Brown, C. (2001) 'If we want social sochietion we need a sense of identity', interview with David Blunkett, Independent on Sunday, 9 December, p. 4.
Buchan, J., T. Parkin and J. Sochalski (2003) *International Nurse Mobility: trends and policy implications.* <www.rcn.org.uk/downloads/InternationalNurseMobility accessed 30 March 2004.
Cameron, C. (2003) *Care work in Europe: future needs.* Paper presented at Careworkers: matching supply and demand. Employment Issues in the Care of Children and Older People Living at Home. Sheffield Hallam University, 20–21 June.
Cancedda, L. (2001) *Employment in Household Services.* European Foundation for the Improvement of Living and Working Conditions, Dublin.
Caritas (2001) *Immigrazione Dossier Statistico 2001.* Caritas, Rome.
Castles, S. and M. Miller (2003) *The Age of Migration. International Population Movements in the Modern World* (3rd ed.). Palgrave Macmillan, London.
Castells, M. (1996) *The Rise of the Network Society, vol. 1.* Blackwell, Oxford.
CERC (1999) *Immigration, emploi et chomage: un etat de lieu empirique et théorique.* Paris: les dossiers de Cerc no 3.
Chang, K. and L. Ling 2000. 'Globalization and its intimate other: Filipina domestic workers in Hong Kong." in M. Marchand and A. Sisson Runyan (eds.), *Gender and Global Restructuring. Sightings, Sites and Resistances.* Routledge, London.
Charbit, Y. and C. Bertrand 1985. *Enfants, Familles, Migrations.* INED Cahier 110, Presses Universitaires de France, Paris.
Cox, R. (2006) *The Servant Problem,* I.B. Tauris, London.
Crawley, H. (2001) *Refugees and Gender. Law and Process.* Jordans, Bristol.
Daly, M. and J. Lewis (2000) 'The concept of social care and the analysis of contemporary welfare states', *British Journal of Sociology,* vol. 51, no. 2, pp. 281–98.
Dayan-Herzbrun, S. (2000) 'The issue of the Islamic headscarf', in J. Freedman and C. Tarr (eds.), *Women, Immigration and Identities in France.* Berg, Oxford.
De Hart, B. (1999) '"It just went according to the rules with us." Binational families, marriage, migration and shifting identities' Paper presented at the conference on Migrant Families and Human Capital Formation in Europe, Leiden, 19–21 November.
Delacroix, C. (1997) 'Mediatrices socio-culturelles, citoyennes innovantes', in N. Bentichcou (ed.), *Les femmes de l'immigration au quotiden.* l"Harmattan, Paris.
Deol, R. (2004) 'Who cares?' *The Guardian* 4 February, pp. 11.

Dietz, G. and N. El-Sohoumi (2002). 'Door to door with our Muslim sisters: intercultural and inter-religious conflicts in Granada, Spain', *Studi Emigrazione*, vol. XXXIX, pp. 77–105.
Deutsche Welle (2005) First German immigration law takes effect, accessed 18 February 2005, from http://www.dw-world.de/dw/article/0,1564,1442681,00.html
Ehrenreich, B. and A. R. Hochschild (eds.). 2003. *Global Woman. Nannies, maids and sex workers in the new economy*. Metropolitan Books, New York.
Erdem, E. and M. Mattes (2003) 'Gendered policies-gendered patterns: female labour migration from turkey to Germany from the 1960s to the 1990s', in Rainer Ohliger, Karen Schönwälder and Triadafilos Triadafilopoulos (eds.), *European Encounters 1945–2000: Migrants, Migration and European societies since 1945*. Ashgate, Aldershot.
Erel, U. and E. Kofman (2003) 'Professional Female Immigration in Post-war Europe: counteracting an historical amnesia', in R. Ohliger, K. Schönwälder and T. Triadafilopoulos (eds.), *European Encounters 1945–2000: Migrants, Migration and European societies since 1945*. Ashgate, Aldershot.
Erel, U. (2000) 'Skilled migrant women and citizenship', in M. Morokvasic-Müller, U. Erel and K Shinozaki (eds.), *Crossing Borders and Shifting Boundaries. Vol 1. Gender on the Move*. Leske and Budrich, Opladen.
Escrivá, A. (2005) 'Aged global care chains: a Southern-European contribution to the field', Conference on Migration and Domestic Work in Global Perspective, Wassenaar, 26–29 May 2005.
Esping-Andersen, G. (1990) *Three Worlds of Welfare Capitalism*. Polity Press, Cambridge.
European Council for Refugees (2001) *Gender Sensitive Integration Practice*. ECRE, Brussels.
European Foundation for the Improvement of Living and Working Conditions (2003) *Care workers: matching supply and demand. Employment issues in the case of children and older people living at home*. Dublin.
European Industrial Relations Observatory (2003) *Migration and Industrial Relations*. Accessed 30 March 2004., from http://www.eiro.eurofound.eu.int/2003/03/study/tn0303105s.html
Fagnani, J. and M-T. Letablier (2005) 'Social rights and care responsibility in the French welfare state', in B. Pfau-Effinger and B. Geissler, *Care and Social Integration in European Societies*, Policy Press, Bristol, pp. 135–53.
FASILD (2003) *Femmes immigrées et issues de l'immigration*. FASILD, Paris.
Fassano, L. and F. Zucchini (2002) *Local implementation of the consolidated law on immigration. The Seventh Italian Report in Migration 2001*. Fondazione ISMU, Milan.
Federal Institute for Vocational Training (2000) *New Employment Opportunities for Female Migrants*. Federal Institute for Vocational Training, Bonn.
Freedman, J. (2004) 'Secularism as a barrier to integration, The French dilemma', *International Migration*, vol. 42, pp. 4–27.
Geissler, B. and B. Pfau-Effinger (2005) 'Change in European care arrangements', in B. Pfau-Effinger, and B Geissler (eds.), *Care and Social Integration in European Societies*, Policy Press, Bristol, pp. 3–20.
Hardill, I. and S. MacDonald (1998) 'Choosing to relocate: an examination of the impact of expatriate work on dual career households', *Women's Studies International Forum*, vol. 21, pp. 21–9.
Haut Conseil à l'Intégration (2006) *Le bilan de la politique d'intégration 2002–2005*. La Documentation Française, Paris.

Hauge Byberg, I. (2002) *Immigrant Women in Norway. A summary of findings on demography, education, labour and income*. Statistics Norway, Norway.

Hess, S. and A. Pukhaber (2004) 'Big sisters are better domestic servants? Comments on the booming au pair business', *Feminist Review* no. 77, pp. 65–78.

Hill Maher, K. (2004) 'Globalized social reproduction: women migrants and the citizenship gap', in A. Brysk and G. Shafir (eds.), *People Out of Place. Globalization, Human Rights, and the Citizenship Gap*. Taylor and Francis, New York/London.

Hillmann, F. (2005) "Migrants' care work in private households, or the strength of bilocal and transnational ties as a last(ing) resource in global migration," in B. Pfau-Effinger and B. Geissler (eds.), *Care and Social Integration in European Societies*, Policy Press, Bristol, pp. 93–112.

Hochschild, A. (2000) 'Global care chains and emotional surplus value', in W. Hutton and A. Giddens (eds.), *On the Edge. Living with Global Capitalism*. Jonathan Cape, London.

Home Office (2006) Accesssioning Monitoring Report.

Institute for Public Policy Research (2005) *Selecting Wisely. Making managed migration work for Britain*. Institute for Public Policy Research, London.

Institute of Working Lives KAGU (2005) Women regugees: from volunteering to emploees: a research project on paid and unpaid work in the volutary sector. London.

IOM. (1996) *Traffacking of women in the European Union: characteristics, trends and policy issues*. Conference on Trafficking in Women, 10–11 June. Vienna.

Kingma, M. (2001) "Nursing migration: global treasure hunt or disaster-in-the making?" *Nursing Inquiry*, vol. 8, no.4, pp. 205–212.

Knocke, W. (1999) 'The labour market for immigrant women in Sweden: marginalised women in low-valued jobs', in John. Wrench, A. Rea and N. Ouali (eds.), *Migrants, Ethnic Minorities and the Labour Market — Integration and Exclusion in Europe*. Macmillan, London.

Kofman, E. (2004a) 'Family-related migration: a critical review of European studies", *Journal of Ethnic and Migration Studies*, vol. 30, no. 2, pp. 243–62.

Kofman, E. (2004b) 'Gendered global migrations: diversity and stratification", *International Feminist Journal of Politics*, vol. 6, vo. 4, pp. 642–64.

Kofman, E. (2002) 'Contemporary European migrations, civic stratification and citizenship', *Political Geography*, vol. 21, no. 8, pp.1035–1054.

Kofman, E. (2000) "The invisibility of female skilled migrants and gender relations in studies of skilled migration in Europe", *International Journal of Population Geography*, vol. 6, no.1, pp. 45–59.

Kofman, E. A. Phizacklea, P. Raghuram and R. Sales (2000) *Gender and International Migration in Europe*. Routledge, London.

Kofman, E. and P. Raghuram (2006) 'Gender and global labour migrations: incorporating skilled workers', in *Antipode* 38(2): 282–303.

Koninklijke Nederlandse Akademie Wetenschappen (2001) Solidarity between the sexes and the generations: transformations in Europe, Amsterdam, 28–29 June.

Lazaridis, G. (2001) 'Trafficking and prostitution: the growing exploitation of migrant women in Greece', in *European Journal of Women's Studies*, vol. 8, no.1, 67–102.

Leira, A. (2001) 'Public family and caring state: family change and policy reform in the Nordic countries', Conference Solidarity between the sexes and the generations: transformations in Europe, Amsterdam 28–29 June.

Letablier, T. (2003) 'Les politiques familiales des pays nordiques et leurs ajustements aucchangements socio-économiques des années quatre-vingt-dix', *Revue Française des Affaires Sociales* vol. 57, no.4, pp. 487–514.

Lethbridge, J. (2005) Care Services in Europe, Public Services International Research Unit, University of Greenwich.

Leon, M. (2005) 'Welfare state regimes and the social organisation of labour: childcare arrangements and the work/family balance dilemma'. *The Sociological Review*, vol. 53 (Suppl. 2), pp. 204–18.

Lister, R. (2003) *Justice, equality and dependency: a critical social policy perspective*. Symposium on Nancy Fraser's work, University of Warwick, 22 March 2003. Accessed 30 March 2004, from http://www2.warwick.ac.uk/fac/soc/sociology/gender/events/symposium/lister/

Lutz, H. (1993) 'In between or bridging cultural gaps? Migrant women from Turkey as mediators', *New Community*, vol. 19, no.3, pp. 485–492.

Mahroum, S. (2001) 'Europe and the immigration of highly skilled labour', *International Migration*, vol. 39, no.5, pp. 27–43.

Menz, G. (2002) 'Patterns in EU labour immigration policy: national initiatives and European responses', *Journal of Ethnic and Migration Studies*, vol. 28, no.4, pp. 723–742.

Moreno-Fontes Chammartin, G. (2004) Situacíon laboral de las mujeres migrantes en Espana, Perspectovas sobre migraciones laborales 4, ILO, Geneva.

Morokvasic, M. (2003) "Transnational mobility and gender: a view from post-wall Europe." In M. Morokvasic-Müller, U. Erel and K.Shinozaki (eds.). *Crossing Borders and Shifting Boundaries. Vol 1. Gender on the Move.* Leske and Budrich, Opladen.

Morokvasic, M. (1996) 'Entre l'est et l'ouest, des migrations pendulaires', in M. Morokvasic and R. Hedwig (eds.), *Migrants. Nouvelles mobilités en Europe.* L'Harmattan, Paris.

Morris, L. (2002) *Managing Migration. Civic stratification and migrants' rights.* Routledge, London.

Nussbaum, M. (2003) 'Women's capabilities and social justice', in M. Molyneux and S. Razavi (eds.), *Gender Justice, Development and Rights.* OUP, Milton Keynes.

OECD (2002) *International Mobility of the Highly Skilled.* OECD Policy Brief, Paris.

Ouali, N. (2003) 'Les marocaines en Europe: diversification des profils migratoires', *Hommes et Migrations*, vol. 1242: pp.71–82.

Parrenas, R. (2001) *Servants of Globalization, Stanford University Press: Women, migration and domestic work.* Stanford CA: Stanford University Press.

Parrenas, R. (2005) *Children of Global Migration*, Stanford, CA: Stanford University Press

Pfau-Effinger, B.and B. Geissler (2005) (eds.), *Care and Social Integration in European Societies.* Policy Press, Bristol.

Phizacklea, A. (2003) 'Transnationalism, gender and global workers', in M. Morokvasic-Müller, U. Erel and K. Shinozaki (eds.). *Crossing Borders and Shifting Boundaries. Vol 1. Gender on the Move.* Leske and Budrich, Opladen.

Pratt, G. and B. Yeoh (2003) 'Transnational (counter) topographies', *Gender, Place and Culture*, vol. 10, no.2, pp. 159–166.

Raghuram, P. (2004) 'Migration, gender and the IT sector: intersecting debates', *Women's Studies International Forum*, nol 27, vo. 2, pp. 163–176.

Raghuram, P. and E. Kofman (2002) 'State, labour markets and immigration: overseas doctors in the UK', *Environment and Planning A*, vol. 34, pp. 2071–2089.

Regnard, C. (2006) *Immigration et presence étrangere en France en 2004*, La Documentation Française, Paris.

Riano, Y. (2003) 'Migration of skilled Latin American women to Switzerland and their struggle for integration', In Y. Mutsuo (ed.), *Latin American Emigration: Interregional Comparison among North America, Europe and Japan*. JCAS Symposium Series 19, Japan Centre for Area Studies, National Museum of Ethnology, Osaka.

Rosewarne, S. and D. Groutsis (2003) 'Challenges to the integrity of a European migration program: Greece as a recalcitrant', Paper at Challenges of Immigration and Integration in the European Union and Australia, Sydney, 18-20 February.

Runnymede Trust (1997) *Islamophobia: a challenge to us all*. Runnymede Trust, London.

Sainsbury, D. (ed.) (1999) *Gender and Welfare State Regimes*, Oxford University Press, Oxford.

Salt, J. (2000) 'Trafficking and human smuggling: a European perspective', *International Migration*, vol. 38, no. 3, pp.31–56.

Sargeant, G. et al. (1999) *Turning Refugees Into Employees. Research into the barriers to employment perceived by women refugees in London*. Industrial Society, London.

Sarti, R. Forthcoming. 'Conclusion. Domestic service and European identity'. In S. Paselau and I. Schopp (eds) with R.. Sarti. *Proceedings of the Servant Project*, Editions de l'Universié de Liege, Liege, vol. V.

Sassen, S. (2000) 'Women's burden: counter-geographies of globalization and feminization of survival', in *Journal of International Affairs*, vol. 53, no. 2, pp. 503–524.

Schierup, C.U., P. Hansen, and S. Castles (2006) *Migration, Citizenship and the European Welfare State*. Oxford: Oxford University Press.

Sciortino, G. (2004) 'Immigration in a Mediterranean welfare state: the Italian experience in a comparative perspective' *Journal of Comparative Policy Analysis*, vol. 6, no. 2, 111–29.

Simmons, T. (2004) 'Skills, sexual citizens and the UK's family reunion provision', in *Feminist Review*, no. 77, pp. 172–4.

SOPEMI (2001) *Trends in International Migration*. OECD, Paris.

SOPEMI (2004) *Trends in International Migration*. OECD, Paris.

SOPEMI (2006) *International Migration Outlook*, OECD, Paris.

Theobold, H. (2005) 'Labour market participation of women and social exclusion: contradictory proesses of care employment in Sweden and Germany', in B. Pfau-Effinger and B. Geissler (eds.), *Care and Social Integration in European Societies*. Policy Press, Bristol, pp. 195–214.

Tobio, C. (2001) *Kinship support: gender and social policy in France and Spain*. Paper presented at Solidarity between the sexes and the generations: transformations in Europe, Amsterdam, 28–29 June.

Tolley, E. (2003) 'The skilled worker class selection criteria in the immigration and refugee protection act', *Metropolis Policy Brief*, 1.

Trydegard, G-B. (2003) 'Les réformes des services de soins suedois dans les années quatre-vingt-dix. Une première evaluation de leurs conséquences pour les personnes agées', *Revue Française des Affaires Sociales*, vol. 57, no. 4, pp. 423–42.

Ungerson, C. and S. Yeandle (2003) Gender and paid care work in modern welfare states: issues of work-life balance. Accessed 30 March 2004, from http://www.leeds.ac.uk/esrcfutureofwork/downloads/events/symposium_2003/Ungerson&Yeandle.ppt

Ungerson, C. (2005) 'Gender, labour markets and care work in the European funding regimes', in B. Pfau-Effinger and B. Geissler (eds.), *Care and Social Integration in European Societies*. Policy Press, Bristol.
UNICEF/UNHCR, OSCE. (2003) *Trafficking in Human Beings in South Eastern Europe*. Belgrade.
Weeks, J., B. Heaphy and C. Donovan (2001) *Same Sex Intimacies. Families of Choice and Other Life Experiments*. Routledge, London.
Westin, C. and Dingu-Kyrklund (2000) *Integration Analysis in Sweden*. EFFNATIS Working Paper 34.
Wetten, J W., C. Catrien, F. Bijleveld, F. Heide and N. Dijkhoff (2001) "Female asylum seekers in the Netherlands: an empirical study." *International Migration*, vol. 39, no.3, pp. 85–98.
Williams, F. (2003) *Rethinking care in social policy*. Paper presented at Annual Conference of the Finnish Social Policy Association, 24 October.
Williams, F. (2005) Intersecting issues of gender, 'race, and migration in the changing care regimes of UK, Sweden and Spain', Annual Conference of International Sociological Committee 19, 8–10 September.
Yeates, N. (2004a) 'A dialogue with 'global care chain' analysis: nurse migration in the Irish context', in *Feminist Review* ,77, pp. 179–95.
Yeates, N. (2004b) "Global care chains. Critical reflections and lines of enquiry' *International feminist Journal of Politics*, 6(3): 369–91.
Zanfrini, L. (2002) "Programming flows for purposes of work." In Fondazione ISMU *The Seventh Italian Report on Migrations 2001*, Milan.
Zappi, S. (2003) *French Government Revives Assimilation Policy*. Migration Information Source, October 2003.
Zlotnik, H. (2003) *The Global Dimensions of Female Migration*. Migration Information Source, March, 2003.
Zontini, E. (2001) 'Female domestic labour migrants and local policies in Bologna: the story of a Filipino woman', In R. Grillo and J. Pratt (eds.), *The Politics of Recognizing Difference. Multiculturalism Italian-style*. Ashgate, Aldershot.

4 Gendered Migration in Oceania
Trends, Policies and Outcomes

Siew-Ean Khoo, Elsie Ho and Carmen Voigt-Graf

INTRODUCTION

Encompassing Australia, New Zealand and the Pacific Island countries, Oceania is a region of considerable migration flows linking these countries with one another and with countries along the Pacific Rim as well as beyond. With many countries being simultaneously sources and destinations of international migrants, the region provides interesting data and patterns for a discussion of gendered migration. Australia and New Zealand, the two more advanced countries in the region in terms of their economy, have had large-scale formal immigration programs for more than 50 years. Their status as countries of settler migration is evidenced by the fact that nearly one-quarter of their current population is foreign-born, most of whom are naturalised citizens or have rights to permanent residence. In recent years, however, they have begun to experience more diversity in their international migration flows. Since the 1990s, there has been increasing temporary migration of skilled workers and students to both countries. As well, increasing numbers of their citizens are departing for lengthy periods of work and residence abroad; many New Zealanders have gone to Australia while Australians have moved to the Northern hemisphere countries. Both countries have become countries of immigration as well as emigration. In contrast to Australia and New Zealand, the Pacific Island countries are mainly sending countries of international migrants. Indeed the economic sustainability of some of these small nation states is largely dependent on the remittances sent back by their emigrants in the larger Pacific Rim countries that include the United States as well as New Zealand and Australia. Although considerable migration flows occur between the Pacific Island countries themselves, they are often of a temporary or circulatory nature.

Countries in the region also have special immigration relationships with one another, thus enhancing the flow of migrants within the region. Because of their historic, economic and cultural ties, Australia and New Zealand have had various arrangements since the 1920s allowing their citizens free movement between the two countries, culminating in the Trans-Tasman Travel Agreement in 1973. The Agreement is considered a critical component of the Closer Economic Relations agreement signed between the two governments which is progressively removing barriers to the free movement of capital, goods and services between the two countries. The Trans-Tasman Travel Agreement allows Australian citizens to migrate to New Zealand, and New Zealand citizens to migrate to Australia, to reside and work without the need for a visa. New Zealand, through its past colonial ties with some of the Pacific Island countries such as the Cook Islands, Niue and Tokelau, also places few restrictions on the immigration of people from these islands. A treaty signed with Western Samoa allows for a quota of Samoans to be admitted to New Zealand as labour migrants each year.

These regional migration arrangements are not selective of gender and neither are the broader immigration policies of Australia and New Zealand. Women now make up about half of all permanent and long-term migrants to Australia although they tend to predominate in some categories of migration such as family reunion or accompanying spouses while forming only a small minority of business and highly skilled migrants. However, there is evidence that their share as primary migrants in skilled migration is increasing as the level of education and labour force participation of women increase in the countries within and outside the region that are the sources of migration to Australia. Although the gender composition of the different migration flows into and out of New Zealand is less well studied, net permanent and long-term migration to New Zealand over the period 1981–2004 has also been about 50 percent female. In the Pacific Island countries, gender related issues have tended to be overlooked in migration studies partly because of the lack of gender-based data[1]; however a few recent studies have begun to focus on some specific female migration flows to and from the Fiji Islands (Chandra 2003; Rokoduru 2004; Scott 2003).

In this chapter we address the issue of gender in the contexts of changing international migration patterns and policies in the major countries of the Oceania region and assess the outcomes for female migrants in relation to their economic participation and social welfare. First, we examine the policy background of international migration to Australia and New Zealand, their implications for gendered migration and the gender composition of the different migration flows in and out of the two countries. We also examine women's participation in the migration flows between the Pacific Island countries and into the island countries from outside the region. This is followed by an examination of the experiences of migrant women in the labour market and an assessment of the factors associated with their labour market integration. In the final section we review some of the recent changes in welfare and other entitlements to new immigrants and discuss their implications for the migration and settlement of women.

Much of the chapter focuses on the situation in Australia where international migration is a significant policy issue and where data and research on migration have also been the most extensive. There are many similarities between Australia and New Zealand in their population and social structures and in their migration policies but also important differences in migration outcomes. The implications of these similarities and differences for gendered migration and immigrant women's experiences are discussed. The Pacific Island countries' situation provides interesting contrasts to the Australian and New Zealand contexts of female migration. In discussing the situation of migrant women in the Pacific Island countries, the focus is on Fiji as both a source and destination country because information is most readily available and accessible. In addition, important trends have recently emerged in the migration patterns of women in Fiji that are likely to mirror the situation in the other island countries.

MIGRATION POLICIES, MODES OF ENTRY AND OUTCOMES BY GENDER

Australia and New Zealand are among a small group of settler countries (that include Canada and the United States) that have maintained a large-scale immigration program that has contributed to a significant portion of their population growth. While settler migration remains an important component of their international migration systems, both countries have also experienced more diverse migration flows since the 1990s that have included the temporary entry of foreign workers and students, irregular migration and increasing emigration of their citizens. While some of the increased diversity in migration flows has been the result of policy shifts, broader changes in the global economy and geo-politics have also contributed to a general increase in the volume and diversity of international migration flows from which the countries of the Oceania region have not been immune.

Settler migration to Australia and New Zealand

Changes in Australia's and New Zealand's immigration policies in the 1970s and 1980s have led to increased diversity in the sources and composition of settler migration to the two countries. The demise of the 'White Australia policy' in the 1970s eliminated race as a factor in immigration policy and the implementation of a policy that does not discriminate in relation to nationality, ethnicity or religion has resulted in diversifying the sources of immigrants to Australia. While immigrants to Australia have traditionally been from the United Kingdom and other European countries, since the 1980s six of the top 10 source countries have been Asian, and significant numbers of migrants have also come from Africa, the Middle East and the South Pacific region. Similarly in New Zealand, a fundamental change in immigration policy in 1986 replaced the 'traditional source' country preference with a system emphasising individual merit over ethnicity or nationality. This has also resulted in significant changes in the shares of permanent and long-term migrant arrivals from traditional and non-traditional sources[2]. Asia has also emerged as a significant contributor of migration flows to New Zealand since the 1990s, which also saw considerable increases in the number of immigrants and refugees from Africa, the Middle East and Eastern Europe.

Australia's permanent immigration program has family reunion, skilled and humanitarian objectives. Annual targets are set by the government within each of the three components of the program that seek a balance between family reunion considerations, the government's social and economic objectives and Australia's international humanitarian obligations. Since the mid-1990s Australia's immigration program has placed particular emphasis on skilled migration. Migration planning levels for 2006–2007 have been set at 46,000 visas for family reunion migration, 97,500 for skilled migration and 13,000 for the humanitarian program (DIMA 2006a; 2006b).

The family reunion component enables Australian citizens and permanent residents to sponsor the migration of family members such as spouses, dependent children, fiancée, parents and other aged dependent relatives. Australia's immigration policy recognises de facto relationships and same sex couples for spouse migration. Skilled and business migrants are selected on a points system based on age, English language proficiency and occupational skills. Australia is also encouraging migrants to locate to areas outside the large cities and the Regional Sponsored Migration Scheme encourages employers in regional areas who are unable to fill skilled positions to sponsor workers from overseas. The Humanitarian component of Australia's program provides for the resettlement of refugees and includes a Special Humanitarian Program for people who have suffered from violation of human rights and whose applications have strong support from an Australian resident or community organisation.

The refugee category also includes a Women at Risk sub-category for women in vulnerable situations, such as those whose husbands have been killed or have died and they are therefore left alone in a refugee camp. The Women at Risk category has normally yielded between 400 and 500 migrants per year. A target of 10.5 percent of refugee visas was allocated to the Women at Risk category in 2002–2003 which was exceeded with 504 visas (11.5 percent of Refugee places) granted. This has represented the highest number of grants in this category in the previous five years (DIMIA 2004f: 32). Women from Afghanistan accounted for more than one-third of all arrivals in this category in 2002-04. Other leading source countries were Sudan, Iran, Iraq, Liberia, Sierra Leone, Ethiopia and Kenya.

The entry of New Zealand citizens to Australia and of Australian citizens to New Zealand is separate from and outside of Australia's visaed migration program as they do not require visas to migrate because of the Trans-Tasman Travel Agreement. New Zealand citizen migration to Australia is in effect the fourth major category of settler arrivals in addition to the family reunion, skilled and humanitarian components of Australia's permanent migration program.

Table 4.1 shows the number of settler arrivals to Australia by category of migration for the years 1991–2005. Family reunion migrants, which have a female majority, made up nearly half of all settler arrivals in the first half of the 1990s. However, family reunion migrants have declined as a proportion of all settler arrivals since 1996 because of increased emphasis being given to skilled migration. In recent years the government has set the number of humanitarian visas at 12–13,000 which includes both visas granted abroad as well as those granted in Australia to applicants for asylum. New Zealand citizen migration was relatively low in the early years of the 1990s decade because of Australia's economic recession at the time. It reached a

Table 4.1 Settler arrivals to Australia by migration category, 1991–2005

Year	Family reunion	Skilled	Humanitarian	New Zealand citizen	Total*
1991–92	48,621	40,334	7,157	8,201	107,391
1992–93	32,102	22,137	10,939	8,355	76,330
1993–94	33,580	12,794	11,350	9,616	69,768
1994–95	37,078	20,210	13,632	13,618	87,428
1995–96	46,458	20,008	13,824	16,234	99,139
1996–97	36,490	19,697	9,886	17,501	85,752
1997–98	21,142	25,985	8,779	19,363	77,327
1998–99	21,501	27,931	8,790	24,680	84,143
1999–00	19,896	32,350	7,267	31,610	92,272
2000–01	21,169	33,084	7,313	42,257	107,366
2001–02	23,344	36,036	6,732	21,458	88,900
2002–03	28,066	38,504	9,569	16,364	93,914
2003–04	29,548	51,529	10,335	18,717	111,590
2004–05	33,182	53,133	13,235	22,379	123,424
1991–92	45.3%	37.6%	6.7%	7.6%	100.0%
1992–93	42.1%	29.0%	14.3%	10.9%	100.0%
1993–94	48.1%	18.3%	16.3%	13.8%	100.0%
1994–95	42.4%	23.1%	15.6%	15.6%	100.0%
1995–96	46.9%	20.2%	13.9%	16.4%	100.0%
1996–97	42.6%	23.0%	11.5%	20.4%	100.0%
1997–98	27.3%	33.6%	11.4%	25.0%	100.0%
1998–99	25.6%	33.2%	10.4%	29.3%	100.0%
1999–00	21.6%	35.1%	7.9%	34.3%	100.0%
2000–01	19.7%	30.8%	6.8%	39.4%	100.0%
2001–02	26.3%	40.5%	7.6%	24.1%	100.0%
2002–03	29.9%	41.0%	10.2%	17.4%	100.0%
2003–04	26.5%	46.2%	9.3%	16.8%	100.0%
2004–05	26.9%	43.0%	10.7%	18.1%	100.0%

*Includes a small number in other special eligibility categories.
Sources: DIMIA (various years).

peak in 2000–2001 reflecting strong economic conditions in Australia at the end of the twentieth century. The decline in New Zealand citizen arrivals since then was likely to be related to two factors: improvements in New Zealand's economy and, since 2001, a two-year waiting period before new settler arrivals can access social security payments.

What are the gender implications of these trends and changes in immigrant arrivals? The gender composition of migrants varies by migration category (Figure 4.1). Women predominate in family reunion migration while the majority of skilled migrants are male. Thus, when the family reunion component of the migration program increases relative to the skill component, the percentage of females among settler arrivals increases. Among all settler arrivals, the percentage who is female reached a peak at 55 percent in 1995–96 when the percentage of family reunion migrants was at its highest. Since then with the decline in family migration relative to skilled migration, the percentage of female settler arrivals has trended downwards although it increased again after 2000 as the number of family reunion migrants rose again as shown in Table 4.1.

Figure 4.1 also shows that the participation of women in skilled and humanitarian migration to Australia increased during the early 1990s before levelling off in recent years. Humanitarian migrants had a male majority in the early part of the 1990s but a more balanced gender composition since 1995. New Zealander migration is also fairly evenly balanced by gender with some minor fluctuations around the 50 percent line. The percentage of female family reunion migrants has increased to more than 60 percent since 1996 when extended family members were transferred to the skilled category because they had to meet skills and English language selection criteria, leaving the family stream dominated by spouses and fiancés who are mostly women. The overall outcome has been that at least half of all permanent migrants to Australia since 1991 have been female.

The percentage female shown in Figure 4.1 includes women as primary migrants and accompanying spouses. The percentage female among skilled migrants is nearly 50 percent because the accompanying spouse (and any dependent children) of a primary migrant in the skilled category is also included in that category. When primary migrants and accompanying spouses are examined separately (Figure 4.2), it is clear that men predominate in business and skilled migration as primary migrants while women in these migration categories are mostly accompanying spouses. The same gender division is seen in the other migration categories with the exception of the preferential family category, which is dominated by spouse migration where the majority of migrants are women.

Since 2001, New Zealand has also established three immigration streams (skilled/business; family sponsored; and international/humanitarian) with each stream being allocated a proportion of places in its overall migration program. Since 2001 there has been greater emphasis on skilled migration with 60 percent of total residence approvals allocated to the skilled/busi-

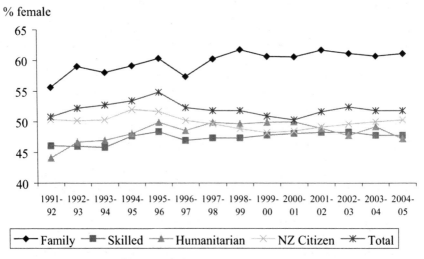

Figure 4.1 Percentage of female settler arrivals to Australia by migration category, 1991–2005.

ness stream, 30 percent to the family sponsored stream and 10 percent to the international/humanitarian stream. In 2002, New Zealand introduced the "Pacific Access Category" (PAC) under which an annual quota of 250 Tongans, 75 Tuvalans and 50 I-Kiribati are granted entry ('Esau & Hirai, 2002: 22). The PAC was extended in 2003 to include a sub-quota for Fiji (250 places) and the number of places for I-Kiribati was increased to 75 (New Zealand Immigration Service, 2003a). Statistics on permanent residence visa approvals by the New Zealand Immigration Service (2003a: 37) in 2002–03 showed a majority of males (52 percent) in the General Skills migration category.

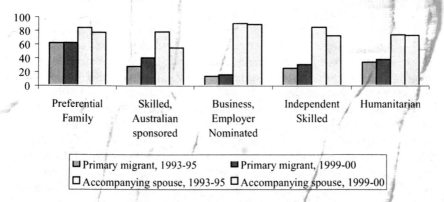

Figure 4.2 Percentage of femal settler arrivals (primary migrants and accompanying spouses) by visa category, Australia, 1993–2005 and 1999–2000.

Temporary migration of workers and foreign students

While Australia's and New Zealand's migration policies have always emphasised permanent settlement, since the mid-1990s there has been a shift in both countries to encourage the temporary entry of skilled workers and overseas students. In 1996, in response to the increasing internationalisation of Australia's economy and lobbying by business that existing procedures for bringing in skilled people for temporary periods were too complex, a new temporary business entry visa was introduced that simplified the procedures allowing employers to sponsor skilled workers from overseas for temporary residence of up to four years (Birrell & Healy, 1997). Holders of the visa can apply to become permanent residents. Employers have to be pre-approved by the Department of Immigration to sponsor and sponsored employees must be in managerial, professional, associate professional or trades occupations. A minimum salary has been set to exclude low skilled workers and employers are closely monitored by the Department of Immigration to ensure compliance with the conditions of sponsorship (Khoo et al. 2003).

In 2004–2005, more than 49,000 temporary business entry long-stay visas were granted, more than half of which was granted onshore to foreigners already in Australia on other types of visitor visas. Over half of the arrivals on the skilled temporary business entry visa are primary applicants (the employees sponsored by their employers); the rest are dependents. There is a clear gender dimension in temporary skilled migration; three-quarters of primary applicants (those who are being sponsored by their employers) are male while two-thirds of their dependents are female (Figure 4.3). The major source countries of people on the temporary skilled business entry visa are UK, India, Japan, US, China, South Africa and Ireland. In comparison with permanent skilled migrants, the majority of whom come from Asian countries, temporary skilled migrants are more likely to come from English-speaking countries. They are also more likely to be young and single (Khoo et al. 2003).

In New Zealand, "skill shortage" permits are issued to address skill and labour shortages and to attract talented individuals to New Zealand (New Zealand Immigration Service 2004a: 13). A labour market test is required to determine that no suitable New Zealand workers are available to do the job a work permit applicant has been offered. In April 2002, New Zealand also introduced "work to residence" policies designed to facilitate temporary entrants whose skills are in demand to apply for permanent residence. During the six years ended June 2003, a total of 73,397 individuals were issued skill shortage work permits. As in Australia, the majority (62 percent) of skill shortage work permit holders in New Zealand were males. The leading source countries were also the same as for Australia (UK, Japan, US, South Africa and India). It would appear that women are still less likely to come to Australia and New Zealand as skilled temporary

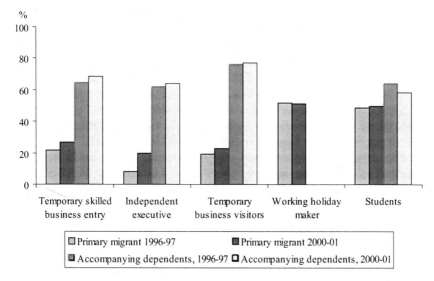

Figure 4.3 Percentage of female temporary migrants and accompanying family members, Australia 1996–1997 and 2000–2001.

migrants, possibly because, aside from nursing, the skills needed tend to be in industry sectors that are male dominant, such as information technology, business and finance and engineering.

Other work permits not requiring a labour market test include those granted for working holidays and to asylum seekers and the spouses and partners of New Zealanders. New Zealand's Working Holiday Schemes currently allow 31,000 young people from 22 countries, aged 18–30, to work in New Zealand for up to 12 months, and for young New Zealanders to work overseas under reciprocal arrangements. This number will increase to 40,000 in 2006. In general, females outnumber males in the Working Holiday and Spouse/Partner categories.

Australia also has reciprocal agreements with some 20 countries that allow their young people to visit and work in Australia for one to two years and young Australians to do the same in those countries. The number of working holiday visas issued each year has increased steadily over the years from around 35,000 in 1994–95 to 104,535 in 2004–2005. The UK is the largest source of working holiday arrivals. Other major source countries are Ireland, Japan, Germany, Canada and Korea. Working holiday makers are mostly single persons aged between 18 and 30 with about equal numbers of women and men (Figure 4.3).

International students are the third major group of temporary arrivals to Australia and they are also becoming a major category of temporary migrants to New Zealand. The majority are from Asian countries. In the last decade, Australian and New Zealand tertiary education institutions, with the encouragement of their governments, have actively promoted their courses overseas, particularly in Asia, to attract full-fee paying students who provide much needed income to the institutions and also contribute to the national economy. In 2001, there was a change in policy to allow foreign students who completed their studies in Australia to apply for permanent residence without leaving the country. This may have led to increasing interest in tertiary education as a pathway to permanent residence in the long-term. Compared with other countries such as UK and US, which are also competing for foreign students, Australia and New Zealand also have an advantage in their lower costs of living and fee structure.

The number of international students coming to Australia and New Zealand has therefore increased steadily. In Australia the number of student visas granted offshore increased from less than 40,000 in 1992–1993 to nearly 117,000 in 2004–2005. The top source countries in 2004–2005 are China, US, India, Korea and Malaysia (DIMA 2006). In the case of New Zealand, 170,840 individuals were issued student visas during the period 1997–2003. The leading source countries are China, Japan, South Korea, Taiwan and Thailand. The gender balance of international students in both countries is fairly even.

In contrast to Australia and New Zealand, the Pacific Island countries admit very few migrants. However, migration into Fiji has increased since the 1987 coup as migrant workers arrive to take up jobs created by new investors and skill loss due to emigration (Raman 1999: 125). There are no quotas on the total number of migrant workers admitted for a specific period of time. Fiji does not give preferential treatment to any category of workers or country. Short-term work permits are valid for six months, ordinary work permits for up to three years and investor permits for seven years (ILO 2003: 172). In 2003, 1,347 work permits plus 970 residence permits were issued in Fiji. China topped the list with 581 work permits, followed by Australia (178), India (111) and New Zealand (96)[3]. Other Pacific Islanders have also moved to Fiji to study at the regional university and to work in the many regional and international organisations located there. Fijians have also migrated to several Pacific Island countries in increasing numbers. After the 2000 coup, the tourism industry in Fiji suffered greatly and some of the employees who lost their jobs have moved to work in the tourism industry in the other Pacific Island countries.

Both Australia and New Zealand have focussed their temporary migration policies on skilled migration where males tend to predominate, rather than on lower or unskilled labour migration such as that of domestic service workers or caregivers where women are likely to be in the majority. However, many women migrate temporarily as accompanying spouses and their participation in temporary skilled migration is likely to increase as skills such as nursing and teaching (in mathematics and science particularly) become more in demand in future. Population ageing in Australia is increasing the demand for nurses in hospitals and aged care nursing homes.

The migration of Australian nurses and teachers to work in other countries (Hugo et al. 2003: 35) has also contributed to a shortage of these skills.

Annual net overseas migration to Australia in recent years (the result of both permanent and temporary long-term arrivals and departures) has been over 110,000 (ABS 2004). In 2002–2003, the sex ratio of net overseas migration to Australia was 94 males per 100 females, a slight majority of women (ABS 2004: 16). In New Zealand, the proportion of women in net migration gain for the period 1982–2004 (a total of 275,000 people) was higher at 58 percent. The gender outcome of net migration to both Australia and New Zealand is therefore very similar, both with just a slight female majority.

Emigration from Australia, New Zealand and the Pacific Island countries

People leaving Australia permanently have been increasing over the years and numbered about 59,000 in the 12 months to June 2004. About half of them were females and this proportion had been fairly constant over recent years (DIMIA 2005: 24). The Australian-born component of permanent departures has also been increasing over the years and was just over 50 percent of all emigrants in 2002-03 (ABS 2004). The remaining were former settlers returning home or immigrating to another country.

Among Australia-born residents departing permanently in 2001–2002, males (12,176) outnumbered females (11,970) slightly but among Australian residents departing long-term (more than 12 months), females (30,392) slightly outnumbered males (29,767) (Hugo et al. 2003: 34). However there are significant differences in the gender composition by destination. Females are more numerous than males in flows to the UK and other European countries. Females also outnumber males in permanent departures to New Zealand and North America, but males are more numerous among long-term departures to these destinations as well as to Asian and Middle East countries where they are likely to be moving to work on contracts. There is, however, a female dominant flow to the United Arab Emirates where many Australian nurses and teachers have gone to work (Hugo et al. 2003: 35).

There has also been extensive emigration of New Zealand citizens in the last two decades. In the 10 years between 1986 and 1996, New Zealand lost 148,725 citizens. Between 1997 and 2001, the net losses of New Zealanders were nearly double those of the previous five years. The majority (60 percent) of net losses of New Zealanders were males. Since 2002 the magnitude of emigration has diminished considerably as emigration to Australia slowed and many New Zealanders who had left in the late 1990s returned. Returnees had a balanced sex ratio. Many were well educated and were returning from Australia and the UK (Lidgard 1993; Lidgard & Gilson 2002).

Emigration is a significant migration issue in the Pacific Island countries. The largest migration flows are from the islands to the developed countries of the Pacific Rim, although there is also some intra-Pacific migration. More than 80 percent of Cook Islanders live in New Zealand, Australia and elsewhere and more Samoans live in New Zealand, Australia and the United States than in Samoa (Crocombe 2001: 66). Due to the huge out-migration flows particularly from Polynesia, the smaller island states have been characterised as MIRAB (Migration, Remittances, Aid and Bureaucracy) states. Their economies are dependent on migration, which stimulates substantial remittance flows. Aid is another significant source of income, and these sources have contributed to the emergence of an urban, bureaucratic society and economy (Bertram & Watters, 1985). In recent years most island states have faced declining economies and a growing dependence on migration and remittances —especially in the case of Fiji — hence the MIRAB system, initially derided, may prove to be more sustainable than other forms of development.

Out-migration from the Pacific Islands is primarily a response to the low wages and lack of opportunities in the islands, particularly for skilled people, and the pull factors of high wages and better job opportunities in the more developed economies of the Pacific Rim countries. The presence of relatives overseas is also a factor, particularly in the choice of destination country.

Before the 1980s, male migration had preceded female or family migration throughout the South Pacific, the main exception being Tokulauan and Cook Islander women migrating to New Zealand as domestic workers (Connell 1984: 966). By the early 1980s, more Pacific Islander women were migrating autonomously as well as to join their husbands (Connell 1984: 968). Today there is generally little gender bias in Pacific Islander migration to the Pacific Rim countries of New Zealand, Australia and the US because people are migrating in family units or young men and women are migrating on student visas. Between 1990 and 2002, just over 50 percent of Indo-Fijian emigrants from Fiji were female; however among ethnic Fijians the proportion of women was slightly higher at 56 percent. There are, however, flows of specific occupational categories which are either male or female dominated. For instance, Fijian women have migrated as domestic helpers and caregivers to the United States while Fijian men have moved overseas as soldiers and employees of private security companies.

The Pacific Island countries have not sought to intervene in emigration and have not tried to curb the loss of skilled and unskilled workers. They are unlikely to do so in the future, given the financial benefits from remittances. Bonding of students who study on government scholarships has been the only policy directed at (temporarily) retaining qualified people. However, the approach of the Fiji government is one which regards emigrants as traitors and there are policies punishing return migrants, for example, migrant nurses having to start on a lower salary upon their re-employment in Fiji compared to before their emigration (Rokoduru 2004). To some extent this policy may discourage the temporary migration of nurses. It also discourages return migration in a sector where there are acute shortages[4].

Irregular migration

The scale of unauthorised migrant arrivals to Australia, New Zealand and the Pacific Island countries is relatively small compared to the situation in Europe and the United States. This is in part a consequence of a 'tyranny of distance', which has made the costs of migration to the Oceania region relatively high for unauthorised or undocumented migrants compared to other destinations. Australia, New Zealand and the Pacific Island countries (with the exception of Papua New Guinea) also do not have land borders. Notwithstanding these geographic barriers, irregular migration does occur and is becoming an issue of concern in the region. Although undocumented migrants are usually more likely to be men, women are over-represented as victims of trafficking.

Australia has strict policies to deal with irregular migration and migrants working illegally. In 1992, in response to a number of boat arrivals carrying undocumented migrants, a mandatory detention policy was introduced that required all unauthorised migrant arrivals be detained in detention centres while their asylum or migration claims are processed. People who have overstayed their visas or are found to be working in breach of their visas are also detained while arrangements are made for their deportation.

In the late 1990s unauthorised boat arrivals increased sharply and peaked at over 4,200 in 2000–2001 but had subsided since then. The migrants were mostly men from Afghanistan, Iraq, Pakistan and Sri Lanka, but there were also family units including women and children.

Overstayers and illegal workers are quite different from the unauthorised or undocumented arrivals by boat. According to the Department of Immigration and Multicultural and Indigenous Affairs (DIMIA 2004d), as at mid-year 2004, some 51,000 people were in Australia illegally, having overstayed their visas. During the 12-month period to 30 June 2004, the Department of Immigration reported having located 20,000 overstayers of whom 39 percent were female. Most of the people who were found working illegally were mainly from countries in the Asia-Pacific region including China, Korea, Indonesia, Malaysia, Thailand, Philippines and Fiji. Female victims of people trafficking who have been found by the Department of Immigration are usually from Asian countries such as Thailand and Korea. In a recent report of police cases involving people trafficking, all 22 victims were women[5] and 14 were from Thailand (Drennan & Wright 2004).

As in Australia, irregular migrants in Fiji are mostly people who have overstayed their tourist, temporary visitor or student visas. There have also been cases of Asian women entering Fiji on student visas and working illegally as sex workers and of Chinese women transiting through Fiji to other Pacific Island countries to work as prostitutes there (*Fiji Times*, 24 January 2004).

Since 2002, on the initiative of the Australian government, a number of ministerial level meetings, consultative groups and workshops to address the issue of illegal migration and people smuggling in the Asia-Pacific region have been organised. Known as the Bali Process, after the first ministerial meeting held in Bali in February 2002 which was co-chaired by Indonesia and Australia, these activities have been attended by representatives of more than 30 countries in the Asia-Pacific region and the United Nations High Commission for Refugees and the International Organisation for Migration. The Bali Process has stressed regional cooperation and consultation in combating irregular migration. There have also been workshops focussed on detecting document fraud and drafting of legislation to prosecute people smuggling and trafficking.

MIGRANT WOMEN AND THE LABOUR MARKET

The labour force participation rate of women in Australia and New Zealand has increased steadily over the last three decades and the majority of women now participate in the labour market. In 2002, 55 percent of women in Australia and 59 percent of women in New Zealand were in the labour force. Many women migrating to these countries, whether as primary migrants or accompanying spouses, also seek to enter the labour market. A survey of recently arrived immigrants in Australia showed that 54 percent of women who arrived during 1999–2000 as primary migrants were in the labour force within 18 months of arrival and 48 percent were employed. This compares with 43 percent and 41 percent respectively of women who migrated as accompanying spouses (Longitudinal Survey of Immigrants to Australia, Second Cohort).

Immigrants and certain types of temporary migrants have work rights while irregular migrants, if working, are working illegally. Therefore, migrant women's experience in the labour market can differ according to whether they are settlers, temporary migrants or irregular migrants. For women migrating to settle permanently, whether as primary migrants or accompanying spouses, labour force participation and employment are important indicators of their labour market integration and a significant aspect of the settlement process. For women on temporary work visas, their employment experience is an important aspect of their migration rather than their settlement. And for those women working illegally in breach of visa conditions, their labour force participation may be an involuntary outcome of migration. It is relevant to examine the labour force status and employment outcomes of migrant women in relation to their migration status as immigrants, temporary migrants or irregular migrants.

Female immigrants' labour market outcomes in Australia and New Zealand

Because of Australia's and New Zealand's long-standing settler migration program, there has been much research and policy interest in the labour market integration of immigrants. Hence there is a large body of research on the labour market experiences of immigrants in both countries where the economic integration of immigrants is considered an important indicator of successful settlement.

Labour force participation and employment rates of immigrants generally increase and unemployment rates decrease with duration of settlement. This is true of both men and women (see Khoo et al. 1994 for example). The Longitudinal Survey of Immigrants to Australia (LSIA) shows that of the cohort of migrants who arrived in Australia in 1993–95, 39 percent of primary female migrants were in the labour force at 6 months of arrival and the proportion increased to 47 percent after three years of residence. Employment rates (of those in the labour force) also increased from 59 percent to 83 percent during the same period while unemployment rates declined from 41 percent to 17 percent. The 1996 Australian census show that after 10 years of residence in Australia, overseas-born women have a labour force participation rate that is very similar to that of Australian-born women of the same age. However, both female and male immigrants still have slightly higher unemployment rates than the Australian-born population even after 10 years of residence. Both female and male migrants who migrated as refugees have much higher unemployment rates than migrants in the family reunion or skilled category regardless of length of residence. The difficulties of former refugees, both women and men, in integrating into the Australian labour market appear to persist even in the long-term and indicate the difficulties associated with their migration and resettlement.

Many studies have shown that female and male migrants' labour force participation rates and employment outcomes vary considerably according to their migration category, English language proficiency and country of origin. Female migrants in the skills category have much higher labour force participation and employment rates than those in the family reunion and humanitarian categories (Cobb-Clark & Chapman 1999; VandenHeuvel & Wooden 1999; Richardson et al. 2001). LSIA data show that 86 percent of female migrants in the Independent skilled category were employed at three to four years after arrival in Australia compared with 38 percent of those in the family reunion category and 31 percent in the humanitarian category. This is to be expected since migrants in the skilled category have been selected based on criteria that emphasised their employability, while migrants in the family reunion and humanitarian categories are not assessed on their skills or English proficiency. Women migrating in the family reunion and humanitarian categories are also more likely to work in unskilled jobs as factory workers and cleaners. The studies have also indicated the importance of English language proficiency in determining employment outcomes of both female and male immigrants in Australia. Migrants who speak English well have higher employment rates than those who do not speak it well, even when other differences in human capital have been taken into account (Cobb-Clark & Chapman 1999; Williams et al. 1997).

Studies based on the 2001 Census in New Zealand also found that employment rates varied by migrants' region of origin and duration of residence (Boyd 2003; New Zealand Immigration Service 2003b; Statistics New Zealand 2004). The employment rate of overseas-born women aged 25–54 years who had lived in New Zealand for less than five years was significantly lower than the rate for New Zealand-born women of the same age (Table 4.2). Recent female migrants from Northeast Asia (that is, China, Korea, and Taiwan) and the Pacific Islands had the lowest employment and labour force participation rates. While migrant women from Asia and the Pacific regions who had been resident in New Zealand for 5–10 years had higher employment and participation rates, only those with more than ten years residence had employment and participation rates that were closer to the rates for New Zealand-born women. Male employment and participation rates showed similar trends but were higher than the female rates.

As in Australia, studies in New Zealand have also shown that educational qualifications and the ability to speak English make a significant difference to the probability of recently arrived migrants gaining employment (Boyd 2003; New Zealand Immigration Service 2003b, 2003c; Statistics New Zealand 2004; Winkelmann & Winkelmann 1998). A much higher proportion of working aged migrant women from Northeast Asia indicated that they could not conduct an everyday conversation in English compared with women from other parts of Asia or the Pacific Islands. The majority of these women from Northeast Asia had no post-school qualifications. Their participation rates and employment rates were lower than for migrant women from elsewhere.

Recent migrant women from Northeast Asia who could speak English were better qualified than their counterparts from the Pacific Islands. Forty-six percent had vocational or university qualifications, compared with only 27 percent of English-speaking recent Pacific Islander females who had these qualifications. However, labour force participation and employment rates for Pacific Islander women with vocational or university qualifications were much higher than those for their Northeast Asian counterparts. Overall, participation rates for English-speaking recent migrant women from the Pacific ranged from 46 percent for those with no qualifications, through to 79 percent for those with university qualifications, and employment rates ranged from 34 percent for those with no qualifications, to 66 percent for those with university qualifications. Labour force participation

Table 4.2 Employment rates, labour force participation rates and unemployment rates for women and men born in Asia and the Pacific Islands, and total overseas-born, aged 25–54 years, by duration of residence in New Zealand, and New Zealand-born aged 25–54 years, 2001

Duration of residence/Region of origin	Female				Male			
	Emp Rate	LFPR	Unemp Rate	Total number	Emp Rate	LFPR	Unemp Rate	Total number
0–5 years								
Pacific Islands	46.7	57.4	10.8	5,355	68.9	80.3	11.4	5,271
Southeast Asia	51.7	59.3	7.7	4,656	68.8	77.2	8.4	2,946
Northeast Asia	32.8	40.6	7.8	11,286	49.0	60.2	11.2	7,686
Southern Asia	48.1	63.0	14.9	3,834	72.0	85.7	13.7	4,119
All overseas-born, 0–5 years	52.7	60.6	7.9	46,565	72.5	81.4	8.9	41,271
5–10 years								
Pacific Islands	55.1	63.5	8.4	2,973	75.9	84.1	8.2	2,592
Southeast Asia	59.9	65.0	5.1	2,922	74.4	81.5	7.1	1,488
Northeast Asia	45.8	51.5	5.7	7,824	66.0	73.8	7.8	5,343
Southern Asia	63.4	71.0	7.6	1,614	62.2	89.9	7.7	1,479
All overseas-born, 5–10 yrs	60.9	66.2	5.3	27,282	80.5	86.4	5.9	22,287
10+ years								
Pacific Islands	61.6	69.3	7.8	24,207	76.7	84.8	8.1	21,522
Southeast Asia	70.5	75.5	4.9	7,473	84.4	89.3	5.0	5,238
Northeast Asia	62.7	66.4	3.7	4,515	79.9	85.1	5.2	3,849
Southern Asia	73.8	77.6	3.8	2,223	84.9	90.1	5.2	2,940
All overseas-born, 10+ yrs	72.5	76.9	4.5	96,366	85.2	90.1	4.9	89,157
NZ Born	73.6	78.1	4.5	613,233	86.3	90.7	4.4	576,690

Source: Boyd (2003): 59.

rate for those without any qualifications and had no conversational English was 32 percent and their employment rate was only 20 percent.

It was also noticeable that over 50 percent of migrant women from Northeast Asia who claimed to speak conversational English and had vocational or university qualifications were not participating in the labour force. The relatively low labour force participation rate among these women compared with migrant women with similar qualifications from other regions suggests that their qualifications may not be directly transferable to the New Zealand labour market. Other studies have also shown that there are a number of "astronaut families" among them (Ho 2002; Ho et al. 1997, 2000a; Lidgard et al. 1998). In these families, the women stay in New Zealand to look after the children while their husbands return to the country of origin to work. The particularly low sex ratio (68 males per 100 females) among working aged migrants from Northeast Asia gives indirect evidence of the "astronaut family" phenomenon. This partly accounts for the low labour force participation rate. The "astronaut family" phenomenon also exists among Northeast Asian migrants in Australia (see Pe-Pua et al. 1996).

The high level of unemployment among recently arrived migrant women from Asia who are competent in English and have vocational and university qualifications suggests that the human capital of these high-skilled women has not been fully utilised. Non-recognition of overseas qualifications and experiences, discrimination by employers, perceived English language difficulties and lack of local knowledge are the main employment barriers faced by recent migrants from non-English-speaking countries (Bedford 2003; Department of Internal Affairs 1996; Ho et al. 2000b; New Zealand Immigration Service 2004b).

Of the migrants from the Pacific Island countries in New Zealand, a higher proportion of women than men had post-school qualifications, according to the 2001 New Zealand census. However, the men had higher labour force participation and employment rates and lower unemployment rates than the women. Women from the Pacific countries are most likely to be employed as clerks (18–25 percent) and service and sales workers (20–29 percent). Men on the other hand were working mostly as plant and machine operators and assemblers (17–25 percent) and in elementary occupations. Despite the greater percentage of females with post-school qualifications, their median income was considerably lower than that of males.

In a study of Asian immigrants in Australia, Khoo et al. (1994) also found differences in the labour market outcomes of migrant women by country of origin. Migrant women from India, Malaysia and Sri Lanka had higher labour force participate rates than Australian-born women while migrant women from Indonesia, Japan, Pakistan and Taiwan had lower participation rates. Unemployment rates were generally higher for migrant women than migrant men. They were also higher for migrant women from Vietnam, Cambodia and Laos than for other Asian migrant women. A likely reason is that migrants from these countries had lower levels of English language proficiency than migrants from other Asian countries as many had arrived as refugees or on family reunion visas and not as skilled migrants assessed on their occupational skills and English proficiency. There were also differences in occupational patterns by origin, which are also likely to be related to differences in education and English language proficiency. A relatively large proportion (20–30 percent) of women from Indochina and China were employed in low skilled occupations compared with less than 10 percent of employed women from Singapore or India. Women migrating from countries such as Singapore, India and Sri Lanka generally have better English language skills and many have professional qualifications. The diversity in the occupational profile of migrant women in Australia reflects the three-pronged immigration program with its family reunion, skills and humanitarian components. Women who are unskilled workers (such as factory workers or cleaners) are likely to have migrated in the family reunion and humanitarian visa categories while those who are in professional or associate professional occupations are likely to have migrated in the skilled visa category.

Temporary residence and employment

The two main groups of temporary migrants to Australia for whom employment is an objective of their migration are skilled temporary business entrants and working holiday makers. Although foreign students are able to work up to 20 hours a week, their primary objective is to obtain an education.

As indicated earlier, women are a minority among skilled temporary migrants working in Australia. There are three times more men than women among primary migrants, and in some occupational groups such as managers and IT professionals, men outnumber women by five to one. Only among nurses do women outnumber men, by a large margin of five to one (DIMIA unpublished statistics 1997–2001).

The top five occupational groups of temporary skilled migrants nominated by employers in 2004–2005 were computing professionals (12 percent), managers (11 percent) registered nurses (9 percent), business and information professionals (4 percent) and chefs (3 percent) (DIMIA 2006: 68). In 2002–2003, registered nurse was the largest single occupation sought by Australian employers and the importance of meeting this demand for nursing professionals was acknowledged by the Department of Immigration in giving priority to processing visa applications for nursing positions (DIMIA 2004f: 64). More than 10 percent of women arriving as skilled temporary migrants are nurses. A large majority (70 percent of those arriving in 2000–2001) of the nurses are from the UK and Ireland. Other major source countries are South Africa, US, Philippines and Sri Lanka. Nurses from the UK, Ireland and US are more likely to have their qualifications approved by the Nursing Federation and nursing registration board for employment in Australia. Many of the nurses are recruited for private hospitals, specialist hospitals and nursing homes by labour recruitment companies although the larger hospitals do their own recruitment. More than 10 percent of female skilled migrants are also managers, associate professionals and IT professionals. Women in trade occupations are mostly hairdressers, which have been identified as one of the skills in demand in Australia.

Of the temporary female migrants in New Zealand who were granted work permits in 2003–2004, nearly one in four were employed in professional occupations, many as nurses and secondary school teachers. The other major occupational group was sales and service workers where some of the occupations filled by the women included travel attendants, tour guides and chefs. More female than male work permit holders were employed in these two occupational groups (Table 4.3).

The working holiday maker program in Australia provides a casual labour force that many employers consider an invaluable resource, especially employers in tourism and horticulture that require additional staff in peak seasons (DIMIA 2004f: 57). Many young women from UK, Ireland

Table 4.3 Occupational classifications of labour market tested work permit holders in New Zealand by gender, 2003–2004

Occupational Classification	Female		Male	
	Number	Percent	Number	Percent
Legislators, Administrators and Managers	526	5	957	6
Professionals	2,505	24	2,788	16
Technicians and Associate Professionals	935	9	1,360	8
Clerks	276	3	177	1
Service and Sales Workers	2,069	20	2,521	15
Agriculture and Fishery Workers	615	6	1,335	8
Trades Workers	59	1	1,878	11
Plant and Machine Operators and Assemblers	140	1	542	3
Elementary Workers (incl. not identifiable, not applicable)	284	3	527	3
Not Recorded	2,999	29	4,933	29
Total	10,408	100	17,018	100

Source: Unpublished Immigration database, New Zealand Immigration Service.

and other European countries on working holidays in Australia work as relief nurses, teachers and clerical workers and filled casual job vacancies in the hospitality industry as waitresses in hotels, resorts and restaurants.

In Fiji, the employment situation of temporary migrant workers is different from that in Australia and New Zealand. In the late 1990s, there were some 2,000 Chinese temporary migrant workers employed in the garment industry as well as smaller numbers from the Philippines, Taiwan and Indonesia (Oxfam New Zealand 2004: 40). They are initially given three-year work permits. The majority of the Chinese workers returned to China eventually, but a few have applied for Fijian citizenship after 10 years of residence in Fiji. Many Chinese garment workers are female, between 20 and 40 years old, and had worked in garment factories before coming to Fiji.

Fijian nurses and teachers have also migrated to other Pacific Island countries such as Kiribati and the Marshall Islands where the salary is higher and work conditions are better. A recent study has found that between 1991 and 2001, 839 nurses left Fiji (Rokoduru 2002: 44). The women frequently took the decision to migrate autonomously, leaving their husbands and children behind (Rokoduru 2002, 2004). They had responded to advertisements in Fijian newspapers and to hiring agents. The nurses and teachers had work permits and work contracts that they signed on arrival and that gave them the status of "legal aliens". Nurses were given two-year contracts and teachers three-year contracts (Rokoduru 2004). In a study of a health centre on the Marshal Islands, 10 out of the 11 Fijian nurses were female (Rokoduru 2002: 45). All were registered nurses with six to 20 years of work experience.

The case of Fijian nurses in the Marshall Islands underlines the increasingly autonomous decision-making and migration of women as migrant workers. A growing shortage of skilled health workers in all Pacific Island countries has contributed to increased intra-Pacific migration with workers migrating to countries offering better work conditions and salaries.

Emigration and the loss of skills from Pacific Island countries

Emigration rates of skilled persons have increased steadily in the Pacific Island countries, as skilled Pacific Islanders respond to overseas demand, particularly for health workers, teachers, accountants and other professionals. The migration of nurses and doctors from Pacific Island countries is a growing concern and has affected the provision of health services in many Pacific Island countries. The migration has come at a considerable cost to the island states because of the high costs of training and the reduction in the effectiveness of health care (World Health Organization 2004).

Women emigrating from Fiji during the period 1990–2002 who stated an occupation were mainly professional and clerical workers (Table 4.4). However, a large proportion gave no occupation and was likely to be not in the labour force. Women made up 40 percent of all professional, technical and related workers who left and they dominated the two sub-categories of "teachers" (55 percent in 2002) and "medical and related workers" (75 percent in 2002) who would be mostly nurses (Chandra 2003: 12).

The loss of skills from the Pacific Island countries is countered by the importance of remittances from emigrants to the economies of these countries[6]. In 2002–2003 net remittances to Tonga were equivalent to 41 percent of the country's Gross Domestic Product (GDP) (Ministry of Finance, Tonga Selected Indicators 2004). The body of literature on remittances in the Pacific makes little reference to the role of women as remitters and none to women as receivers. Where there has been some mention of the role of gender in remittances and where there are data, women are found to be more frequent remitters, despite lacking the capacity to send the same amount as men (Connell 1985: 18). In Samoa, women are considered the most reliable remitters and are therefore particularly encouraged by their families to migrate (Shankman 1976). Fijian nurses in the Marshall Islands remit between one-quarter and one-third of their wages to their families in Fiji (Rokoduru 2002: 46). Research among Tongans in Auckland in 1984 showed that males were more likely to be non-remitters than females. The average sum sent by men was higher than that of women, even though women sent a larger proportion of their (lower) income, possibly because of their greater commitment to families, especially parents (Vete 1995). However, a recent survey among 36 remittance-receiving rural house-

Table 4.4 Occupational categories of emigrants from Fiji by gender, 1990–2002

	Males	Females	Total	% Female
Professional, technical and related	4669	3126	7795	40.1
Administrative and managerial	2878	692	3570	19.4
Clerical, supervisors and related	2249	3540	65789	61.2
Sales workers	1096	673	1769	38.0
Service workers	828	488	1316	37.0
Agricultural, animal husbandry and forestry workers and fishermen	1340	29	1369	2.1
Production workers, transport equipment operators and labourers	5706	1127	6833	16.5
Others not classifiable by occupation	12762	23953	36715	65.2
Total	31528	33628	65156	51.6

Source: Chandra, 2003.

holds in Tonga did not reveal that gender of the remitter was a significant factor determining the volume and regularity of remittances (Voigt-Graf unpublished).

Working illegally

Many people who overstay their visa in Australia are believed to be working illegally. Certainly those overstayers who were located by the Department of Immigration were usually found at the place of their employment, which have included restaurants, factories, farms, construction sites and brothels. In 2004, the Department reported locating 329 illegal migrant workers, of whom 139 (42 percent) were female. Many of the women were located working in the sex industry; men were more likely to be located working on construction sites, factories and farms. Women who are found working in the sex industry are now interviewed to determine if they have been the victims of people trafficking. Australia has recently put in place protocols for victims of people trafficking; these are discussed later in the chapter.

Asian women entering Fiji on student visas have been found working as prostitutes. The immigration director in Fiji told the media he was aware of an Asian prostitution racket operating in Micronesian countries but it was not clear whether prostitutes in Fiji were part of the racket (*Fiji Times*, 16 June 2004).

Many Fijian migrants are working illegally in the United States, the women as caregivers for children and the elderly and the men as maintenance workers and grounds-keepers (Scott 2003: 187). The number of Fijians in the US was estimated at 14,000 in 1994 (Scott 2003: 186) about half of whom are thought to be undocumented. The women generally migrate alone, entering on visitor visas and then overstaying to earn money to send back to their families. Although most plan to return to Fiji, some have regularised their status by marrying US citizens (Scott 2003: 191).

POLICY SHIFTS AND MIGRANT ENTITLEMENTS

Australia and New Zealand's social assistance systems provide for a range of welfare benefits (such as unemployment benefits, sickness benefits and single parent payments) to people with little or no income to enable them to meet their living costs and to participate in the community. People receiving welfare benefits must meet income, residence and other eligible criteria for each type of payment. Migrants to Australia and New Zealand with rights to permanent residence have work and welfare entitlements that are the same as those of native-born or naturalised citizens.

In the 1980s settler arrivals in Australia had access to social security payments such as the unemployment benefit immediately on arrival, with the exception of the aged pension for which a minimum of 10 years residence was required. However, the policy was changed in 1992 to require new immigrants, with the exception of refugees and other humanitarian migrants, to wait for six months after arrival in Australia before they could access unemployment and other social security benefits. Exceptions were made for unforeseen changes in migrants' circumstances in which they could still access special welfare payments. A survey of recently arrived immigrants in 1993–95 showed that over 20 percent of migrants in the skilled migration category were receiving special social security benefits during their first six months of settlement (VandenHeuvel & Wooden 1999: 66).

In 1998 there was another change in policy that extended the waiting period for new migrants (again with the exception of refugees and other humanitarian migrants) to two years before they could access social security income support payments. There is some evidence that this change in policy may have two types of effect. The first is that some potential migrants may have decided not to apply to migrate if they think that they may have some difficulty or may take some time in finding employment and they do not have the means to support themselves in the meantime. The second is that the migrants who arrived after the policy change brought more financial resources with them, particularly those migrants in the skilled category who did not have jobs lined up and had to begin looking for employment after arrival.[7]

Similarly in New Zealand, since 1998 new immigrants with the exception of those arriving in the refugee category are no longer eligible for many social welfare benefits until they have been resident in New Zealand for two years. The two-year waiting period is also required of migrants applying for student grants. These changes followed the policy changes in Australia and particularly affected those migrants from Asia and the Pacific Island countries who often experienced difficulties finding employment in the first few years after arrival in New Zealand. Those who would like to study or to learn English also have difficulties because they are not eligible for study grants in the first two years of residence.

In February 2001 the Australian government extended the two-year waiting period for access to social security income support payments to include immigrants from New Zealand. Previously New Zealand citizens, who do not need a visa to migrate to Australia, could access unemployment benefits and other social security payments immediately after arrival. With the increase in migration from New Zealand to Australia after the mid-1990s, which was also becoming a concern to New Zealand, both the Australian and New Zealand governments agreed to the policy of a two-year waiting period in an effort to reduce the flow of New Zealanders across the Tasman. The change in policy requires New Zealand citizens to obtain a permanent residence visa if they wish to access social security payments or Australian citizenship. It appears that the policy has had some effect in reducing the migration flow from New Zealand although other factors such as the improvement in economic conditions in New Zealand could also have contributed to the reduction in migration (Bedford et al. 2003).

Settler arrivals in Australia have immediate access to the country's universal health care system, Medicare. With the exception of migrants on the provisional spouse visa, they also have the same entitlements as the native-born and naturalised citizens to the education system. This means that their children do not pay fees if attending the public school system. They and their children also qualify for the lower tertiary education fees and the higher education contribution scheme that are available to Australian residents. These entitlements are not available to family reunion migrants while they are on the provisional spouse visa as they are not considered to have permanent residence status during that time. Migrants on the spouse visa have to wait until they are granted permanent residence at the end of their two-year provisional status in order to be entitled to Australian residents' educational fees. Thus some women who are on the provisional spouse visa may have been deterred from undertaking further education until they obtain permanent residence and qualify for the lower fees as Australian residents.

Since 1996, people being sponsored to immigrate on the spouse visa have been granted a provisional visa, with a permanent residence visa to be granted after two years if the couple is still in a genuine relationship[8]. This change to a two-stage process occurred following concerns that some people being granted the spouse visa were not in a genuine marriage relationship[9]. At the same time, a limitation was placed on the number of partners — two — that an Australian resident could sponsor. A person who has previously sponsored a spouse or prospective spouse also has to wait a minimum of five years before being eligible to sponsor another partner. This change was the result of problems with repeat or serial sponsorships of spouses in the early 1990s. A number of relationships involving female migrant spouses, often from the Philippines and other Asian countries, had broken down within a short period of time, sometimes involving domestic violence and leaving the women dependent on welfare (see Iredale 1994; Smith & Kaminskas 1992). The male sponsor had then proceeded to sponsor another spouse, often with the same unfortunate consequences. The five-year gap between spouse sponsorship aims to reduce the likelihood of repeat sponsorship. Since women are the majority among migrants arriving on the spouse visa, these provisions are seen to reduce exposure of women migrants to potential abuse by serial sponsors. While the limitations on serial sponsorship would have reduced the likelihood of women entering into an unhappy relationship with a serial sponsor, the two-year provisional spouse visa excludes its holders from entitlements normally available to migrants on permanent residence visas such as lower tertiary education fees. There is, however, provision for permanent residence to be granted to a migrant spouse whose marriage breaks down due to domestic violence while on the provisional spouse visa. This is to make it possible for migrants to leave an abusive relationship without losing their eligibility to apply for permanent residence. This provision is very much in the interest of female migrant spouses as they are more likely than male migrant spouses to be at risk of domestic violence.

New Zealand also made some changes to sponsorship entitlements in the Family Sponsored category in 2001. Sponsors of parents or adult siblings for migration to New Zealand now must have been resident for at least three years. They must also sign a declaration that they will provide accommodation and financial support for the first two years of the migrant's residence in New Zealand.

Temporary migrants and entitlements

In contrast to immigrants with permanent residence status, temporary residents and their dependents in Australia are not entitled to health and education services and various government payments. Although all temporary migrants have to pay tax in Australia on income earned in the country, they cannot access any social security payments nor receive any payments from the public Medicare health system. Whether they have to pay school fees for their children depends on the state in which they live. Most states' education systems do not differentiate between temporary and permanent residents so children of temporary migrants can attend state schools without paying school fees. However, in a few states full fees are charged for children of temporary residents. This can have a discouraging effect on the migration of people with school aged children to those states, particularly those migrants in associate professional or trades occupations whose salary is not high enough to afford paying the full costs of their children's schooling. As mentioned earlier, spouses of skilled temporary migrants have unrestricted work rights. Women would be the main beneficiaries of this entitlement as they are more likely to be accompanying spouses than to be primary migrants.

To date, just like all countries in the developed world, New Zealand has not yet ratified the 1990 United Nations International Convention on the Protection of the Rights of All Migrant Workers and Members of Their Families (CRMW). This convention has officially become part of international law in 2003 and seeks to ensure protection and respect for the human rights of all migrant workers (Piper & Iredale 2003). However, some types of protection for migrants are already in place in New Zealand, such as the Bill of Rights which offers protection for migrants, and citizenship provisions which enable migrants to become naturalised and full citizens.

With regard to social welfare services, subsidised compulsory education (primary and secondary) is available to the children of work permit holders in New Zealand. Health care access is only possible for those with a work permit of two years or more. The spouses and de facto partners of most classes of work permit holders working in New Zealand for more than six months may be granted work permits that allow them to work for any employer.

None of the Pacific Islands countries has signed or ratified the CRMW. The reason for this may be that they do not acknowledge their status as migrant sending countries. Discussions with government officials in Fiji revealed that an awareness of Fiji as a migrant sending country was growing. However, this has not been translated into policy regulations aimed at protecting Fijian workers abroad. There have been efforts by the Fiji Government and particularly the Ministry of Labour to ensure that Fijians migrating overseas sign contracts with employers before leaving Fiji so that the Ministry of Labour can approve the contracts and can take official action if the conditions are breached. While Fiji has not entered into any bilateral or multilateral agreements with receiving country governments to protect the rights of migrant workers abroad (ILO 2003: 171), it is planned for the future.

A study of Fijian nurses working in the Marshall Islands found that they felt they were disadvantaged compared to local workers in that they did not enjoy equal opportunities for further training (Rokoduru 2004). While women migrants were generally not well informed of their rights as "legal aliens", their civil, social, political and industrial rights were in theory protected. However, due to their comparatively higher salary levels in the Marshall Islands than in Fiji, migrant workers were hesitant to report breaches of their contract regarding work conditions or salaries. The absence of trade unions has effectively closed a legitimate avenue through which migrant workers can air their grievances (Rokoduru 2004).

Migrant workers in Fiji are eligible to use Fiji's national health system of government hospitals and health centres free of charge. However, they are not eligible for unemployment benefits or family benefits that are part of the Fiji Government's social security system. After 10 years residence in Fiji, foreigners are eligible to apply for citizenship; however there are many conditions. One of the most restrictive is that migrant spouses have residence but no automatic work rights. Instead, they must independently find an employer willing to sponsor them. Foreign spouses of Fijian citizens also have no automatic work rights, leading many migrants who have married locally to move to the country of the foreign spouse rather than stay in Fiji. Eleven Indian doctors recently recruited by the Fiji Ministry of Health were contemplating a return to India six months into their three-year contracts. Despite promises that their spouses who were also medical professionals would be given jobs in Fiji, this was not the case and the doctors were getting increasingly impatient, one already returning to India (*Fiji Times*, 28 July 2004).

The situation of Chinese migrants working in garment factories in Fiji can be precarious largely because of their dependence on agents and employers and because they are usually not informed of their rights. Their migration is organised through agents and their wages are usually paid in

China through the recruitment agencies. Some are virtually bonded labourers. The factories arrange and cover all the migrant workers' main expenses including food, accommodation and transport but there are concerns of overcrowding in dormitories and houses (Oxfam New Zealand 2004: 41). Most workers come without their families and some employers have put conditions in the contract threatening dismissal if they marry locally.

Trade unions in Fiji have not provided any specific services to help migrant workers. Rather, the Fiji Trade Unions Council has voiced concern that migrant workers are taking jobs from locals. Indeed, many migrant workers are treated with animosity in Fiji and are blamed for taking jobs from locals and for threatening the work conditions of locals. This attitude on the part of trade unions is not unusual (see chapter 8 in this volume).

Some practical support has been given to Chinese migrant workers by the Fiji Women's Rights Movement (FWRM), a non-governmental organisation that has produced a brochure in Cantonese to educate Chinese garment workers on workplace rights and labour laws. Unions have distributed this brochure in workplaces. The FWRM plans to recruit a Chinese-speaking officer to inform Chinese migrant workers of their rights and assist them in all matters. A major handicap for garment workers is the unavailability of adequate information on Fiji before their migration. Migration is handled by agents in China and some migrants find their work conditions and pay different from what they had been told. Some unregistered agencies also charge excessive fees (Raman 1999: 127).

Irregular migration and working illegally

Irregular migrants and migrants working illegally usually have few entitlements and are likely to be exploited by employers because of their illegal status. Women migrants who are the victims of people trafficking usually fare the worst.

All unauthorised migrants to Australia are detained while their claims are processed. Similarly migrants who are found to be working illegally are detained while arrangements are made for their deportation. Since 2002, family style accommodation (referred to as residential housing projects and consisting of houses or apartments where residents can prepare their meals) has been developed to accommodate women and children so they would not be housed in detention centres where the inhabitants are mostly male.

Detainees have the right to certain entitlements while in detention centres although they do not have work rights. According to the Department of Immigration, the detainees have access to medical and dental services, culturally responsive physical and psychological health services and religious services (DIMIA 2004b). They also have access to telephones, newspapers and television and education programs and English language classes are provided for adults and children. Most children living with their parents in detention centres attend schools in the community. Detainees also have help through the Immigration Advice and Application Assistance Scheme to prepare and lodge protection visa applications (DIMIA 2004b).

Unauthorised arrivals in Australia whose asylum claims are successful are provided with a temporary protection visa that allows them to work. They are not entitled to unemployment benefits but they can access other social welfare and family support payments such as rent assistance, family tax benefits, child care allowance and maternity allowance. They can access the government's job search agency for assistance in finding employment and are also covered by the government's Medicare health system. Most people on temporary protection visas are men, some of whom have left their wives and children behind in their home country. Their temporary protection visa does not allow them to sponsor family members for migration.

Previously temporary protection visa (TPV) holders were not permitted to apply for permanent residence and could only apply for another TPV or return home at the end of their three-year stay. However, in August 2004, the Australian Government changed its policy making it possible for TPV holders to apply for permanent residence. This was in recognition of a number of TPV holders who had found low skilled or seasonal employment in small towns and regional areas in need of workers. The government has amended the skill requirements in the Regional Skilled Migration Scheme so that TPV holders working in regional areas can apply for permanent residence under this scheme (DIMIA 2004e).

TPV holders who are at the end of their three-year stay and who are not able to obtain another temporary protection visa have also been given a further 18 months extension of their visa (DIMIA 2004e). They can use this time to find work in regional areas that will make them eligible to apply for permanent residence under the Regional Migration Scheme or to explore other means of qualifying for permanent residence. They can also now apply for a student visa if they want to undertake further education and have been offered a place in an educational institution (DIMIA 2004e). These recent policy shifts relating to TPV holders reflect a softening of the Australian government's approach to unauthorised arrivals in the context of a reduction in such arrivals since 2001.

Policy shifts in relation to illegal migrant workers are directed mainly at those who are considered to be the victims of people smuggling or trafficking. Until recently victims of people trafficking who were caught working illegally, many of whom were women, were treated as illegal migrants and simply deported. However, following extensive media reports of a Thai woman who died in a detention centre after having been found working illegally in the sex industry, the Australian Government has introduced new protocols to deal with illegal migrant workers in the sex industry who are found to be victims of people trafficking.

A number of Australian government agencies are now cooperating to implement a plan of action directed at people trafficking that was introduced in October 2003. The agencies involved include the Department of Immigration, the Office of the Status of Women, AusAID (the Australian government's overseas development assistance agency) and the Attorney General's Department. New visa arrangements have been introduced for people identified as trafficking victims to allow them to stay in Australia to receive medical treatment, counselling and temporary accommodation and to assist police with their investigation. Foreign-born women who are found to be working illegally in the sex industry are now interviewed by Department of Immigration staff to determine if they are the victims of trafficking. If so, the police are informed and the women are provided with bridging visas and access to support services. A special 23-member police taskforce, the Transnational Sexual Exploitation and Trafficking Team, has been set up to prosecute cases of people trafficking. AusAID is also working with the International Organisation for Migration to provide re-integration assistance to those women who return to their home countries (Australian Government 2004).

These initiatives are only a beginning in addressing the increase in people smuggling and cross-border trafficking, particularly of women, in the region. There is recognition that Australia as a receiving country of cross-border trafficking victims needs to do more to address both the supply and demand factors associated with the cross-border trafficking of women. The action plan has called for development assistance directed at the countries of origin as well as domestic deterrence efforts that include the introduction of further legislation to criminalise all aspects of human trafficking (Australian Government 2004: 12). Australia is a signatory to both the United Nations Convention against Transnational Organised Crime and the Protocol to Prevent, Suppress and Punish Trafficking in Persons, especially Women and Children, and plans to ratify the Protocol in 2004 following consultations with state and territory governments (Australian Government 2004: 5).

Return migration and entitlements

With the rise in temporary migration and the return migration of some settlers, particularly after retirement, to their country of origin, the international portability of pensions and other entitlements has become an important issue for an increasing number of migrants. It is not a gendered migration issue however, as any policy in this area affects female and male migrants in the same way. In reality, because of women's longer life expectancy, the issue of access to such entitlements as the aged pension or widow's pension may have implications for more female than male migrants.

In recognition of the increasing propensity of people to move between countries during and after their working life, Australia has signed agreements with 16 countries relating to social security coverage, and is in the process of negotiations with several more countries on similar agreements.

Under the agreements, a pension from one country can be accessed in the other country and responsibility for social security is shared between the two countries based on the number of years of working life that a person has spent in each country[10]. For example, the social security agreement signed with Slovenia allows former Australian residents now living in Slovenia to claim Australian pensions while Slovenians living in Australia will be able to claim Slovenian pensions through Centrelink, Australia's social security payments agency.

Former settlers who have spent most of their working life in Australia and have become citizens are likely to continue receiving their pensions when they return to their country of origin upon retirement. Where the country of origin has no international agreement with Australia, continued access to welfare entitlements depends on a number of factors including the length of absence and whether the migrant continues to maintain ties with Australia. Factors indicating continuing ties with Australia include having immediate family remaining in Australia, retention of property and bank accounts and length of residence in Australia before departure. Access will cease only if there is evidence that the return migration is permanent and the person no longer has any continuing ties with Australia.

CONCLUSION

As in other regions, Oceania is experiencing an increase in international population movements. There has been more migration between the countries in the region, a greater diversity of the origins of immigrants to Australia and New Zealand, and increasing outmigration from the region to North America, Europe and Asia. The pattern of international migration to Australia and New Zealand has also become more diverse, with a shift to more temporary movements, a greater focus on skilled migration, and increasing exposure to irregular or undocumented migration.

Women are becoming increasingly important participants in all these migration flows, as part of family units and as autonomous labour migrants, highly skilled migrants and undocumented migrants. Most migration flows in the region have a fairly balanced gender composition, an indication that women are participating in migration at a similar level as men, at least on a numerical basis. Their labour force participation rates may be lower than male migrants, because many are accompanying spouses, but for those migrating autonomously for economic reasons they are also participating in the work force on par with male migrants. As for male migrants, the situation of female migrants in the Oceania region in terms of their labour market outcomes is largely dependent on their migration status and skill level. Migrants, regardless of their gender, also differ in terms of their entitlements according to their migration and residence status. While migrants with permanent residence status usually have the same entitlements in terms of access to government services as the nativeborn and naturalised citizens, temporary migrants usually do not and are more dependent on their employers for any entitlements. Women migrants in low skilled employment or working illegally are most vulnerable to exploitation.

The main issues facing migrant women in Australia, New Zealand and the Pacific Island countries are therefore also related to their migration status. For women who have migrated as settlers with permanent residence, their participation in the labour force according to their skills and qualifications is an important part of their settlement process. That some migrants face barriers in transferring their skills to their new country of residence is a loss in productivity for both migrants and the receiving country. For women who migrate temporarily, those who work in higher skilled occupations are likely to face fewer problems in relation to work place entitlements. However, for those who are in lower skilled employment such as Pacific Islander women working as caregivers or Chinese women working in garment factories in Fiji there is scope for exploitation by employers when governments have no firm policies on the conditions of their migration and employment or are unable to monitor or enforce existing policies. The situation of irregular migrants is understandably of most concern, particularly if the women have been trafficked. In relation to this issue, there is a need to focus on the situation of the women in both sending and receiving countries. There is therefore much scope for international action and regional cooperation to reduce the exposure of and the pressure on women to migrate and seek employment in such precarious conditions in foreign countries a long way from home and family.

NOTES

1. Official statistics are often not available by gender. For instance in Fiji, data on work permit issues are disaggregated by nationality but not by gender.
2. Traditional sources are Australia, United Kingdom, Pacific Islands, Northern and Western Europe and North America. These are the countries from which most immigrants to New Zealand were drawn before the policy changes in the mid-1980s. The non-traditional sources are countries in Asia, Africa, South and Central America and Southern and Eastern Europe.
3. It was not known if any of the Australians or New Zealanders included former migrants from Fiji who were returning as Australian or New Zealand citizens.
4. Most emigrants have been Indo-Fijians who are unlikely to return. It is only in recent years that ethnic Fijians have started to migrate in greater numbers. It is possible that the adverse effects of these policies on return migration have not been fully realised by the decision makers in Fiji. On the other hand, it may be unwise to encourage return migration as this would reduce the very substantial contribution of remittances to the Fijian economy.
5. Current Australian legislation allows for the criminal prosecution of only one aspect of human trafficking — sexual exploitation, where the victims

are likely to be women. There is no legislation that allows police to prosecute traffickers of men and women to work in construction, factories, agriculture or any sector other than the sex industry (see Piper 2005).
6. This substantial flow of remittances has probably quietened any debate in the islands on the issue of compensation for the loss of skilled people, unlike in other regions.
7. The evidence came from the Department of Immigration's Longitudinal Survey of Immigrants to Australia. A comparison of two cohorts of immigrants in the survey, the first arriving before the two-year waiting period and the second after, showed that the second cohort found jobs faster than the first cohort and that they also brought more money with them, particularly those in the Independent skilled visa category.
8. It is possible for a permanent visa to be granted in less than two years if at the time of visa application the couple has been in a relationship for at least five years or at least two years if there are children from the relationship.
9. A few cases came to the courts and resulted in prosecution for visa fraud.
10. The specific conditions of the agreements may vary with different countries. Details are available from the Australian Government's Department of Family and Community Services website http://www.facs.gov.au

REFERENCES

Australian Government. (2004) *Australian Government's Action Plan to Eradicate Trafficking in Persons*. Canberra: Attorney General's Department.

Australian Bureau of Statistics (ABS) *Australian Demographic Statistics*. Canberra: various years.

Bedford, C. (2003) "Skill Shortages in New Zealand: Public and Private Sector Responses," *New Zealand Population Review*, 29 (2): 63–88.

Bedford, R, E. Ho and G. Hugo (2003) "Trans-Tasman Migration in Context: Recent Flows of New Zealanders Revisited," *People and Place,* 11 (December): 53–62.

Birrell, B. and E. Healy (1997) "Globalisation and Temporary Entry," *People and Place* 5 (December): 43—52.

Boyd, C. (2003) *Migrants in New Zealand: An Analysis of Labour Market Outcomes for Working Aged Migrants Using 1996 and 2001 Census Data*. Wellington: Department of Labour.

Brinsdon, S. (1999) *Patterns in the Sponsorship of Social Migrants*. Commissioned Report for New Zealand Immigration Service. Wellington: Department of Labour.

Chandra, D. (2003) *Fiji's International Migration in the Context of Human Development: Gender Trends, Motivations and Strategies*. Report prepared for Economic and Social Commission for Asia and the Pacific, Ad Hoc Expert Group Meeting on Migration and Development. Bangkok: ESCAP.

CM Research. (1999) *Migrants' and Parents' Experiences of Sponsoring*. Qualitative Research Report prepared for the New Zealand Immigration Service. Wellington: New Zealand Immigration Service.

Cobb-Clark, D. and B. Chapman (1999) *The Changing Pattern of Immigrants' Labour Market Experiences*. Centre for Economic Policy Research Discussion Paper no.396. Canberra: Australian National University.

Connell, J. (1984) "Status of Subjugation? Women, Migration and Development in the South Pacific," *International Migration Review*, 18 (December): 964–83.

———. (1985) *Migration, Employment and Development in the South Pacific: Country Report No. 4 Fiji*. Noumea: South Pacific Commission.

Crocombe, R. (2001) *The South Pacific*. Suva: University of the South Pacific.

Department of Immigration and Multicultural Affairs (DIMAa) *Government Successfully Matching Skilled Workers to Employers*. Media Release, 1 May 2006.

———. (DIMAb) *Another 13,000 Refugees to Call Australia Home*. Media Release, 2 May 2006.

Department of Immigration and Multicultural and Indigenous Affairs (DIMIA) *Immigration Update*. Canberra, various years.

———. *Migration Program Planning Levels*. Fact Sheet 20. (2003a) Canberra: Department of Immigration and Multicultural and Indigenous Affairs.

———. *Submission to Joint Standing Committee on Migration, Review of Skilled Labour Migration Programs*. (2003b) Canberra: The Parliament of the Commonwealth of Australia.

———. *Australia's Refugee and Humanitarian Program*, Fact Sheet 60. (2004a) Canberra: Department of Immigration and Multicultural and Indigenous Affairs.

———. *Immigration Detention*, Fact Sheet 82. (2004b) Canberra: Department of Immigration and Multicultural and Indigenous Affairs.

———. *Initiatives to Combat Illegal Work in Australia*. Fact Sheet 87. (2004c) Canberra: Department of Immigration and Multicultural and Indigenous Affairs.

———. *Overstayers and People in Breach of Visa Conditions*, Fact Sheet 86. (2004d). Canberra: Department of Immigration and Multicultural and Indigenous Affairs.

———. "New TPV Measures to Commence on 27 August 2004", Media Release VPS 12/2004. (2004e). Canberra: Department of Immigration and Multicultural and Indigenous Affairs.

———. *Population Flows: Immigration Aspects*. (2004f). Canberra: Department of Immigration and Multicultural and Indigenous Affairs.

———. *Population Flows: Immigration Aspects*. (2006). Canberra: Department of Immigration and Multicultural and Indigenous Affairs.

Department of Internal Affairs. (1996) *High Hopes : A Survey of Qualifications, Training and Employment Issues for Recent Immigrants in New Zealand*. Ethnic Affairs Service Information Series 2. Wellington: Department of Internal Affairs.

Drennan, P. and S. Wright. (2004) "Transnational networking for detection and law enforcement." Presentation at the Conference on People Trafficking, Human Security and Development, Canberra.

'Esau, R. L. and S. Hirai. (2002) "Contemporary migration research in Tonga, trends, issues and the future", in *5th International APMRN Conference, Fiji 2002: Selected Papers*, ed. Kerry Lyon and Carmen Voigt-Graf. APMRN Working Paper No. 12. Wollongong: APMRN.

Fiji Times. "Sex workers in transit", 24 January 2004.

———."Sex in the city", 16 June 2004.

———. "Indian doctors claim raw deals", 28 July 2004.

———. "Zinck probes worker abuse", 30 August, 2004.

Ho, E. S. (2002) "Multi-local Residence, Transnational Networks: Chinese "Astronaut" Families in New Zealand," *Asia and Pacific Migration Journal*, 11 (1): 145–64.

Ho, E. S., R. D. Bedford and C. Bedford. (2000) "Migrants in their Family Contexts: Application of a Methodology". *Population Studies Centre Discussion Paper 34*. Hamilton: University of Waikato.

Ho, E. S., R. D. Bedford and J. E. Goodwin. (1997) "'Astronaut' Families: A Contemporary Migration Phenomenon", in *Northeast Asian New Zealanders: Research on New Migrants,* ed. W. Friesen, M. Ip, Elsie Ho, Richard D. Bedford and J.E. Goodwin. Aotearoa/New Zealand Migration Research Network Research Paper 3. Auckland: Department of Sociology, Massey University at Albany.

Ho, E. S., E.Cheung, C. Bedford, and P. Leung. (2000) *Settlement Assistance Needs of Recent Migrants.* Commissioned report for New Zealand Immigration Service. Wellington: Department of Labour.

Hugo, G., D. Rudd and K. Harris. (2003) *Australia's Diaspora: Its Size, Nature and Policy Implications.* CEDA Information Paper No 80. Melbourne: Committee for the Economic Development of Australia.

International Labour Office. (2003) *ILO Migration Survey 2003: Country Summaries.* Geneva: ILO.

Iredale, R. (1994) "Patterns of Spouse/Fiance Sponsorship to Australia," *Asian and Pacific Migration Journal,* 3 (4): 547–66.

Khoo, S. E. and P. McDonald. (2001) *Settlement Indicators and Benchmarks.* Report to the Department of Immigration and Multicultural Affairs. Canberra: DIMA.

Khoo, S. E., Kee P., T. Dang and Jing Shu. (1994) "Asian Immigrant Settlement and Adjustment in Australia," *Asian and Pacific Migration Journal,* 3 (2–3): 311–38.

Khoo, S. E., C. Voigt-Graf, G. Hugo and P. McDonald. (2003) "Temporary Skilled Migration to Australia: the 457 Visa Subclass," *People and Place,* 11 (December): 27–40.

Lidgard, J. M. (1993a) "Neglected International Migrants: A Study of Returning New Zealanders," *New Zealand Population Review,* 19 (3&4): 99–128.

———. (1993b) "Tagging Along? An Examination of the Experiences of Returning New Zealand Women". In *Ethnicity and Gender: Population Trends and Policy Challenges in the 1990s. Proceedings of a Conference, Wellington.* Wellington: Population Association of New Zealand and Te Puni Kōkiri, 1993b.

Lidgard, J. M. and C. Gilson. (2002) "Return Migration of New Zealanders: Shuttle and Circular Migrants". *New Zealand Population Review,* 28 (1): 99–128.

Lidgard, J. M., E. S. Ho, Y. Chen, J. E. Goodwin, and R. D. Bedford. (1998) "Immigrants from Korea, Taiwan and Hong Kong in New Zealand in the mid-1990s: macro and micro perspectives" *Population Studies Centre Discussion Paper 29.* Hamilton: University of Waikato.

New Zealand Immigration Service. (2000) *Humanitarian Category Circumstances.* Wellington: New Zealand Immigration Service, Department of Labour.

———. (2003a) *Trends in Residence Approvals. 2002/2003. Volume 3.* Wellington: New Zealand Immigration Service, Department of Labour.

———. (2003b) *Migrants in New Zealand: An Analysis of 2001 Census Data.* Wellington: New Zealand Immigration Service, Department of Labour.

———. (2003c) *Skilled Migrants: Labour Market Experiences.* Wellington: New Zealand Immigration Service, Department of Labour.

———. (2004a) *New Zealand Work Policy: Meeting Talent, Skill and Labour Needs.* Wellington: New Zealand Immigration Service, Department of Labour.

———. (2004b) *Migrants' Experiences of New Zealand. Pilot Survey Report. Longitudinal Immigration Survey: New Zealand.* Wellington: New Zealand Immigration Service, Department of Labour.

———. (2004c) *Refugee Voices: A Journey Towards Resettlement.* Wellington: Department of Labour.
Pe-Pua, R., C. Mitchell, R. Iredale and S. Castles. (1996) *Astronaut Families and Parachute Children: The Cycle of Migration between Hong Kong and Australia.* Canberra: Australian Government Publishing Service.
Piper, N. (2005) *A Problem by a Different Name? A Review of Research on Trafficking in Southeast Asia and Oceania* in: *International Migration,* vol. 43(1/2): 203–33.
Piper, N. and R. Iredale (2003) *Identification of the Obstacles to the Signing and Ratification of the UN Convention on the Protection of the Rights of All Migrant Workers 1990 The Asia Pacific Perspective.* Report funded by UNESCO. Wollongong: APMRN.
Raman, J. (1999) "Fiji", in *Report and Conclusions: ILO Asia Pacific Regional Trade Union Symposium on Migrant Workers, 6–8 December 1999, Kuala Lumpur,* ed. International Labour Office. Geneva: Bureau for Workers Activities, ILO.
Richardson, S., F. Robertson, and D. Ilsey (2001) *The Labour Force Experience of New Migrants.* Canberra: Department of Immigration and Multicultural Affairs.
Rokoduru, A. (2002) "The Contemporary Migration of Skilled Labour from Fiji to Pacific Island Countries (PICs)", in *5th International APMRN Conference, Fiji 2002: Selected Papers,* ed. Kerry Lyon and Carmen Voigt-Graf. APMRN Working Paper No. 12. Wollongong: APMRN, pp. 43–48.
———. (2004) *Emerging Women's Issues in the Pacific – Migrant Women Workers.* Research paper prepared for the Secretariat of the Pacific Community and presented during the Ninth Triennial Conference of Pacific Women, Nadi, Fiji, 16–19 August, 2004.
Scott, G. G. (2003) "Situating Fijian Transmigrants: Towards Racialised Transnational Social Spaces of the Undocumented," *International Journal of Population Geography,* 9: 181–98.
Shankman, P. (1976) *Migration and Underdevelopment: The Case of Western Samoa.* Boulder: Westview.
Smith, A. and G. Kaminskas (1992) "Female Filipino Migration to Australia: An Overview," *Asian Migrant,* 5 (3): 72–81.
Statistics New Zealand. (2004) *Degrees of Difference: The Employment of University-qualified Immigrants in New Zealand.* Wellington: Statistics New Zealand.
Tonga Ministry of Finance (2004) *Tonga Selected Economic Indicators.*
VandenHeuvel, A. and M. Wooden. (1999) *New Settlers Have Their Say: How Immigrants Fare over the Early Years of Settlement.* Canberra: Department of Immigration and Multicultural Affairs.
Vete, M. F. (1995) "The Determinants of Remittances among Tongans in Auckland," *Asian and Pacific Migration Journal,* 4 (1): 55–68.
Voigt-Graf, C. (2003) "Fijian Teachers on the Move: Causes, Implications and Policies," *Asia Pacific Viewpoint,* 44 (2): 163–74.
Williams, L. S., J. Murphy and C. Brooks. (1997) *Initial Labour Market Experiences of Immigrants.* Canberra: Department of Immigration and Multicultural Affairs.
Winkelmann, L. and R. Winkelmann. (1998) "Immigrants in New Zealand: A Study of Their Labour Market Outcomes." *Labour Market Policy Group Occasional Paper 1998/1.* Wellington: Department of Labour.

5 Gender, Migration and Livelihoods
Migrant Women in Southern Africa
Belinda Dodson

INTRODUCTION

The movement of people between countries in Southern Africa has ebbed and flowed in response to social, political and economic changes in the region, of which the collapse of apartheid in South Africa in the 1990s is but the most recent. Colonial expansion and settlement, the discovery of diamonds and gold in South Africa in the nineteenth century, industrialization, urbanization and agrarian change all led to significant migrant flows within and across the region's borders. Those borders are themselves the products of historical geopolitical forces extending well beyond the African continent. States and their boundaries were superimposed on pre-existing geographies of ethnicity, settlement and mobility. Indeed it could be argued that mobility is a characteristic feature of this region, with multi-local households and migration-dependent livelihoods having long been features of most Southern African societies. Transnationalism, far from being anything unusual or novel, is here a well-established practice, and while formal immigration levels are relatively low, various forms of short-term, temporary or cyclical cross-border migration are commonplace.

As in the past, while there is some movement between other countries, it is South Africa, with its relative economic strength, which is the lure for most of the region's migrants. Much of this chapter, therefore, is concerned with migration to South Africa. Particular attention is paid to the socio-political transformation of South Africa since the collapse of apartheid and how this has affected the nature, volume and gendering of migrant flows from the wider Southern African region.

The chapter begins by considering the neglect of female migrants in official, academic and popular imaginations, seeking both to retrieve the history of women's migration as well as to place current female migration in appropriate historical context. It goes on to examine the gender dynamics of contemporary cross-border migration, pointing to some important differences between male and female migrants in terms of their demographics as well as their motives, patterns and experiences of migration.

The third major section of the chapter presents a gender analysis of South African immigration policy as set out in the 2002 Immigration Act, 2004 Immigration Amendment Act and the subsequent regulations. The chapter concludes with a brief discussion of the connections between gender, migration, livelihoods and development, using this to argue for a move away from the current 'fortress South Africa' mentality to a more flexible and gender-equitable policy framework.

MIGRATION PAST AND PRESENT: CONTINUITY, CHANGE AND REFEMINIZATION

Historical migration patterns

Migration in Southern Africa has deep-rooted and inter-connected race, class and gender dimensions. The most long-established form of cross-border migration within the region is African labour migration to South Africa from its neighbouring countries, a system dating to the beginning of the South African diamond and gold mining industries in the nineteenth century and continuing to this day (Crush 1987; Crush, Jeeves & Yudelman 1991; Crush & Tshitereke 2001; Harries 1994; Moodie 1994). Given this long association with the mining industry, both the reality and the perception of regional cross-border migration have been heavily male biased. Recent scholarship has challenged the androcentric, 'kraal to compound'[1] logic of much of the regional labour migration literature, putting this forward as one of the main explanations for the relative neglect of women in Southern African migration studies (Barnes 2002). Certainly the highly formalized, organized and collective system of male labour migration makes it easier to monitor and study, while the more informal, less structured cross-border movement of women has been inherently less visible. In consequence, much of the research on women's cross-border migration in this region has been qualitative and historical (Barnes 2002; Bonner 1990; Cockerton 1996; Coplan 2001; Miles 1991; Walker 1990); or alternatively has been concerned with the women left behind as 'gold widows' in Lesotho and elsewhere by male labour migrants (Murray 1981). There has been a considerable amount of research on *internal* rural-urban migration by women within individual Southern African countries (Bozzoli 1991; Elder 2003; Francis 2002), but Southern African women as *international* migrants in their own right have only recently begun to attract due academic attention.

In reality, added to the highly regularized system of male labour migration have always been various alternative forms of movement across Southern Africa's borders. Much of this movement has involved significant numbers of women (Barnes 2002; Bonner 1990; Cockerton 1996; Coplan 2001; Miles 1991; Walker 1990). Miles (1991) reveals the hitherto hidden history of women who migrated to South Africa from Swaziland over much of the twentieth century, at least until the constraints of apartheid made it more difficult. Cockerton (1996) has done the same for women from Bechuanaland (today's Botswana). As Cockerton, Miles and others demonstrate, many migrant women historically found employment in domestic service, while others engaged in agricultural labour or various forms of informal-sector economic activity. Bonner (1990), for example, describes how migrant women from Lesotho secured their livelihood through activities such as beer brewing, cooking, laundry and sex work in the towns and cities of South Africa's Witwatersrand mining belt between 1920 and 1945.

As these and other authors make clear, female migration to South Africa is not a purely post-apartheid phenomenon, although it is true to say that it was severely restricted, or at least driven further underground, during the apartheid era. Nor have female migrants always been passive or dependent 'accompanying persons' coming with male partners or family members. Rather, women migrants past and present have employed migration as a means of independently finding employment or otherwise seeking their own livelihoods, often with the deliberate intent of escaping patriarchal control and gender-based discrimination or abuse (Bozzoli 1991; Wright 1995).

Given these gendered migration flows, it is clear that the category of 'labour migrant' in this region needs to be reconceptualized to include women as well as men. Of course male labour migration has implications for women too, as well as for gender roles and relations in both source and destination areas. Most domestic and foreign male mineworkers come from rural areas. Many of them leave behind partners and families — the 'gold widows' so evocatively described by Colin Murray (1981), bearing the burdens of child care, agricultural labour and household maintenance. Male labour migration brings significant household economic benefits in the form of remittances, but often comes at considerable cost to personal and family relations. Divided families and single-sex migrant streams contribute to the high rates of HIV among migrant workers and their sexual partners — including their female partners at home in South Africa and neighbouring countries (Campbell 1997; Lurie 2006). Nationally and regionally, male labour migration has high socio-cultural significance (Elder 2003; Moodie 1994). It is perceived as a male rite of passage, not least as a means by which single men can earn money to pay "brideprice" or *lobola*. Whether as migrants themselves or as migrants' wives and partners, the lives of women in Southern Africa, today as in the past, are bound up in numerous ways with the migration process.

Post-apartheid changes in regional migration flows

Male mine labour migration from neighbouring countries has continued virtually unchanged since the end of apartheid, albeit with some reduction in volume and a shift in the geography of labour sourcing and recruitment (Crush & Tshitereke 2001; Tshitereke 2004). But the end of apartheid certainly brought dramatic changes to international migration flows within the wider Southern African region, and especially to movement to (and from) South Africa. As Landau (2005: 6) argues, '[a]lthough migrant labour continues to make critical contributions in mining and agriculture, post-apartheid mobility is more than the intensification of long-standing migration patterns. Because of these movements, the country's cities have, for the first time, become the primary destinations for people from beyond South Africa's borders'. Once the official apartheid policy of race-based discrimination had been removed, both internally and in terms of immigration policy, South Africa as the region's most powerful economy became a highly desirable destination for cross-border migrants from other African countries. There has been an increase not only in the number of migrants to South Africa but also in the variety of forms of cross-border migration: short-term and long-term, documented and undocumented, voluntary and forced, and from an increasingly diverse range of source countries both in Southern Africa and further north on the continent (Crush 2003; Gotz & Simone 2003; Landau 2005; McDonald et al. 1998; Simone 2000; Western 2001). These new and expanded flows of people include both men and women, albeit in different proportions in the various migrant streams.

This diversity of form, legality and temporality of contemporary cross-border migration makes it impossible to state the number of foreign nationals living in South Africa with any accuracy. Certainly few of these contemporary migrant flows take the form of formal, permanent immigration. This has in fact shown a marked decline even while it has undergone increasing Africanization since the termination of the apartheid era's racially restrictive immigration policy (Mattes, Crush & Richmond 2002; Peberdy 1999 and 2001). Official estimates of the number of foreigners living in South Africa have been grossly exaggerated, at one time presenting improbable figures of four to seven million *illegal* immigrants alone (Crush & Williams 2003). This contributed to media portrayals of a flood or tidal wave of immigrants descending on South Africa from countries to the north and to corresponding anti-immigrant, even xenophobic, public sentiment (Danso & McDonald 2001). Far from the official estimates, Crush and Williams (2003) estimated the figure of non-nationals living in South Africa in 2001 at 850,000. The national census taken that same year indicated that there were just over a million people living in South Africa who were born in other countries. This represents just over 2 percent of the country's total 2001 population of approximately 45 million (Statistics South Africa 2004) — far from the "flood" in popular media representations, although still almost certainly an underestimate of the true number. The South African Human Sciences Research Council (HSRC), which had earlier produced the estimates of millions of illegal immigrants living in the country, later retracted its reported figures and admitted using a flawed methodology in arriving at their inflated numbers. Recently, with the ongoing political and economic crisis in Zimbabwe, the South African media have again been putting out figures of two to three million Zimbabwean nationals being in South Africa illegally (*Mail and Guardian* online 24 March 2005). The real number of foreign nationals living in South Africa, including its gender composition, is simply unknown.

From the limited evidence available, it does seem that post-apartheid migrant flows to South Africa have involved a degree of feminization (Dodson 1998), in keeping with trends in other regions of the world. Yet the inter-linked factors of race, gender and geography are difficult to disentangle. Comparing the 1996 and 2001 censuses presents some interesting trends.[2] In 1996, there were 582,096 foreign-born men recorded as living in South Africa and 376,090 foreign-born women. By 2001, those figures had increased to 610,394 foreign-born men and 414,702 foreign-born women. This represents a 5 percent increase in the number of foreign-born men, but a 10 percent increase in the number of foreign-born women. Although this meant that the proportion of foreigners in the country who are women had increased only slightly, it does suggest that the 'new', post-apartheid immigrant streams are more female than those that previously prevailed, and that more women than men moved to South Africa during this five-year period. Given that the actual levels of in-migration are in all likelihood higher than those obtained in the official census, the real figure for the feminization of migration may well be higher still.

The official figures, while unreliable in any absolute sense, also present tantalizing evidence of a strongly gendered geography of migration. A regional breakdown by the place of birth of foreign-born people in South Africa shows highly uneven gender proportions. Of those giving their country of birth as Southern African Development Community (SADC) countries[3], who made up over half the total number of foreign-born residents, only 32 percent were women in 1996. This had increased to 37 percent by 2001, still a heavily male-dominated migrant flow but a significant change nevertheless. For the other major sources of immigrants, the proportions of women in 2001 were 34 percent of the migrants from the rest of Africa (i.e. outside SADC), 49 percent of the migrants from Europe, and 42 percent of those from Asia. For the other three listed regions of origin, North America, Central and South America, and Australia and New Zealand, the proportion of men and women was more or less equal, although these regions were all relatively minor sources of immigrants. The 'country of birth' statistics were further broken down by race, providing additional insight into the shifting gender dynamics of post-apartheid immigration. Of the SADC-origin immigrants categorized as 'black African', 27 percent were female in 1996, increasing to 33 percent by 2001. Interestingly, for people classified as 'black African' from countries in the 'rest of Africa', the percentage of women decreased slightly between 1996 and 2001, from 31 percent to 28 percent. While other writers have focused on the dramatic *Africanization* of migration to South Africa since the end of apartheid (Gotz & Simone 2003; Landau 2005; Simone 2000; Western 2001), this can mask the racially and geographically patterned *gendering* of migration flows, with African-origin migrant streams, except for those from the southern portion of the continent, tending to be relatively more male than those from other regions of the world.

However inaccurate in absolute terms, the census data seem to indicate both an Africanization and a feminization of migration to South Africa, but with a particular increase in migration by women from SADC countries: 169,255 SADC-born women living in South Africa in 1996, according to the census; 257,244 in 2001. This means that 62 percent or almost two-thirds of all the recorded foreign-born women in South Africa come from the neighbouring Southern African region[4]. It is impossible to obtain accurate figures for either current or historical migrant flows, particularly given the undocumented nature of some of those flows and the reluctance of 'illegal' immigrants to be recorded in any official census, but the significant increase even in the *official* number of SADC-born women living in South Africa suggests a refeminization of cross-border migration from the region. This perhaps signals a return to the situation described by Miles, Cockerton, Bonner and others for the early to mid-twentieth century.

Factors driving new migrant flows

What, then, are the factors driving contemporary migration to South Africa, including its gender characteristics? It is likely that the observed refeminization of migration from the Southern African region is in part a response to the reduction of male migration in certain economic sectors. Most significant has been the downsizing of the South African mine workforce, which has led to a reduction in male labour migration to mining areas, especially from certain countries (Crush & Tshitereke 2001; Tshitereke 2004). The resulting loss of household income appears to have led to an increase in both internal and international migration by female household members in a quest for alternative sources of individual and household livelihood. Women migrating from Lesotho to work on the farms of South Africa's eastern Free State province, for example, do so in part to make up for the loss of income from male household members formerly employed in the mining industry (Ulicki & Crush 2000).

New economic opportunities have also been a driver of increased cross-border migration, and especially of the growth in migration by women. Greater regional economic integration since the end of apartheid has led to a dramatic expansion in regional cross-border trade, of which a significant volume is informal trading by small-scale individual entrepreneurs (Peberdy 2000; Peberdy & Crush 1998). Petty traders come to South Africa from neighbouring countries to purchase a variety of consumer goods which they then sell back in their home countries, as well as to sell goods such as handicrafts which they have produced. Many of those involved are women from countries such as Mozambique and Zimbabwe. This has led to a dramatic increase in the number of people crossing South Africa's borders on cross-border passes, which allow entry for the purposes of visiting, tourism, or conducting business (Crush 2003). The volume and value of goods traded, while not readily quantifiable, are certainly significant. They are even more significant in terms of household livelihoods, and in particular of the livelihoods of women and female-headed households. Similar if smaller movements of traders occur across other borders in the regions, for example between Zimbabwe and Botswana.

As described above, formal contract labour migration to the mines of South Africa from Botswana, Lesotho, Mozambique and Swaziland continues much as before, if in reduced numbers. The employment of foreign labour in agriculture also continues, although numbers and trends are difficult to specify. Significant numbers of foreign workers are employed (legally or illegally) in farming areas close to the borders with Zimbabwe, Mozambique and Lesotho (Crush et al. 2000). While the mine workforce remains almost 100 percent male, there is a considerable female presence in migrant agricultural labour, both legal and undocumented. Another significant source of employment, although impossible to quantify given its dispersed, fragmented and individualized nature, is domestic service. This is similar to the situation in many other parts of the world, as described elsewhere in this volume.

In other employment sectors, the deracialization of the South African labour market, along with the removal of racial restrictions in immigration policy, has seen increasing movement of skilled 'non-white'[5] immigrants to South Africa to take advantage of professional employment opportunities (Mattes, Crush & Richmond 2002). This particular migrant stream, however, appears to be predominantly male, especially for skilled migrants from African countries (Dodson 2002). Deracialization and Africanization of formal immigration appears to have been accompanied by a masculinization rather than a feminization, and by a trend toward migration by single professionals rather than family-class migrants (Dodson 2002)[6]. Male bias in skilled migration is unsurprising given the criteria of education and training applied in immigrant selection, with access to education continuing to favour men, and especially so in the African context. There is a much smaller reverse stream of skilled migration from South Africa to other Southern African countries, for example in the form of intra-company transfers as South African companies expand into regional and continental markets. As in other parts of the world, this too is likely to be predominantly male. At the same time, skilled Southern Africans, especially South Africans, are immigrating in large numbers to countries like Australia, Britain, the United States and Canada (Brown, Kaplan & Meyer 2002; Crush, McDonald & Williams 2000). Much of this takes the form of family migration, including men and women as well as children. Interestingly, South African women across race groups seem to act as a brake on skilled emigration's 'brain drain', with women (more than men) citing family ties as a reason for not wishing to leave the country and generally proving to make more reluctant emigrants (Dodson 2002). This seeming gender difference may be one reason why individuals' stated likelihood of emigration is not always turned into actual migration behaviour.

Refugees and asylum seekers are another source of international migrants within and to the region. People escaping conflict further north on the continent, for example in Rwanda and the Democratic Republic of Congo, have made their way southward, many to South Africa, where some have been granted asylum (Landau 2005). Difficult anywhere, the distinction between political refugees and economic migrants is especially so in Southern Africa, where political oppression is often implemented through economic means, and where poor governance at national level has had such devastating economic consequences. The worsening political and economic situation in Zimbabwe, for example, has led to a growing diaspora, both in neighbouring states such as Botswana and South Africa and further afield, notably the United Kingdom. While the total number of Zimbabweans living in South Africa remains unknown, given the undocumented nature of much of this migration in addition to the ongoing disagreement about their legal status as refugees or asylum-seekers, unofficial estimates in the media put the figure at two million (*Mail and Guardian* online, 24 March 2005). One change noted by human rights lawyer Kaajal Ramjathan-Keogh, quoted in the same *Mail and Guardian* article, is that 'more women, some accompanied by children, are now illegally crossing the border'.

Undocumented or 'irregular' migrants have long been part of regional migration flows. For many women, migration is the only viable livelihood strategy when other means of support fail, such as after divorce, abandonment or widowhood. The following extract describes one undocumented female migrant's experience:

> Mrs Ndhlovu was born in 1955 in Kezi, a rural area of Matabeleland in southwestern Zimbabwe. By 1993 she was a divorcee with nine children, and in that year she decided to cross to South Africa in search of employment. She borrowed some South African currency, said goodbye to her children, and set out alone, on foot, without passport or visa, for the promised land. She paid a South African guide to get her through the border fences; she then made her way to Johannesburg,

where she lodged with members of a network of distant relations until she found employment. After about a year she found a good job at a daycare center in central Johannesburg. Her employers did not ask for South African identification documents and she did not bring the subject up. She has since settled down, found a boyfriend, and acquired identity documents. In 1995 she gave birth to her tenth child. (Barnes 2002:181)

This experience echoes those described by Miles (1991) in her work on female Swazi migrants to South Africa in the period 1920–1970, thus demonstrating the continuity between earlier female migration and current flows — albeit with something of a hiatus during the height of apartheid in the 1970s and 1980s. Quite how 'Mrs Ndhlovu' acquired identity documents, and whether this was through legal channels, is not made clear. For several women coming to the 'promised land', the experience is rather more bitter, as they encounter harassment and abuse, exploitative working conditions and, for some, detention and deportation. Lindela deportation centre near Johannesburg has become notorious for its poor conditions and maltreatment of detainees, who include a growing proportion of women (*Mail and Guardian* online, 24 March 2005). Trafficking of women is also a growing problem, with many ending up working in the sex trade in Johannesburg and other cities (*Mail and Guardian* online, 20 April 2006).

It is to be hoped that further research, along with improvements in official data collection, will yield a more comprehensive picture of both cross-border migration in general and of its gender composition in particular. Nevertheless, even with the limited data available, it is possible to assert with some confidence that female cross-border migration in this region has seen a significant increase since the end of apartheid in both absolute and relative terms, and that women make up a significant proportion of most migrant streams, whether refugees, undocumented migrants, temporary sojourners or holders of official residence permits. Factors driving the increase in regional migration since the end of apartheid include both pushes and pulls, many of them acting differently on men and women. The following section explores some of those gender dynamics, emphasizing the particular motives, experiences and circumstances of female migrants.

GENDER DIFFERENCES AND GENDER DYNAMICS IN CONTEMPORARY MIGRATION

Comparing the demographics of male and female migrants

Data from surveys conducted by the Southern African Migration Project[7] (SAMP) since the late 1990s present snapshots of the demographic profile of male and female migrants to South Africa from neighbouring countries. Rather than interviewing migrants actually living in South Africa, these surveys asked people in neighbouring countries about their experience of migration to South Africa, including their own previous migration experience and the past or current migration of other household members. Overall, the survey results confirm how long-standing and well-established a practice cross-border migration is in the region, with fully 42 percent of respondents in a 1997 survey having visited South Africa at least once themselves and 34 percent saying that at least one of their grandparents had been to South Africa (McDonald et al. 1998). That and more recent surveys also demonstrate the short-term, purpose-driven nature of much of the migration from the region, along with a low probability of future migration on a long-term or permanent basis. Most respondents in 1997 said they would prefer to raise their families in their home country and that they considered the overall quality of life to be higher in their home country than South Africa[8].

Comparisons between male and female respondents yielded interesting contrasts, indicating that the migration experiences of men and women differ in terms of migration motives, patterns and practices (Dodson 1998). The male dominance in migration was evident in the breakdown of the survey samples. There was an over-representation of women in the economically active age groups which have 'missing men' away in South Africa as migrant workers and thus not present to be included in the survey. This male bias seemed likely to persist, as male respondents were much more likely than female respondents to express a desire to migrate to South Africa in future, whether for a short time or more permanently. Women reporting personal migration experience tended to be older and more educated than men reporting migration experience, while women migrants' marital status suggests that divorce, marital breakdown and widowhood, along with other factors giving women the status of head of household, are all important drivers of female migration. While the majority of both male and female migrants were married, the incidence of migration among unmarried men was much higher than that among unmarried women. Based on the SAMP survey data, two significant migrant 'types' in this region are the young, unmarried male migrant worker, perpetuating a long tradition of male labour migration with its associated socio-cultural meaning and economic significance, and older women migrating when circumstances place them in the position of household head or otherwise make them primarily responsible for household livelihood. While not yet comprehensively analysed, more recent SAMP surveys on migration, poverty and remittances indicate continuity in these patterns and confirm the significance of both male and female migrants' remittances in household livelihoods and poverty alleviation.

Motives, patterns and experiences of male and female migration

The hints provided by the demographic analysis of men's and women's different migration motives were further borne out by the stated factors encouraging or discouraging migration, together with the different temporal and geographical patterns of male and female migration. The majority of male migrants go to South Africa for reasons associated directly with employment, while women's motives for migration include a far wider range of reasons, including shopping, trading, accessing health care, and visiting friends and relations, in addition to employment. This was true not only collectively but also individually, with individual women's stated motives for migration often including several of the above categories. This, of course, reflects the multiple social and economic roles fulfilled by women, including both productive and reproductive responsibilities. Unlike the structurally and geographically rigid system of male labour migration, women's migration is much more multi-purpose, making it hard to separate out 'labour migration' as a distinct category for female migrants.

Reflecting the diversity of women's migration motives are the temporal and spatial patterns of female migration. Women migrants make more frequent but shorter trips to South Africa, for example for purposes of trading or shopping. Male migration, by contrast, being more closely tied to employment, tends to be for longer periods of months or even years at a time. This was true both for reported previous migration and for intended future migration. Geographically, too, men's migration was more likely than women's to be tied to particular places of employment, such as specific mining towns, while women migrate to a wider range of places, including towns close to the borders of the countries concerned as well as major cities such as Johannesburg and Durban where there are greater opportunities for trading and shopping. The types of employment in which many migrant women are engaged, such as agricultural labour or domestic work, are also by their nature dispersed rather than concentrated.

Whereas male migrants stated mining and industry as their favoured type of employment in South Africa, hawking and trading are the most common economic activities for women migrants (Peberdy 2000; Peberdy & Crush 1998). This is borne out repeatedly in SAMP survey data as well as by anecdotal 'street' evidence in South Africa's towns and cities. Even where women stated 'shopping' as the reason for crossing the border into South Africa, this is far from conventional consumption of goods. Rather, women travel to South Africa to purchase goods for resale back in their home countries as a means of earning an income:

> Caroline [not her real name] from Harare comes to Jo'burg twice a month to shop. She does not like the place, but needs to come here to support her family. "I buy things here so I can sell them in Zimbabwe,"

says Caroline, who mostly buys industrial goods, such as rubber, for making couches. Her reasons for coming to Johannesburg are a wider variety and lower prices. There are thousands of so-called cross-border shoppers like Caroline who come to Jo'burg every year. They buy fridges, televisions, computers, clothes, food, household goods and personal care products. (Pelgrim 2006)

Among the problems faced by women like Caroline are the lack of affordable accommodation, fears for their personal safety, police harassment, and xenophobia from South Africans, especially those with whom they are seen to be in competition (Hunter & Skinner 2003; Pelgrim 2006). They are also faced with legal and bureaucratic obstacles, for example the restrictions on foreigners opening bank accounts in South Africa. Men also engage in such cross-border trade, but it is an especially important source of income for women, who have relatively less access to legal, formal employment in South Africa.

'Farm worker' was another category stated as a preferred form of employment, especially by women. Crush et al (2000) document the experiences of male and female migrants working in the agricultural sector: Mozambicans in Mpumalanga province, Zimbabweans in Limpopo province, and people from Lesotho in the Free State. Each of these areas has significant demand for seasonal agricultural workers, especially for fruit and vegetable picking and processing. Some of these workers are legal, documented migrants, while others are undocumented workers. Crush et al. report the exploitative working and living conditions endured by most farm workers in South Africa, but in particular by migrant workers and even more so by women. In addition to low wages and poor housing and living conditions, migrant farm workers reported incidences of verbal, physical and even sexual abuse.

Domestic work is another form of employment in South Africa for women from other countries, although competition for such employment from South African women is high and immigration policy does not technically allow 'unskilled' labour by foreigners except in areas of recognized labour shortage. Where undocumented migrants are employed as domestic workers in private homes, employment conditions are highly variable, being essentially at the whim of the employer, and with employees being in a particularly weak and vulnerable position. While hard evidence is lacking, it would be surprising if there were no cases of exploitation or abuse. Farm work and domestic work are still obviously more favourable that the sex work that some female migrants find themselves engaged in. 'Without legal documents, and far from their homes in Zimbabwe, Zambia, Mozambique, Lesotho and elsewhere, newly arrived female migrants are often forced into sex work simply because they lack alternatives' (*Mail and Guardian*, 20 April 2006).

Despite the obstacles and problems faced by female migrants in South Africa, a number of 'push' factors drive women to cross the country's borders: their individual personal and family circumstances, the lack of social and economic opportunities in their home countries, and widespread poverty and deprivation, exacerbated by the high incidence of Human immunodeficiency virus/Acquired Immune Deficiency Syndrome (HIV/AIDS) and other diseases. In such conditions, many of them experienced more acutely by women than by men, migration to South Africa represents a choice for women; a literal 'way out' of adverse situations, even if one bearing considerable risk and no guarantee of reward. Research on women's internal migration within South Africa points to the growing number of female-headed or even female-only households and to a parallel increase in female migration for purposes of employment or other income-earning activity (Casale & Posel 2002). It is reasonable to assume that similar changes in household composition are occurring in South Africa's neighbouring countries, and that these are driving increased female participation in internal as well as cross-border migration.

IMMIGRATION POLICY REFORM IN SOUTH AFRICA SINCE 1994

Policy reform: From alien control to skills import

Immigration policy reform in South Africa has been a slow, opaque and arduous process, and one in which the gender implications have been largely ignored. The early post-apartheid removal of racial and gender restrictions on would-be immigrants was countered by an initially reactionary, 'fortress South Africa' mentality, perhaps the product of an insecure sense of national identity as the new South Africa emerged from the deeply divided and discriminatory social order that had prevailed during apartheid (Peberdy 1999, 2001). Reflecting this sense of xenophobia, and fed by the prevailing idea that there were millions of illegal immigrants in the country, the 1995 Amendment of the 1991 Aliens Control Act employed both the language and the logic of immigration *control*.

The policy reform process then went through the requisite stages of a Green Paper in 1997, a White Paper in 1999 and a Bill in 2000. The Immigration Act was eventually passed by Parliament only in 2002, and underwent subsequent amendment in 2004. Public participation in immigration policy development was limited and came only late in the process. Barely any of the limited number of public interventions argued for changes on the basis of likely gender bias. The Immigration Act (2002) and subsequent Immigration Amendment Act (2004) dropped the xenophobic tone of the earlier policy and legislative instruments. Instead they are characterized by hard-nosed economic imperatives that see immigrants as temporary sojourners bringing needed skills, rather than as men and women to be included as full members of South African society. As argued below, these imperatives are likely to result in *de facto* gender discrimination, as women lack many of the financial and skills-based qualifications required to be admitted to the country legally as temporary or permanent residents. The women described above, seeking a livelihood in South Africa as a means of escaping or alleviating poverty at home, are certainly not the type of immigrant the country hopes to attract, and indeed are among the people the Acts seek to keep out on anything but a temporary basis.

The underlying premises and objectives of the Act have to reconcile sometimes contradictory aims. Skilled migrants have to be admitted, but unskilled migrants kept out. South African labour has to be protected from unfair competition, while industry has to have access to the labour it requires at the lowest cost. South Africa has to compete globally for skilled workers in certain categories, at the same time as it is losing many of its own skilled citizens to other countries. And, of course, both national security interests and the human rights of migrants have to be protected. This is a tough balancing act to achieve. Yet even on its own terms, explicitly prioritizing economic motives, the Act risks failure by its narrow interpretation of skills and its refusal to acknowledge either the social embeddedness or the straightforward embodiment of skills in individual, flesh-and-blood, *gendered* human beings.

These economic imperatives are clearly set out in the 2002 Act's preamble. The Act 'aims at setting in place a new system of immigration control which ensures that…the needs and aspirations of the age of *globalization* are respected' and 'the *South African economy* may have access at all times to the full measure of *needed contributions by foreigners*' (my italics); but also that 'the contribution of foreigners in the South African labour market does not adversely impact on existing labour standards and the rights and expectations of South African workers' and 'a policy connection is maintained between foreigners working in South Africa and our nationals'. This is modified in the 2004 Immigration Amendment Act, which 'aims at setting in place a new system of immigration control which ensures that… economic growth is promoted through the employment of *needed foreign labour*, foreign investment is facilitated, the entry of *exceptionally skilled* or qualified people is enabled [and] *skilled human resources* are increased' (my italics). While the statement about globalization has been excised, the emphasis on labour and skills is, if anything, reinforced. In its provisions, too, the Immigration Amendment Act reduces some of the onerous requirements of certification and monitoring for companies wishing to employ foreign nationals. It thus further demonstrates the official construction of immigration first and foremost as an engine of *national economic growth*. Given the gendering of the labour market in particular economic sectors, the way in which 'needed foreigners' are identified

Gender, Migration and Livelihoods

and labour and skills shortages are determined results inevitably in gender-biased migrant streams.

The 2002 and 2004 Immigration Acts: Discrimination by default?

While not intentionally or overtly discriminatory on gender or other grounds, the new immigration policy regime as enshrined in the 2002 and 2004 Acts are likely to discriminate against women in numerous ways. It is too early to tell what their actual impact will be in gender terms, as the regulations and procedures governing the administration and enforcement of the Acts is only now coming into effect. Most of the provisions of the Acts, rather than being about permanent immigration, are instead about various forms of temporary residence, with strict controls on the employment status and length of residence in each of a host of different permit categories. Many of the categories prohibit employment altogether, and the multiple categories and sub-categories of permit allowing employment reflect the juggling act required to try and attract and accommodate 'needed foreigners' while keeping out 'un-needed foreigners'.

The main permit categories for temporary residence are the following, each having gender implications not only for the individual permit-holder but also for any partner or family member they might want to bring with them to South Africa.

- Work permits
- Treaty permits
- Corporate permits
- Business permits
- Student permits
- Retirement permits
- Exchange permits
- Asylum seekers
- Visitor's permits
- Cross-border passes
- Relative's permits

Permit categories allowing employment include four different types of work permit (quota, general, exceptional skills and intra-company transfer), the treaty and corporate permits that allow the continued import of foreign labour and access to 'needed' foreign employees, and business permits that allow individual foreigners to set up businesses in South Africa. Student, retirement and exchange permits allow only limited work activity, while visitor's permits, cross-border passes and relative's permits explicitly prohibit employment. This 'salami' approach, slicing immigration into ever-thinner and more tightly defined and demarcated categories, is a growing

Table 5.1 Maximum number of people to be admitted in quota work permit categories (Republic of South Africa, 2003).

Postgraduate degree and 5 years experience	90,000	Certificate and 5 years experience	70,000
Graduate degree and 5 years experience	75,000	Certificate and 5 years entrepreneurship etc.	70,000
Graduate degree and 2 years experience	70,000	5 years entrepreneurship, craftsmanship or management	75,000
Degree and 5 years experience	70,000	5 years of skills acquired through training	90,000
Degree and 2 years experience	70,000	Skills acquired through training	60,000

trend around the world, as described in other chapters in this volume. In effect it creates a system of 'influx control' based on skills, qualifications and other abilities to meet particular labour market needs.

Closer examination of each of these categories reveals the potential for gender discrimination and the creation or perpetuation of male-dominated migrant streams. Within the temporary residence permits, the quota work permit categories were originally expressed in terms of qualifications, skills, training and experience (see Table 5.1). More recently, in February 2006, the Department of Home Affairs published revised categories of professions and occupational classes permitting entry under the quota permit system. The list could almost be one outlining the global economy's most male-dominated employment sectors. Too lengthy to reproduce here, it is nevertheless worth describing in summary form. The primary categories in the schedule are Science and engineering, Education professions, Information technology professions, Health and medical sciences professions, Agricultural sciences, and Management and commerce professions. Each is divided into specific sub-categories, for example avionics engineers (for which the quota is 250), astrophysicists (200) and foundry metallurgists (500). Under education, the sole designated category is math and science teachers (1000). The only identified category in which there might realistically be expected to be a female majority is that of jewelry designer (250).

Given the widespread gender differential in access to education and training, particularly in the areas identified as sectors experiencing skilled labour shortage, the implementation of such a quota system is likely to reinforce the existing male bias in skilled migration to the country. Further, as noted above, this male bias in educational attainment is especially marked on the African continent, source of a growing proportion of migrants to South Africa. The quotas are intended to be reviewed annually by the Minister of Home Affairs in consultation with the Ministers of Labour and Trade and Industry. However revised and redefined, they demonstrate the 'salami' approach to immigration, the prioritization of certain types of highly-skilled immigrant, and the resulting likelihood of a male-dominated migrant flow in the quota permit category. Bringing no associated rights of residence for partners or family members, except under short-term visitors' permits prohibiting employment, this particular work permit category is likely to encourage migration by unaccompanied males.

Corporate and treaty permits are equally or even more likely to result in male-dominated migrant flows. These categories of permit were explicitly designed to perpetuate the migrant labour system, and in particular to allow the mining industry to continue to draw labour from neighbouring countries such as Lesotho and Mozambique (Crush & Tshitereke 2001). These permits bring no rights of residence for family members. The men who come into the country in these categories are in South Africa to provide labour, and are expected to return home when their term of employment expires. The other categories of work permit (general work permits, exceptional skills permits, and intra-company transfers) are also likely to create or perpetuate male-dominated migrant streams, if not as extreme as in the case of quota, treaty and corporate permits. The criteria of capital assets for business immigrants are likewise likely to discriminate in favour of men. Overall, then, male migration under the new policy regime is likely to be concentrated at the two ends of the skills spectrum: providing difficult and dangerous manual labour at one end and high-skilled intellectual labour at the other. Not only does this perpetuate the situation during apartheid, albeit with the racial dimension removed, but it mirrors the pattern found in many other parts of the world, as outlined elsewhere in this volume.

There is more to the gender implications of these permit categories than the probable male dominance amongst holders of temporary residence permits. The selection of immigrants in terms of abstract categories of skills, capital and labour market need is to deny the tying of skills to individual persons and persons to other persons in bonds of family, friendship and social networks. Thinking through each of the work permit categories in social terms, and especially in terms of gender and gender relations, immediately throws up a number or potential problems. Without associated rights of residence and employment for partners or family members, except under visitors' permits, most of the temporary residence permit categories are likely to create male-dominated migrant streams. Given that more men than women are likely to be the primary applicants for residence permits, these provisions are in effect likely to discriminate against women, many of whom will be legally prohibited from seeking employment if they have come to South Africa accompanying their male partners. Work-permit holders who have partners and families may thus be forced to leave them behind in their country of origin, thereby creating complicated and problematic transnational family structures. These restrictions are likely to act as disincentives to the type of skilled foreigner the policy was designed to attract.

For the women of the region, the most significant permit category in the new immigration regime is that of cross-border passes. This category of entry is for citizens of prescribed foreign countries which share a border with South Africa, but who do not hold a passport, and in effect are equivalent to a multiple-entry visitor's permit. They allow tourism, education, business, medical treatment and visiting relatives but *not* work. Thus while prohibiting formal employment, they do permit precisely the sort of shopping and trading activities engaged in by large numbers of women from the region as a source of income and livelihood. These cross-border passes are especially significant in facilitating women's multi-purpose migration, which often combines social functions, such as visiting friends or relatives, with some business activity, such as buying goods for resale in their home country. This is perhaps the only permit category under the Immigration Act and its subsequent regulations that might be said to favour — or at least not to disfavour — women. Along with the bilateral labour treaties and corporate permits that undergird the mine labour system, it is also one of the few sections of the Act that acknowledges the particular needs and claims of South Africa's neighbouring countries.

CONCLUSION

South Africa's new immigration policy prioritizes narrowly-defined labour market need over other possible criteria for entry to the country. Beyond the categories of cross-border passes and permits allowing mine labour, it is largely irrelevant to regional migration realities. The Act is certainly not beneficial to women, setting up the potential for a marked male bias in almost every permit category. The hurdles of education, professional category, and ownership of capital are all effectively higher for women, especially for women from the region. It is, in other words, a classic case of state masculinism. To quote my own conclusion from a previous publication:

> The two normative models the Act implies are of a skilled male worker with a dependent female spouse and children; and an 'unskilled' male migrant worker unaccompanied by spouse or family. Looking at the reality of female migration in the region, there is little in the Act that will make life easier for the Zimbabwean domestic worker in Johannesburg, the Basotho farmworker in South Africa's Free State province, or the wife of the migrant Mozambican mineworker. Where is the flexibility that might facilitate the multi-purpose migration practised by Southern African female migrants, migration that might include some work even when it is not undertaken primarily for the purposes of employment? The Act is out of step with the reality of Southern African migrants' lives and needs, and especially of female migrants' lives and needs. (Dodson & Crush 2004: 115)

Yet people from neighbouring countries continue to cross South Africa's borders, regardless of what the Act decrees. Although the Act constrains their livelihood options and serves to 'illegalize' their employment, Southern African women are re-establishing earlier patterns of cross-border migration. In so doing, whether legally or otherwise, they are strengthening their own and their households' livelihoods and contributing to poverty alleviation. While it is important to avoid either over-valorizing female migrants as a resilient socio-economic safety net or presenting them as hapless victims of patriarchy and gender discrimination, an appreciation of the social and economic significance of women's migration adds to the arguments for establishing a more flexible, gender-equitable, *developmental* regional migration regime.

NOTES

1. 'Kraal' is a South African term referring to the traditional African homestead in rural areas, while 'compound' is the term used to describe mine labourers' housing at their place of employment. The use of these two terms, which are becoming increasingly obsolete, is used here to signify that this system of migration, while entrenched and long-standing, is no longer the sole dominant form of regional population movement.
2. Given the notorious unreliability of census figures on immigrants and in particular the unlikelihood of capturing undocumented migrants in census data, these figures should not be taken as accurate in any absolute sense. They may, however, be illustrative of general trends, and in particular of trends in the gender composition of migration flows.
3. SADC is the Southern African Development Community, consisting of Angola, Botswana, Democratic Republic of Congo (DRC), Lesotho, Malawi, Mauritius, Mozambique, Namibia, Seychelles, South Africa, Swaziland, Tanzania, Zambia and Zimbabwe.
4. The proportion of Southern African migrants in male migration is even higher at 71 percent, but this reflects the dominance of mining in formal labour migration.
5. This term, while obviously problematic, and especially so in the South African context, is used here to indicate that the deracialization of South Africa's immigration policy has allowed access to people who were formerly denied entry, including immigrants from many different African and Asian countries.
6. This is also a reflection of the gender discrimination in apartheid-era immigration legislation, which gave rights of permanent residence to the wives of male South African citizens but not to the husbands of female South African citizens, thus (ironically) encouraging female immigration. Immigrants of whichever gender of course also had to be assimilable into the country's white population.
7. The Southern African Migration Project is a research, training and policy network with partners in Canada, South Africa, Namibia, Botswana, Lesotho, Swaziland, Zimbabwe, Mozambique and Malawi. It is funded by the Canadian International Development Agency and the UK's Department for International Development.

8. Of course if the same survey were to be conducted today, findings might be rather less positive, especially in Zimbabwe.

REFERENCES

Barnes, T. (2002) 'Virgin territory? Travel and migration by African women in twentieth-century Southern Africa'. In J. Allman, S. Geiger and N. Musisi (eds.), *Women in African Colonial Histories*. Bloomington and Indianapolis: Indiana University Press.

Bonner, P. (1990) 'Desirable or undesirable Basotho women? Liquor, prostitution and the migration of Basotho women to the Rand, 19201945'. In C Walker (ed.), *Women and Gender in Southern Africa to 1945*. Oxford: James Currey, Cape Town: David Philip.

Bozzoli, B., with M. Nkotsoe (1991) *Women of Phokeng: Consciousness, Life Strategy and Migrancy in South Africa, 1900–1983*. Portsmouth, NH: Heinemann.

Brown, M., D. Kaplan and J-B Meyer (2002) 'The brain drain: an outline of skilled emigration from South Africa'. In McDonald, D. A. and Crush, J. S. (eds.), *Destinations Unknown: Perspectives on the Brain Drain in Southern Africa*. Pretoria: Africa Institute.

Campbell, C. (1997) 'Migrancy, masculine identities and AIDS: The psycho-social context of HIV transmission on the South African gold mines'. *Social Science and Medicine* 45(2): 273–281.

Casale, D. and D. Posel (2002) 'The feminization of the labour force in South Africa: An analysis of recent data and trends'. *South African Journal of Economics* 70(1): 156–184.

Cockerton, C. M. (1996) 'Less a barrier, more a line: the migration of Bechuanaland women to South Africa, 1850–1930'. *Journal of Historical Geography* 22: 291–307.

Coplan, D. (2001) 'You have left me wandering about: Basotho women and the culture of mobility'. In D. Hodgson and S. McCurdy (eds.) *"Wicked" Women and the Reconfiguration of Gender in Africa*. Portsmouth, NH: Heinemann, Oxford: James Currey, Cape Town: David Philip.

Crush, J. S. (1987) *The Struggle for Swazi Labour*. Montreal and Kingston: McGill-Queen's University Press.

——— (2000) 'The dark side of democracy: Migration, xenophobia and human rights in South Africa'. *International Migration* 38: 103–134.

——— (2003) 'South Africa: New nation, new migration policy?' *Migration Information Source*, June 2003. Accessed online at http://www.migrationinformation.org.

Crush, J. S. and B. J. Dodson (forthcoming) 'Another lost decade: The failure of South Africa's post-apartheid migration policy'. *Tijdschrift voor Economische en Sociale Geografie*.

Crush, J. S., A. Jeeves and D. Yudelman (1991) *South Africa's Labor Empire*. Boulder, CO: Westview Press.

Crush, J. S., D. A. McDonald and V. Williams (2000) *Losing Our Minds: Skilled Migration and the South African Brain Drain*. SAMP Migration Policy Series no. 18. Kingston: Southern African Migration Project, Cape Town: IDASA.

Crush, J. S. (editor) with C. Mather, F. Mathebula, D. Lincoln, C. Maririke and T. Ulicki (2000) *Borderline Farming: Foreign Migrants in South African Commercial Agriculture*. SAMP Migration Policy Series no. 16. Kingston: Southern African Migration Project, Cape Town: IDASA.

Crush, J. S. and C. Tshitereke (2001) 'Contesting migrancy: The foreign labor debate in post-1994 South Africa'. *Africa Today* 48(3): 49–70.
Crush, J. S. and V. Williams (2003) 'Making up the numbers: Measuring "illegal immigration" to South Africa'. *SAMP Migration Policy Briefs* no. 3.
Danso, R. and D. A. McDonald (2001) 'Writing xenophobia: Immigration and the print media in post-apartheid South Africa'. *Africa Today* 48(3): 115–137.
Dodson, B. J. (1998) *Women on the Move: Gender and Cross-Border Migration to South Africa*. SAMP Migration Policy Series no. 9. Kingston: Southern African Migration Project, Cape Town: IDASA.
Dodson, B. J. (2002) *Gender and the Brain Drain from South Africa*. SAMP Migration Policy Series no. 23. Kingston: Southern African Migration Project, Cape Town: IDASA.
Dodson, B. J. and J. S. Crush (2004) 'A report on gender discrimination in South Africa's 2002 Immigration Act: Masculinizing the migrant'. *Feminist Review* 77: 96–119.
Elder, G. S. (2003) *Hostels, Sexuality and the Apartheid Legacy: Malevolent Geographies*. Athens: Ohio University Press.
Francis, E. (2002) 'Gender, migration and multiple livelihoods: Cases from Eastern and Southern Africa'. *The Journal of Development Studies* 38(5): 167–190.
Gotz, G. and A. Simone (2003) 'On belonging and becoming in African cities'. In Tomlinson, R., R. A. Beauregard, L. Bremner and X. Mangcu (eds.). *Emerging Johannesburg: Perspectives on the Postapartheid City*. New York and London: Routledge.
Harries, P. (1994) *Work, Culture and Identity: Migrant Labourers in Mozambique and South Africa c. 1860–1910*. Portsmouth, NH: Heinemann.
Hunter, N. and C. Skinner (2003) 'Foreign street traders working in inner-city Durban: Local government policy challenges'. *Urban Forum* 14(4): 301–319.
Landau, L. B. (2005) *Urbanization, Nativism and the Rule of Law in South Africa's "Forbidden" Cities*. Vancouver Centre of Excellence, Research on Immigration and Integration in the Metropolis, Working Paper Series no. 05-05.
Lurie, M. (2006) 'The epidemiology of migration and HIV/AIDS in South Africa'. *Journal of Ethnic and Migration Studies* 32(4): 649–666.
Mail and Guardian online (24 March 2005) 'SA is revolving door to desperate Zimbabweans'. Accessed online at http://www.mg.co.za.
Mail and Guardian online (20 April 2006) 'Migrants find sex trade a dead-end street'. Accessed online at http://www.mg.co.za.
Mattes, R., J. S. Crush and W. Richmond (2002) 'The brain gain and legal immigration to South Africa'. In McDonald, D. A. and Crush, J. S. (eds.) *Destinations Unknown: Perspectives on the Brain Drain in Southern Africa*. Pretoria: Africa Institute.
McDonald, D. A., J. Gay, L. Zinyama, R. Mattes and F. de Vletter (1998) *Challenging Xenophobia: Myths and Realities about Cross-Border Migration in Southern Africa*. SAMP Migration Policy Series no. 7. Kingston: Southern African Migration Project, Cape Town: IDASA.
Miles, M. (1991) *Missing Women: A Study of Swazi Female Migration to the Witwatersrand, 1920–1970*. Unpublished MA thesis, Queen's University, Kingston, Ontario.
Moodie, T. D. (1994) *Going for Gold: Men, Mines and Migration*. Berkeley: University of California Press.
Murray, C. (1981) *Families Divided: The Impact of Migrant Labour in Lesotho*. Cambridge: Cambridge University Press.
Peberdy, S. (1999) *Selecting Immigrants: Nationalism and National Identity in South Africa's Immigration Policies, 1920–1998*. Unpublished PhD thesis, Queen's University, Kingston, Ontario.

Peberdy, S. (2000) 'Border crossings: Small entrepreneurs and cross-border trade between South Africa and Mozambique'. *Tijdschrift voor Economische en Sociale Geografie* 91(4): 361–378.

Peberdy, S. (2001) 'Imagining immigration: Inclusive identities and exclusive policies in post-1994 South Africa'. *Africa Today* 48(3): 15–32.

Peberdy, S. and J. S. Crush (1998) *Trading Places: Cross-Border Traders and the South African Informal Sector.* SAMP Migration Policy Series no. 6. Kingston: Southern African Migration Project, Cape Town: IDASA.

Pelgrim, R. (2006) 'A (week-long) trip to the shops'. *Mail and Guardian* online (14 April 2006). Accessed online at http://www.mg.co.za.

Republic of South Africa, Department of Home Affairs (2003) Immigration Act 2002 (No. 13 of 2002): Draft Immigration Regulations. *Government Gazette* vol. 453 no. 24587. Pretoria, 14 March 2003.

Republic of South Africa, Department of Home Affairs (2006) Immigration Act 2002 (No. 13 of 2002): Specific Professional Categories and Specific Occupational Classes. *Government Gazette* no. 28480. Pretoria, 8 February 2006.

Republic of South Africa, The Presidency (2002) Immigration Act: No. 13 of 2002. *Government Gazette* vol. 443 no. 23478. Cape Town, 31 May 2002.

Republic of South Africa, The Presidency (2004) Immigration Amendment Act: No. 19 of 2004. *Government Gazette* vol. 472 no. 26901. Cape Town, 31 May 2002.

Simone, A. (2000) 'Going South: African immigrants in Johannesburg'. In Nuttall, S. and C-A. Michael (eds.), *Senses of Culture: South African Culture Studies.* Oxford and Cape Town: Oxford University Press.

Statistics South Africa (2004) *Census 2001: Primary Tables South Africa, Census '99 and 2001 Compared.* Pretoria: Statistics South Africa (report no. 03-02-04).

Tshitereke, C. (2004) *GEAR and Labour in Post-Apartheid South Africa: A Study of the Gold Mining Industry, 1987–2004.* Unpublished PhD thesis, Queen's University, Kingston, Ontario.

Ulicki, T. and J. S. Crush (2000) 'Gender, farmwork and women's migration from Lesotho to the new South Africa'. *Canadian Journal of African Studies* 34(1): 64–79.

Walker, C. (1990) 'Gender and the development of the migrant labour system c. 1850–1930'. In C. Walker (ed.). *Women and Gender in Southern Africa to 1945.* Oxford: James Currey, Cape Town: David Philip.

Western, J. (2001) 'Africa is coming to the Cape'. *Geographical Review* 91(4): 617–640.

Wright, C. (1995) 'Gender awareness in migration theory: Synthesizing actor and structure in Southern Africa'. *Development and Change* 26(4): 771–791.

6 Feminised Migration in East and Southeast Asia and the Securing of Livelihoods

Nicola Piper and Keiko Yamanaka

INTRODUCTION

Since the 1980s labour migration from Southeast Asia to other sub-regions in Asia[1] has become increasingly feminised linked to changes in the composition of labour markets and availability of jobs. The specific socio-economic developmental paths chosen by governments in Southeast and East Asia have resulted in producing employment opportunities and constraints differentiated by sex (Gills & Piper 2002). Migration policies, too, have been designed to address specific labour market needs which are often gendered. Migrant women work largely in informal service economies of the countries of destination whose governments are primarily concerned with national survival in global competition. As a result little, if any, attention is paid to international labour standards and human rights. At the places of origin, it is often male un- or underemployment which creates the need for more and more women to enter the labour force (Oishi 2005; Sassen 2003). Cross-border migration is an important means of securing livelihoods in the absence of jobs 'at home' or a deficit in 'decent work' — and according to the ILO, the latter should be at the core of social and economic development (ILO 1999). Given the current state of affairs, access to, and the ability to remain in, paid overseas work is a priority for many migrant women (Briones 2006).

Feminist scholarship has demonstrated that economic independence and security of livelihoods are of vital importance in order for women to be empowered and to claim their rights, but it has also been acknowledged that economic rights have to be addressed in tandem with political and social rights if women are to reach full potential (IDRC 2006). Empowerment is, thus, linked to rights and socio-economic development. This is also evident in the context of international migration, but further complicated by migrants moving across borders and thus involving origin and destination countries. Socio-economic empowerment, rights and development, therefore, have to be approached from two ends at least (transit countries too are folded into this). Creating jobs and livelihoods in low-income countries, for instance, is vital if migration is to become more of a choice than a necessity (GCIM 2005). At the destination, it is the recognition and implementation of migrant women's labour rights which contributes to their socio-economic empowerment (see also Piper, chapter 8 of this volume).

These issues — rights and development as they relate to international migration – have also appeared on the global policy scene. The International Labour Office (hereafter ILO) has developed guidelines for a rights-based approach to labour migration and the UN called a High Level Dialogue on 'International Migration and Development' in September 2006, which was the first event of this kind dealing exclusively with this subject. What these initiatives have done is provide an overview of the complex issues involved in the discussion on how to maximize the positive outcomes of migration. Concrete solutions, however, have not yet been provided by these initiatives — and it is probably too early to expect any. Neither does our paper provide any answer. Our aim is more modest: to highlight the relevance of the current policy debate to migrant women in the specific context of regional migratory flows in East/Southeast (E/SE) Asia.

Despite being global in scope, the most significant flows of migration still occur within the same region, generally from low-income to mid-income or high income countries in the developing world (UN 2004, 2006). This can also be observed with regard to cross-border migratory movements within Asia. Our analysis of gendered labour migration, therefore, takes an intra-regional approach that links source and destination countries in their exchange of labour and formation of their migration policies. We do not discuss the flow of Asian migrants to destinations beyond Asia.

We begin by outlining the quantitative and qualitative aspects of the feminisation of migration in E/SE Asia to then shift to a more detailed assessment of migration policies and the major categories by which women migrate. What follows is a discussion of the global policy discourse and its emphasis on management and developmental aspects of migration under the overarching concern for migrant women's ability to secure livelihoods.

FEMINISATION OF MIGRATION

According to the 2006 UNFPA report on women and international migration, Asia as a whole is one of the two regions in this world[2] where there are still slightly more male than female migrants by the year 2005, but the number of women migrating from some countries in Asia has surpassed that of men (2006:23). Another UN report states that "female migrants are particularly underrepresented in Asia" (2006:33). Men, by contrast, migrate from almost all developing countries in Asia, whereas there are only three source countries from which the bulk of female migrants originate: the Philippines, Sri Lanka, and Indonesia. This is partly a reflection of the demand structure. Many jobs are in the construction sector, security services, or in specific service jobs as drivers in West Asia, and in the construction, plantation or shipyard sectors in Southeast Asia. The relatively low numbers of South Asian women (with the exception of Sri Lanka)[3] migrating as domestic or factory workers has largely to do with the strict social norms imposed on lower and unskilled women restricting their mobility. Another reason is that statistics often capture only formalised jobs under temporary contract schemes. Women are mainly represented in these as domestic workers although they also migrate in other informal streams which are not captured by official statistics.

The feminisation of migration in Asia is in fact usually associated with out-going flows from Indonesia, Sri Lanka and the Philippines where women make up 62–75 percent of workers who are deployed legally on an annual basis (Asis 2005).[4] If, however, unauthorized migrants were factored in, the feminisation of migration would involve more countries. Thai women, for example, are underrepresented in statistics of legal migration, but they predominate among irregular migrants or those presumed to be trafficked. Thailand has also been the destination for unauthorized migrant women, such as Burmese women working as domestic workers. There are, however, important gender variations with regard to unauthorized migration: in the context of Indonesia, most unauthorized migrants are men going to neighbouring Malaysia to work on plantations and in the construction sector. In the Philippines, men and women are more or less equally represented in unauthorized migration streams (Asis 2005). In addition, if the increasing number of international marriages between Asians were included, the gendered landscape of migration within Asia would take on a different dimension.[5]

The demand for domestic workers and so-called 'entertainers' in E/SE Asia has also been an important driving force behind the feminisation of migration. Changes are gradually becoming evident not only with regard to the increased volume of female migrants, but also with regard to the diversified patterns of their migration, including source, destinations, working conditions and skill levels. The largest proportion of these women, documented and undocumented, continue to work in job categories characteristically assigned to female migrants such as live-in maids, care givers, entertainers, sex workers and other service employees (e.g., *Asian and Pacific Migration Journal* 2003). A smaller but substantial proportion of women work in the garment sector as well as agricultural and fish farm hands. It seems as if it is in particular women from South Asia — Bangladesh and Sri Lanka — who have been deployed in Malaysia and the Middle East as garment workers (Dannecker 2005; Dias & Wanasundera 2002; INSTRAW & IOM 2000). Vietnam has become a source country of male and female factory workers in Korea and Taiwan and more recently also of a small number of domestic workers to Taiwan (Dang 2000). Very little is known about Cambodian out-migrants who seem to be mainly destined for Thailand. Their flows are divided into short-term/range border crossing (typically seasonal agricultural workers, the majority of whom are women) and longer-term/range movements (mainly by construction workers, porters, factory and food processing workers, most of whom men) (Sophal & Sovannarith 1999). Fewer but increasing numbers of women migrate to other Asian countries as wives of male citizens (Piper & Roces 2003). Recently, skilled and professional women have migrated in response to expanding employment opportunities in business, health, education, and services (Raghuram 2000; Willis & Yeoh 2000; Thang et al. 2002). But the overall numbers of skilled women moving within Asia appears to be small.

Short-term contract work (and it has to be noted that such contract work is both a characteristic of lesser skilled sectors such as domestic work as well as highly skilled workers in the IT sector) leads women to migrate and re-migrate repeatedly. Likewise, a considerable number of women manage to obtain extensions on their contracts adding up to a period of many years, if not decades, abroad. In the absence of family reunification policies in Asia, migrant families often become transnationally "split households", either with one parent working abroad or both doing so in different countries. Their mothers, while working abroad, experience a phenomenon referred to as "transnational motherhood" (Hondagneu-Sotelo & Avila 1997; Hondagneu-Sotelo 2001; Hochschild 2002). The reversed gender roles in which a wife becomes the family's breadwinner while her husband attends to the children and household, have frequently resulted in marital conflict. Such role reversal has often challenged the masculinity of men, especially those who are permanently unemployed in a stagnant economy (Gamburd 2001; Parreñas 2001).

Although the issue of whether or not 'sex and entertainment' related jobs should be categorized as 'labour migration' is highly contested among feminists, we do not wish to engage with this debate in this chapter (see Piper 2005b for a more detailed discussion) but simply want to mention here the fact that a significant number of Southeast Asian (and other) women have been entering East Asian countries, especially Japan and Korea, in response to a great demand for sexual labour. In order to let these women enter legally (albeit limited to a period of six months), the already existing visa category for artists or entertainers was broadened in the 1980s to include bar hostesses (who constitute potential sex workers). As a result, migrant women, mostly from the Philippines, Thailand and Korea, have entered East Asian countries to work in the lucrative sex and entertainment industries via both legal and illegal channels.

STATISTICS OF FEMINISED MIGRATION: 1970S TO 2000S

Outflow of women from Asia

Although international migration has gradually become a global phenomenon since the 1970s, reliable information is lacking in many countries and areas of the world (United Nations 2003:1). Asia is no exception. International migration emerged in the 1980s as a policy concern to the Gulf countries. There were immigration regulations in many Asian countries inherited from the colonial period which were not rewritten after independence. There were also restrictions on emigration, as in India from 1922. For postcolonial nations conflictual border identities led to migration policies inflicted on the basis of the borders that they felt needed most policing. Until the 1970s, migration and settlement were often frequent and informal, primarily in areas where people could cross borders on foot or by boats to settle among others of similar language and culture. As a result of rapid industrialisation, a larger inexpensive and flexible labour force was required in countries such as Malaysia and Singapore so that governments began to legislate new policies on migration.

The presence of large numbers of irregular migrants throughout the region has made it difficult to estimate accurately the volume, direction and characteristics of migrants. Sex comprises a crucial piece of information in understanding the nature, process and consequence of international migration, yet it is frequently ignored in sources of migration data (United Nations 2003). In Asia, one cause of the under-representation of women in official statistics is the state-imposed restrictions and periodic bans on the out-flow of women (INSTRAW & IOM 2000). As a result, many women use unofficial channels.

Using the most reliable statistics available, Table 6.1 shows outflows of female migrant workers, mostly live-in domestics, from the four major sending countries in Asia from 1979 to 1996: Sri Lanka, Indonesia, Philippines and Thailand (United Nations 2003: 44–47). These data suggest that feminisation of migration began as early as the late 1970s, when Sri Lanka sent 12,000 to 30,000 women migrants (about 50 percent of the total annual flow of both sexes) as domestic workers, mostly to the Middle East. Feminisation of migration has accelerated world-wide since the 1980s as more women have joined the global labour force. By the mid-1990s, totals of 86,000 Indonesian women and 42,000 Thai women had left their countries, accounting for 66 percent and 20 percent, respectively, of each country's total outflow. In 1994, 154,000 Filipino women, 59 percent of the Philippine's total migrants, left their country. In 1995, 126,000 Sri Lankan women, 73 percent of the Sri Lanka's total migrants, did so. In 2001, 650,000 Sri Lankan women, 70 percent of the country's overseas population, worked as domestics in eight Middle Eastern countries, five Asian countries and three European countries (Saroor 2003: 209–10).

The Philippines has emerged as the world's largest labour exporting-country, overtaking Mexico. It has always had the most dispersed workforce — as of 2000, approximately 5 to 7 million overseas workers, the majority of them women, in more than 160 countries (Lindio-McGovern 2003: 514).

Table 6.1 Number of unskilled female migrant workers by sending country and proportion of females in total outflows, 1979–1996*

	Sri Lanka		Indonesia		Philippines		Thailand	
	Total number	% of females	Total number	% of females	Total number	% of females	Total number	% of females
1979	12,251	47.3	–**	–	–	–	–	–
1980	14,529	50.8	–	–	3,862	18.0	–	–
1981	30,135	52.5	–	–	–	–	–	–
1982	5,400	24.0	–	–	–	–	–	–
1983	7,819	43.2	12,018	48.4	–	–	–	–
1984	5,762	36.7	20,425	48.0	–	–	–	–
1985	11,792	95.1	39,960	49.4	–	–	–	–
1986	5,150	31.4	39,078	47.7	–	–	7,194	6.4
1987	5,474	34.0	44,291	49.0	180,441	47.2	9,752	9.2
1988	10,119	54.9	49,586	48.6	–	–	15,062	12.7
1989	16,044	58.4	–	–	–	–	–	–
1990	27,248	63.9	–	–	–	–	–	–
1991	43,612	67.0	–	–	–	–	–	–
1992	29,159	65.3	–	–	–	–	–	–
1993	31,600	64.8	85,696	66.0	138,242*	54.0	41,830	19.4
1994	43,796	72.8	–	–	153,504*	59.2	–	–
1995	125,988	73.3	–	–	124,822*	58.3	31,586	15.6
1996	119,456	73.5	–	–	111,487*	54.2	28,642	13.3

*Numbers of newly hired only; **Numbers of migrants by sex are frequently unavailable.
Source: United Nations Economic and Social Affairs 2003:4 5–46.

STOCK OF MIGRANT WOMEN IN E/SE ASIA

Turning to the stock of female migrants in Asia's major labour importing countries, Table 6.2 lists by country the number and proportion of females to the total migrant population in various occupations.[6] Table 6.2 indicates that, by 2002 there were at least a total of 1.4 million foreign women working in the major seven labour importing countries of the region (Singapore, Malaysia, Thailand, Taiwan, Hong Kong, Korea and Japan). Singapore has the highest ratio of foreign migrants to the local population (30%). Among the approximately 500,000 to 600,000 foreign workers, at least 180,000 are male construction workers and approximately 140,000 are domestic workers (Huang & Yeoh 2003:82), mostly from the Philippines, Indonesia and Sri Lanka. Apart from domestic work, the health sector constitutes another significant employer of foreign women (Piper 2005a). According to the Singapore Nursing Board's Annual Report of 2003, there were a total of 18,392 Registered (RN) and Enrolled nurses (EN), of whom 2818 RNs and 1807 ENs were foreign. They were mainly from the Philippines, Republic of China, Malaysia and others like Myanmar and Sri Lanka. The numbers have apparently not changed much in the past few years (Piper, email communication, Singapore Nursing Association, July 12, 2005).

By 1995 Malaysia had become the largest importer of labour in Asia in terms of overall numbers. Between 1997 and 2002, the manufacturing and domestic sectors housed the largest shares of documented migrants (37% and 22%, respectively) (Narayanan and Lai 2005: 37). Although women entirely staff the latter and are well represented in the former, it is estimated that Malaysia's entire foreign workforce is 68 percent male (Piper 2005c). In 2001, approximately 162,000 women from Indonesia and the Philippines were employed as domestic workers (Chin 2003). The country receives the largest number of its unauthorised workers from its neighbours, Indonesia, Philippines and Thailand. Their easy access makes it difficult to estimate accurately the number of migrants (Battistella & Asis 2003: 5–6). There are a few foreign nurses in Malaysia (a small number of whom from Bangladesh, INSTRAW & IOM 2000:15), but no concrete data could be found.

Thailand receives large numbers of migrant workers from neighbouring Burma, Laos and Cambodia, most of whom are unauthorised. According to a Thai governmental report, between 1996 and 2001, 568,000 irregular migrants registered themselves to obtain work permits. Females numbered 244,000 (43 percent) of those "registered irregular migrants" (Tantiwiramanond 2002: 29; also see Battistella & Asis 2003: 5–6).[7]

In 2001, Hong Kong hosted more than 184,000 domestic workers who accounted for the overwhelming majority (95%) of the unskilled migrant labour force (Hong Kong Census and Statistics Department 2003:111). Seventy percent of them were from the Philippines, followed by those from Indonesia, Thailand, and other countries (also see Ogaya 2003: 11). In

Table 6.2 Occupation, immigration status, country of origin, and number of unskilled female migrant workers by receiving country/economy and percentage of total number in the early 2000s

Receiving country/ economy	Major occupation	Immigration status	Major country of origin	Number of women	% of women to total number of migrant workers
Singapore	Domestic worker	Contract worker	Philippines, Indonesia, Sri Lanka	140,000	43.8
Malaysia	Domestic worker	Contract worker	Indonesia, Philippines, Thailand	162,000	20.5
	Unknown	Unauthorized migrant		–	–
Thailand	Domestic worker	Registered migrant	Myanmar, Laos, Cambodia	244,000	43.0
	Unknown	Unauthorized migrant		–	–
Hong Kong SAR	Domestic worker	Contract worker	Philippines, Indonesia, Thailand, Sri Lanka, Nepal, India	184,000	95.0
Taiwan Province of China	Domestic worker and care giver	Contract worker	Indonesia, Philippines, Viet Nam, Thailand	170,000	56.0
Republic of Korea	Factory worker	Industrial trainee, Unauthorized migrant	China, Philippines, Mongolia, Viet Nam, Thailand, Indonesia	35,000	35.1
	Service worker	Unauthorized migrant	China	43,000	–
	Entertainer	Entertainer	Philippines, Russia, Uzbekistan, Kazakhstan	5,000	–
	Unknown	Unauthorized migrant	Philippines, Thailand, Mongolia	19,000	–
	Immigrant wife	Spouse of citizen	China, Philippines, Thailand, Viet Nam	57,000*	–
Japan	Factory worker	Long-term Resident	Brazil, Peru	120,000	45.1
	Entertainer	Entertainer	Philippines, Russia, Republic of Korea	40,000	84.1
	Unknown	Unauthorized migrant	Republic of Korea, Philippines, Thailand, China	106,000	47.3
	Immigrant wife	Spouse of citizen	China, Philippines, Republic of Korea, Thailand	89,000**	–
			TOTAL	1,414,000	

*Total for 2000 and 2001; **Total for 1989 to 1999; – n/a.
Source: Huang and Yeoh (2003); Chin (2003); Tantiwiramanond (2002); Hong Kong Census and Statistics Department (2002); Lan (2003a); Lee (2003) and Yamanaka (2003a).

Taiwan by the end of 2002, the number of registered migrant workers exceeded 305,000, of whom over 170,000 (56%) were females employed for domestic work (Lan 2003). Most of these women were from Indonesia, the Philippines, Vietnam and Thailand. Throughout the 1990s, Korea witnessed rapid growth of its migrant worker population, of whom, by 2000, women numbered 110,000 (35 percent) (Lee 2003). These women, the majority of whom were unauthorised, came from Thailand, the Philippines, Mongolia, Vietnam, Russia, Uzbekistan, Kazakhstan and others. They were employed as assembly line operators, entertainers and other service workers. Recently, an increasing number of women from China, Philippines and other Asian countries have been admitted as wives of Korean men: 24,000 in 2001 and 32,900 in 2002 (Lee 2003: 142).

In Japan in 2001, 132,000 (84%) of 157,000 Filipino migrants were women, most of whom worked as entertainers or overstayed their short-term visas or married to local citizens (Japanese Ministry of Justice 2003). According to immigration records, from 1989 to 1999, a total of 89,000 women from China, Philippines, Korea and other Asian countries resided in the country as wives of Japanese men (Sadamatsu 2002:44). Japanese-Brazilians in Japan numbered more than 225,000 of whom 120,000 (45%) were females most of them working in factories (Yamanaka 2003). There were also an estimated 224,000 undocumented workers from several countries of whom 106,000 (47%) were women. Many of these undocumented women were assumed to be employed as entertainers, other service workers and factory workers (Japanese Ministry of Justice 2003). In the 1980s, Japan also implemented a so-called 'trainee system' that was originally aimed at technology transfer but came to be tacitly misused to supply unskilled workers. Korea followed suit by establishing a similar program in 1992. Women account for about 10 percent of the trainees in each country (JANNI 2001; Lee 2003).

In sum, adding to the large but unknown numbers of unauthorised female migrant workers, especially in Malaysia and Thailand, the total number of migrant women working in E/SE Asia may have reached two million in the beginning of the 2000s (Yamanaka & Piper 2003: 6). This figure does not include the large numbers of women from Sri Lanka, Philippines and Indonesia working in the Middle East. Clearly, the feminisation of migratory flows in and from Asia has progressed rapidly since the mid-1990s when Lim and Oishi (1996) estimated a total of approximately 1.5 million Asian women, both authorised and unauthorised, working abroad. According to Battistella (2002: 406), by 2000 the stock of authorised migrants in the seven major labour importing countries in E/SE Asia was approximately 3.7 million, while unauthorised migrants in the same countries were estimated at 2.4 million. Based on these statistics, an estimated two million women account for an unprecedented one third of the 6.1 million migrant workers in this region.

MIGRATION POLICIES

Government policies in Asia have focused on regulating the migration dimension (i.e. departure and entry) by neglecting work- or employment-related aspects (i.e. labour standards and rights) of international labour migration. Unlike the government-to-government arrangements in Western European guest-worker programs, the system that evolved in Asia did not involve governments as such. Rather, recruitment has largely been left to private agencies and a dense network of brokers and intermediaries, a practice that exposes the migrants to rampant human and financial exploitation at all stages of the migration process (Asis 2005). It also causes high levels of collusion among members of business and government circles (Piper & Iredale 2003). Furthermore, Asia contrasts with Europe and traditional immigration countries in that Asian governments practice temporary migration schemes only and thus officially prevent migrants in the less skilled category from settling and reuniting with their families in the host country.[8] Consequently, acquisition of permanent residence status, let alone citizenship, is out of reach for most migrants in Asia.

At the receiving end of migration existing policies typically categorise migrant workers into three broad groups: (1) registered professionals or highly skilled workers; (2) unskilled workers that are on contract, and are therefore authorised; and (3) unskilled workers, with neither contract nor permission of entry or work, who are therefore unauthorised. In forming policies on unskilled migration, governments are especially determined to control their foreign labour forces while at the same time providing local employers with a pool of flexible labour to assist them cope with market fluctuations and pressures.

Comparisons of migration policies and their implementation among E/SE Asian host countries reveal that despite many similarities, there has been a great deal of variation regarding aims and policies for dealing with less skilled foreign workers. Broadly speaking, there have been two types of migration policies in E/SE Asia. The first is found in Singapore, Malaysia, Taiwan and Hong Kong, where migrants enter to work on contract at well-defined jobs for a specified number of years. This may be called a 'front door' policy (Yamanaka 1999). Under such a policy, governmental regulations designed to manage immigration flows require employers to pay a levy upon hiring each employee and a security bond to ensure his or her exit upon completion of contract. Governments also determine quotas for numbers of workers per industry and for each country of origin (Wong 1997). Moreover, governments adopt strict exclusionary policies by which less skilled migrants are prohibited not only from obtaining social welfare services and from establishing permanent residence, but also from integrating with the local population through marriage (Wong 1997).

The second type of immigration policy has been operative in Japan and Korea since the 1990s. In contrast to Singapore, Malaysia, Taiwan and

Hong Kong, these two East Asian countries do not officially admit low skilled migrants to work on contract, while encouraging skilled foreigners to work in selected occupations. However, the rhetoric and official policy of banning unskilled foreigners notwithstanding, both countries have been home for many years to two to three hundred thousand migrants working in lower skilled jobs (Lee 1997). Through many 'back' or 'side' doors (Yamanaka 1999) available to entrants, migrants arrive legally as residents, students, industrial trainees, entertainers, tourists, business travellers, etc. many of whom remain to work in an unauthorized manner. Unknown numbers of workers also gain illegal entry smuggled by boat or other means.

MAJOR CATEGORIES OF MIGRANT WOMEN WORKERS

The two types of migration policies have resulted in six major categories of migrant women workers in E/SE Asia that entail distinct types of movement and characteristics of the women involved. The first five of the six collectively comprise the less skilled, and numerical majority: (1) domestic workers; (2) entertainers; (3) unauthorised workers; (4) immigrant wives; (5) Japanese-Brazilians and Korean-Chinese. There are also small but increasing numbers of: (6) skilled migrant women in Asia's newly prospering global cities. These six categories of migrant women differ in the conditions for their admission to these countries, and for their employment, residence and welfare. Consequently, they also differ in their impacts on women's livelihood, socioeconomic status, social mobility, and personal freedom.

DOMESTIC WORKERS

In Asia and elsewhere, domestic work has been the major occupation for migrant women on contract and their situation has been subject to considerable research — so much so that Asian FDWs have become the most researched group of Asian women migrants. International and local NGOs have also produced reports on the working and living conditions of FDWs in various parts of Asia (Human Rights Watch 2004 and 2006; WAO 2003).

There are differences between countries as to whether they recognize the domestic sector as an area of employment. In E/SE Asia some countries and territories, such as Hong Kong, Singapore, Malaysia, Taiwan recognize domestic work for visa purposes, while others do not (e.g. Korea, Japan). However, legal status (work permit) does not entail any rights as it does not automatically entail recognition by national labour laws. In fact, domestic work is widely excluded from national labour legislation. With the exception of Hong Kong, the national employment act or labour standard law typically does not recognise their work as a legitimate form of labour. This effectively excludes domestic work from legal protection under law (Chin 2003; Huang & Yeoh 2003; Lan 2003).[9] Foreign workers in industries such as construction and manufacturing in Taiwan are covered by industrial relations legislation (in Taiwan's case, the Labour Standards Law), but women working as domestic helpers or carers are not (Loveband 2004). Thus, national employment acts or labour standard laws do not recognise domestic work as a legitimate form of labour.

Moreover, the receiving state in its attempt to exert control over its population officially prohibits FDWs marrying citizens or permanent residents of the host society.[10] In an extreme form of control of female bodies, some states require migrant women to take periodic pregnancy tests and to leave the country immediately if they become pregnant (Wong 1997: 161).[11] The imposition of a security bond (repaid upon end of contract and departure of the FDW) by the government makes employers responsible for monitoring the whereabouts of their domestic helpers. This shapes the ways in which employers, especially female employers, monitor and control the daily behaviour and spatial movement of their live-in employees (Yeoh, Huang & Gonzalez 1999; Wong 1997; Constable 1997; Lan 2003).

In Singapore, Malaysia, Hong Kong and Taiwan, foreign domestic workers (hereafter FDWs) and caregivers are usually given two-year (often renewable) contracts that tie them to one specific employer.[12] If problems arise, the women are not allowed to change employers, but have to return home and re-apply from there. This means that they must either again pay recruitment fees or remain in the host country clandestinely as undocumented workers. Hong Kong is an exception to this rule. There, FDWs are subject to a 'grace period' of two weeks during which they have the opportunity to find a new employer before facing deportation.

Working and residing in private homes, live-in maids incur the risk of suffering violation of contract terms and abuses by employers and family members with few avenues available for recourse (Cox 1997; Shah & Menon 1997; Yeoh, Huang & Gonzalez 1999; Huang & Yeoh 2003). Employers' practices of illegally undercutting wages, requiring longer working hours and demanding that more tasks be performed than initially agreed upon, are common. If a migrant woman is unwilling to comply with her employer's demands, emotional and physical assaults may be used to force her compliance (Constable 1997).

ENTERTAINERS

As has been mentioned above, Japan and Korea officially prohibit contract work by less skilled foreigners. In these countries, a legal avenue by which foreign women can enter and work, usually up to six months, is by obtaining an 'entertainer' or 'artist' visa.[13] Although these women, mostly from the Philippines or Thailand, enter the country as 'skilled workers', the majority are rarely trained as professional entertainers or performing artists.[14] Upon arrival, they work as hostesses and dancers in bars and cabarets where their employers are frequently associated with criminal gangs. Upon expiry of their short-term visas, these entertainers must return home and, if they wish to return, reapply for the same visa one year later. As short-term migrant workers, these women are ineligible for public services including access to inexpensive health care and social welfare programs. They are defined as performers (not workers), and are therefore not covered by protective provisions of labour standards law. How widespread the trafficking of women for the purpose of sexual exploitation is, is unclear. According to the latest report by United Nations Office on Drugs and Crime (UNODC 2006: 88), Japan ranks very high in the citation index as destination country in global comparison.

Very complex and highly controversial issues surround the human rights of migrant women in the sex and entertainment industry. Feminists are broadly divided into two camps, (1) the abolitionists who argue that all prostitution is a violation of women's human rights and (2) the protagonists of 'sex workers' rights'. This is an ideologically charged and in many ways older debate which often overlooks the multi-layered structure of this 'industry,'[15] as well as silencing the voices of those most directly affected (Piper 2005b; Augustín 2005).

UNAUTHORISED WORKERS

In Japan and Korea, female (and male) migrants can enter the country with a variety of short-term visas (in addition to that for 'entertainers') that allow them to stay up to three months. Upon their arrival, a significant proportion of holders of these visas (issued for tourists, business travellers, trainees and students) overstay their visas to work. In Japan, throughout the 1990s, the number of visa-overstayers remained between 200,000 and 300,000, of whom more than 40 percent were females and many of whom worked in the sex industry (see Table 6.2). Without permission to stay and work in the country, these women, some of them having been trafficked, are not entitled to any protective measures. As a result, they often suffer significant abuse and exploitation, as discussed above.

In Korea, during the 1990s, the number of undocumented workers and visa over-stayers, both men and women, increased rapidly to the extent that in 2002, 289,000 (86%) of 335,000 foreign workers were unauthorised (see Table 6.2). Women numbered 102,000 of whom 88 percent were unauthorised, mostly engaging in manufacturing and service occupations (Lee, 2003:137). This is largely attributable to the company or industrial 'trainees' system in which trainees receive visas for internships of up to two years.[16] In practice, they simply serve as a reservoir of inexpensive and flexible workers, earning far less than market wages and experiencing little, if any, substantive training during their stay (Lee 2003; Kim 2003). Because they are defined as 'trainees' rather than workers, they are excluded from protective provisions of labour standards law and frequently meet harassment, abuse, violence, and delayed or unpaid wages. Consequently, many trainees 'escape' from the company to which they are contracted, and through personal networks find illegal employment in other companies.

There are also large numbers of undocumented workers in Southeast Asia, especially in Malaysia and Thailand. Because of uneven economic development accompanied by shared history, language and religion among neighbouring countries, borders have been porous among Malaysia, Indonesia and the Philippines, and among Thailand, Burma, Laos, Vietnam and Cambodia. Although reliable information is unavailable, the total number of unauthorised workers in these areas is estimated at roughly 1.5 to 2 million (Battistella & Asis 2003: 5). Recent studies of undocumented migration in Southeast Asia report significant numbers of migrant women from the Philippines, Indonesia, Burma and Laos working under strenuous conditions with little legal protection in a wide range of occupations, including domestics, vendors, plantation workers, factory workers, construction labourers and fish farm hands (see Battistella & Asis 2003). The borders between Thailand, Burma and neighbouring countries host large numbers of women (often of ethnic minority origins) who engage in sexual labour often akin to slavery (e.g., Asia Watch and Women's Rights Project 1993).

IMMIGRANT WIVES

The inconsistent implementation of rigid immigration control promulgated in Japan and Korea brought to both an influx of women from other countries, with the unexpected result of a rapid increase in formal and informal unions between these foreign women and local men and the families that resulted (Piper 1999; Lee 2003; Suzuki 2002, 2003). A chronic 'shortage of brides' in these countries also prompted international match-making services to provide male citizens with the means to marry women from less developed Asian countries, mostly from China, Philippines and Thailand. The 'global hypergamy phenomenon' has recently spawned research on the causal link between labour migration and international marriage (e.g., Association for Asian Studies 2001). In the context of rigid immigration and visa policies in Asia, marriage to a local citizen constitutes an important strategy for migrant women (and men) to achieve legal and economic security in the host country (Piper 1999; Piper & Roces 2003).[17]

In Korea, until 2002, immigration and nationality laws had treated the two genders unequally in their access to permanent residence and work permits. When a female citizen married a migrant, she and her family lost out in this regard; when a male citizen married a migrant, he and his family benefited (Lee 2003). With amendment of the Nationality Law in 1998 and establishment of the visa rules of 2002, gender inequality has been reduced. In Japan, when international marriage is registered, the foreign spouse is given a two-year residence visa before a spousal visa is issued. In the event of divorce, foreign spouses are allowed to remain in the country only if the marriage has produced a child. Lacking institutional support and unequal power, marriages between Japanese men and Asian women are reported to face serious problems. These include wife's cultural maladjustment, husband's physical abuse of wife, in-laws' intervention in the couple's privacy, children's identity crises, etc. (Sadamatsu 2002: 44).

Migration to Taiwan for the purpose of marriage has increased quite dramatically in recent years, with foreign brides now numbering about 300,000. They mostly come from China and Southeast Asia. Vietnamese women have also married Taiwanese men in rising numbers: since the 1990s, nearly 100,000 (UNFPA 2006: 25). As the above trends indicate, these unions usually involve men from the wealthier countries in Asia and women from the lower developed countries.

JAPANESE-BRAZILIAN AND KOREAN-CHINESE

In 1990, in response to growing demand for unskilled workers, and an increasing number of unauthorised workers, Japan implemented an immigration policy that granted second and third generations of foreign nationals of Japanese ancestry (*Nikkeijin*) long-term residence visas for a stay of up to three years, with unlimited access to the labour market. Pulled by an explosive demand for labour in the manufacturing industries and pushed by economic and political instability in Latin America, more than 200,000 *Nikkeijin* from Brazil (and substantially fewer from Peru) arrived in Japan within the next five years (Yamanaka 2003). From the beginning of this migration boom, the Brazilian *Nikkeijin* population in Japan included a high proportion of women, reaching 45 percent in 2001. The proportion of children went up from five percent in 1990 to 15 percent in 2001 (Yamanaka 2003). A majority of *Nikkeijin* women and men work as assembly line operators in the automobile parts and electrical appliance industries. Their Japanese ancestry and legal status notwithstanding, without Japanese citizenship most Japanese-Brazilian workers receive neither benefits of public services (including social welfare programs, national healthcare insurance and old age pension plans), nor are they covered by regulations for the well-being of workers (Miyajima & Higuchi 1996).[18]

In Korea, there is a similar category of migrants, Korean-Chinese, who are considered more welcome than other non-Korean Asians. Unlike Japanese-Brazilians in Japan, Korean-Chinese in Korea have not been granted visa privileges by the Korean government.[19] Many Korean-Chinese women are unauthorised workers who are employed as domestics in private households because they share culture and language with their employers (Lee 2003:136, 2004).

SKILLED WORKERS

From the onset of expanding global migration in the 1970s, Asian women have migrated overseas as skilled workers.[20] Significant numbers of Filipino and Korean nurses have worked in the United States, Europe and the Middle East to alleviate severe labour shortages in those countries (e.g., Ong & Azores 1994).[21] With the rise of Asia's global capitalism since the 1980s, small but increasing numbers of Asian women in a broad range of immigration statuses (as spouse, student, long-term resident) and professional experience (in business, finance, education, health, etc.) have migrated to Asia's major global cities (Hong Kong, Kuala Lumpur, Shanghai, Singapore, Tokyo, to name a few). Such examples include Singaporean women in China (Willis & Yeoh 2000), Japanese women in Hong Kong (Sakai 2000) and Singapore (Thang, MacLachlan & Goda 2002), and many other nationalities in many locations (Yeoh & Khoo 1998; Lee & Piper 2003). Because the phenomenon is relatively recent and seems to affect relatively few, it has yet to attract much scholarly attention. There is, for instance, anecdotal evidence of short-term skilled migration involving Indian women to IT processing zones such as in Malaysia[22] but no detailed research has been conducted on this. The inattention also reflects the existing division of labour by gender that separates individuals' lives between the 'public' and 'private' spheres.[23] Women are discursively constructed within privatised spaces and the discourse then centres predominantly on their role within these spaces, rendering women, regardless of their skills and experience, vulnerable to the belief that they are inherently responsible for home making roles throughout their lives.

Recent studies suggest that cross-border migration for skilled women is growing in frequency and is diversified in the attendant patterns of motivation and experience, legal status and entitlements, and coping strategies with which to confront the barriers they face in foreign countries (Yeoh & Khoo 1998; Raghuram 2000; Sakai 2000; Willis & Yeoh 2000; Yeoh & Willis 2004; Thang, MacLachlan & Goda 2002; Lee & Piper 2003; Ono & Piper 2004). Commonly, these studies reveal that Asia's regional migration of skilled workers is highly gender-segregated, and is also characterised by institutional barriers based on nationality, ethnicity, language, religion and class. The literature indicates that despite governmental encouragement for skilled foreigners to relocate, immigration and labour policies are inexplicably intertwined with traditional gender ideologies that view and treat most women as 'dependants' of expatriate men who cross borders for career and business. Such a policy, in turn, significantly reduces women's chances of obtaining residence and working visas and being employed as professionals. As a result, they confront far greater obstacles than their male counterparts in pursuit of careers abroad. Men are able to upgrade their careers through foreign employment, while their skilled wives often experience unemployment and underemployment at their destinations. Eventually, they are likely to give up their aspirations for employment to concentrate on housekeeping, child rearing and community service (Yeoh & Khoo 1998).

Migrant women also labour as factory workers in countries such as Malaysia and Singapore. Some research has been conducted on Bangladeshi women in Malaysian garment factories (Dannecker 2005), but no research has been done on Singapore's factories. There is only anecdotal evidence of Malaysians working in Singapore-based manufacturing companies. A study by Dias and Wanasundera (2002) provides descriptive information on Sri Lankan women working as skilled machine operators in garment factories in places such as Oman. On the whole, however, there is a dearth of systematic research on migrant women in these sectors.

CHANGES IN FEMALE MIGRATION

These statistics and recent studies point to at least two important changes in women's migration that are directly relevant to our discussion.

First, the most evident of these is the diversified nationalities of migrant women. As demands for migrant women's labour increased in the region, opportunities opened up for women from countries that had not previously been sources of migrant labour. These new faces included: Vietnamese and Thai in Taiwan, Cambodians in Malaysia, and Mongolians, Russians, Uzbekistanis and Kazakhstanis in Korea. The seeking of new sources of migrant labour is not only related to demand in terms of numbers, but also to demand for a different kind of workers: those less expensive, more docile (which is also a racialised position) and/or less 'rights' conscious. Successful campaigns for, and enforcement of, workers' protective mechanisms and/or rights in some countries have brought about unintended consequences in the nationality composition of their immigrant work forces. A good example is that of Filipino domestics in Hong Kong who have been partially replaced by less organised, and thus less vocal and assertive, nationality groups[24], such as Indonesians and Sri Lankans (Ogaya 2003). Similarly, in Taiwan the proportion of Filipino women in the country's foreign domestic worker population has plummeted significantly between 1998 and 2002 as they are being replaced by less expensive Indonesian and Vietnamese women (Lan 2003). These changes in the proportions of women's nationalities among migrants suggest their vulnerability to unpredictable changes in labour market forces and governmental policy. As a result, a new stratification is emerging, whereby women are ranked in the scale of demand and wages according to their nationality, ethnicity, class, educational level, and available support networks.

Second, despite the absence of official settlement policies, changes are apparent in the prolonged duration of employment and residence among migrant women in receiving countries. For example, since 2002 Taiwan has allowed migrant workers "with good records" to re-enter the country to work for up to six years (Lan 2003:105). In Hong Kong, the number of Filipinas staying between five years and 15 years is increasing as more of them choose to remain there rather than returning to the Philippines (Sim & Wee 2004). There has also been a considerable rise in the numbers and types of migrant women whose legal visa status grants them the right to reside and work indefinitely in the country to which they have migrated. This is evident in the rising numbers of women who arrive as wives of citizens in countries, such as Japan (Piper 1999; Nakamatsu 2003), Korea (Lee 2003) and Taiwan (UNFPA 2006). In these societies, a lack of local women willing to marry men deemed to be undesirable and prolonged singlehood among the younger generations have spawned commercial or community services to promote international marriage (Piper & Roces 2003).[25] These developments require re-consideration of the socio-legal understanding of what citizenship is all about.

GLOBAL POLICY DISCOURSE, RIGHTS AND DEVELOPMENT

The continuing salience of economic migration (in addition to forced migration owing to persecution which we do not discuss here) is evident from the push within the global policy discourse toward the "management of migration" in form of international cooperation of all countries implicated. The (re-) emerging concern with the elaboration of an international framework for migration management is related to a number of initiatives, such as the recent Berne Initiative, the establishment of the Geneva Migration Group[26] and the work and final report (October 2005) of the Global Commission on International Migration (GCIM). The main objective of this global agenda is to promote cooperation among states in dealing with various dimensions and the complexity of international migration.

A parallel development is the recent framework to labour migration developed by the ILO aimed at addressing the protective deficit for migrants in current policy practices by individual states. Taking a human rights perspective on economic wellbeing and livelihoods reflects a normative framework in form of so-called 'rights-based approaches' (RBA) that has been emerging in relation to a number of global issues, such as development (adopted by the UN General Assembly in 1986), health (as championed by the World Health Organisation), and now migration (ILO 2006). In the broader framework of promoting decent work for all, the ILO's RBA to migration aims to foster cooperation and consultation not only among states, but also between states and social partners, reflecting its tripartite constituency which is a unique set-up (UN 2006). The role of trade unions is discussed in the chapter by Piper (chapter 8 of this volume).

In addition the ILO's attempt to revive a human rights framework to migration, the Office for the High Commissioner on Human Rights (OHCHR) set up the Migrant Committee in 2004, the Treaty Body in charge of monitoring the 1990 UN Convention on the Rights of All Migrants and their Families which came into force in September 2003, having finally reached the required minimum number of ratifications. As a result of these, new developments or revived initiatives (in addition to two UN reports 2004, 2006) have resulted in bringing the issue of migrants' rights onto the global policy agenda.

In the attempt to improve the benefits of migration for all, the global policy debate has also taken up the linkages between migration and development (GCIM 2005; UN 2006). Although the focus is often predominantly on the developmental impact of out-migration for origin countries (in form of remittances, investment, skill transfers), the need for enhanced development has also been discussed in terms of alleviating the pressure to migrate in the first place.

MANAGEMENT OF MIGRATION — AN ISSUE OF CONTROL OR PROTECTION?

The agenda behind managing migration is to a large extent about the control of entry and exit of migrant workers. This is as such not new — the control of migration has preoccupied the minds of policy makers since the 1970s and more forcefully since the late 1980s and 1990s. Although this shift in the migration policy debate to focus on international cooperation is primarily concerned with control over entry and exit as well as prevention of irregular migration[27], broader human rights issues as well as the rights of foreign workers have also entered into the discussion (GCIM 2005; IOM and FOM 2005) and thus, a concern for the basic units of analysis of migration: the migrants themselves. But it is yet to be seen whether this is a matter of paying mere lip service or whether there is in fact a serious concern with migrants' human rights and efforts toward implementation are made.

States typically take a utilitarian approach to migration prioritising their economic interests: origin countries are often driven by the desire to increase foreign remittances and to reduce unemployment; destination countries are interested in solving labour market shortages in certain sectors by ensuring a highly flexible and compliant workforce. As a result, governments usually take less notice of migrant workers' needs and concerns as opposed to those of employers — and sometimes not even of those employers who are in favour of increasing legal migration of lower skilled workers. There are, therefore, competing societal demands which are rooted in real socio-economic needs, but the economic, social, political and distributional consequences of migration, and their implications for gender, at the micro level have not yet been explored and are thus not fully understood.

On the issue of cooperation between destination and origin countries, there is the option of negotiating bilateral agreements or Memoranda of Understanding (MoUs), but examples of 'good practices' with regard to the inclusion of gender sensitive rights clauses are few and far between. Moreover, the problem with bilateral agreements and MoUs is that they give preferential treatment to a specific group of migrants, and by not promoting universal standards across all nationality groups, a hierarchy among migrant workers often emerges.[28] Also, international agreements affecting migration at global, regional and national levels are more likely to be more favourable towards skilled than low skilled migrants (Skeldon 2004) leaving many female migrants who dominate the latter category at a disadvantage. UN Development Fund for Women (UNIFEM) in Bangkok has facilitated the establishment of an implementing mechanism for MoUs between Jordan-Indonesia and Jordan-Philippines that contain rights protection for FDWs. It remains to be seen what the concrete outcome of this promising endeavour will be. There are also MoUs in place between Thailand and its neighbours Laos and Cambodia which are said to contain clauses on migrants' rights (UNFPA 2006).

An important development in the Asian region is the holding of three ministerial level consultations (labour ministries) by Asian labour sending countries — in Colombo (April 2003), Manila (September 2004) and Bali (2005) — to discuss issues of common concern, including the protection of migrant workers. Concrete action has not been taken, other than the plan for a feasibility study on the establishment of a Common Migrant Resource Centre in the Gulf Cooperation Council Countries. The final statement of the Bali ministerial consultation, however, directly refers to the 'management of migration' which is defined as "orderly labour movement and employment policies consistent with the welfare of workers". Four areas of management are highlighted as essential: (1) ensuring the welfare and well-being of vulnerable overseas workers, especially women, during recruitment employment; (2) optimising benefits of organised labour flows, including the development of new markets; (3) building institutional capacity and inter-ministerial coordination to meet labour movement challenges; (4) increasing cooperation between countries of origin and destination countries in ensuring the welfare of overseas workers. More specifically, one area of cooperation is to aim at "establishing minimum wage levels and ensuring safe and decent conditions of employment for contract workers, particularly women, in low skill and low wage sectors." This finally constitutes a clear recognition of the rampant abusive employment practices.

The challenge which lies ahead is to translate this rhetorical statement into action.

LINKING MIGRATION AND DEVELOPMENT

The 2004 UN report on women and migration highlights the two main elements of the migration-development nexus: (1) the ways in which development processes can reduce pressures for migration and (2) the ways in which migrants can be a resource for poverty reduction and sustainable development in their home communities (UN 2004: 24). This has also been touched upon by the 2006 UN report on migration and development stating that all countries should strive to create more jobs, and decent jobs, to allow everyone the option of staying at home. This is at least partially to be achieved through a process of "co-development". Co-development refers to various initiatives between origin and destination countries aimed at boosting development in the former. This debate seems to be largely concerned with development at the macro and community level.

On an individual level, it has been noted in a generalized manner that "although all migrants can be agents of change, migrant women are more likely to have their personal development thwarted" (than men) (UN 2006: 15). Respecting women's rights as part of economic and social development is seen as the best long-term solution to reduce the pressures of out-migration. Measures to improve the benefits of migration for women include providing them with independent legal status and permission to work when admitted for family reunification. As vital, we would argue, is the issue of improvement of skills. One of the important ways of protecting migrants and guaranteeing 'successful' migration is via the acquisition of skills. This does not only refer to work skills (language, job training) but also financial skills (budgeting, planning and strategizing for the future). In this regard, it would be interesting to study in greater detail the training and skill programmes offered to FDWs by various non-profit organizations in Singapore and Malaysia as well as a strategy developed by Filipino NGOs called 'Migrant Savings for Alternative Investment' (Macabuag & Dimaandal 2006).

On a broader level, a direct link between a rights-based approach to labour migration and a rights-based approach to development, however, has not been established by global policy makers which must be mainly connected to the politically sensitive nature of the underlying global inequalities at play. A deeper normative and empirical analysis of the political and economic processes and linkages between gender, migration and development, however, are required and could ultimately assist non-governmental activists to make these connections in their advocacy work and lead to new or extended coalitions between various civil society organisations nationally and transnationally.

CONCLUDING REMARKS

Aiming to improve their livelihoods and that of their families, increasing numbers of women seek work in foreign countries in different types of occupations. This is not necessarily their first choice but at times a reflection of male un- or under-employment and specific job opportunities abroad in highly gendered job categories. Under restrictive migration policies and the prevalence of temporary contract schemes, with many migrant women's economic and social contributions being undervalued and their work being legally not recognized, their full potential or ability to secure livelihoods and their chances for personal socio-economic empowerment are somewhat limited. The full implications of migration on women's social and economic development have not been explored in sufficient detail. This chapter offered an initial discussion of these linkages in reference to the feminisation of intra-regional migratory flows in E/SE Asia.

As a general observation, migration poses a new challenge in the subject area of women's rights, development and citizenship, for research and policy-makers alike (as also highlighted by IDRC 2006). Especially the conceptual and normative linkages between women's social and economic rights as related to migration need further exploration in specific geographic or cultural settings. For instance, the limits to mobility imposed on women in much of South Asia are typically couched in terms of the rights of women to 'safety'. Rights to protection by origin countries are often based on legality of migration rather than on their nationals' origins meaning that legality/illegality become a key vector of differentiation. This means that women have to use their multiple identifications in pursuing their rights. On the policy level, a deeper political analysis of policy making processes and the identification of good practices in specific countries is needed to inform relevant policy developments and political advocacy elsewhere (Poniatowski & Jimenez 2006).

NOTES

1. This refers to East and West (i.e. the Gulf states) Asia. A note on terminology is required here: we refer to 'Asia' when we make broader observations valid for the whole region; otherwise we use the phrase E/SE Asia to refer to the two sub-regions most of our discussion focuses upon. East Asia excludes the People's Republic of China which we do not discuss (hence the difference to the phrase "Northeast Asia" used in chapter 4).
2. The other region is Africa.
3. See Nana Oishi (2005) and Dannecker (2005) for a more detailed discussion on women's restricted mobility in South Asia.
4. South Asia is mainly a labour exporting sub-region where women's (official) mobility is subject to serious restrictions (with the notable exception of Sri Lanka). Hence, countries such as Bangladesh predominantly send male migrants. It has to be noted, however, that mobility is not limited per se but

shaped by sector and skill level. In India and Bangladesh, for instance, skilled women' migration is not limited, but there are limits on domestic workers. In all these countries, women internal migrants outnumber men because of marriage migration. In view of this, it is the specific nature of the mobility that is restricted and this is done through official controls (sex and domestic work) and unofficial discursive limits on single female mobility because of social construction of femininity, gendered social order that increased women's workload which is then not easily redistributed outside of the family because of patrilocality etc. We owe these insights to Dr. Parvati Raghuram (personal conversation, 27 September 2006).

5. It might appear odd to include foreign wives into the discussion of economic migration, but as argued by Piper (2003) and Piper and Roces (2003), the two streams are inter-related.
6. Information in Table 6.2 was provided by participants in the conference, "Gender, Migration and Governance in Asia," held December 5-6, 2002 at the Australian National University, Canberra. For a summary of the conference, see Yamanaka and Piper (2003). For original sources of information, see Huang and Yeoh (2003); Chin (2003); Tantiwiramanond (2002); Hong Kong Census and Statistics Department (2002); Lan (2003); Lee (2003), and Yamanaka (2003).
7. According to Khruemanee (2002: 1), in 2001 for the first time the Thai government allowed the registration of irregular migrant domestic workers for a work permit. Thailand also is host to a considerable number of migrant workers who have not registered. In 1997, the Asian Research Centre for Migration of Chulalongkong University estimated that only 45 percent of the migrant population was registered (Khruemanee, 2002: 2).
8. However, according to Parreñas (2004), many European countries prohibit migrant domestic workers from reuniting with their families at their destinations also. Notable exceptions are Italy and Spain.
9. Using Singapore as an example, Huang and Yeoh (2003) discuss extensively how gender makes a difference in governmental policy and public receptions towards migrant men and women. The majority of women labour as domestic workers in isolated private homes, as a result of which they are subject to labour contract violation and harassment by their employers. In contrast, men working in construction under the state's supervision are provided dormitories for their residence and leisure programs for their off-day activities. The government is reported to be concerned about 'productivity' and 'welfare' of male construction workers while neglecting the same concerns for FDWs.
10. This is the same for un- or semi-skilled male migrant workers. This seems, therefore, to be an issue of class rather than gender.
11. Throughout Asia, despite governmental efforts to control migrant women's behaviours and bodies, there have been increasing incidents of them having developed informal and sometimes formal domestic relationships with local men. In Hong Kong, FDWs in such relationships can now remain in the territory (Piper, interview with senior officials of the Hong Kong government, February 2003, Hong Kong). In Singapore, couples often marry abroad after which the former FDW wives return to the city state with a spousal visa. In Bintan Island of Indonesia near Singapore, small but increasing numbers of Indonesian wives/partners establish a home from where their Singaporean husbands/partners commute to work in Singapore (Lindquist 2004). In Malaysia, where there has been a rising incidence of South Asian men becoming intimately involved with Malaysian women, the government has imposed

a ban specifically on male Bangladeshi workers (Piper, interview with Tenaganita, an NGO in Kuala Lumpur, February 2003). These relationships are constructed as a 'social problem' (e.g., Dannecker 2005).
12. As mentioned earlier, in Taiwan since 2002, migrant workers are permitted to re-enter and work up to six years.
13. In the Philippines, the government classifies women departing on the entertainer visa as professional 'overseas performing artists'.
14. A recent study by the International Organisation for Migration (2003: 65) describes the classifications of entertainers as professional or skilled as an "anachronism".
15. The issue of work in this area could be approached from the viewpoint of a short-/medium-term versus long-term solution, advocating for minimum work standards to provide some level of immediate protection and some kind of regulation workers in this 'sector' and NGO advocates can hold onto. Unlike in the case of domestic workers (see e.g. Colombo Declaration), however, activists have not produced many concrete ideas how to go about this.
16. Japan began this practice in the late 1980s, based on an existing visa category for company trainees that was originally aimed at technology transfer but came to be tacitly misused and in the 1990s officially endorsed, to supply unskilled foreigners to the workforce (Oishi 1995). Korea implemented a similar program of industrial trainees in 1992. Most "trainees" come from China, Indonesia, Philippines, Thailand and other Asian countries. Women account for about 10 percent of the trainee entrants in each country (JANNI 2001; Lee 2003).
17. International marriage between Japanese women and Asian immigrant men is also on the rise. In a recent study, Sakurai (2003) discusses the growing Moslem community in Japan in which an increasing number of Japanese women participate as wives of migrant workers from Bangladesh, Pakistan and Iran. For studies of marriage between Japanese women and Moslem South Asian men, see Terada (2001), Takeshita (2001), Fukuda (2004).
18. By law Japanese-Brazilians are eligible for many public services. In practice, however, most of them are unable to use these services because of administrative, institutional and cultural barriers that exclude them. As the duration of stay is extended, many Japanese-Brazilian families face problems in educating their children as they grow up in Japan (Yamanaka 2003).
19. In 2004, Korea is to implement the amended Act of the 1998 *Immigration and Legal Status of Overseas Koreans*, which is designed to provide ethnic Koreans from China and Russia with legal privileges defined by the Act (Lee 2003: 135).
20. The Philippines began sending nurses to the United States as early as the 1960s. According to Espiritu (2003: 145), between 1966 and 1991 nearly 25,000 Filipino nurses left for the United States, followed by another 10,000 between 1989 and 1991.
21. In the Philippines, a host of vocational institutions have been established in order to provide applicants with training to become nurses and other health-related workers (Ong and Azores 1994). Nursing is still an occupation dominated by women, but it has also attracted males as it enables them to migrate to the United States and elsewhere where they can earn higher wages than are available in the Philippines. There have been "second-courses" programs in the Philippines in which skilled Filipino workers in other occupations will be retrained to become nurses. Anecdotal evidence suggests that some Filipino male doctors have been retrained as nurses in such programs in order to be posted overseas when the demand and the wages are relatively high

(Piper, personal communication with Dr. Maruja M.B. Asis, Manila, February 2004).
22. Personal email communication with Dr. Parvati Raghuram, Open University (15 September 2006).
23. See Caufield (1981) for a brief and incisive discussion of the relationship between gender and mode of production. She defines the "public sphere" as the one of "production for exchange" which, in capitalist societies and economies, means the marketplace, as contrasted with the "private sphere" that is the one of "production for use" which, in such societies and economies, means the family and the household.
24. The reasons for such variable "national assertiveness" are themselves interesting.
25. In 1996, the average age at marriage among Japanese women was 27.5 (29.9 for men) (Asahi Shimbun 2000:62). In contemporary Japan (and Korea), young women shun marriage with farmers co-residing with their parents in remote agricultural communities, and men of lower socioeconomic status or with other 'undesirable' characteristics in urban areas (Nakamatsu 2003).
26. This is a forum bringing together the heads of several major UN agencies (ILO, UNCTAD, UNHCR, OHCHR, UNODC).
27. See e.g. Global Consultation on International Protection, *Refugee Protection and Migration Control: Perspectives from UNCHR and IOM*, 31 May 2001; www.unhrc.ch/prexcom/globalcon.htm.
28. This is particularly evident in the case of foreign domestic workers in Asia. Filipinas are usually given the best deal, followed by Indonesians and Sri Lankans (e.g. Wee and Sim 2005).

REFERENCES

Asahi Shimbun (2000) *Japan Almanac 1999*, Tokyo: Asahi Shimbunsha.
Asian and Pacific Migration Journal (2003) 'Gender, Migration Governance in Asia', Special Issue, vol. 12, no. 1-2 (whole issue).
Asia Watch and Women's Rights Project (1993) *Modern Form of Slavery: Trafficking of Burmese Women and Girls into Brothels in Thailand*, New York: Human Rights Watch.
Asis, M. M. B. (2005) 'Recent Trends in International migration in Asia and the Pacific', in: *Asia-Pacific Population Journal*, vol. 20(3): 15–38.
Association of Asian Studies (2001) 'Asia, Global Hypergamy, and the Politics of Transnational Marriage', Session 151, the Annual Meeting of the Association for Asian Studies, Chicago, March 22–25, 2001.
Augustin, L. (2005) 'Migrants in the Mistress' House: other voices in the "trafficking" debate', *Social Politics*, vol. 12(1): 96–117.
Battistella, G. (2002) 'International migration in Asia vis-à-vis Europe: An introduction', in: *Asian and Pacific Migration Journal*, vol. 11(4): 405–414.
Battistella, G. and M. M. B. Asis (eds) (2003) *Unauthorised Migration in Southeast Asia*, Quezon City: Scalabrini Migration Centre.
Briones, L. (2006) 'Beyond agency and rights: capability, migration and livelihood in Filipina experiences of domestic work in Paris and Hong Kong', *Unpublished PhD Thesis*, Centre for Development Studies, Flinders University of South Australia.
Caufield, M. D. (1981) 'Equality, sex, and mode of production', in Gerald D. Berreman (ed.), *Social Inequality: Comparative and Developmental Approaches*, New York: Academic Press.

Constable, N. (1997) *Maid to Order in Hong Kong: Stories of Filipina Workers*. Berkeley: University of California Press.
Cox, D. (1997) 'The vulnerability of Asian women migrant workers to a lack of protection and to violence', in: *Asian and Pacific Migration Journal*, vol. 6(1): 59–75.
Dannecker, P. (2005) 'Transnational Migration and the Transformation of Gender Relations: the Case of Bangladeshi Labour Migrants', in: *Current Sociology*, vol. 53(4): 655–674.
Dias, M. and L. Wanasundera (2002), *Sri Lankan Migrant Garment Factory Workers: Mauritius and Sultanate of Oman*, Study Series No. 27, Colombo/Sri Lanka: Centre for Women's Research (CENWOR).
Fukuda, T. (2004) 'Kokusai Kekkon to Ethnic Business ni Miru Gender Kankei: Tainichi Pakistanjin Dansei to Nihonjin Josei wo Jirei Toshite', in: Ruri Ito (ed.), *Gendai Nihon Shakai ni okeru Kokusai Imin to Gender Kankei no Saihen ni Kansuru Kenkyu*. Tokyo: Institute of Gender Studies, Ochanomizu University, pp. 155–181.
Gamburd, R. (2001) *The Kitchen Spoon's Handle: Transnationalism and Sri Lanka's Migrant Households*, Ithaca, NY: Cornell University Press.
Gills, D-S. and N. Piper (eds.) (2002) *Women and Work in Globalising Asia*, London: Routledge.
Global Commission on International Migration (2005) *Migration in an interconnected world: New directions for action*', Geneva: GCIM.
Hochschild, A. R. (2002) 'Love and Gold', in: B. Ehrenreich and A. R. Hochschild Russell (eds.), *Global Woman: Nannies, Maids and Sex Workers in the New Economy*. New York: Metropolitan Books.
Hondagneu-Sotelo, P. (2001) *Doméstica: Immigrant Workers Cleaning and Caring in the Shadows of Affluence*, University of California Press: Berkeley.
Hondagneu-Sotelo, P.and E. Avila (1997) 'I'm Here, but I'm not There': The Meaning of Latina Transnational Motherhood', in: *Gender and Society*, vol. 11(5): 548–571.
Hong Kong Census and Statistics Department (2002) *2001 Population Census*, Special Administrative Region, People's Republic of China, Hong Kong.
Huang, S. and B. Yeoh (2003) 'The difference gender makes: State policy and constract migrant workers in Singapore', in: *Asian and Pacific Migration Journal*, vol. 12(1-2):.75–97.
Human Rights Watch (2006) *Maid to Order — Ending Abuses Against Migrant Domestic Workers in Singapore*, New York: HRW.
Human Rights Watch (2004) *Help Wanted – Abuses against Female Migrant Domestic Workers in Indonesia and Malaysia*, New York: HRW.
International Development Research Centre (IDRC) (2006) *Women's Rights and Citizenship — Program Initiative*, Ottawa: IDRC.
International Labour Office (ILO) (2005) *ILO Multilateral Framework on Labour Migration — Non-binding principles and guidelines for a rights-based approach to labour migration*, Geneva: ILO.
International Labour Office (ILO) (1999) *Report of the Director-General: Decent Work*, Geneva: ILO.
INSTRAW (United Nations International Research and Training Institute for the Advancement of Women) and IOM (International Organisation for Migration) (2000) *Temporary Labour Migration of Women: Case Studies of Bangladesh and Sri Lanka*, Dominican Republic: Amigo del Hogar.
IOM (International Organisation for Migration) (2003) *World Migration 2003*. IOM: Geneva: IOM.

IOM (International Organisation for Migration) and FOM (Federal Office for Migration Switzerland) (2005) *The Berne Initiative — International Agenda for Migration Management*, IOM: Geneva.
Japanese Ministry of Justice (ed.) (1998) *Shustunyukoku Kanri* (Admission and exit control). Tokyo: Printing Office of the Ministry of Finance.
Japanese Ministry of Justice (2003) Accessed 10 June 2005, from http://www.moj.go.jp/
JANNI (Japan NGO Network on Indonesia) (2001) *Technical Interns or Menial Labourers? The Reality of Indonesian Trainees and Technical Interns*, Tokyo: JANNI.
Kim, J. (2003) 'Insurgency and advocacy: Unauthorised foreign workers and civil society in South Korea', in: *Asian and Pacific Migration Journal*, vol. 12(3): 237–269.
Lan, P-C. (2003) 'Political and social geography of marginal insiders: Migrant Domestic Workers in Taiwan', in: *Asian and Pacific Migration Journal*, vol. 12(1-2): 99–125.
Lee, H-K. 2004. *Migrant Domestic Workers in South Korea: An Unpopular Option?"* Paper presented in the International Conference on Transnational Domestic Workers Workshop. *National University of Singapore. February 23–25, 2004*.
Lee, H-K. (2003) 'Gender, Migration and Civil Activism in South Korea', in: *Asian and Pacific Migration Journal*, vol. 12(1-2): 127–153.
Lee, H-K. (1997) 'The Employment of Foreign Workers in Korea: Issues and Policy Suggestion', in: *International Sociology*, vol. 12(3): 353–371.
Lee, M. and N. Piper (2003) 'Reflections on Transnational Life-Course and Migratory Patterns of Middle Class Women — Preliminary Observations from Malaysia', in: N. Piper and M. Roces (eds.), *Wife or Worker?: Asian Women and Migration*, Lanham, MD: Rowman & Littlefield Publishers.
Lim, L. L. and N. Oishi (1996) 'International labour migration of Asian women: Distinctive characteristics and policy concerns', in: *Asian and Pacific Migration Journal*, vol. 5(1): 85–116.
Lindio-McGovern, L. (2003) 'Labour export in the context of globalisation: The experience of Filipino domestic workers in Rome', in: *International Sociology*, vol. 18(3): 513–534.
Loveband, A. (2004)'Nationality Matters: SARS and Foreign Domestic Workers' Rights in Taiwan Province of China', *International Migration*, vol. 42(5): 121–139.
Macabuag, L. and J. M. Dimaandal (2006) 'Working Together for Migrants' Empowerment, in: *Asian and Pacific Migration Journal*, vol. 15(3): 415–424.
Miyajima, T. and N. Higuchi (1996) 'Iryo, Shakai Hosho: Seizonken no Kanten kara', in: Kajita Takamichi and Miyajima Takashi (eds), *Gaikokujin Rodosha kara Shimin he*, Tokyo: Yuhikaku.
Nakamatsu, T. (2003) 'International marriage through introduction agencies: Social and legal realities of 'Asian' wives of Japanese men', in: N. Piper and M. Roces (eds.), *Wife or Worker? Asian Women and Migration*, Lanham, MD: Rowman & Littlefield Publishers.
Narayanan, S. and Y-W Lai (2005) 'The Causes and Consequences of Immigrant Labour in the Construction Sector in Malaysia", *International Migration*, vol. 43(5): 31–57.
Ogaya, C. (2003) 'Feminisation and empowerment: Organisational activities of Filipino women workers in Hong Kong and Singapore', in: M. Tsuda (ed.), *Filipino Diaspora: Demography, Social Networks, Empowerment and Culture*, Quezon City: Philippine Social Science Council and UNESCO.

Oishi, N. (2005) *Women in Motion — Globalization, State Policies, and Labor Migration in Asia*, Stanford: Stanford University Press.

Ong, P.L and T. Azores (1994) 'The migration and incorporation of Filipino nurses', in: P. Ong, E. Bonacich and L. Cheng (eds.), *The New Asian Immigration in Los Angeles and Global Restructuring*, Philadelphia: Temple University Press.

Ono, H. and N. Piper (2004) 'Japanese women studying abroad: The case of the United States', in: *Women's Studies International Forum*, vol. 27(2): 101–118.

Parreñas, R. S. (2001) *Servants of Globalisation: Women, Migration and Domestic Work*, Stanford: Stanford University Press.

Piper, N. (2005a) 'Gender and Migration', *Paper prepared for the Policy Analysis and Research Programme of the Global Commission on International Migration*, Geneva: GCIM (accessed September 2006, from http://www.gcim.org/en/ir_experts, September 2006)

———. (2005b) 'A Problem by a Different Name? A Review of Research on Trafficking in Southeast Asia and Oceania', in: *International Migration*, vol. 43(1/2): 203–233.

———. (2005c) 'Country Study: Malaysia', *Unpublished Paper presented at the Workshop on Foreign Migrant Workers in Southeast Asia*, Friedrich Ebert Foundation and the Asia Research Institute, 20–21 August 2005, Singapore

———. (2003) 'Bridging gender, migration and governance: Theoretical possibilities in the Asian context', in: *Asian and Pacific Migration Journal*, vol. 12(1-2): 21–48.

———. (1999) 'Labor Migration, Trafficking and International Marriage: Female Cross-Border Movements into Japan', in: *Asian Journal of Women's Studies*, vol. 5(2): 69–99.

Piper, N. and R. Iredale (2003) *Identification of the Obstacles to the Signing and Ratification of the UN Convention on the Protection of the Rights of All Migrant Workers 1990: The Asia Pacific Perspective*, APMRN Working Paper No. 14, University of Wollongong.

Piper, N. and M. Roces (2003) 'Introduction: Marriage and migration in an age of globalisation', in: N. Piper and M. Roces (eds.), *Wife or Workers? Asian Women and Migration*, Lanham, MD: Rowman & Littlefield Publishers, pp. 1–22.

Poniatowski, B. and C. Jimenez (2006) *Workshop on Gender and Migration: Domestic Workers from Asia and Latin America — Report*, Tokyo: United Nations University.

Raghuram, P. (2000) 'Gendering Skilled Migratory Streams: Implications for Conceptualisations of Migration', in: *Asian and Pacific Migration Journal*, vol. 9(4): 429–457.

Sadamatsu, A. (2002) 'Kokusai Kekkon ni Miru Kazoku no Mondai (Problems with the family in international marriage)', in: T. Miyajima and H. Kano (eds.), *Henyo suru Nihon Shakai to Bunka* (Japanese society and culture in transformation). Tokyo: Tokyo Daigaku Shuppankai.

Sakai, C. (2000) '*National boundary ni okeru kosho*: Hong Kong de hataraku Nihonjin no katari kara', in: *Shakaigaku Hyoron*, vol. 51(3): 314–330.

Saroor, S. (2003) 'Advocating for the voting rights of Sri Lankan migrant workers', in: *Asian and Pacific Migration Journal*, vol. 12(1-2): 209–216.

Sassen, S. (2003) 'The feminisation of survival: Alternative global circuits', in: M. Morokavsic-Müller, U. Erel and K. Shinozaki (eds.), *Crossing Borders and Shifting Boundaries*, Opladen: Leske+Bude, pp. 59–78.

Shah, N. M. and I. Menon (1997) 'Violence against women migrant workers: Issues, data and partial solutions', in: *Asian and Pacific Migration Journal*, vol.6 (1): 5–30.
Skeldon, R. (2004) 'More than Remittances: Other Aspects of the Relationship between Migration and Development', *UN/POP/MIG/2004* (9 November 2004), New York: Population Division of the United Nations, UN.
Sophal, C. and S. Sovannarith (1999) 'Cambodian Labour Migration to Thailand: A Preliminary Assessment', *Working Paper No. 11*, Phnom Penh: Cambodia Development Resource Institute.
Suzuki, N. (2002) 'Gendered surveillance and sexual violence in Filipina pre-migration experiences to Japan', in: B. S.A. Yeoh, P. Teo and S. Huang (eds.), *Gender Politics in the Asia-Pacific Region*, London: Routledge.
Suzuki, N. (2003), 'Transgressing 'victims': Reading narratives of 'Filipina brides' in Japan', in: *Critical Asian Studies*, vol. 35(3): 399–420.
Takeshita, S. (2001) 'Nihonjin-tuma no Islam eno Tekio: Gaikokujin Moslem wo Otto ni Motsu Tsuma no Jirei Bunseki kara', in: *Aichi Gakuin Daigaku Kyo-yobu Kiyo*, vol. 48(3): 157–172.
Tantiwiramanond, D. (2002) 'Situation analysis of out-migration from Thailand and the role of GOs, NGOs and academics', *Paper presented at the Conference 'Gender, Migration and Governance in Asia'*, Australian National University, Canberra, December 5–6.
Terada, K. (2001) 'Kyosei e muketa Shien no Tenkai: Nihonjin Moslema no Seikatsu Kadai to sono Taio karano Kosatsu', Unpublished PhD Dissertation, Department of Sociology, Tokyo University, Tokyo.
Thang, L. L., E. MacLachlan and M. Goda (2002) 'Expatriates on the margins: A study of Japanese women in Singapore', in: *Geoforum*, vol. 33 (44): 539–551.
United Nations (2006) *International migration and development — Report of the Secretary-General*, New York: UN.
United Nations (2004) *World survey on the role of women in development — Women and international migration*, New York: UN.
United Nations (2003) *Levels and Trends of International Migration to Selected Countries in Asia*, New York: Department of Economic and Social Affairs Population Division, United Nations.
UNFPA (2006) *A Passage to Hope — Women and International Migration*, New York: UNFPA.
United Nations Office on Drug and Crime (UNODC) (2006) *Trafficking in Persons and Global Patterns*, Vienna: UNODC (accessed 11 September 2006, from http://www.unodc.org/pdf/traffickinginpersonsreport2006ver2.pdf
WAO (Women's Aid Organisation) (2003) 'Protection of Foreign Domestic Workers in Malaysia: Laws and Policies, Implication and Intervention', *Paper prepared for Programme Consultative Meeting on the Protection of Domestic Workers Against the Threat of Forced Labor and Trafficking*, Hong Kong SAR, February 16–10.
Wee, V. and A. Sim (2005) 'Hong Kong as a destination for migrant domestic workers', in: S. Huang, B.S.A. Yeoh and N. Abdul Rahman (eds.), *Asian Women as Transnational Domestic Workers*, Singapore: Marshall Cavendish.
Willis, K. D. and B. Yeoh (2000) 'Gender and transnational household strategies: Singaporean migration to China', in: *Regional Studies*, vol. 34(3): 253–264.
Wong, D. (1997) 'Transience and settlement: Singapore's foreign labour policy', in: *Asian and Pacific Migration Journal*, vol. 6(2):135–167.

Yamanaka, K. (1999) 'Illegal immigration in Asia: Regional patterns and a case study of Nepalese workers in Japan', in: D. W. Haines and K. E. Rosenblum (eds.), *Illegal Immigration in America: Handbook*, Westport, CT: Greenwood Press.

Yamanaka, K. (2003) 'Feminised migration, community activism and grassroots transnationalisation in Japan', in: *Asian and Pacific Migration Journal*, vol. 12(1-2): 155–187.

Yamanaka, K. and N. Piper (2003) 'An introductory overview', in: *Asian and Pacific Migration Journal*, vol. 12(1-2):1–19.

Yeoh, B.S.A., S. Huang and J. Gonzalez III (1999) 'Migrant female domestic workers in the economic and political impacts in Singapore', in: *International Migration Review*, vol. 33(1): 114–136.

Yeoh, B.S.A. and L-M Khoo (1998) 'Home, work and community: Skilled international migration and expatriate women in Singapore', in: *International Migration*, vol. 36(2): 159–186.

Yeoh, B.S.A. and K.D. Willis, (2004) 'Gendering transnational communities: a comparison of Singaporean and British migrants in China', in: *Geoforum*, vol. 33(4):553–565

7 Gendered Migrations in the Americas
Mexico as Country of Origin, Destination, and Transit[1]

Martha Luz Rojas Wiesner and Hugo Ángeles Cruz

In any study examining international migration in Mexico, regardless of the particular point of view, women — migrating women and the women who, as part of the family strategy, remain at home — inevitably play a central role, both quantitatively and qualitatively. In considering migrant women, two distinct types of situations must be taken into account. One concerns women whose journey is linked to that of other migrants, i.e., women who travel, alone or accompanied, as wives, mothers, sisters, or daughters, in a quest to reunite their families. The other involves relatively independent women traveling alone (i.e., without other family members) to perform or seek work.

In Mexico, as in other countries, efforts to study the role of women in migration began only a few years ago — though the subject of male migration has experienced a similar neglect. The theoretical approaches prevalent prior to the 1960–70 period provided no basis for examining the differential participation of men and women in migration. An entire line of developments in the social sciences, including the field of social statistics, was necessary before these differences could be recognized, categories could be deconstructed, data could be disaggregated, and the potential relationships between multiple variables could be discerned. In the 1980s, approaches to the study of everyday life, the collective imagination, the subjectivity, gender differences, gender inequalities and gender-based oppression, among other issues, led to the first targeted studies of the role of women in production and social reproduction, and to a general realization that a gender perspective and other conceptual orientations were essential tools in gaining a more complete understanding of complex social phenomena.

The most recent studies of female migration and gender show that women also migrate alone (see, among others Barrera and Oehmichen 2000; Rojas 2001, 2002; Woo 2002), and that they do so as part of a complex decision-making process that takes place within the family. The determining factors in this process, as well as the decision-making modalities and consequences, are not necessarily the same for women as for men (Woo 2002; Martínez 2003).

In the case of Mexico, taking a gender perspective has made it possible to focus on women's role in migration and to clarify how this differs from migration in the male population. Ivonne Szasz's (1999) assessment of current knowledge regarding female migration in Mexico, however, shows that while major progress has been achieved, much remains to be done. In particular, there has been, to date, little work structured specifically around gender. Research has also been limited in terms of geographic coverage and in examining the different migratory flows involving women.

This chapter attempts to examine the role of women in international migration in Mexico, taking into account not only Mexican women directly or indirectly involved in international migration, but also women of other nationalities who enter Mexico for various purposes. For some of these women, Mexico is a stepping stone to the United States. Others arrive with the intention of remaining on a short- or long-term basis to work or study, or as members of families or households — as mothers, daughters, sisters, etc.

Though the term *migrant* has generally carried a labour connotation (Perruchoud 2001: 276), the present chapter considers not only international migrant women who travel to work or seek work, but also those who accompany men migrating for work-related purposes. Women who remain in their families' place of origin also play a role, as do those who migrate domestically — traveling to border areas but remaining on the Mexican side while their husbands or other family members cross the border to work in the United States (for the latter case see, for example, the work of Velasco 1995). The available statistical information is insufficient to document the status of women who remain in Mexico, though some sociological and anthropological studies have focused on the issue within specific communities and groups.

While there is ample literature on migration to the United States, studies dedicated to women's role in this migratory flow are still few and fragmentary. There are, however, special sources[2] that deserve to be more fully explored and utilized, since they provide data disaggregated by sex and have become more accessible.[3] In the case of migratory activity at Mexico's southern border, though the contrast is greater still, there are historical reasons for the lack of attention, as will be seen. This region of Mexico, which has experienced an increase in migratory activity in recent years, warrants greater study. Despite an increase in interest since the end of the 1990s and the start of the new century in the peculiarities of migration at the southern border, much remains to be achieved in terms of generating information.

The present chapter is divided into five sections, focusing on the various roles of women in the migratory process in Mexico. The first section describes Mexico's triple role in international migration over the last few years. The second provides a general description of Mexican emigration (primarily to the United States, but including, also, recent emigration to Canada). The third section outlines major features of immigration to Mexico and examines Mexico's role as a receiving country. The fourth focuses on migration at Mexico's southern border, looking at the triple role this region plays (as does Mexico generally) in the phenomenon of international migration. The fifth and final section details concerns regarding the human rights of migrant women.

Women's role in migration is examined here on the basis of existing information, drawing comparisons with the situation of men where possible.

MEXICO'S TRIPLE ROLE IN THE MIGRATORY PROCESS

Mexico is a country of migrants. Though it is not the only such country, it represents a special case, inasmuch as it borders the United States, which has served as a magnet for Mexicans as well as for people from other, primarily Central American countries. Proximity to the United States has clearly been a decisive factor in producing the migratory patterns evident in Mexico today.

The complexity and diversity of population movements in Mexico can be traced to Mexico's triple role in migration: as a source of emigration, a country of immigration, and a transit corridor. As such, it faces special challenges, not only vis-à-vis migrants, but in relation to a broader universe of players linked to the phenomenon of international migration.

There is extensive literature, in both Mexico and the United States, on Mexico as a country of origin and on its emigrants (primarily those migrating to the United States). This migration has, in fact, become an essential part of Mexico's twentieth-century history. Its impact, at both the micro and macro levels, has been enormous, with significant economic, social, cultural and political impact on the country as a whole. The experience of migration to the United States has played a defining role in Mexican culture, and in the creation of new identities, both for those who remain on "the other side" and for those who continue to live in their places of origin.

As a receiving country, Mexico also has played a historic role. Population groups from different parts of the world have come to Mexico for a variety of reasons, some temporarily, and others for longer periods of time. Some arrive and subsequently leave; others come repeatedly; yet others settle permanently in Mexico, which is well known as a country of refuge. In the 1980s, this country received thousands of Guatemalan refugees, of whom some have returned to Guatemala over time, while others have remained as permanent residents, opting for Mexican citizenship.

Mexico, because of its geography, plays a third strategic role in international migration: as a country of transit for migrants from Central America, other Latin American countries and even other parts of the world who have been attracted by the "American dream" and are attempting to gain access to the United States. They are obliged to cross the immense expanse that

Mexico represents, and to face a series of often life-threatening obstacles. From the Suchiate River, which marks the border between Guatemala and the Mexican state of Chiapas, to the Rio Bravo/Rio Grande which constitutes a portion of the Mexico-United States border, increasing numbers of documented and undocumented migrants from third countries have traversed Mexico in attempts to enter the United States.

Mexico's triple role in international migration has been particularly noteworthy in the last few years. Its role as a transit country was particularly evident in the wake of the 1998 natural disasters in Central America, and as a result of the economic crises precipitated by the decline in international coffee prices. Men and women of different age groups and nationalities attempted to reach the United States without documentation, and without support networks, as migration statistics covering a period of merely a few months reveal.

MEXICO AS ORIGIN AND DESTINATION

Mexico's proximity to the United States has clearly contributed to the international migration patterns of its citizens. This magnet on the "other side" of the country's northern border has exerted such a strong attraction that the prevalence of a single destination has become one of the distinctive features of Mexican emigration, which points predominantly toward the United States.

As Durand and Massey (2003: 57) observe, this is corroborated by a recent survey conducted by the Federal Electoral Institute regarding voting among Mexicans abroad. According to these data, the United States is the destination of 98 percent of Mexican emigrants. Similarly, estimates of the IMILA (Investigation of International Migration in Latin America) project, based on Latin American censuses and data from the United States Current Population Survey (CPS), indicate that, as of 2000, the United States accounted for 93.3 percent of the Mexican emigrants (7,893,271 persons), in 10 Western Hemisphere countries, for whom there are records (Pizarro 2003: 73).

Given this singular vector, the Mexican presence in countries other than the United States is insignificant, though the number of Mexicans in Canada, according to that country's last census (1996), was slightly over 30,000, making Canada the country with the second-largest population of Mexican immigrants. Among the remaining countries on the continent, Bolivia stands out, with a Mexican population of nearly 10,000 according to Bolivia's 2001 census (Pizarro 2003).

Mexico also plays a role as a destination for international migrants, though the volume of this flow is much lower. According to the 1990 census, Mexico was home to 340,000 foreign nationals, representing 0.4 percent of the country's total population. This proportion seems to be relatively stable over time. Statistics show that when Mexico became independent in the mid-nineteenth century, it had a foreign population of 0.44 percent (Navarro 1994: 271), with that proportion remaining stable over the second half of the nineteenth and throughout the twentieth century.

MEXICO–UNITED STATES MIGRATION

Mexican migration to the United States is part of a current global process, in which increasing numbers of people — generally seeking better living conditions for themselves and their families — cross international borders.

As various authors have indicated, however, understanding the dynamics of migration from Mexico to the United States requires knowledge of the historical events that have shaped the flow and direction of migration (see, among others, Verduzco 2000 and Alba 2001). This history is a long one and has contributed to the increasing complexity of migratory patterns. It reflects the geographic proximity of the two countries, with structural roots on both sides of the border. According to Durand and Massey (2003), a third essential element (in addition to history and proximity) is the growing, indeed massive, number of Mexicans migrating to the United States.

The marked wage asymmetry between the two countries — along with their unequal job-creation capacities and other economic and social factors — has perpetuated this massive flow of Mexicans northward over time.[4]

> The *Report of the Mexico-United States Binational Migration Study* underlines the binational nature of the various factors — historical, economic, social and cultural — behind this phenomenon. However, the catalyst for Mexican emigration lies in the United States as an engine of job creation. (Alba 2001: 44)

Labour demand in the United States has contributed to the strength and pattern of Mexican emigration. Various sectors depend on Mexican labour, and it is anticipated that this dependency will continue. According to estimates by the U.S. Bureau of Labour Statistics, the country's demographics indicate that by the first decade of the twenty-first century there will be as many as 5 million unfilled jobs, while 57 percent of the jobs created will require minimal skills and less than a high-school or college-preparatory education (cited in Tuirán et al. 2002: 12). The need for labour could increase in the medium and long term as a result of the aging of the U.S. population, and it is anticipated that this demand will be met by Mexican workers.

Meanwhile, as a result of the recurrent crises and profound restructuring of the Mexican economy that has occurred since the early 1980s, the economic factors that encourage Mexican migration to the United States have intensified. The Mexican development model has had a decisive effect on the country's job-creation capacity, as well as on wage levels and working conditions — leading to increasing and entrenched migration to the United States.

The export-oriented development scheme formulated over the last two decades in Mexico has increased the socioeconomic gaps between states, regions, economic sectors and social groups, resulting in differences in both domestic and international migration patterns. Thus,

> the regions and cities whose economies grow as a result of greater competitive activity in the domestic or export market are experiencing rapid job growth, which operates as a magnet for migratory flows. In contrast, the supply of jobs tends to contract in those regions and cities whose productive activities have borne the brunt of economic crises and trade liberalization, and their capacity to absorb workers is diminished. This is reflected in growing unemployment and under-employment rates, and in deteriorating living conditions and well-being, thus encouraging emigration. (Tuirán et al. 2002: 13)

The history of migration between Mexico and the United States manifests a set of features that, while they have been stable, now coexist with recent changes (Tuirán et al. 2002), namely:

- more complex, diverse and larger migratory flows, including different types of migration;
- increasing regional diversification of the flows, as the geographic origin of migrants moves beyond traditional areas and municipalities. Thus, for example, Puebla, Hidalgo, the state of Mexico, the Federal District and Morelos, which do not have historic traditions of migration, have been the source of a significant share of migrants to the United States in recent years;
- the presence of emigrants from urban areas, which is increasingly pronounced. There is evidence that the great urban centers and a number of medium-sized cities are not only absorbing internal emigrants from rural areas and other urban regions, but are also becoming the source of migration to the United States;
- increasing occupational and sectoral diversity among emigrants, in both Mexico and the United States. At both the source and the destination, agricultural workers no longer represent a majority; and
- Mexican migrants are increasingly likely to prolong their stay in the United States or to establish residence there.

In these changes, the Immigration Reform and Control Act (IRCA), of 1986, was a decisive factor. Its principal objective was to legalize the foreign population undocumented as of 1982. The reform played a role in changing the traditional pattern of migration to the United States, provoking a significant increase in the volume of both documented and undocumented migrants, and encouraging geographic dispersion (Verduzco 2000; Durand and Massey 2003). Tight border controls during the 1990s were also important. The border area was transformed, and migratory routes changed, as the risk and cost of crossing the border rose. Migrants' length of stay in the United States also increased (Durand and Massey 2003).

One important change in the traditional pattern concerns the age of migrants and their distribution by gender: female migration became more important following the IRCA:

> The Bracero Program was successful in terms of generic male selectivity. Subsequently, during the period of undocumented migration, female migration became more widespread. It was with IRCA, however, that it became truly significant. IRCA legalized 43 percent of the women in the program (LAW), for the first time incorporating a large number of women (15%) in an agricultural workers' program (SAW). (Durand and Massey 2003: 173)

Though the profile of the Mexican migrants to the United States has become more diverse, now including a range of different groups, two types of flows can be distinguished: temporary workers who regularly enter and leave the United States, and Mexicans who are more or less settled there. The latter group includes migrants born in Mexico who have become U.S. citizens.

Temporary workers account for the largest portion of migration to the United States. CONAPO (the National Population Council of Mexico) estimates that, between 2001 and 2003, an annual average of approximately 437,000 Mexican migrants currently work in the United States on a temporary basis. Ninety-seven percent of these workers that returned to Mexico were men; almost 53 percent were between 25 and 34 years of age; 50 percent had at least a secondary education; 79 percent entered the U.S. without working papers; 40 percent worked in the service sector, while only 20 percent were employed in the primary sector; and 53 percent came from urban areas. In light of tighter border controls, temporary migrants have increased their average stay in the United States from 5.5 to 12.2 months, and have changed to riskier crossing points. Increasingly, people without previous migratory experience are migrating, and the proportion of those who resort (at ever increasing prices) to the services of third parties (more commonly known in Mexico as "coyotes" or "polleros") to help them cross the U.S. border has risen (CONAPO 2005).

The number of migrants of the second type — those who, for varying reasons, decide to take up residence in the United States — has increased systematically and steadily since the 1960s. Thus, according to a combination of sources, the number of Mexicans who decided to stay in the United

States rose from 260,000 to 290,000 between 1960 and 1970, from 1.20 to 1.55 million between 1970 and 1980, and from 2.10 to 2.60 million between 1980 and 1990, reaching nearly 3.3 million between 1990 and 2000 and nearly 1.6 million between 2000 and 2004. Thus, the net annual flow has risen from 26,000–29,000 in the 1960s to over 300,000 in the 1990s and almost 400,000 in the first years of the new century (Tuirán 2002; Alba 2004; Corona 2004; CONAPO 2005).

These estimates imply a systematic loss of population in Mexico, and a community in the United States that comprises an estimated 26.7 million individuals of Mexican origin as of 2003. Of these, it has been estimated that 9.9 million (living with or without official authorization in the U.S.) were born in Mexico, while the other 16.8 million were born in the United States[5] (Tuirán 2002: 78, CONAPO 2005).

Based on the 2003 United States CPS, CONAPO (2005) has drawn inferences regarding various features of the Mexican-born population living in the United States. Only slightly over one half (53.8%) are men, and the proportion of women is steadily increasing. The 1999 estimates based on the CPS show women representing 45.6 percent of the total. Average age is 34 years, and 87.1 percent are between 15 and 64 years of age. The majority, however, are between 20 and 44 years of age, i.e., of productive/reproductive age. A majority (67%) entered the United States between 1986 and 2003, particularly between 1994 and 2003 (42%). Over 60 percent live in either California or Texas (39.3% and 23%, respectively), followed by Illinois (6.5%). Geographic locations have diversified however, as documented by Durand and Massey, in a dynamic process of concentration and dispersion that has led to a pattern of new destination regions for migrants. Approximately one-fifth (21.8%) of Mexican immigrants (24% of the women and 21% of the men) have acquired U.S. citizenship, and these tend to have more schooling than do temporary migrants. Only 12 percent have a fourth-grade education or less; 29 percent have completed fifth through eight grades; 21 percent have completed ninth through eleventh grades; and almost 40 percent have 12 years or more of schooling. Nearly half of resident immigrants (53%) lack health insurance. The migrants are primarily (69%) economically active individuals, of which 62 percent are employed. The majority works in low-paying manual jobs (service occupations; construction and mining/oil extraction occupations; production, transportation, and material-moving occupations). Only one out of 10 economically active migrants is unemployed (Alba 2004; CONAPO 2005).

Regardless of their particular form of migration to the United States, it is clear that these Mexicans are large in number, a fact which has enormous impact on the lives of their compatriots in Mexico. This is confirmed by recent CONAPO estimates, made by experts on the subject.

Nearly 18 percent (nearly 4 million) of Mexico's households have or have had immediate family members in the United States, or have received remittances from the United States. Thus, one out of five Mexican households has had some type of connection with migration to the United States, though the proportion varies depending on the particular state or region.[6] In areas that have traditionally been a source of migration to the United States, the figure is 37 percent. The proportion in the north is 22 percent, in the central region, 12 percent, and in the southeast, only 4 percent[7] (Tuirán 2002: 79; Tuirán et al. 2002: 30). These disparities are certain to diminish in the coming years, as the process of migration becomes more entrenched in the southeast part of the country.

In view of the complexity and growth of migration to the United States during the last few years, CONAPO decided to refine the measurement of this demographic phenomenon and generate data to reflect figures for states and municipalities. With this in mind, Tuirán et al. (2002) created an estimated migratory intensity index (MII) based on information from Mexico's Twelfth General Population and Housing Census (2000) (see Tuirán et al. 2002:31, for more detail on the MII) . The index classifies Mexico's 32 states in 5 levels, from those with the least to those with the greatest intensity of migration (Table 7.1)[8] On the extremes of this scale are Zacatecas (the greatest migratory intensity) and Chiapas and Tabasco (the least).

MII data at the municipal level show that migration no longer originates exclusively in regions with a history of migratory activity, but extends, in varying degrees, to the entire nation. According to the index, only 93 municipalities in the country's south and southeast (out of Mexico's total of 2,443 municipalities) show no connection with migration to the United States — i.e., have no household member who has migrated to the United States or who receives any remittances from that country. The remaining 2,350 municipalities (96% of the total) do show some relationship or contact with U.S. migration. Of these, 492 fall in the categories of high or very high migratory intensity, 392 in the medium-intensity category, and 1,466 in the low or very low category (Tuirán et al. 2002: 36; Tuirán 2002: 81).

In geographic terms, the MII estimates corroborate the persistence of migration to the United States in those regions that have traditionally been a source of such migration. Indeed, the phenomenon is evident in an increasing number of municipalities — in states such as Durango, Guanajuato, Michoacán and Jalisco, over half of the municipalities. States such as Aguascalientes and Zacatecas have surpassed even this figure, and close to 75 percent of the municipalities are involved in U.S. migration (Tuirán et al. 2002).

As indicated above, this pattern has continued over time, with a series of changes occurring over the last few years, including (as cited above) the diversification of migrants' places of origin:

> Mexico's southern states and other regions where emigration was not traditional, such as Morelos, Hidalgo, Guerrero and Oaxaca, are rapidly joining the category of 'migration states'. (Alba 2004)

Table 7.1 Mexico. Index and degree of migratory intensity by state, 2000

State	Migratory Intensity Index	Degree of migratory intensity	Region
Zacatecas	2.58352	Very high	Traditional
Michoacán	2.05950	Very high	Traditional
Guanajuato	1.36569	Very high	Traditional
Nayarit	1.27041	Very high	Traditional
Durango	1.09000	Very high	Traditional
Aguascalientes	1.03883	High	Traditional
Jalisco	0.88785	High	Traditional
Colima	0.80260	High	Traditional
San Luis Potosí	0.67344	High	Traditional
Morelos	0.51921	High	Center
Guerrero	0.42772	High	South-southeast
Hidalgo	0.39700	High	Center
Chihuahua	–0.00082	Medium	North
Baja California	–0.00104	Medium	North
Querétaro	–0.04158	Medium	Center
Oaxaca	–0.26377	Medium	South-southeast
Sinaloa	–0.26620	Medium	North
Puebla	–0.42263	Medium	Center
Tamaulipas	–0.42994	Medium	North
Coahuila	–0.47955	Medium	North
Sonora	–0.63929	Low	North
Nuevo León	–0.66630	Low	North
Veracruz	–0.70717	Low	South-southeast
Tlaxcala	–0.73806	Low	Center
México	–0.74732	Low	Center
Baja California Sur	–0.86423	Low	North
Distrito Federal	–0.90984	Very low	Center
Yucatán	–1.08207	Very low	South-southeast
Quintana Roo	–1.14632	Very low	South-southeast
Campeche	–1.19328	Very low	South-southeast
Chiapas	–1.24572	Very low	South-southeast
Tabasco	–1.27065	Very low	South-southeast

Source: Tuirán et al. 2002: Table A.

Both the MII and data from other projects show that municipalities in the center of the country (in states such as Mexico, Morelos, Guerrero, Puebla and Oaxaca) are registering levels of migratory intensity as high as those seen in the municipalities of the traditional emigration areas (Tuirán et al. 2002: 36, Durand and Massey 2003).

FEMALE MEXICAN MIGRANTS TO THE UNITED STATES

The role of women has attracted little attention in the context of this continuing and changing migration to the United States, in part because migration seemed to be predominantly a male phenomenon, and partly because of a lack of information. Complete national data are unavailable, and existing data are not disaggregated by sex — an obvious obstacle when attempting to identify the features and dynamics of female migration. This problem has not been exclusive to Mexico, nor is it a technical problem. As mentioned above, the invisibility of female migration was a result of the conception of the female role, both in migration and in relation to extra-domestic and domestic activities.

Women began to gain visibility when conceptions of their role changed, and as more women migrated to the United States seeking work. However, it is important to note that the increased number of women migrants cannot be designated a "feminization of migration." This label, in the authors' opinion, is part of a process in which only one segment of the female migrant population is made visible, while other women, who are equally a part of the migratory phenomenon, remain invisible as "companions" or "economic dependents." What is seen here is not, therefore, a "feminization of migration," but rather a process of "quantitative feminization," as Martínez Pizarro (2003) has stated.

At the global level, quantitative evidence of female migration has only recently become available. It was not until 1998 that the United Nations Population Division first provided global estimates by sex for the 1965–1990 period, and only in 2002 did it publish estimates for the 1960–2000 period, showing that there were almost as many women migrants as men (Zlotnik 2003). The concern for statistical evidence has also become important in Mexico, and there are ongoing efforts to gather data on the role of women, through a number of national-level surveys and by means of the census process. This quantitative visibility, though important, must be a part of a wider process that examines the particular conditions and circumstances under which both women and men migrate.[9]

Recent CONAPO estimates have been based on a study of data from the 1992 and 1997 National Survey on Demographic Dynamics (Encuesta Nacional de la Dinámica Demográfica or ENADID), with supplementary data from databases created by the Survey on Migration at the Northern Border (Encuesta sobre Migración en la Frontera Norte or EMIF).

ENADID estimates have provided unprecedented information on female migration in Mexico. One of the most important results has undoubtedly been the finding that the phenomenon of Mexican women migrating temporarily to the United States for the purpose of work or residence predates the Bracero Program, rather than being a result of immigration reforms (IRCA) (Ávila et al. 2000; CONAPO 2000). The 1992 ENADID data (based on a retrospective survey that collects information on habitual household members) estimated that in that year there were 1.8 million Mexicans living in Mexico who had gone to the United States at least once to work or seek work on a temporary basis (see Figure 7.1). By 1997, according to the later ENADID, this figure was 2.2 million. In the aggregate, for both of those years, the percentage of Mexican women with migratory experience of this type was nearly 15 percent (15.4% in 1992 and 13.8% in 1997). While this figure may appear low, the absolute numbers are notable: 276,009 women in 1992 and 304,931 in 1997.

According to ENADID data, international migration by Mexican women dates from a century ago, and though it represented only a small proportion of migration at that time, there was significant female migration for purposes of work well before the 1940s. Over time, the proportion has increased, though remaining rather low in percentage terms, as compared with men. According to the 1992 ENADID, the number of female temporary migrants rose from 864 before 1942 to a total of 148,521 for the 1987–1992 period (see Figure 7.1). According to the 1997 ENADID, the figures were 250 women before 1942 and over 115,000 for the 1992–1997

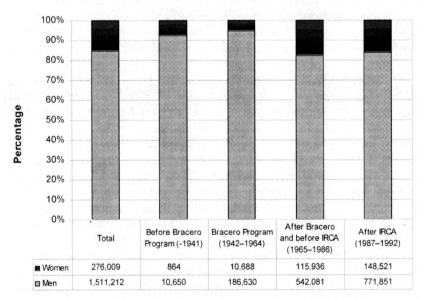

Figure 7.1 Mexico. Temporary work-related migrants residing in Mexico by sex, according to the time period of their most recent trip to the United States. Source: Elaboration of the authors, based on CONAPO (Ávila et al., 2000: table 1).

Table 7.2 Mexico. Temporary work-related migrants residing in Mexico, by sex and various sociodemographic characteristics, according to the time period of their most recent trip to the United States.

Sex and selected characteristics	Total	Bracero Program (1942–1964)	After Bracero Program and before IRCA (1965–1986)	After IRCA (1987–1992)
Men				
Average age as of most recent trip to U.S. (years)	29.5	28.4	30.0	29.7
Age groups	100.0	100.0	100.0	100.0
12–20 years	19.6	16.5	17.1	22.1
20 years or more	80.4	83.5	82.9	77.9
Average schooling (grades completed)	6.7	4.0	5.5	6.9
Marital status at time of most recent trip	100.0	100.0	100.0	100.0
Single	31.0	34.1	27.5	32.7
Has at some point been married	69.0	65.9	72.5	67.3
Women				
Average age as of most recent trip to the U.S. (years)	27.3	22.5	25.8	28.7
Age groups	100.0	100.0	100.0	100.0
12–20 years	32.4	53.5	36.7	27.6
20 years or more	67.6	46.5	63.3	72.4
Average schooling (grades completed)	6.9	4.5	6.1	7.6
Marital status as of most recent trip	100.0	100.0	100.0	100.0
Single	40.9	65.5	46.8	34.7
Has at some point been married	59.1	34.5	53.2	65.3

Source: CONAPO estimates, based on ENADID, in Ávila et al. 2000: Table 3.

period. This increase is accompanied by a general increase in migration to the United States, in which men also play a large role (CONAPO 2000).

ENADID data have also highlighted some of the characteristics of this migrant population (see Table 7.2). First, the migrants are young. This has remained true over time. The average age at different periods analyzed by

ENADID is close to 30. Women are slightly younger than men, and their average age has varied more than that of men. In some periods, such as that of the Bracero Program, the average age was close to 20. More recently, women's average age is not very different from that of men. For 1992–1997, it was 28.1 years, while men's average age was 29.7 (CONAPO 2000).

One notable feature relates to the marital status of temporary migrants at the time of their most recent trip to the United States. In general, the men were living with, or married to women (67.5%), and this proportion remains essentially unchanged over time. In the case of women, the percentage of single individuals is greater (40.9%) than in the case of men (31%), but there has been greater change over time. Thus, during the Bracero Program, there were more single women (65.5% according to the 1992 ENADID) than women living with, or married, to men. For the period following the IRCA (1987–1992), there was a lower proportion (34.7%) of single women (Ávila et al. 2000: 155). This change coincides with the higher average age registered recently among women, suggesting that at the time of their last trip to work in the United States they were no longer single.

The ENADID data call into question the perception that was dominant until the 1970s regarding the role of migrant women as economic dependents or companions, a perception that identified them as an economically inactive population. The historic record of their work-related migration clarifies their role in the migratory process.

These same ENADID data suggest questions regarding the degree of autonomy that women were able to achieve in their ability to migrate, and questions about their migration in association with men. Marital status is not, in itself, a determining factor in permitting "single" (unmarried, separated, divorced, widowed) women to migrate with more autonomy or to undertake their journeys independent of men's migrations. However, answers to these questions about women's autonomy open the door to investigating the supposed historic pattern in which migrant women were in a passive role as companions to men.

Using a different methodology from ENADID, and providing different coverage, the EMIF[10] also contributes to recent knowledge about migration to the United States. In particular, it helps to identify continuities and changes in patterns of temporary migration, highlighting both causes and effects of migratory policy (Ávila et al. 2000: 156).

Based on EMIF, CONAPO has estimated that between 1993 and 1997 an annual average of 464,432 workers who had temporarily migrated to the United States returned to Mexico, while the figure for the 1998–2000 period was 331,334 (CONAPO 2000: 3). The percentage of women in these annual returns is low, though there was an increase between the two periods (from 3.5% to 6.4%), which is consistent with the growing proportion of women migrants registered by ENADID (see Table 7.3).

Table 7.3 Mexico. Percentage distribution of temporary migrant women who return from the United States, according to various characteristics, 1993–1997 and 1998–2000

Characteristics	1993–1997	1998–2000
Total	3.5% (16,217)	6.4% (21,108)
Age groups	100.0	100.0
12–24 years	29.7	40.5
25–34 years	36.4	30.5
35 years or more	33.9	29.0
Average age (years)	31.6	30.8
Schooling	100.0	100.0
Did not complete primary	31.8	21.5
Completed primary	17.1	21.5
Secondary or higher	51.1	57.0
Average schooling by grades completed	6.9	7.4
Marital status	100.0	100.0
Single	31.8	44.0
Has at some point been married	69.4	56.0
Head-of-household status	100.0	100.0
Head	30.1	39.7
Not head	69.9	60.3
Region of residence	100.0	100.0
Traditional	30.0	37.6
North	48.7	49.3
Center and South-southeast	11.3	13.1
Type of locality of residence	100.0	100.0
Urban	61.9	72.2
Nonurban	38.1	27.8
Previous migration experience	100.0	100.0
Prior experience	61.6	27.4
No prior experience	38.4	72.6

Source: CONAPO estimates, based on EMIF 1993–1997, in Ávila et al. 2000: Table 4

EMIF data on temporary migrants indicate an average age slightly above that suggested by ENADID's findings, which was 33 for men and 31 for women in the 1998–2000 period.

The data show that the women have a higher level of schooling than the men — grade 7.4 on average at the turn of the century, as against men's

6.6. This has been true since the time of the Bracero Program (1942–1954), when women's average level of schooling was grade 4.5 (though this was only 0.5 years above the male average). With time, schooling levels rose for both men and women, while the gap between them increased to almost one year by 1998–2000. Disaggregated schooling data for this period show that a greater percentage of women than men had some (but not complete) secondary schooling (57% versus 45%). For 1993–1997, EMIF showed a majority of men as not having completed primary schooling (Ávila et al. 2000; CONAPO 2000). This gap could be associated with the greater proportion of urban women than urban men in the flow of workers (62% versus 56%). EMIF data reflect this urban-versus-rural gender disparity over time, with almost 80% of migrant women being from urban settings in 1998–1999 (STPS et al. 2004).

Migrants' places of residence consist principally (75.2%) of two regions in Mexico: 53 percent of men are from the so-called traditional emigration areas (see note 8 above), while women come predominantly (49%) from the northern area bordering the United States, though a significant number (38%) are from the traditional area (CONAPO 2000; STPS et al. 2004). A majority of these workers spend most of their time, while in the United States, in Texas and California. For 1998–2000, this was true of seven out of 10 migrants, independent of gender. Of the seven out of 10 men, half stayed longer in Texas, the other half in California, while for women, the respective figures for these temporary work stays were four in Texas and three in California (CONAPO 2000: 5).

EMIF data show a major change in the head-of-household status of migrant women between the 1993–1997 period and the 1998–2000 period, with the percentage stating that they were heads of household increasing from 30 percent to 40 percent. This is consistent with the greater proportion of non-married women (unmarried, separated, divorced, or widowed). It does not necessarily indicate an increase in the proportion of unmarried women, since a breakdown of the "non-married" category shows a moderate increase over time in the proportion of non-single women (Corona 2000; STPS et al. 2004). The data would have to be analyzed in more depth to determine the characteristics of the women who are heads of household, and the conditions under which they migrate. Information obtained at Mexico's southern border, for instance, has revealed a high percentage of women who identify themselves as single or "unmarried" (without partners) migrating to the United States to seek work. Many have children and are forced to leave them in the care of family members, or even neighbors of friends, as part of the migration strategy.

The EMIF indicates an important change in the percentage of Mexicans emigrating for the first time to the United States. Between 1993 and 1997 and from 1998 to 2000, this percentage increased from 29 percent to 52 percent. In the case of the women, this change is notable. During the first period, four out of ten women who emigrated to the United States had no migratory experience, while in the second period, seven out of ten women lacked such experience. In the case of men, there was also an increase in the number of migrants without experience, though in smaller percentages than for women. Thus, from one period to the next, the number emigrating without previous migratory experience grew from 30 percent to 50 percent.

Between 1998 and 2000, over half of migrant workers entered the United States without authorization or without documentation (57.2% of men and 45% of women). The majority also lacked U.S. work papers (65% of men and 79% of women). This latter percentage also includes Mexicans entering legally but without permission to work. Despite this, the average working stay was six months for men and almost eight months for women. During their stay in the U.S., the majority of both men (79%) and women (95%) received some type of support from family or friends who had a more settled status in the United States (CONAPO 2000: 6).

However, the migratory process involves not only those who successfully arrive at their destination and procure paid work, but also those who attempt to enter the United States and are turned back by immigration authorities. Most of the latter share social and demographic features (and certain travel conditions) with the former. Between 1998 and 2000, EMIF shows a yearly average of 639,459 individuals being turned back by the border patrol. Of these, 82.4 percent were men and 17.4 percent women (CONAPO 2000: 8). The earlier EMIF surveys (1993–1997) show women as representing roughly 14 percent of the forced returns (STPS et al. 2004: 92). The men and women turned back in the 1998–2000 period were primarily going to the United States to work or seek work. This was the case for 9 out of 10 men and seven out of 10 women. The majority did not pay anyone for help in crossing the border (eight out of 10 men and seven out of 10 women), and for the majority (six out of 10 men and eight out of 10 women), this was their first attempt to enter the United States. Of those who were turned back, seven out of 10 men and six out of 10 women attempted to cross the border again.

In the Mexico–United States migration process, it is important to take into account individuals who have migrated and, for different reasons, have decided to remain more or less permanently in the United States. This population will not be examined in depth, since other papers in the present book deal with immigration to the United States. However, some general features may be noted. Six out of 10 women are married or living with a man as a couple; nearly five out of 10 (47%) are economically active; and 90 percent of these have a job, in most cases a wage-earning job (94%). On average, they work a few hours less per week than do men (37 versus 41), while their monthly wage is disproportionately less (on the order of US$500 less). This comparison may, however, be distorted by the wages of men who work more than 45 hours per week (which is the case for 22.3 percent of the men, while it is true for only 9% of the women). As

CONAPO (2000) states, the data on this female labour force in the United States demand more thorough analysis. At the same time, there needs to be an analysis of the context and conditions governing the lives and work of this group of women, including social and demographic characteristics, gender issues, age, class, ethnic group and migratory status, both in relation to their Mexican peers and in comparison with other women doing similar work.

MIGRATION OF MEXICAN WOMEN TO CANADA

Canada is the second most common destination for Mexican emigrants. The total number of Mexicans in Canada tripled in 15 years, from 13,845 in 1986 to 36,575 at the time of the most recent Canadian census, in 2001 (IME 2005). It is estimated that close to half of the later figure (52%) represents Mexican women (Martínez 2003).

According to the Institute of Mexicans Abroad (Instituto de los Mexicanos en el Exterior or IME), which is a part of the Ministry of Foreign Affairs:

> The Mexican community in Canada is highly diverse, including women married to Canadians, individuals working in the service sector, personnel of the National Autonomous University of Mexico (UNAM) and more recent migrants, who are principally young professionals with families, working in science and technology. (IME 2005: 26)

The 2001 Canadian census showed Mexicans throughout Canada, and while, in some provinces, they are few in number, the fact that they are found in places as remote as the Yukon Territory (where there were 35 in 2001) is certainly notable. The great majority (92.2%) live in the four provinces of Ontario (42.3%), British Columbia (23.1%), Quebec (17.7%) and Alberta (9.1%) (IME 2005).

The migration to Canada also includes temporary workers. This is the result of a 1974 bilateral agreement for the hiring of unskilled labour known as the Temporary Agricultural Workers Program or Mexican Temporary Agricultural Workers Job Program. As the name indicates, the purpose of this program is to ensure a supply of intensive labour needed to plant, care for and harvest fruit, tobacco and vegetables in nurseries and greenhouses, as well as for apiculture. The rules governing the temporary work agreements, which workers sign, provide that employers shall hire workers for no less than 240 hours per six or fewer weeks, and for no more than eight months per year. The period for these temporary jobs begins in January and ends on December 15 of each year (STPS 2005).

Workers applying to the program must meet the requirements of Mexico's Ministry of Labour and Social Welfare (Secretaría del Trabajo y Previsión Social or STPS) and of Human Resources and Skills Development Canada. Hiring decisions may be influenced by the evaluation of the Canadian employers, who submit STPS reports on workers' performance. In the reports, employers may request the return of particular workers for the following year (STPS 2005). According to Sook Lee (2003), this evaluation process, in practice, prevents workers from lodging complaints regarding the poor living and working conditions that Mexican workers experience at some Canadian farms and nurseries.

The requirements and number of Mexican workers participating in the program from year to year depend on the needs and number of requests of Canadian employers. For 1995, for example, workers were required to be at least 18 years old (SRE and MRHDH 1995), while in 2005 they were to be between 22 and 45 years old:

> Women and men who meet the following criteria are eligible to participate in this program:
> - campesinos, day workers or manual labourers whose current job is agriculture-related. Apiculture workers must have technical knowledge and a minimum of five years experience. Women must have experience in strawberry harvesting.
> - Age 22 to 45.
> - Residents of rural areas. (STPS 2005)

As indicated in Table 7.4, the program began in 1974 with 203 male workers, but has increased to 10,681 Mexican workers (10,342 men and 339 women). Female temporary workers only appeared in 1989, when 37 were hired. Since then, women have been hired as part of this temporary program, but only in 1998 did a steady increase in their numbers begin to occur (Becerril 2003).

Workers are selected and hired through the STPS's State Employment Service. Most of the 10,681 workers hired by the offices of this agency in 2002 came from the states of Mexico (22.5%), Tlaxcala (17.2%), Guanajuato (9.5%), Puebla (7.8%), Morelos (7.0%) and Hidalgo (6.1%). The principal destination of these workers — and those who are hired yearly — is Ontario, which is Canada's most important farming province. After Ontario, in order of numbers, Mexican workers are hired to provide intensive labour in Quebec, Manitoba and Alberta (Becerril 2003; Pickard 2004).

The increasing number of female Mexican workers in Canadian agriculture is the result of employers' needs and market demands. The demand for this type of labour has tended to be focused on certain crops and tasks that require "special care," such as selecting and packing fruits and vegetables. Despite the recognized skill of women in this type of activity, women are less hired than men, according to Barrón (Barrón 1999, quoted in Becerril 2003: 6), due to the strict sexual and ethnic division of labour that pre-

Table 7.4 Mexico. Mexican agricultural workers working in Canada, by sex, 1974–2002

Year	Total	Men	Women
Total	101,495	99,680	1,815
1974	203	203	
1975	402	402	
1976	533	533	
1977	495	495	
1978	543	543	
1979	553	553	
1980	678	678	
1981	655	655	
1982	696	696	
1983	615	615	
1984	672	672	
1985	834	834	
1986	1,007	1,007	
1987	1,538	1,538	
1988	2,623	2,623	
1989	4,414	4,377	37
1990	5,143	5,067	76
1991	5,148	5,071	77
1992	4,778	4,701	77
1993	4,866	4,794	72
1994	4,910	4,862	48
1995	4,886	4,830	56
1996	5,211	5,154	57
1997	5,647	5,580	67
1998	6,486	6,341	145
1999	7,574	7,409	165
2000	9,175	8,945	230
2001	10,529	10,160	369
2002	10,681	10,342	339

Source: STPS, Reports from 1974–2002.

vails on Canadian farms, where gender is a determinant in the places, jobs, tasks, work schedules, opportunities and job duration given to workers (Becerril 2003: 6).

More study is needed regarding the characteristics and working conditions of both male and female temporary workers in Canada, in order to identify the differences that account for the disadvantage that women experience in employment opportunities as compared to men. It is also important to research the backgrounds of women participating in the program, for although the STPS requirements do not so stipulate, Sook Lee (2003) and other writers indicate that only unmarried or widowed women are hired. If this is indeed the case, it raises questions about changes in marital status and the strategies women adopt in order to migrate, particularly when they have children. According to Becerril (2003), it has already been shown that women migrating to Canada are principally single mothers who leave their children with their grandmothers, aunts, or older sisters. Research is needed, however, regarding not only this, but also the working conditions under which these women operate in Canada.

MEXICO AS A DESTINATION

Mexico has historically received large groups of immigrants from different parts of the world. Though the number of individuals involved is much lower than the numbers of Mexicans who emigrate, the presence of a foreign-born population has been important in various spheres of the national life — social, economic, cultural, and political.

The percentage of foreign residents in the Mexican population, according to the country's first censuses (1895, 1900 and 1910), was 0.43 percent (Navarro, 1994: 271). This immigrant population was principally male: seven out of 10 according to the 1895 census, a proportion confirmed again in the 1910 census. Gender distribution varied significantly as a function of immigrants' continent of origin, but in almost all cases there were some women. Only in the case of Asian immigrants were men overwhelmingly more numerous (which explains the intense attention Mexicans gave to the arrival of the first Chinese women) (Navarro 1994: 271).

In the twentieth century, immigration to Mexico continued to be slight in relative terms. However, it acquired new meaning as Mexico became a refuge for Spaniards and people fleeing conditions in other Latin American countries, and with the increase in the numbers of Mexicans, along with their U.S.-born children, returning from the United States. From the end of the 1930s to the end of the 1940s, Mexico's General Directorate of Statistics registered 22,123 Spaniards entering the country, including 18,758 adults (42.2% of whom were women) and 3,365 children under 14 (Lida 1997: 58). Spaniards began entering in 1936, fleeing the political violence associated with the Spanish Civil War. The government of Lázaro

Cárdenas provided these people with various forms of support, including granting Mexican citizenship to those who desired it. According to Lida (1997: 112), nearly 80 percent of the Spanish immigrants took advantage of this offer. Though the number of Spaniards entering Mexico between 1936 and 1948, as well as the number of other foreigners who came to Mexico in the 1970s fleeing repression in their countries, did not represent significant percentages of the population, their presence was qualitatively significant. The Spanish influence was felt not only in the arts, the sciences and culture, but also in finance, trade and industry (Lida 1997: 99 and 111). Exiles from Argentina, Uruguay and Chile have had a recognized influence, in particular, in the area of cultural and social sciences.[11] (Alba 2004: 42)

In the 1980s, Mexico once again received foreign nationals fleeing political violence. Though some of these were not unlike those who had fled to Mexico in earlier times (academics, political activists, intellectuals), most were of another type. They came from nearby countries, rather than distant places, and were largely of rural origin, either peasants or indigenous persons. They sought asylum principally in the state of Chiapas, fleeing the persecution that had been unleashed in Guatemala as a result of government counter-insurgency policies. After incursions into Mexican territory by the Guatemalan army, which Guatemala justified as an attempt to hunt down guerillas, the Mexican government relocated nearly half of the refugees to camps in the border states of Campeche and Quintana Roo. Those refugees who refused relocation remained in Chiapas (Kauffer 2002; Kauffer 2003: 126).[12] The presence of the Guatemalan refugees in Mexican localities near Guatemala brought attention to Mexico's southern border. It was not only the government that became interested, for political and administrative reasons related to the demarcation of the international border and with national security: academics were also drawn to the challenge of documenting the make-up of the border and studying the economic, political and social issues in the border region (among others see Castillo 1990, 1992, 1995; Hernández and Sandoval 1989; and De Vos 1993, for more details).

Given the general increase in Mexico's population, this growing flow of immigrants did not raise the historical level of immigrants as a proportion of the total population, remaining unchanged at 0.4 percent, as reflected in the 1950, 1970, and 1990 censuses (INEGI 2005). Meanwhile, the number of women immigrants rose practically to parity with men in the second half of the century. While, in 1950, women represented 42.8 percent of immigrants, the figure reached nearly half (49.4% and 49.6%, respectively) by the time of the 1970 and 1990 censuses.

At the beginning of the twenty-first century, slightly over a hundred years after the first census data on immigration to Mexico became available; the percentage of foreign-born individuals residing in Mexico is slightly over the historical percentage, at 0.5 percent (492,617 individuals) of the total population. The predominant country of origin, representing

69 percent of the immigrants, is the United States,[13] which is followed by Guatemala (5.6%), Spain (4.1%), Cuba (1.4%), Canada (1.4%), Colombia (1.3%) and Argentina (1.3%), with other countries registering lower percentages (CONAPO 2005).

The immigrant population includes nearly equal numbers of men (50.3%) and women (49.7%). According to estimates by CONAPO (2005), the nationalities with slightly more women than men are El Salvador (55.1%), Colombia (54.5%), Guatemala (52.2%), Cuba (52.1%) and Argentina (51.8%). The regions of Mexico attracting the largest proportions of women immigrants are Chiapas (52.9%), the Federal District (51.9%), Yucatán (51.6%) and Quintana Roo (51.5%). In Chiapas, the greater number of women is associated with the flow of Central American women resulting from forced displacement in Guatemala during the 1980s, and with the migration of foreign women living in the state who maintain family links on both sides of the border. In Quintana Roo, the greater number of women is associated with job opportunities in the service sector in tourist centers such as Cancún.

The age composition of the immigrant population is worthy of note. The group with the largest population of persons 10 years of age or less consists of individuals who state that they were born in the United States but reside in Mexico (57%). In contrast, the group with the greatest percentage (53%) of individuals 55 years of age and older consists of the Spanish immigrant population, in which adults 65 years old and above represent 36 percent of the population. Cubans, Canadians and Germans have also begun to show higher percentages of persons over 55 years of age. The largest percentage of Colombians and Argentines falls within the 30 to 44 age range (CONAPO 2005).

With the exception of immigrants from the United States and Guatemala, the immigrant population in Mexico is characterized by a high level of schooling. The highest levels (college or above) among Latin American immigrants are found among Colombians (68%), Argentines (51.4%) and Cubans (54.4%). The unemployment rate among the immigrants is generally low (1.3%), though more than half are economically inactive (55%) because they are students, homemakers, pensioners, or people who have some impediment to working (CONAPO 2005). Economically active immigrants working in an activity or job fall primarily in the category of "employees or labourers" (58.5%). Only those of Guatemalan origin have a greater proportion of day labourers or farm workers (36%), as a result of their greater participation in the primary sector. In nearly all cases, one fourth of immigrants are own-account workers.

In concluding this section on immigration to Mexico, it is important to note that immigrant workers who arrive at Mexico's southern border to work temporarily in agriculture, construction or services are also an important presence. Either with or without documentation, these workers enter Mexico at various times of the year based on the needs and demands of Mexican employers. As indicated above, this particular flow of migrants will be considered below, in the section on the southern border.

MEXICO'S SOUTHERN BORDER: MIGRANTS' DESTINATION, TRANSIT, AND ORIGIN

The southern border as a site of international migration

Mexico's southern border exemplifies a set of phenomena, associated with international migration that has received little study but is of great social, economic and cultural importance, both for the population living in this area, and for those participating in the process as international migrants either arriving, crossing, or leaving the region.

For a number of reasons, little attention had been paid to this border. In various forums and contexts (governmental, media, and even academic) a variety of expressions are used in which the phrase "the border" is used to refer to Mexico's northern border with the United States, as though Mexico bordered and interacted with only one country. This does not mean that the southern border is unimportant, but that relations with Mexico's northern neighbor have driven the attention of Mexicans in regard to their territorial boundaries. That attention has generated better and greater knowledge of the social, cultural, economic and political phenomena associated with the northern border and the country to which Mexico is connected (or from which it is separated). In particular, greater knowledge is reflected in the terminology associated with migration, which, because of its impact on the life of the migrants themselves and on affairs of national interest, have been more fully documented.

In contrast, the southern border only recently began to be considered geopolitically strategic and to be targeted for research by academics (such as De Vos 1993 and 1994; Boivn 1997; Kauffer 2002; Villafuerte 2004) interested in documenting and explaining its historic development, the different "borders" that comprise it, its diversity, the distinct faces of its multicultural nature, etc., as well as the complexity of social, economic, and political phenomena that characterize this part of Mexico, which both unites the country with, and separates it from, its nearest neighbors (Belize and Guatemala, and Central America as a whole, in addition to other countries that, in recent years, have begun to have a presence in the border area).

The strategic character of the border, in terms of national security, became a major issue in the early 1980s, when the Guatemalan army made numerous incursions into Mexican territory on the pretext of hunting down Guatemalan guerillas (Kauffer 2003: 126). Those were years of forced migration in Guatemala, when thousands of people fled the political violence generated by the government and entered Mexico to protect their lives and families. This was perhaps one of the first events in Mexico's history to call attention to its southern border (a number of academics have documented this process; among others, see Aguayo 1985; Kauffer 1997, 2002 and 2003). Though a process of "rediscovery" of "the south" had begun some years earlier, it was less comprehensive, focusing primarily on exploiting the natural wealth of the Border States' oil and water, as well as the tourist potential of Mexico's Caribbean region.

Over a decade ago (in 1994), the armed Zapatista movement in Chiapas again brought attention to the south, not only for Mexico's people and government, but for the international community. More recently, Mexico's free trade agreements with some Central American countries (Costa Rica, and Guatemala-Honduras-El Salvador) and the promotion of the so-called Plan Puebla-Panama have once again made the southern border a focus of interest to various sectors of government and of society overall.

In addition to these factors, the number of migrants in the region has increased, particularly since 1998. The policy that has developed in response has created more controls in the border area.[14] This intensified after September 11, 2001. Thus, international migrants seeking to cross Mexico's southern border must now seek out more intricate and dangerous routes, exposing them to multiple risks.[15] More recently, interest in the region has focused on the presence of gangs, which have found this, and other areas in Mexico, a convenient place to locate. Coming from Central America, and called "*maras salvatruchas*," these gangs have increased their presence in Mexico as a result of special programs in El Salvador and Honduras to combat the presence of these groups (Ángeles and Martínez 2006).

Thus, a combination of situations has led to the "rediscovery" of the southern border, fostering a recognition of this area as a multi-regional one (Fábregas 1997), shaped by multiple borders (De Vos 2002):

> The southern border of Mexico is an area of convergences, where history is shared with the Central American and Caribbean peoples. (Fábregas 1997: 349)

In this area of convergence, some portions of the border have become more important than others, due to the volume and intensity of trade or movement of persons across the border. This is true at both the Belize and Guatemalan borders, particularly as related to the so-called Soconusco region of Chiapas.

The history of the Mexico-Belize border area is unique. Since at least the second half of the nineteenth century, it has turned on the exploitation of the natural wealth of the forests. The relationships this produced led gradually to a border area that, though it lacks the intensity of the Soconusco region in Chiapas, has its own cultural practices and social structures, which have been intertwining for more than a century (Higuera 1994). The population dynamics of the region have received little documentation, particularly as concerns international migration. Quintana Roo, which borders Belize, has experienced growth in the last few decades as a result of tourist activity, but little is known about the use of this region by Belizean and Central American migrants to enter Mexico, either to work in the tourist service sector in Cancún (which is in the border state of Quintana Roo), or as a stepping stone to the United States.

In contrast, we know that the border region between the department of San Marcos in Guatemala and the Soconusco region in Chiapas has some of the most intense migratory activity of any area along the southern border. To a lesser extent, the region between the department of Huehuetenango in Guatemala and the so-called "border region" of Chiapas also has historically received (and continues to receive) some of the agricultural workers destined for the farms near the Chiapas state capital of Tuxtla Gutiérrez. The recent increase in the migratory control in this border area has redirected some of the flow of undocumented migrants who previously used these two regions as transit corridors, and who now are forced to find new routes through the department of Quiche in Guatemala to the Chiapas cross-border highway, and through the department of Petén in Guatemala to the Mexican states of Tabasco and Campeche (Lorenzana 2004).

THE MEXICO-GUATEMALA BORDER AS A FOCUS OF MIGRATORY INTENSITY

The history of population movements on the Mexico-Guatemala border is as old as the borders themselves. The current pattern of interchange between the two countries illustrates the role that population movements have played here and the importance they have acquired (Castillo 1997: 206). The steady increase in flow, which began as early as the nineteenth century, has created heightened interest in this border and, in particular, in the Soconusco region. One must not lose sight, however, of other parts of the southern border with major migratory activity, which calls for greater documentation.

In the late nineteenth century, a process began that was to prove fundamental in the history and economy of Chiapas, as well as in the dynamics of migration between Chiapas and its neighbor, Guatemala. After the Mexican government created the Colonization Law in 1883, a group of German farmers from Guatemala settled in the Soconusco area to create large-scale, labour-intensive coffee-growing operations (González 1994; Castillo 1997; De Vos 2002). Since then, Guatemalan seasonal farm workers have played a key role in the region's economy. These migratory workers laboured primarily in harvesting coffee; however, they also harvested cacao and bananas on plantations where labour was needed. Until the early decades of the twentieth century, these people and indigenous workers from the highlands of Chiapas carried out this work in roughly equal numbers. However, in Guatemala, export crops requiring labour drained a considerable portion of the flow of Guatemalan workers, so that by the 1930s, indigenous workers had become essential to the economy of the Soconusco region in Chiapas (Rodríguez 1989). Guatemalan workers continued to arrive, but represented a much smaller portion of the workforce than they had at the beginning of the century.

Until the mid-twentieth century, the Mexico-Guatemala border was the principal entry and departure point for these temporary workers, who came primarily from neighboring Guatemalan towns. The border experienced the everyday movement of persons and goods typically found in this type of area. The people in this area, in addition to their involvement in trading products produced on only one side of the border, moved about for family-related reasons. The political/administrative line that had divided the two countries since the nineteenth century had effectively separated families and communities linked in a variety of ways.

As the second half of the twentieth century began, a number of factors combined to free up agricultural labour in Guatemala. Workers found their way to Mexican cotton, banana and coffee plantations. Meanwhile, in Mexico, the flow of indigenous workers from the Chiapas highlands to Soconusco farms diminished. One element in changes in the movement of indigenous people from the highlands was the opportunity to obtain their own land, with the implementation of incentives, around this time, to encourage the settling of the Lacandona jungle (Rodríguez 1989). Thus, seasonal migration by Guatemalan workers began gaining momentum in the 1950s and continued even more intensively in the 1960s.

The 1970s saw profound social change in Guatemala, and major impacts were felt in the areas bordering Mexico. The crisis that led to armed conflict in the late 1970s gave rise to a counterinsurgency movement, with deep and widespread repercussions. The violence reached a peak in 1981–1983, when military operations, which had initially targeted opposition groups, indiscriminately targeted segments of the civilian population. One result was a massive displacement of families — and even communities — moving to Mexico. This was a factor in what some writers have called the "redrawing of the southern border of Mexico" (Hernández & Sandoval 1989).

At approximately the same time, the Mexico-Guatemala border became the scene of a new phenomenon in which undocumented persons from Guatemala, other Central American countries and, to a lesser extent, other parts of Latin America attempted to reach the United States in search of better opportunities than those available in their home countries. This began in the 1960s and gained force in the 1970s.

> Silently, Honduran men and women had long been leaving their country in search of better options... Before the 1970s, in cities such as La Ceiba, Tela, Puerto Cortés, Trujillo and the town of Garíguna, covering almost the entire Atlantic coast of Honduras, it had become a

source of pride and prestige to have relatives working in the United States. (Arias Foundation 2000: 5)

Statistics of the United States Immigration and Naturalization Service (INS) show that the number of Guatemalan immigrants admitted to the United States doubled from 1976 to 1977, and that from that point through the 1980s, but especially from 1983 on, Guatemalan immigration reached massive proportions. (Rincón et al. 2000)

This flow gradually increased as a result of political violence in Central America and poverty and unemployment in Guatemala, Honduras, El Salvador and Nicaragua. Nicaraguan migration, however, has been directed primarily toward Costa Rica, rather than the United States (Morales 1997; Alvarenga 1997).

Thus, some portions of Mexico's southern border, due to their proximity to Guatemala, play a dual role in international migration — as both a destination and a transit area — and the role of women in both types of flows is of special relevance to the present document.

LABOUR FLOWS AT THE CHIAPAS-GUATEMALA BORDER

According to the last Mexican census (INEGI 2000), Chiapas is home to 17,416 foreign-born persons (3.5%), among a total of 492,617 residing in Mexico overall.[16] Accordingly, Chiapas ranks ninth (out of 32 states) in the number of foreign-born residents. The great majority of these are from Guatemala, with women representing slightly over half (53%) of the immigrants. As has occurred in other border regions, the Soconusco population was composed of indigenous Mam and immigrants from other states and countries. The main foreign groups have been Guatemalans, Germans, Japanese and Chinese. The presence of these different cultures is very noticeable in the region, and is particularly evident in the everyday life of the city of Tapachula, which is the region's nodal center.

The state of Chiapas is the major recipient of temporary, migrating seasonal workers from Central America (especially from Guatemala). However, this traditional group is not the only one contributing to the stream of migrants. Two other groups may be considered traditional as well: female domestic workers, and vendors who sell vegetables in local markets. Though the characteristics of this migrant group have not been studied, it is known to be made up of members of peasant/indigenous families from western Guatemala, primarily women (mothers and daughters) who sell in local markets in the Soconusco border area of Chiapas. These groups share a common denominator: they are largely campesinos and indigenous persons from areas around Guatemalan towns located near or on the Mexican border.

Other migrants are also in evidence, though in lesser numbers. These include men and women working as street vendors or as workers in the service sector (stores, restaurants, workshops, etc.). There is a notable presence of children and adolescents within this migratory group, who work in the informal economy as porters, shoe shine boys, street vendors, helpers in stores and workshops, etc. Some of these children work at corners as jugglers or windshield cleaners. While most of the migrants are Guatemalan, a small number come from Honduras and El Salvador. Some of these children have been associated with sexual exploitation, as well as with drug dealing and use (Azaola 2000).

Little systematic information is available on this second group of temporary migrants, but their presence and productive activity are a constant, particularly in the region's urban areas. They are present where merchandise is loaded and unloaded, but they are most active in street vending, where they offer a range of merchandise made in Guatemala, Mexico and, above all, China, including candy, cigarettes, towels, pots and pans, shoes, and clothing. Migrants also work in construction as masons or assistants, and in auto repair and carpentry, where they primarily work as helpers and apprentices.[17]

GUATEMALAN AGRICULTURAL WORKERS AND THE ROLE OF WOMEN

From the late nineteenth century, when they began coming to Chiapas to work, until the 1980s, agricultural workers entered Mexico from Guatemala without any form of migration papers, as no documentation was required for this labour force. However, the political conflict in Guatemala and the thousands of refugees seeking asylum in Mexico, as well as increasing numbers of migrants in transit, created a need to legalize this type of labour and seasonal migration. At the same time, no comprehensive policy covering this particular type of migrants was seen as necessary. The legalization process did not presuppose a binational work program, such as that created in the United States and Canada, with standards for supervision and control designed to guarantee (at least on paper) workers' rights and working conditions. Nevertheless, the legalization was an initial effort to come to grips with some of the features of migratory activity and call attention to migrants' situations and working conditions (CNDH 1996; Castillo 1997).

As the indigenous people of the Chiapas highlands ceased to migrate in mass to work in the Soconusco plantations, which still needed a workforce, the flow of agricultural labourers became a survival strategy for many campesinos and indigenous families in western Guatemala. At the same time, it also became an indispensable element of the economy of this region of Mexico. This migratory pattern has been so integrally linked with the development of the region's agricultural economy that neither of the two processes can be understood without the other. Guatemalan workers in the late nineteenth century were hired primarily in connection with the large-scale coffee-growing operations. In the twentieth century, other crops began to generate a demand for labour. As the twenty-first century begins, while work on coffee plantations retains its dominance for Guatemalan workers, they also are employed in the agricultural cycles of other crops in the region (bananas, mangos, papaya, tobacco, etc.), as well as in certain livestock-related activities. Nor is it only on large plantations that they are in evidence. Mexican campesinos with small coffee-producing operations hire Guatemalan labourers. Between January and April of 2000, for example, the office of the National Institute of Migration (INM) in Ciudad Hidalgo, Chiapas, registered the entry of documented Guatemalan workers destined for 33 *ejidos* in the region, while the remainder of the documented workers entering there were heading for some 250 farms scattered over 21 towns in the Soconusco, Coastal, Frailesca and Sierra de Chiapas regions. These data are taken from a list that the INM compiles based on the entries it authorizes. For 2000, the list was entitled "Relation of Producers on the coast of Chiapas who document Guatemalan agricultural workers, with Agricultural Visitors Migration Form [Forma Migratoria de Visitantes Agrícolas] (FMVA). Year 2000". With the current trend for campesinos from Chiapas to migrate to the United States, some small producers are hiring Guatemalan workers with the money sent to them by their children in the United States.[18]

A number of factors have led to a reduction in the flow of documented Guatemalan agricultural labourers to Chiapas. These include changes in coffee production and marketing due to the falling prices on the international market, policies that do little to stimulate the farm economy, and the failure of governments in the region to give support to peasant growers and other small producers (see Figure 7.2). It appears that this trend will continue in the coming years, given the region's persistent state of economic crisis (Ángeles 2002).

(At present, there is no available estimate of the number of Guatemalan agricultural workers migrating to Chiapas on a temporary basis. Mexico's National Institute of Migration records the entry of documented workers,[19] but undocumented workers are not accounted for. Most of these go to the towns closest to the border, where farming creates a demand for their labour. Some of these workers — known as "volunteers" — arrive without the involvement of intermediaries.

The hiring process is carried out through intermediaries — known as "contractors," "recruiters," or "enablers" ["*habilitadores*"] — though some farms no long use this type of intermediary:

> It used to be necessary to recruit. There were specialized people who went to San Cristóbal. There were even recruiters living there ... who

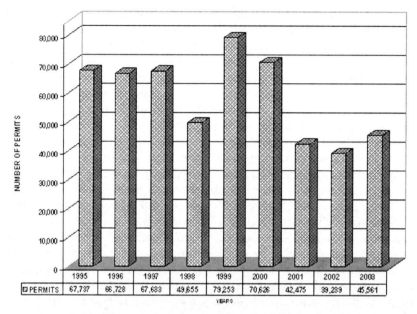

Figure 7.2 Chiapas–Entry of documented Guatamalan agricultural workers, 1995–2003. Source: Statistics of INM, Chiapas, 1995–2003.

were called "*habilitadores*"... We had an *habilitador* in a city south of Comitán, which I believe is now called Trinitaria... He got people and sent them to us. Some workers still come, but they come on their own. We don't need *habilitadores* or anything any more... though I know of farms that have six *habilitadores* (Walter P., interview with a farm owner, December 8, 2001).

One of the objectives of Mexican migration authorities in changing documentation mechanisms was to end this intermediation. However, it persists, not only because, for the great majority of growers, it is a way of guaranteeing the labour they need, but also because the contractors, who are unionized, resist efforts to change the system, since not only they, but a series of helpers involved in the recruitment process, as well, depend on the work. This recruitment process has many features in common with the mode of hiring prevalent in the early twentieth century.

The flow of workers consists primarily of young adults. The median age is 26.5. Approximately one-third are illiterate, and a similar percentage speak an indigenous language (primarily Mam). Approximately 90 percent of the migrants are male, though this proportion has changed slightly, since the women who were previously recorded by Mexican migration officials as "companions" gradually recognized as workers in their own right. It is now estimated that roughly 16 percent of the workers are women (Castillo & Ángeles 2000). A study conducted between 1999 and 2001[20] to shed light on the female component of this migratory flow revealed certain characteristics of the population involved. The great majority of the women (75%) are under 30. Their average age is 25, with a median age of 22. Half (51%) are illiterate, and their average level of schooling is a third-grade education. Single women (unmarried, widowed, and separated) and women who are married or live with a man are represented in comparable numbers (49.8% and 50.2%, respectively). Single women constitute 37 percent of the total number of women in this group of migrants.

Guatemalan women who arrive in the Soconusco region and obtain authorization to enter Mexico already have previous histories of migration. A significant percentage (41%), have at least experienced a change of residence and no longer live where they were born. Specifically, 65 percent have lived in a place other than their birthplace, and 20 percent have lived in two or more such places. Of these women who have left their birthplace at least once, 87 percent have gone to Mexico and 45 percent to places within Guatemala. The women surveyed in the study came from 8 of Guatemala's 22 departments. However, these data are based only on a sampling of the many agricultural workers who arrive in the region throughout the year. To mention only one example, in the growing year 1997–1998, the women who entered with papers at the National Institute of Migration (INM)'s station at Ciudad Hidalgo came from 19 of the 22 departments (Castillo & Ángeles 2000), though three departments accounted for most of the workers (San Marcos, 63%; Quetzaltenango, 19%; Retalhuleu, 9%).

Most of the women state that they are coming to Mexico to work (84%). A small number (9%) say that they are coming to seek work, and a mere 6 percent identify themselves as being companions of workers. Their reasons for migrating is primarily that "they pay better here than in Guatemala" (64%); that "there is reliable work" here (38%); and because "they feed you here" or "the food isn't always the same" (11%).[21] The women carry out activities required by the region's agriculture (coffee, bananas, papaya and other fruits). Though they are primarily hired for the coffee harvest, they also perform a wide range of other tasks, including cleaning, fertilizing, harvesting and selection, and even cooking for the workers.

Walter: For some field work we prefer women, who perform better. The selection of coffee, for instance, is done exclusively by women. In addition, only women are used in grafting the coffee plants, which is something new, provided that they have gone through a training course previously.

Hugo: And why did you choose women for this type of work?

Walter: Well, they are the only ones who do it well, very efficiently, more so than men. It is work that requires dedication, meticulous, you might say. You work with recently germinated plants. The stalks are the thickness of a match, and cuts have to be made in them... after which they have to be bound. Imagine, you just do this and the plant breaks. So in practice, we have seen that women produce high yields. Of 100 plants grafted by women, 95 take. If I do it, I may not even reach 40%." (Hugo Ángeles Cruz interview with farm owner Walter P., December 8, 2001)

The great majority of women state that they will receive payment for their work. On average, they report a wage of 33 pesos per day,[22] but individual figures range from five to 60 pesos. As of January 2005, this has not changed. For the current harvest, average pay is 35 pesos, and the highest pay is between 48 and 52 pesos.[23]

The contractors themselves acknowledge the difference between men's and women's pay for the same work.

Interviewer: "Could you give an example of how many pesos they pay at this time? How much per day do they pay a man, and how much do they pay a woman?"
Contractor: "Well, before [in 2000], they were paying 25 pesos, but what we have heard now is that they are paying from 20 to 18."
Interviewer: "That is for women?"
Contractor: "Yes."
Interviewer: "And men?"
Contractor: "Men are getting 30, 31 pesos."
(Interview with contractor in Tecún Umán, Guatemala 2001)

[Minors,] if they are paid at all, get no more than what women get, which is less than what men get.

(Interview with contractor in Tecún Umán, Guatemala 2001)

The workday begins between three and six in the morning for most women. Some finish at two, three or four in the afternoon, but others continue until nine, 10 or 11 at night. They sleep mostly in sheds. Slightly less than half say that they sleep on the floor, and one-third say they sleep on wooden beds with no mattresses. Over half sleep in the same place as the other workers.

Additional information from the Fray Matías de Córdova Human Rights Center (CDHFMC) and from the records of the Beta-Tapachula Migrants' Protection Group show that most complaints by agricultural workers (male and female) concern failure to comply with contracts, as well as the withholding of pay and documents (Rojas 2002).

WOMEN IN DOMESTIC SERVICE

No documentation currently exists as to when young Guatemalan women began performing domestic work in Mexican border towns, or when their numbers increased. The percentage of women from other Central American countries doing such work is also unknown, though some cases of Honduran women are confirmed.

In the city of Tapachula, as well as in nearby urban areas (Cacahoatán, Tuxtla Chico, and Ciudad Hidalgo), a high percentage of families employ Guatemalan women on a full-time basis (i.e., living in). Many young women from western Guatemala, facing a lack of jobs and poverty at home, respond to the demand for this type of work in Mexico as a personal and family choice. Most are indigenous and young. Their average age is 19, and most began to work before the age of 14. They come primarily from the border department of San Marcos. The majority are single (95%), and some are mothers (15%) who are compelled to leave their children with relatives at home. Over half of these workers are older daughters of poor families with six to nine members. They come to Mexico to work and provide economic assistance to their families, and because pay is better in Mexico than in Guatemala (CDHFMC 1999; Garrido 2001; Ángeles et al. 2004).

Information from the CDHFMC (1999), which provides legal aid to these female workers, indicates that some have been abused in the houses where they are employed. Such abuse is largely verbal, though excessive work, low pay and insufficient or inadequate food are also issues. A 2004 study shows that nearly half of the women (45%) were subject to some type of violence in their first experience as domestic workers (Ángeles et al. 2004). Though some recognize violations of their human rights, many do not conceive of themselves as persons with rights, but simply as individuals obliged to fulfill obligations. Thus, being a woman, undocumented, with little education, and of indigenous origin (isolated in an entirely foreign setting) creates a situation of defenselessness and exploitation for these women, whose work contributes to the social reproduction of the region's families (Rojas, 2002).

MIGRANTS IN TRANSIT

The population movements currently recorded between Guatemala and Mexico include flows of migrants in transit, most of whom enter via the Soconusco region in an attempt to reach the United States, as a part of a strategy to improve their economic situation.

As mentioned above, this type of migration increased markedly in the 1990s, particularly as a result of the economic crisis in the region and the precarious economic situation of families, aggravated by the natural disasters of 1998. The increased flow was accompanied by a diversification of the migrants' countries of origin. Though Central Americans continue to constitute the majority of migrants in transit, migration from other Latin American countries, and even from the Middle East and Asia, is also occurring.

Table 7.5 Mexico. Cases of "aseguramiento" [detention] of foreigners, according to regional INM office, 2001–2003

2001		2002		2003	
Regional Office	%	Regional Office	%	Regional Office	%
Total	100.0 (150,530)	Total	100.0 (138,061)	Total	100.0 (187,537)
Chiapas	53.2	Chiapas	45.5	Chiapas	39.0
Tabasco	11.3	Tabasco	10.8	Distrito Federal	18.0
Oaxaca	8.4	Oaxaca	10.3	Tabasco	9.2
Veracruz	7.7	Veracruz	10.2	Veracruz	7.5
Tamaulipas	2.6	Tamaulipas	3.4	Oaxaca	5.8
Chihuahua	2.3	Querétaro	2.7	Edo. México	2.4
Sonora	1.6	Distrito Federal	1.2	Tamaulipas	2.3
Distrito Federal	1.3	Chihuahua	2.2	Hidalgo	1.6
Quintana Roo	1.3	Hidalgo	1.8	San Luis Potosí	1.6
Querétaro	0.7	Sonora	1.4	Chihuahua	1.5
Hidalgo	0.5	Quintana Roo	1.1	Sonora	1.5
San Luis Potosí	0.5	San Luis Potosí	1.1	Querétaro	1.1
Other	8.6	Other	8.3	Other	8.3

Source: INM, 2004.

Given the conditions under which most transit migration occurs, and the complex factors that affect this flow, only an approximation of the magnitude of the phenomenon along Mexico's southern border is currently available, using the statistics of the National Institute of Migration (INM). In particular, figures on the detention or *"aseguramiento"*[24] of individuals entering Mexico without papers can be used in producing such an approximation, since a comparison of the number of these events recorded by the National Institute of Migration (INM)'s different regional offices indicates that the southern border is the principal place of entry for migrants wishing to reach the United States (see Table 7.5).

In the last few years, the Chiapas Regional Office registered the greatest proportion of detentions of undocumented foreign migrants, with over half of these events occurring in either Chiapas or Tabasco. Considering, in addition, that Oaxaca and Veracruz form part of the transit corridor of undocumented workers from Central America, and taking into account the nationalities of the detainees in those states, one can conclude that the international migrants who use Mexico as a route to the United States enter at Mexico's southern border, and that the southern border is therefore a focal point of intense migratory activity.

Transit migration occurs through the border state of Chiapas, where over half of the detentions of undocumented migrants occurred. The situation appears to have changed in 2003, however, with aggregate detentions in the states of Chiapas, Tabasco, Oaxaca, and Veracruz diminishing to 61.5 percent (from 80.6% in 2001 and 76.8% in 2002). Chiapas, in particular, showed a notable decline between 2001 and 2003, while percentages rose in central Mexico (Federal District, 18%; state of Mexico, 2.4%) (see Table 7.5).

These changes may be associated with a number of factors, but they relate specifically to measures taken by migratory authorities at locations in the center of the country that lie along the route taken by migrants seeking to enter the United States. These measures have increased the number of detentions in this part of the country, which functions as a node connecting the southern and northern borders of the country.

Given the limited sex-disaggregated migratory statistics available, little can be stated with certainty about the role of women in this migratory flow. However regional INM offices, such as the one in Chiapas, are now gathering this type of data. Sex-disaggregated information is important not only in being able to quantify the characteristics of migrant groups, but also in the vital task of bringing to light the role of women and minors — the groups most vulnerable to trafficking.

Based on this information, as shown in Table 7.6, in the state of Chiapas a considerable percentage of undocumented foreign women are detained: 15.3 percent in 2001, and 15.9% in 2002. The greatest number of migrants in transit through Mexico come from Central America. Almost all of the women detained are from Central America (98% in 2001, and 99% in 2004). However, although the number of detained women from other countries detained represents only a small percentage of the total number, it should be noted that the number of migrant women from South America and the Caribbean has increased as a percentage of all migrants from their region. Thus, they now represent a greater percentage of their region's migrants than is the case with Central American migrant women.

As indicated by the data in Table 7.7, three countries—Guatemala, Honduras and El Salvador—account for the bulk of detentions: 96.5 percent of detentions in Chiapas in 2001 and 98% in 2004. Guatemala has accounted for a rising proportion of detentions in recent years, as the number of women detained in Chiapas during 2001 and 2004 indicate. In those two years, Guatemalan women accounted for 46.4 percent and 48.6% of detentions for the two years, respectively, while Honduran women accounted for

Table 7.6 Chiapas. Cases of "aseguramiento" [detention] and holding of foreign women, by region of origin, 2001 and 2004

Region of origin	2001		2004 (*)	
	Total	Women	Total	Women
Total	80,022	12,283	84,691	13,442
Central America	78,363	12,019	84,016	13,296
South America	1,211	223	367	83
Caribbean	90	10	231	45
United States & Canada	79	10	35	8
Asia	179	9	13	3
Africa	20	0	15	2
Europe	53	9	8	3

* January to October 2004
Source: INM Chiapas 2004.

23.3 percent and 27.7 percent and Salvadoran women for 26.8 percent and 21.4 percent.

A breakdown of detained migrants by sex shows practically no variation in the ratio between the men and women over the last few years, though the overall numbers have risen. Thus, of the 80,022 detentions registered in 2001, 12,283 (15.3%) involved adult women, while three years later the number was 13,442 out of a total of 84,691 detentions (a slightly higher percentage, representing 15.9%). Thus, for every 100 men detained in Chiapas, 19 women were detained in 2001, and 20 in 2004 (see Table 7.7).

In 1999, a group of organizations working to protect the rights of migrants conducted a survey of 992 undocumented migrant women in transit to the United States,[25] from which some conclusions can be drawn about the characteristics of, and conditions surrounding, migrant women. According to the study, 95 percent of women in transit come from Central America (primarily Guatemala, 35%; Honduras, 29.2%; and El Salvador, 28.6%), as indicated, also, by the above-mentioned INM detention statistics. Three quarters of the women are under 30, and the majority (86%) is able to read and write. Slightly over half (52%) have only a primary school education, though some have higher levels of schooling, including, in some cases (2.3%), university-level education. Only approximately one quarter of the women are married or living with a man, while most are unmarried (56.6%) or living alone, either by virtue of being separated, divorced or widowed (14.6%). Sixty-five percent have at least one child, and roughly 40% have children under five years of age. For this reason, only a small percentage (13%) travel with their children. The remainder stated that they had left their children with a family member in their country of origin in

Table 7.7 Chiapas. Cases of "aseguramiento" [detention], according to principal country of origin, by sex, 2001 and 2004

Country of origin	2001			2004 (*)		
	Total	Men	Women	Total	Men	Women
Total	80,022	64,387	12,283	84,691	67,307	13,442
Guatemala	37,409	30,169	5,695	47,600	38,659	6,527
Honduras	21,866	18,011	2,859	21,530	16,805	3,724
El Salvador	18,018	14,054	3,297	13,923	10,575	2,871
Nicaragua	1,026	791	163	925	731	169
Ecuador	992	770	195	282	216	62
Cuba	24	19	3	212	159	45
Peru	101	89	9	31	21	10
United States	76	40	10	35	15	8
Colombia	91	66	19	29	21	8
Belize	8	7	1	16	11	5
Other	411	371	31	108	94	13

** January to October 2004
Note: The "total" comprises the sum of women, men and people under 18 years old.
Source: INM Chiapas 2004.

order to make migration possible. Sixteen percent intended to bring their children to the United States once they became established. This percentage coincides roughly with the percentage of women who expressed the intention to remain permanently at their destination (13.3%). The great majority intended only to migrate temporarily for the purpose of work.

Women migrate essentially for economic reasons, intending to work in the United States. Only one out of 10 stated that their purpose was to reunite their families. Women leave their countries not only to provide a living for their children and parents, but also because of domestic violence and as a result of having been abandoned by their partners. Approximately 80 percent of the women stated that their decision to migrate was not influenced by family members or other people. The majority were financing their travel with their own savings (43%), with loans (29%) or by the sale of property (2%). Only some 15% were emigrating because their husband, or another relative (1.8% and 12%, respectively), had sent them money. The vast majority was traveling without migration documents (89%), and some were traveling with counterfeit documents (3.8%). For most (76%), this was their first migration.

Like other migrant women, women in transit face a series of problems. Because they are undocumented, they are extremely vulnerable and are exposed to a gamut of risks, including assault, extortion, sexual violence, illness and death. It is paradigmatic, as the cited study shows, that of the women detained by migration authorities (84%), 22 percent stated that they would continue to attempt to cross until they succeeded, 41 percent stated that they would return home and 14 percent said that they intended to remain in Mexico to work (Sin Fronteras et al. 2000).

INTERNATIONAL MIGRANTS' REGION OF ORIGIN

The floods in the Soconusco region in September 1998, which were caused by a tropical depression that preceded Hurricane Mitch, were a watershed in the recent history of the economy of peasants — particularly the micro producers of coffee in this part of the country, who were soon to be affected by a crisis in coffee prices. The peasant farming crisis that had already developed in the two preceding decades, affecting the region's small producers, was aggravated by these natural disasters, and families who depended on the land were impelled to seek economic alternatives.

One of the most visible manifestations of this situation has been a steady increase in the migration of the region's peasants, both to Mexico's northwestern states, where they work on farms growing commercial crops, and to the United States, where they seek employment alternatives. This phenomenon has barely begun to be studied:

> The situation in the southeast is undoubtedly in its initial phase, but its potential for growth is enormous if it follows the pattern of cases such as Veracruz. However, indications suggest that the migration will principally consist of undocumented workers. (Durand & Massey 2003: 88)

The southern border region as a whole had experienced very little migration, but the situation is now intensifying in the state of Chiapas, where even towns right on the Guatemalan border (the most distant towns in Mexico from the Rio Grande or other sections of the United States border) are now a source of actual and potential U.S.-bound migrants.

Data from the field research of the "Chiapanecos p'al Norte" project (carried out by Hugo Ángeles Cruz at the Colegio de la Frontera Sur since 2003) reflect the participation of peasants in migration to states such as Jalisco, Nayarit, Sinaloa, Sonora, Baja California and Baja California Sur to work on commercial farms. Young people also play a role, but they primarily travel to the northern border to work in the *maquila* industry or in services, while another portion of this migratory flow is directed to the United States. This process has unfolded over a period of a very few years, and some communities have already established family and social networks that facilitate and encourage the migration of new family members to various destinations in the United States. Informants in the communities visited stated that they had relatives, friends and neighbors working in New York, Chicago and Los Angeles. For example, Nájar (2002) reports that one fourth of the population (500 inhabitants) of the Chimalapa *ejido*, which is located in the border town of Motozintla, is now in one of the U.S. states of Tennessee, Georgia or California.

The signs of migration in communities of origin have proliferated rapidly. Many travel agencies can be seen in communities and towns in Soconusco and other southern border areas, currency exchanging businesses have appeared, remittances have increased, public telephones and calling centers have proliferated wildly, and calls are made from these places to family members in the United States, etc. (Nájar 2002).

Meanwhile, according to the assessment by the "Chiapanecos p'al Norte" project (cited above), the economy of the region's rural population depends increasingly on remittances from family members in the United States, or on economic aid that results directly from recent migration of family members to other Mexican cities and states. This situation reveals not only looming changes in the region's productive activities and labour market, but also the beginning of a migratory process that will solidify in the coming years through support networks and the emergence of social and cultural phenomena associated with migration.

EMERGING HUMAN RIGHTS ISSUES IN MEXICO

In a country such as Mexico, where there are various types of migration, and where the intensity and complexity of migratory phenomena are steadily increasing, it is crucial to identify the specific characteristics of different types of migrants, and to pinpoint the vulnerabilities and risks they may face, whatever the type of migration and geographic area involved. They encounter obstacles in their areas of origin, as well as in transit and at their destinations, but their movement is not one that can be contained. People seek to improve their living conditions, and will take whatever measures are necessary to pursue that objective.

Networks, chains, circuits, flows, currents, etc. are not inappropriate categories with which to address a phenomenon in which people are driven to cross borders. However, not all people can create and recreate the migration networks, chains and circuits needed to surmount certain obstacles. Many fail even to glimpse the possibility, because their efforts are nipped in the bud. The risk of accident or death in border crossing attempts is always present for undocumented migrants, on both Mexico's northern and southern borders.

At the United States border, operations to control migration (Operations Hold the Line, Gatekeeper, Safeguard, and Rio Grande) have increased the incidence of abuse and risk, as well as death, among migrants. For example, violence and abuse directed at Mexican migrants by certain members of the Border Patrol have been reported in various forums, documents and press outlets. At the same time, the search for new crossing points or alternate routes has brought migrants to locales and regions where geographic conditions are more difficult. The risks they face include death by overexposure to sun, dehydration, hypothermia, animal bites and drowning. The control operations have also created a context for extortion, deception and abuse, which has raised the cost of migrating to the United States (Oceguera 2001: 18; UNHCHR 2003: 174). These conditions led to the death of approximately 2,355 Mexican migrants between 1995 and 2003 as they attempted to gain access to the United States (figures from the California Rural Legal Assistance Foundation's Border Project cited in UNHCHR 2003: 174).

The situation is similar at Mexico's southern border. U.S. measures to control migration have had repercussions here, since the southern border has become the first line at which to stop migrants who are in transit to the United States (Oceguera 2001). In the last few years, the portion of Mexico between the Guatemala and Belize border and the Isthmus of Tehuantepec has become a strategic area for Mexican migration policy, which has taken advantage of the narrowness of this area — a natural filter, as it were — and has increased operations to control migrants in transit.

In July 2001, the National Institute of Migration inaugurated its so-called "Southern Plan" to combat trafficking in migrants in the south, fight illegal trafficking in, and exploitation of, children and promote and consolidate a culture of respect for the law and human rights in southern Mexico. However, the implementation of the plan led to an intensification of border controls and increased the presence of various police forces on the traditional routes by which persons and merchandise enter Mexico.

As was the case at the northern border, the increased controls have had negative effects on migrants from other countries, as well as on Mexicans. It has led to a portion of the flow of undocumented migrants being rechanneled to more inhospitable and risky areas (Lorenzana 2004), and migrants have been forced to pay large sums to hire *polleros* or *coyotes*, who often abandon them or take advantage of their vulnerability (UNCHR 2002: 15 and 16). According to the National Institute of Migration, there were 102 migrant deaths in 1999, and 136 in 2000 (cited by Oceguera 2001: 19), though Central American consulates reported 260 victims in 2000.

Since the mid-1990s, various social and civic organizations in Mexico and Central America, as well as governmental organizations and numerous writers and press outlets, have called the attention of the public and of the region's governments to the need to address the serious deterioration of respect for the dignity and rights of migrants — those in transit to the United States, those coming to work in Mexico and those who remain (or are forced to remain) "parked" at the border (CNDH 1996; Informe 1999; Foro Migraciones 2002).

Abuse is committed both by bands of criminals and by individuals connected with migrants through some commercial or other activity, as well as by government officials at various levels. This ranges from threats, blackmail and extortion to armed assault and rape — leading in many cases to the death of migrants (CNDH 1996; Foro Migraciones 2002; Ruíz 2004). Thus, Mexico's southern border

> has become one of the most difficult and hazardous crossings for undocumented migrants coming, in the main, from Guatemala, Honduras, El Salvador and Nicaragua. In particular, the Soconusco coastal route, which runs from Ciudad Hidalgo to Tonalá, is notable for its concentration of dangers. The multiple threats that migrants face there, including assault, rape, theft and loss of limb as a result of falling from trains (to mention but some of the hazards), make this region one of extraordinarily high risk for those attempting to traverse it. (Ruiz 2004: 2)

The assessment of the United Nations High Commissioner for Human Rights in Mexico explicitly recognizes the problem of human rights at the southern border:

> From the point of view of human rights, the most serious situation [in Mexico] is at the southern border. (UNHCHR 2003: 174)

Various types of accidents are associated with the situation of migrants who have little in the way of economic resources, contacts or support networks. The most frequent accidents are related to traveling, or attempting to travel, by train, especially on the route that stretches from Ciudad Hidalgo, at the Guatemalan border, to the Isthmus of Tehuantepec area. The accidents principally involve attempts to board moving trains, either as travel begins or in an attempt to evade authorities at migration control or police inspection points. Falls commonly end in mutilation or death.

Another point that deserves attention is the interception, detention and deportation of migrants. Detention conditions vary from one location to another and based on the number of people detained. People are often detained in improvised facilities, many of which are inadequate to house the number of migrants involved. This is especially true in the southeast and on the southern border. The situation is further aggravated by the poor medical attention that migrants receive. Detained undocumented migrants of different cultures, religions and ethnic groups receive discriminatory and humiliating treatment (UNCHR 2002).

In the labour flows of the Soconusco area, on the southern border, conditions of discrimination and abuse arise daily. In the specific case of agricultural workers of both sexes, violations of labour rights are frequent, despite the fact that this population technically falls under the regulation of migration authorities. The working and living conditions of women are particularly bad on the farms of the Soconusco border area in Chiapas. In general, women are paid less than men, and piecework predominates, forcing the entire family group to work in order to maximize pay. The majority of agricultural workers' complaints relate to failure to comply with contracts and withholding payment and documents. One factor contributing to these abuses by employers is the lack of attention on the part of labour authorities. Only one staff member of the Ministry of Labour and Social Welfare is present in the city of Tapachula to oversee employers' compliance with contracts—in an area in which over 250 farms employ Guatemalan agricultural workers (Rojas 2002; Ángeles and Rojas 2002).

Female domestic workers receive extremely low wages, with long work days, no benefits, physical and verbal abuse, unjustified firings, retention or non-payment of wages, fabrication of crimes, threats, sexual harassment, and racial discrimination (Ángeles et al. 2004). Testimony from domestic workers and from others who have witnessed the treatment to which the workers are subject reveals deplorable working conditions in border towns and cities. Being a woman, indigenous, Guatemalan (i.e., foreign), undocumented, illiterate, and a domestic worker are all elements that lead to discrimination and abuse in this part of the country (CDHFMC 1999; Rojas 2002).

Another highly vulnerable group of Central American migrant women are those working, either voluntarily or as a result of trickery, in bars and brothels in the Chiapas border area. Many are minors, and they frequently suffer extortion at the hands of health authorities, as well as sexual abuse, exploitive conditions, violence, lack of protection from sexually transmitted diseases including HIV/AIDS and discrimination. Many are subject to extortion because they are undocumented. Others are forced to remain in this type of work to pay debts to their employers that they have incurred (Bronfman et al. 2001; Oceguera 2001: 17).

Paradoxically, the Mexican government is demanding better treatment of Mexicans in the United States while these human rights violations are being documented in its own territory. There must be consistent principles and practices to improve the conditions of migrants in the various phases of their journey, and recognition of their legitimate right to seek work and to attempt to improve their own and their families' economic situation.

United States policies and programs to combat terrorism and drug trafficking identify the Mexican border as one of the principal places to target people attempting to attack the country's national security and the health of its population. One direct consequence of these programs is that migrants, especially undocumented migrants, are seen as either real or potential allies of drug traffickers and criminal groups. Hence, detaining and deporting them becomes a routine administrative task within a strategic, patriotic mission (Oceguera 2001: 7).

Thus, the association made between migrants and crime is reinforced by the construction of a sophisticated infrastructure at the U.S. border. In this context, the abuse and death of migrants occur with impunity. There is a tendency, in some segments of the U.S. population, to equate undocumented migrants with criminals and drug traffickers who represent a threat to the national security. In the wake of the events of September 11, 2001, these people think of undocumented migrants as potential terrorists. The xenophobic and racist attitudes that U.S. ranchers evince toward migrants all along the border is reflected in the detention of undocumented workers passing through their land, as well as in incidents of intimidation and even shooting (UNCHR 2002: 14).

The violations to which Mexican migrants are subject occur from the time they are preparing their journey, continuing throughout the voyage to the northern border, the crossing, the stay in the United States and the return to Mexico. Even attempts to send remittances to family members in Mexico may provoke violations. Violations are committed by Mexican authorities and private individuals, especially in border states, where many people arrive intending to cross the border but fail to do so because they are cheated or robbed of their money or tricked. According to the National Human Rights Commission, however, the most aggressive violations are committed by United States authorities and private parties when migrants cross the border (CNDH 1999: 71).

The report of the CNDH (1999) on violation of the human rights of Mexican migrants emphasizes the problems of women, whether traveling alone or with children, husbands or other family members. They include physical, sexual, and psychological aggression, work discrimination and constraints, arrest and deportation, and other problems and obstacles that are part of the vulnerability to which women, in attempting to migrate to the United States, are subject (CNDH 1999: 127 and 128).

Despite laws and regulations in the United States regarding the equality of women, female Mexican workers in the late 1990s (to cite but one example) received monthly wages up to $250 less than those of men, and 87 percent lacked any benefits (Oceguera 2001: 12). This vulnerability is aggravated, as a result of cultural and linguistic differences, when women are undocumented or indigenous.

Very little attention has been given to the costs of migration in terms of lost human resources and the impact on families, e.g., the disintegration of many Mexican families (CDHNU 2002). The chances that a family will disintegrate are greater for undocumented migrants since, if they visit their families in Mexico, they face new risks and costs in attempting to re-enter the United States. Even when migrants are working in the United States legally, however, various conflicts arise in families. When husbands migrate, women are generally left with additional responsibility and work. In addition to domestic work, they are responsible for the education and health of children, family finances and caring for land and animals. In many cases, unaccompanied women become victims of sexual harassment. The situation is more complicated when the men are away for years, forget about their families or, as happens in many cases, end up living with another woman in the United States (Oceguera 2001: 13; Villaseñor & García 1999: 21–22).

The common experience of men and women entering and leaving Mexico in search of better work opportunities and living options includes abuse, accidents and violations of human rights, and has become a focus of attention for various national and international organizations[26] and institutions[27]. Monitoring and follow-up activity to enforce rights and safeguard the lives of migrants have led to a series of measures and agreements. These instruments include the International Convention on the Elimination of All Forms of Discrimination Against Women, the Inter-American Convention of Belem do Para and the International Convention on the Protection of the Rights of All Migrant Workers and Members of their Families. In 2004, Mexico also ratified the Protocol on Trafficking in Persons, Particularly Women and Children, as a follow-up to which Mexico has signed the Memorandum of Understanding for the Protection of Women and Minors who are Victims of Trafficking in Persons on the Mexico-Guatemala Border (see Carral 2004, Rodríguez Oceguera 2001).

The signing of these instruments should translate into concrete steps, including campaigns to promote respect for Mexican and foreign migrants, ongoing training of public employees and officials whose work is directly related to migrants, among many other measures. Creating a comprehensive policy and updating some of Mexico's legislation are pending tasks requiring an effort to create consistency between demands for the human rights of Mexican migrants, and action to guarantee respect for foreign migrants in Mexico.

FINAL OBSERVATIONS

Women's role in migration today is of various types, and any classification or examination of the issue should include at least three groups of women: (1) those migrating "in association with" a migrating man, whether as a companion or to reunite a family; (2) those migrating independently of men; and (3) those who remain in the community of origin of their migrating family members. In the case of Mexico, attention must also be paid to similarly motivated women from Central America and other countries, who enter at the southern border either accompanying migrants, or seeking work in the region, or trying to reach the United States.

The phenomenon of international migration in Mexico, of whatever type, will continue to intensify, change and become more complex, as a result of the country's simultaneous flows of emigration, immigration and transit migration. This triple role, which many of the world's countries and regions play, presents enormous challenges. The need to ensure respect for migrants' human rights stands out as a priority. People migrate as a result of structural factors that are consequences of the particular development of national and regional economies. Hence, measures to regulate and control migration at international borders must consider the causes of migration, while taking into account the right of all human beings to seek a life of dignity for themselves and their families.

NOTES

1. This chapter was originally written in Spanish and translated by Paul Keller.
2. A review of the Mexican sources for the study of migration to the United States is available in Corona and Tuirán (2000a), two writers who have contributed to resolving many of the theoretical and methodological problems involved in measuring this demographic phenomenon in Mexico.
3. In very recent years, the development of the Internet and the use of CDs have facilitated the dissemination of statistical information. Information on Mexico may now be accessed online at the websites of official sources of data such as the Institute of Statistics, Geography and Informatics (INEGI), the National Population Council (CONAPO) and the National Institute of Migration (INM), as well as through academic institutions that provide the public with online databases from research projects. Even international sources may be consulted online. This technological development has led to the creation of electronic networks and forums through which first-hand information on migration is available on a timely basis. This is particularly true for types of information that were previously restricted to the local area in which the events occurred, e.g., the violation of migrants' human rights.
4. Durán and Massey (2003: 47–48) identify five phases of Mexican emigration to the United States, revealing a pendulum swing, from the opening of the border and recruitment of workers, to partial closing of the border with tighter controls and deportations. The five phases are: (1) the *"enganche"* or "recruitment period" (1900–1920); (2) the "deportation" period (1921–1939); (3) the "Bracero" period or period of documented workers (1942–1964); (4) the "undocumented" period (1965–1986); and (5) the legalization and clandestine migration period (1987 to the present). With some differences in the earlier periods, CONAPO also identifies five historical periods: (1) late 19th century to the years of the Great Depression; (2) Great Depression to 1941; (3) 1942 to 1964, with the Bracero Program; (4) 1964 to the late 1980s; and (5) late 1980s to the present. The first four periods feature the traditional pattern of migration to the United States, with the last representing the "new era" (CONAPO 2005; also see Verduzco 2000).
5. Differences may be found in estimates of the number of Mexicans migrating to the United States, depending on the sources and methodologies used. Having refined methods and reviewed a variety of sources, CONAPO has now provided what may be considered the most reliable figures. Experts in migration, such as Rodolfo Corona and Rodolfo Tuirán, have been involved in the process. On the subject of the estimation process, see Corona and Tuirán (2000a and 2000b), Corona (2000) and Corona (2004).
6. Mexico is divided into 32 political/administrative units known as "federal entities" or "states." These, in turn, are divided into smaller units known

as "municipalities." Various criteria may be used to group the states into regions. For the purpose of studying migration, the most frequently used approach divides Mexico into four regions: traditional, northern, central and south-southeast. Writers such as Durand (see Durand and Massey, 2003: 71) combine geographic and migratory criteria, describing these regions as: historical, border, central and southeast. These divisions will surely change as the numbers of migrants from "emerging" migratory areas increase and are statistically documented.

7. The classification of states into migration-based regions is as follows: (1) **Traditional**: Aguascalientes, Colima, Durango, Guajanuato, Jalisco, Michoacán, Nayarit, San Luis Potosí and Zacatecas; (2) **Northern**: Baja California, Baja California Sur, Coahuila, Chihuahua, Nuevo León, Sinaloa, Sonora and Tamaulipas; 3. **Central**: Federal District [D.F.], Guerrero, Hidalgo, México, Morelos, Oaxaca, Puebla, Querétaro and Tlaxcala; (4) **South-southeast**: Campeche, Chiapas, Quintana Roo, Tabasco, Veracruz and Yucatán.

8. Ordering the states from greater to lesser MII values, they are as follows: **Very high** (5 states): Zacatecas, Michoacán, Guanajuato, Nayarit and Durango; **High** (7): Aguascalientes, Jalisco, Colima, San Luis Potosí, Morelos, Guerrero and Hidalgo; **Medium** (8): Chihuahua, Baja California, Querétaro, Oaxaca, Sinaloa, Puebla, Tamaulipas and Coahuila; **Low** (6): Sonora, Nuevo León, Veracruz, Tlaxcala, Estado de México and Baja California Sur; **Very low** (6): Federal District, Yucatán, Quintana Roo, Campeche, Chiapas and Tabasco (Tuirán et al. 2002: 32–35).

9. A great deal of what is known about female migration to the United States is derived from more specific local and regional studies (González et al. 1995, Szasz 1999, Barrera and Oehmichen 2000, Tuñón 2001).

10. EMIF began in 1993, and is a project of CONAPO, the Ministry of Labour and Social Welfare (STPS) and the Colegio de la Frontera Norte (COLEF). The project continually generates statistical information on the labour migration of Mexicans to the United States and to Mexico's northern border towns, in an attempt to determine the number and sociodemographic characteristics of migrants at given points in their migration (Corona and Tuirán 2000a: 42–43)

11. On the experience of South American exiles in Mexico, see the book by Yankelevich (1998).

12. Between 1980 and 1984, the Mexican Commission for Aid to Refugees (COMAR) and the United Nations High Commissioner for Refugees (UNHCR) documented nearly 45,000 persons (Saayavedra 2001: 123). However, this estimate would seem to be low. The Catholic Church, for instance, counted 93,000 refugees, and other institutions suggest even higher figures (see Saayavedra 2001 and Kauffer 2003). In the environment created by recent programs to regularize the status of migrants, implemented by Mexico's INM with the support of civil society organizations, an indeterminate number of persons are thought to have arrived in border areas seeking protection during the same period. These fall in the category of "dispersed unrecognized refugees" who found protection in places other than those inhabited by people who were initially placed in camps.

13. This high percentage of immigrants is associated largely with the return of Mexican migrants with children born in the United States (see CONAPO 2005). As will be seen, disaggregating figures on immigrants' ages shows that nearly 6 out of 10 immigrants in the United States are under 10 years of age. This high number could be a reflection of the children of returning Mexicans, though establishing such a relationship would require more documentation.

14. Such controls have become a common denominator in other Central American countries, where migration controls have become tighter. In Guatemala, for example, controls on the Salvadoran and Honduran borders have been tightened as part of a policy to limit migration. Like other countries in the region, Guatemala has become a transit country for migrants attempting to reach the United States.
15. Regarding the vulnerability and risks that the migrant population faces, see the work of Olivia Ruíz, who has documented cases of migrants from Central America who entered Mexico via the Soconusco area of Chiapas, which borders Guatemala and has the most intense migratory activity along the southern border of Mexico (Ruíz 2001 and 2004). Also of interest in this connection is the work of Mexico's National Institute of Public Health (INSP) in the context of its HIV/AIDS project and mobile populations, conducted in Mexico and Central American countries, initially coordinated by M. Bronfman and now being overseen by Rubén Leyva (see http://www.insp.mx)
16. As to the other three states in the region, the 2000 census records 8,901 immigrants in Quintana Roo, 4,678 in Campeche and 1,179 in Tabasco. If Mexico's states are listed in order of the number of resident immigrants, these three occupy, respectively, 16th, 24th and 31st place. Women constitute approximately half of this population, though they represent a somewhat lower percentage in Tabasco (the percentages being 51.5%, 48.6%, and 44.9 % for the three states, respectively).
17. Though not as part of a specific study, the authors have been gathering information on certain types of migrant workers through informal interviews with informants, and by observation in various border communities in the Soconusco region. The information on migrants in carpentry comes from informal conversations with a master carpenter in Tapachula, named Manuel. On various occasions between 2001 and 2003, the authors discussed the quality of carpentry in Guatemala with him, as well as the issue of discrimination against undocumented migrants.
18. Field observations by Hugo Ángeles in 2002–2003.
19. Since October 1997, the so-called "migratory form for agricultural visitors from Guatemala" (FMVA) has been in use. Before this, authorization for the entry of workers was obtained by the owner of a farm or *ejidatario* making application to the INM. The request was delivered by a contractor commissioned to provide a certain number of workers. To the request the contractor appended a list of workers compiled in Guatemala and authorized by one of the offices of the Guatemalan Ministry of Labour near the border (in Tecún Umán or El Carmen) (Rojas and Ángeles 2002).
20. The authors surveyed 491 migrant women and minors in migration offices as they waited for approval of their migration form for agricultural visitors (FMVA). Of these, 44.6% were migrant women (Rojas and Ángeles 2002).
21. In other words, at least once a week something different from the other days is included in the food provided to workers by the employer. The change may be no more than a piece of meat in a diet that consists of beans, tortillas and coffee.
22. In year-2000 Mexican pesos, 9.90 of which equal one US dollar.
23. Year-2005 Mexican pesos, 11.2 of which equal one US dollar.
24. Migration officials, following the General Population Law, use the category, known as *"aseguramiento,"* to refer to the temporary detention of a migrant in their facilities because the migrant lacks papers to remain in Mexico. Here, the word "detention" is used.

25. Mexicali (Baja California) Desert Youth Hostel, Fray Matías de Córdova Human Rights Center, Tepeyac Human Rights Center and Sin Fronteras. See Sin Fronteras IAP et al. (2000).
26. Various organizations and academics making up the Migration Forum, as well as the Coalition for the Defense of Migrants, the Migrants' Human Rights Center [Centro de Derechos Humanos del Migrante, A.C.] in Ciudad Juárez, Chihuahua, and the Center for the Care of Migrants in Need in Altar, Sonora, have participated in this effort to formulate and provide follow-up to guarantee the human rights of migrants. In particular, they have contributed to the current formulation of the National Human Rights Plan through their reasoned and critical participation on the Migrants' Human Rights Subcommittee [Subcomisión de los Derechos Humanos de los Migrantes], which was formed in 2004 to fulfill commitments in this area. See, for example, the document *Propuestas para el mejoramiento de los derechos humanos de los migrantes en México para el programa nacional sobre derechos humanos* [Proposals for the improvement of the human rights of migrants in Mexico for the national human rights program], October 18, 2004, at http:// www.gobernacion.gob.mx/comisiondh.
27. The visit of the United Nations Special Rapporteur on the Human Rights of Migrants in 2002, as well as the establishment (also in 2002) of a UNHCHR office in Mexico, reflect this concern and efforts to monitor human rights (see UNCHR 2002a and 2002b, UNHCHR 2003).

REFERENCES

Aguayo, S. (1985). *El éxodo centroamericano, consecuencias de un conflicto*. Secretaria de Educación Pública (SEP), Mexico D.F.
Alba, F. (2001) *Las migraciones internacionales*. Consejo Nacional para la Cultura y las Artes, Mexico D.F.
Alba, F. (2004) *México: un difícil cruce de caminos*. March. Retrieved 5 October 2004, from http://www.migrationinformation.org.
Alvarenga, P. (1997) "Cultura y sobrevivencia: la migración nicaragüense a Costa Rica." In Philippe Bovin (coord.), *Las Fronteras del Istmo. Fronteras y sociedades entre el Sur de México y América Central*. Centro de Investigaciones y Estudios Superiores en Antropología Social, and Centro Francés de Estudios Mexicanos y Centroamericanos, Mexico D.F, pp. 221–229.
Ángeles Cruz, H. (2001) "Los flujos migratorios laborales en la frontera sur de México." In *Población y Desarrollo Sustentable*. Consejo Estatal de Población del Estado de Guanajuato, Guanajuato, pp. 103–106.
Ángeles Cruz, H. (2002) "Migración en la frontera México-Guatemala. Notas para una agenda de investigación." In Edith Kauffer Michel (ed.), *Identidades, migraciones y género en la frontera sur de México*. El Colegio de la Frontera Sur, San Cristóbal de las Casas, Chiapas, pp. 193–214.
Ángeles Cruz, H. (2003) "La migración internacional a través de la frontera sur. La dimensión de las estadísticas para la región del Soconusco." *Ecofronteras*, No. 19, El Colegio de la Frontera Sur, San Cristóbal de las Casas, Chiapas, pp. 5–8.
Ángeles Cruz, H., and S. Martínez (2006) "Violencia social y pandillas. Las maras en la región fronteriza del Soconusco, Chiapas." In Daniel Villafuerte y Xóchitl Leyva (coords.), *Geoeconomía y geopolítica en el área del Plan Puebla-Panamá*.

Ángeles Cruz, H., C. Robledo and A. I. Soto. (2004) *Trabajo y migración femenina en la frontera sur de México. Las trabajadoras domésticas guatemaltecas en la ciudad de Tapachula, Chiapas.* "Paper presented at Seminario Internacional Mujer y Migración", Federación Mexicana de Universitarias A. C. (FEMU), Hermosillo, Sonora, 11–13 November.
Ariza, M. (2000a) *Ya no soy la que dejé atrás... mujeres migrantes en la República Dominicana.* Instituto de Investigaciones Sociales-UNAM and Editorial Plaza y Valdés, Mexico D.F.
Ariza, M. (2000b) "Género y migración femenina: dimensiones analíticas desafíos metodológicos." In Dalia Barrera Bassols and Cristina Oehmichen Bazán (eds.), *Migración y relaciones de género en México.* GIMTRAP and Instituto de Investigaciones Antropológicas-UNAM, Mexico D.F., pp. 33–62
Ávila, J. L., C. Fuentes, and R. Tuirán. (2000) "Mujeres mexicanas en la migración a Estados Unidos." In Rodolfo Tuirán (coord.), *Migración México-Estados Unidos: continuidad y cambio,* Consejo Nacional de Población, Mexico D.F., pp. 149–172.
Azaola, E. (2000) *Infancia robada. Niñas y niños víctimas de explotación sexual en México.* DIF, UNICEF and CIESAS, Mexico D.F.
Barrera Bassols, D., and C. Oehmichen (eds). (2000) *Migración y relaciones de género en México.* GIMTRAP and Instituto de Investigaciones Antropológicas-UNAM, Mexico D.F.
Becerril Quintana, O. (2003) *Relaciones de género, trabajo transnacional y migración temporal: trabajadores y trabajadoras agrícolas mexicanos en Canadá.* "Paper presented at the Primer coloquio internacional Migración y Desarrollo: transnacionalismo y nuevas perspectivas de integración", Zacatecas, Mexico, 23–25 October.
Bilac, E. D. (1995) "Género, familia y migraciones internacionales". *Revista de la OIM sobre migraciones en América Latina,* Vol 13, No. 1, pp. 3–9 (Véase versión en inglés en la misma revista, pp. 13–20).
Boyd, M. and E. Grieco. (2003) *Women and migration: incorporating gender into international migration theory.* Paper presented at the Migration Policy Institute, 1 March. Retrieved 5 October 2004, from http://www.migrationinformation.org.
Bronfman, M. and R. Leyva (2002) *Poblaciones móviles y VIH/SIDA: Respuesta social en la Frontera México-Guatemala.* "Paper presented at the Encuentro sobre la Población en el Sureste de México", El Colegio de la Frontera Sur and Sociedad Mexicana de Demografía, Tapachula, Chiapas, 15–16 August.
Bronfman, M., P. Uribe, D. Halperin, and C. Herrera. (2001) "Mujeres al borde... vulnerabilidad a la infección por VIH en la frontera sur de México." In Esperanza Tuñón Pablos (coord.), *Mujeres en las fronteras: trabajo, salud y migración (Belice, Guatemala, Estados Unidos y México).* El Colegio de la Frontera Sur, El Colegio de Sonora, El Colegio de la Frontera Norte, and Plaza y Valdés, Mexico D.F., pp. 15–31.
Bovin, P. (coord.). (1997) *Las Fronteras del Istmo. Fronteras y sociedades entre el Sur de México y América Central.* Centro de Investigaciones y Estudios Superiores en Antropología Social and Centro Francés de Estudios Mexicanos y Centroamericanos, Mexico D.F.
Carral, M. (2004) *El enfoque de género en las políticas migratorias.* "Palabras de la Comisionada del Instituto Nacional Migración presentadas en el Seminario Internacional "Mujer y Migración"," Federación Mexicana de Universitarias A. C. (FEMU), Hermosillo, Sonora, 11–13 November.
Carrillo, J. H. and A. Hernández. (1988) "Migración femenina hacia la frontera norte y los Estados Unidos." In Gustavo López Castro (ed.), *Migración en el occidente de México.* El Colegio de Michoacán, Zamora, Mich., pp. 85–111.

Casillas, R. (1997) "Redes sociales y migraciones centroamericanas en México." In Philippe Bovin (coord.), *Las Fronteras del Istmo. Fronteras y sociedades entre el Sur de México y América Central.* Centro de Investigaciones y Estudios Superiores en Antropología Social, and Centro Francés de Estudios Mexicanos y Centroamericanos, Mexico D.F., pp. 213-220.
Castillo, M. Á. (1990) "Población y migración internacional en la frontera sur de México: evolución y cambios." *Revista Mexicana de Sociología,* Año LII, N° 1, January-March, pp. 169-184.
Castillo, M. Á. (1992) "Frontera sur y migración: estado actual, necesidades y prioridades de investigación." In Consejo Nacional de Población (CONAPO), *Migración internacional en las fronteras norte y sur de México.* CONAPO, Mexico D.F., pp. 267-290.
Castillo, M. Á. (1995) "Las migraciones en la frontera sur de México." In Adrián Guillermo Aguilar, Luis Javier Castro, and Eduardo Juárez (Coords.), *El desarrollo urbano de México a fines del siglo XX.* Instituto de Estudios Urbanos de Nuevo León and Sociedad Mexicana de Demografía, Mexico D.F., pp. 209-225.
Castillo, M. Á. (1997) "Las políticas migratorias de México y Guatemala en el contexto de la integración regional." In Philippe Bovin (coord.), *Las Fronteras del Istmo. Fronteras y sociedades entre el Sur de México y América Central.* Centro de Investigaciones y Estudios Superiores en Antropología Social, and Centro Francés de Estudios Mexicanos y Centroamericanos, Mexico D.F., pp. 203-212
Castillo, M. Á. (1999) "La vecindad México-Guatemala: una tensión entre proximidad y distancia." *Estudios Demográficos y Urbanos* (40), Vol. 14, N°. 1, January-April, pp. 193-218.
Castillo, M. Á. (2001) "Mujeres y fronteras: una dimensión analítica." In Esperanza Tuñón Pablos (coord.), *Mujeres en las fronteras: trabajo, salud y migración (Belice, Guatemala, Estados Unidos y México).* El Colegio de la Frontera Sur, El Colegio de Sonora, El Colegio de la Frontera Norte, and Plaza y Valdés, Mexico D.F., pp. 33-49.
Castillo, M. Á. and H. Ángeles Cruz (2000) *La participación laboral de los trabajadores agrícolas guatemaltecos en el Soconusco, Chiapas.* Paper presented at the VI Reunión de Investigación Demográfica en México: "Balance y Perspectivas de la Demografía Nacional ante el Nuevo Milenio", Sociedad Mexicana de Demografía, Mexico D.F., 31 July-4 August.
CDHFMC (Centro de Derechos Humanos Fray Matías de Córdova) (1999) *Encuesta a trabajadoras del servicio doméstico.* CDHFMC, Tapachula (Documento interno no publicado).
CDHNU (Comisión de Derechos Humanos de Naciones Unidas) (2002a) *Grupos e Individuos Específicos: Trabajadores Migrantes. Informe presentado por la Relatora Especial Sra. Gabriela Rodríguez Pizarro, de conformidad con la resolución 2002/62 de la Comisión de Derechos Humanos. Adición Visita a México* (E/CN.4/2003/85/Add.2).
CDHNU (Comisión de Derechos Humanos de Naciones Unidas) (2002b) *Grupos e Individuos Específicos: Trabajadores Migrantes. Informe presentado por la Relatora Especial Sra. Gabriela Rodríguez Pizarro, de conformidad con la resolución 2002/62 de la Comisión de Derechos Humanos. Adición Misión a la frontera entre México y los Estados Unidos* (E/CN.4/2003/85/Add.3)
Chiarotti, S. (2003) *La trata de mujeres: sus conexiones y desconexiones con la migración y los derechos humanos.* Serie Población y Desarrollo No. 39, CELADE
CNDH (Comisión Nacional de Derechos Humanos) (1996) *Informe sobre violaciones a los derechos humanos de los inmigrantes. Frontera sur.* CNDH, México.

CNDH (Comisión Nacional de Derechos Humanos) (1999) *Estudio sobre las violaciones a los derechos humanos de la mujer mexicana que migra hacia Estados Unidos de América*, CNDH, Mexico, D. F.

CNDH (Comisión Nacional de Derechos Humanos) (2003) *Prevención de la violencia, atención a grupos vulnerables y los derechos humanos: los derechos de los migrantes*. Fascículo 5. CNDH, Mexico D.F.

CNDH (Comisión Nacional de los Derechos Humanos) (2004) *Transición democrática y protección a los derechos humanos. Fascículo 6: Migración.* CNDH, México D.F.

CONAPO (Consejo Nacional de Población) (2000) *Mujeres en la Migración a Estados Unidos. Migración internacional*, Año 5, No. 13.

CONAPO (Consejo Nacional de Población) (2005) *Migración mexicana hacia Estados Unidos*. Retrieved 1 February 2005, from http://www.conapo.gob.mx/mig_int/03.htm.

Corona, R. (2000) "Estimaciones del número de emigrantes permanentes de México a Estados Unidos, 1850–1990." In Rodolfo Tuirán (coord.), *Migración México-Estados Unidos: continuidad y cambio*. CONAPO, Mexico, pp. 45–62.

Corona, R. (2004) *Cantidad de emigrantes mexicanos en Estados Unidos alrededor de 2000*. "Paper presented at the Seminario Migración México-Estados Unidos: implicaciones y retos para ambos países", CONAPO, El Colegio de México, CIESAS, and Universidad de Guadalajara, Mexico D.F., 30 November.

Corona, R. and R. Tuirán. (2000ª) "Fuentes mexicanas para el estudio de la migración México-Estados Unidos." In Rodolfo Tuirán (coord.), *Migración México-Estados Unidos: continuidad y cambio*. CONAPO, Mexico, pp. 33–44.

Corona, R. and R. Tuirán. (2000b) "Medición directa e indirecta de la migración mexicana hacia Estados Unidos, 1990–1995." In Rodolfo Tuirán (coord.), *Migración México-Estados Unidos: continuidad y cambio*. CONAPO, Mexico, pp. 63–75.

De Vos, J. (1993) *Las fronteras de la frontera sur. Reseña de los proyectos de expansión que figuraron la frontera entre México y Centroamérica*. Universidad Juárez Autónoma de Tabasco and Centro de Investigaciones y Estudios Superioes en Antropología Social, Villahermosa, Tabasco.

De Vos, J. (1994) *Vivir en frontera. La experiencia de los indios de Chiapas*. Centro de Investigaciones y Estudios Superioes en Antropología Social and Instituto Nacional Indigenista, México D.F.

De Vos, J. (2002) "La frontera sur y sus fronteras. Una visión histórica." In Edith F. Kauffer Michel (ed.), *Identidades, migraciones y género en la frontera sur de México*. El Colegio de la Frontera Sur, San Cristóbal de las Casas, Chiapas, pp. 49–67.

Domingo, A. (2000) "Visibilidad estadística y población extranjera." In Maria-Àngels Roque (dir.), *Mujer y migración en el Mediterráneo occidental*. Icaria and ICM, Barcelona, pp. 291–304.

Donato, K. M. (2001) "A dynamic view of mexican migration to the United States." In Rita James Simon (ed.), *Immigrant women*. Transaction Publishers, New Bruswick, pp. 151–174.

Durand, J. and D. S. Massey. (2003) *Clandestinos. Migración México-Estados Unidos en los albores del siglo XXI*. Universidad Autónoma de Zacatecas and Miguel Ángel Porrúa, Mexico D.F.

Flores A., C. (1993) "La frontera sur y las migraciones internacionales ante la perspectiva del Tratado de Libre Comercio." *Estudios Demográficos y Urbanos* (23), Vol. 8, núm. 2, May–August 1993.

Foro Migraciones (2002) *Migración: México entre sus dos fronteras, 2000-2001*, Foro Migraciones, Mexico, D. F.
Fundación Arias para la Paz y el Progreso Humano (2000) *La migración y l@s migrantes hondureñ@s*. CNUAH-Habitat, International Development Research Center, and Postgrado Latinoamericano en Trabajo Social-Universidad Autónoma de Honduras, San José, Costa Rica, http://www.arias.or.cr
Garrido G., P. (2001) *Redes sociales de reciprocidad de las trabajadoras guatemaltecas en la ciudad de Tapachula*. Tesis de Maestría en Ciencias Sociales, El Colegio de Michoacán, Zamora, Mich.
González, S., O. Ruíz, L. Velasco, and O. Woo (comps.) (1995) *Mujeres, migración y máquila en la frontera norte*. El Colegio de México and El Colegio de la Frontera Norte, Mexico,
González Navarro, M. (1994) *Los extranjeros en México y los mexicanos en el extranjero 1821-1970*. Vol 2. El Colegio de México, Mexico D.F.
Higuera Bonfil, A. (1994) *Migración nacional e internacional hacia la frontera México-Belice*. "Paper presented at VIII Coloquio de la Sociedad Nacional de Estudios Regionales: Los extranjeros en las regiones," Oaxaca, Oax., 23-25 March.
Hernández Palacios, L. and J. M. Sandoval (comps.) (1989) *El redescubrimiento de la frontera sur*. Universidad Autónoma de Zacatecas and Universidad Autónoma Metropolitana, Mexico D. F.
Informe Migración (1999) *México entre sus dos fronteras*. Senado de la República LVII Legislatura, México D.F.
IME (Instituto de los Mexicanos en el Exterior). (2005) *Población mexicana en Canadá*. Retrieved 28 January 2005, from http://www.sre.gob.mx/IME.
INEGI (Instituto Nacional de Estadística, Geografía e Informática) (2000) *XII Censo de Población y Vivienda 2000*. México.
INEGI (Instituto Nacional de Estadística, Geografía e Informática) (2005) *Indicadores seleccionados de la población nacida en otro país residente en México, 1950-2000*. Sistema de información municipal y bases de datos (SIMBAD). Retrieved 28 January 2005, from http://www.inegi.gob.mx.
INM Chiapas (Instituto Nacional de Migración. Delegación Regional en Chiapas) (2004) *Estadísticas migratorias (preliminares)*. INM, Tapachula, Chiapas.
INM (Instituto Nacional de Migración) (2004) *Estadísticas migratorias (preliminares)*. INM, México D.F.
Kauffer Michel, E. (1997) "Refugiados guatemaltecos y conformación de la frontera sur de Chiapas en los años ochenta." In Philippe Bovin (coord.), *Las Fronteras del Istmo. Fronteras y sociedades entre el Sur de México y América Central*. Centro de Investigaciones y Estudios Superiores en Antropología Social, and Centro Francés de Estudios Mexicanos y Centroamericanos, Mexico D.F., pp. 162-170.
Kauffer Michel, E. (2002) "Movimientos migratorios forzosos en la frontera sur: una visión comparativa de los refugiados guatemaltecos en el sureste mexicano." In Edith F. Kauffer Michel (ed.), *Identidades, migraciones y género en la frontera sur de México*. El Colegio de la Frontera Sur, San Cristóbal de las Casas, Chiapas, pp. 215-242.
Kauffer Michel, E. (2003) "Los refugiados guatemaltecos y los derechos humanos." In Comisión Nacional de Derechos Humanos (CNDH). 2003. *Prevención de la violencia, atención a grupos vulnerables y los derechos humanos: los derechos de los migrantes*. Fascículo 5. CNDH, Mexico D.F., pp. 121-130.
Lara Flores, S. M. (2003) "Violencia y contrapoder: una ventana al mundo de las mujeres indígenas migrantes, en México". In *Estudios Feministas*, No. 11 (2), July-September, Florianópolis, pp. 381-397.

Lida, C. E. (1997) *Inmigración y exilio. Reflexiones sobre el caso español.* Siglo XXI Editores, Mexico D.F.
Lorenzana, J. D. (2004) *Población migrante.* "Paper presented at Seminario sobre Migración y Salud." Conferencia Regional sobre Migración. Guatemala, 18–19 October. Retrieved 3 February 2005, from http://www.crmsv.org/sem_MigSalud_presentaciones.htm..
Malgesini, G. (comp.) (1998) *Cruzando fronteras. Migraciones en el sistema mundial.* Icaria, Barcelona.
Martínez Pizarro, J. (2000) *La migración internacional y el desarrollo en la era de la globalización e integración: temas para una agenda regional.* CEPAL, Santiago de Chile. Serie Población y Desarrollo, 10, LC/L.1459-P.
Martínez Pizarro, J. (2003) *El mapa migratorio de América Latina y el Caribe, las mujeres y el género.* CEPAL, Santiago de Chile. Serie Población y Desarrollo, 44, LC/L.1974-P.
Mas, F. (2001) *Rompiendo fronteras. Una visión positiva de la inmigración.* Intermón, Barcelona.
Morales Gamboa, A. (1997) "Cruzar la raya: frontera y redes sociales entre Costa Rica y Nicaragüa." In Philippe Bovin (coord.), *Las Fronteras del Istmo. Fronteras y sociedades entre el Sur de México y América Central.* Centro de Investigaciones y Estudios Superiores en Antropología Social, and Centro Francés de Estudios Mexicanos y Centroamericanos, Mexico D.F., pp. 267–275.
Mummert, G. (1988) "Mujeres de migrantes y mujeres migrantes de Michoacán: nuevos papeles para las que se quedan y para las que se van." In Thomas Calvo and Gustavo López (coords.), *Movimientos de población en el occidente de México.* El Colegio de Michoacán and Centre d'Etudes Mexicaines, Zamora, Mich., pp. 281–295.
Nájar, A. (2002) "La Costa y la Sierra se vacían. Chiapas: migrar a puños." *Masiosare 236 [Suplemento semanal]. La Jornada,* 30 June.
Nash, M. (2000) "Construcción social de la mujer extranjera." In Maria-Àngels Roque (dir.), *Mujer y migración en el Mediterráneo occidental.* Icaria and ICM, Barcelona, pp. 275–290.
OACNUDH (Oficina del Alto Comisionado de las Naciones Unidas para los Derechos Humanos) (2003) *Diagnóstico sobre la situación de los derechos humanos en México.* OACNUDH, Mexico D.F.
Perruchoud, R. (2001) "Normas legales para la protección de los trabajadores migrantes." *Notas de población,* Año XXIX, No. 73, pp. 273–303.
Pedrazzini, C. (1999) "Migración interna". In *Informe Migración: México entre sus dos fronteras.* Senado de la República LVII Legislatura, Mexico D.F., pp. 4–17.
Pessar, P. (1999) "Engendering Migration Studies." *American Behavioral Scientist,* Vol 42, No. 4, January, pp. 577–600.
Pickard, M. (2003) "Los trabajadores mexicanos en Canadá: mano de obra "semiesclava" que Fox quiere impulsar en EEUU (I/II)". *CIEPAC: Chiapas al día,* No. 387, 18 december 2003. Retrieved 2 February 2005, from http://www.ciepac.org/bulletins/301-%20500/bolec387.htm. Pickard, M. (2004) "Los migrantes mexicanos en Canadá: el programa de "semiesclavos" pronto se expandirá en Estados Unidos (II/II)". *CIEPAC: Chiapas al día,* No. 398, 03 March 2004. Retrieved 2 February 2005, from http://www.ciepac.org/bulletins/301-%20500/bolec398.htm..

Poggio, S. and O. Woo. (2000) "La invisibilidad de las mujeres en la migración hacia Estados Unidos." In Sara Poggio and Ofelia Woo, *Migración femenina hacia EUA: cambio en las relaciones familiares y de género como resultado de la migración, EDAMEX*, Mexico D.F., pp. 7–19.

Rincón, A, S. Jonas, and N. Rodríguez. (2000) *La inmigración guatemalteca en los EE.UU., 1980–1996*. "Paper presented at the 2000 Meeting of the Latin American Studies Association." LASA, Miami, 16–18 March.

Rodríguez, E. (1989) "En torno a los hilos delgados de la Frontera Sur: la agudización de los problemas agrarios en Chiapas durante la década de los ochenta." In Luis Hernández Palacios and J. M. Sandoval (comps.). (1989). *El redescubrimiento de la frontera sur*. Universidad Autónoma de Zacatecas and Universidad Autónoma Metropolitana, Mexico D. F., 139–152.

Rodríguez Oceguera, P. (2001) "Abuso contra migrantes y defensa de su dignidad y derechos. El Caso de México", Paper for Comisión Ciudadana de Estudios contra la Discriminación, Universidad Abierta. Retrived 5 OIctober 2004, from http://www.universidadabierta.edu.mx.

Rojas Wiesner, M. (2000) *Mujeres trabajadoras agrícolas de Guatemala en la región del Soconusco, Chiapas*. "Paper presented at the VI Reunión de Investigación Demográfica en México: Balance y Perspectivas de la Demografía Nacional ante el Nuevo Milenio", Sociedad Mexicana de Demografía, Mexico D.F., 31 July–4 August.

Rojas Wiesner, M. (2001) "Mujeres trabajadoras agrícolas guatemaltecas en la frontera sur de México." *Entre Redes*, Boletín Trimestral Nº 5, Sin Fronteras I.A.P., Mexico D. F., pp. 19–21.

Rojas Wiesner, M. (2002) "Mujeres migrantes en la frontera sur de México." In *Migración: México entre sus dos fronteras, 2000–2001*. Foro Migraciones, Mexico D.F., pp. 93–101.

Rojas Wiesner, M. and H. Ángeles Cruz. (2002) *Participación de mujeres y menores en la migración laboral agrícola guatemalteca a la región del Soconusco*. Informe Técnico al Sistema de Investigación Benito Juárez (SIBEJ), EL Colegio de la Frontera Sur, Tapachula, Chiapas.

Rojas Wiesner, M. and H. Ángeles Cruz. (2003) "La frontera de Chiapas con Guatemala como región de destino de migrantes internacionales." *Ecofronteras*, No. 19, El Colegio de la Frontera Sur, San Cristóbal de las Casas, Chiapas, pp. 15–17.

Ruíz Marrujo, O. (2001) "Riesgo, migración y fronteras: una reflexión." Estudios Demográficos y Urbanos, No. 47, May-June.

Ruíz Marrujo, O. (2004) *La migración centroamericana en la frontera sur: un perfil del riesgo en la migración indocumentada internacional*. Center for U.S.-Mexican Studies. Retrieved 26 November 2004, from http://repositories.cdlib.org/usmex/ruiz.

Saayavedra, G. (2001) "Mirando al sur del sur: las mujeres guatemaltecas refugiada en Chiapas". In Esperanza Tuñón Pablos (coord.), *Mujeres en las fronteras: trabajo, salud y migración (Belice, Guatemala, Estados Unidos y México)*. El Colegio de la Frontera Sur, El Colegio de Sonora, El Colegio de la Frontera Norte, and Plaza y Valdés, Mexico D.F. pp. 121–141.

SRE & MRHDH (Secretaría de Relaciones Exteriores and Ministerio de Recursos Humanos y Desarrollo de Habilidades de Canadá) (1995) *Memorandum de entendimiento entre el gobierno de los Estados Unidos Mexicanos y el gobierno del Canadá relativo al programa de los trabajadores agrícolas mexicanos temporales*. Retrieved 2 February 2005, from http://www.tratados.sre.gob.mx/tratados/B270495A.pdf.

STPS, CONAPO & COLEF (Secretaria del Trabajo y Previsión Social, Consejo Nacional de Población and El Colegio de la Frontera Norte) (2004) *Encuesta sobre migración en la Frontera Norte de México 2000–2001*. STPS, CONAPO and El Colegio de la Frontera Norte, Mexico D.F.

STPS (Secretaría del Trabajo y Previsión Social) (2005) *Información sobre el Programa [de Trabajadores Agrícolas Mexicanos Temporales]*. Retrieved 2 February 2005, from http://www.stps.gob.mx/01_oficina/03_cgai/triptico.pdf.

Sin Fronteras I.A.P, Albergue Juvenil del Desierto de Mexicali, Centro de Derechos Humanos Tepeyac, and Centro de Derechos Humanos Fray Matias de Córdova (2000) *Mujeres y menores migrantes en México*. Documento preparado por las ONGs mexicanas miembros de la Red No Gubernamental para las Migraciones, para el Seminario-Taller "Mujeres, niños y niñas migrantes", San Salvador, El Salvador, 24 y 25 de febrero.

Sook Lee, M. (2003) "Canadá, los otros braceros". *Masiosare 301 [Suplemento semanal]. La Jornada*, 28 September. Retrieved 28 January from, http://www.jornada.unam.mx/2003/sep03/030928/mas-cano.html.

Szasz, I. (1999) "La perspectiva de género en el estudio de la migración femenina en México." In Brígida García (coord.), *Mujer, género y población en México*. El Colegio de México, Mexico D.F., pp. 167–210.

Trigueros, P. (2003) "La diferenciación de los migrantes mexicanos en Estados Unidos y sus derechos humanos". In *Prevención de la violencia, atención a grupos vulnerables y los derechos humanos. Los derechos de los migrantes. Fascículo 5*. CNDH, México D.F., pp. 87–108.

Trigueros, P. and J. Rodríguez. (1988) "Migración y vida familiar en Michoacán (un estudio de caso)." In Gustavo López Castro (ed.), *Migración en el occidente de México*. El Colegio de Michoacán, Zamora, Mich., pp. 201–221.

Tuirán, R. (2002) "Migración, remesas y desarrollo." In Consejo Nacional de Población (CONAPO), *La situación demográfica de México, 2002*. CONAPO, Mexico D.F., pp. 77–87.

Tuirán, R., C. Fuentes, and J. L. Ávila (2002) *Índice de Intensidad Migratoria México-Estados Unidos, 2000*. CONAPO, Mexico D.F.

Tuñón Pablos, E. (coord.). (2001). *Mujeres en las fronteras: trabajo, salud y migración (Belice, Guatemala, Estados Unidos y México)*. El Colegio de la Frontera Sur, El Colegio de Sonora, El Colegio de la Frontera Norte, and Plaza y Valdés, Mexico D.F.

United Nations Secretariat (2004) *Report of the Secretary-General on the review and appraisal of the progress made in achieving the goals and objectives of the Programme of Action of the International Conference on Population and Development, 2004*. POPULATION Newsletter, No. 77, June. Retrieved 15 October 2004, from http://www.unpopulation.org .

Velasco Ortíz, L. (1995) "Migración femenina y estrategias de sobrevivencia de la unidad doméstica: un caso de estudio de mujeres mixtecas en Tijuana." In Soledad González, Olivia Ruíz, Laura Velasco, and Ofelia Woo (comps.), *Mujeres, migración y máquila en la frontera norte*. El Colegio de México and El Colegio de la Frontera Norte, Mexico D.F., pp. 37–64.

Verduzco, G. (2000) "La migración mexicana a Estados Unidos: estructuración de una selectividad histórica." In Rodolfo Tuirán (coord.), *Migración México-Estados Unidos: continuidad y cambio*. CONAPO, Mexico D.F., pp. 11–32.

Villafuerte Solís, D. (2004) *La frontera sur de México. Del TLC México-Centroamérica al Plan Puebla-Panamá*. Instituto de Investigaciones Económicas-UNAM and Plaza y Valdés, Mexico D.F.

Villaseñor, B. and R. García Zamora. (1999) "Migración en las comunidades de origen". In *Informe Migración: México entre sus dos fronteras*, Senado de la República LVII Legislatura, Mexico D.F., pp. 18–28.
Woo Morales, O. (2001a) "Redes sociales y familiares de las mujeres migrantes." In Esperanza Tuñón Pablos (coord.), *Mujeres en las fronteras: trabajo, salud y migración (Belice, Guatemala, Estados Unidos y México)*. El Colegio de la Frontera Sur, El Colegio de Sonora, El Colegio de la Frontera Norte, and Plaza y Valdés, Mexico D.F., pp. 303–323.
Woo Morales, O. (2001b) *Las mujeres también nos vamos al Norte*. Universidad de Guadalajara, Guadalajara, Mexico.
Woo, O. and J. Moreno. (2002) "Las mujeres migrantes y familias mexicanas en Estados Unidos." In *Migración: México entre sus dos fronteras, 2000–2001*. Foro Migraciones, Mexico D.F., pp.105–113.
Yankelevich, P. (coord.). (1998) *En México, entre exilios. Una experiencia de sudamericanos*. Secretaria de Relaciones Exteriores, ITAM, and Plaza y Valdés.
Zlotnik, H. (1998) "La migración de mujeres del sur al norte". In Graciela Malgesini (comp.), *Cruzando fronteras. Migraciones en el sistema mundial*. Icaria, Barcelona, pp. 113–145.
Zlotnik, H. (2003) *The global dimensions of female migration*. Paper presented at the Migration Policy Institute, 1 March. Retrieved 5 October 2004 http://www.migrationinformation.org..

8 Political Participation and Empowerment of Foreign Workers
Gendered Advocacy and Migrant Labour Organising in Southeast and East Asia[1]

Nicola Piper

INTRODUCTION

The "import" and "export" of steadily increasing numbers of foreign workers in general, and the feminisation of migration in specific, has created a myriad of problems and challenges that require attention by governments, trade unions and NGOs in origin and destination countries. These major challenges arise particularly in contexts where migration is characterized by widespread informalisation, temporariness and/or illegality where migrants, as a result, are not organised politically. Migrant associations, trade unions and other civil society institutions have an important role to play in the empowerment of migrants, especially female migrants. This has been recognized by academics (see Ford and Piper in press for Asia; Basok 2005 for Latin America) as well as policymakers (ILO 2004; GCIM 2005). These different types of organisations have their respective strengths and weaknesses, based on their organisational 'histories' and processes, offering different opportunities and posing different limitations for advocacy and labour organising. In recent years, trade unions have begun taking a new approach to migrant workers, leading to some promising developments which include new strategies which have begun to emerge in the form of intra-organisational policy shifts or reform processes and inter-organisational alliances within and across borders. Part and parcel of these changes is the need to address gender issues in the political organising of migrants which has come to the fore. This also constitutes an important area for academic inquiry which has so far largely neglected the political aspects of migration from a gender perspective (Piper 2006b).

As the previous chapters in this volume show, the incorporation of migrants into the labour market is gendered, as are the processes and dynamics involved in political responses to the widespread non-recognition and violation of migrants' rights. By drawing on the specific situation in Southeast and East Asia, this chapter aims to illustrate the fact that labour relations and the incorporation of migrant workers into advocacy by trade unions and grassroots organisations are gendered processes. The objective is, thus, to contribute to the specific issue of political participation and the political organising of, and by, migrant workers to seek equal treatment for all workers regardless of citizenship or legal status — and the gender dynamics involved in this. The ways in which migrants engage as civic and political actors in the process of migration are often mediated by gendered norms, expectations, and opportunities for agency. In addition, the gendered nature of organisational structures involved in the political struggle for the recognition of migrants' rights does not only reflect gender segregated labour markets but also the gendered nature of law (see also Satterthwaite, this volume).

The issue of political participation and organising points to the importance of institutions or organisations. In the realm of work, the labour movement through trade unions constitutes an important institution for the representation of workers' interests and the right to organize or join trade unions is firmly established in international human rights law. Apart from the general problem of the erosion of workers' rights globally, the additional problem for foreign workers, however, is their status as non-citizens. Trade unions have historically been rather anti-immigration, blaming foreign workers for low wages and deteriorating working conditions. In addition, many of today's labour migrants work on short-term contracts and/or in an undocumented manner — conditions which pose a specific challenge to labour union organising. The feminisation of migration and women's position in mainly informal sector jobs is another area that trade unions have long neglected or found difficult to address. As a result, the organising of migrant labour, or the lack thereof, highlights serious limitations of conventional trade unionism. A number of scholars working on Asia have in fact argued that it is alternative organisations such as migrant worker organisations or NGOs working on migrant issues that have taken on an important role in filling this gap (Ford 2004; Piper 2003; Wee & Sim 2005).

A holistic approach to migrant worker political organising (in the sense of bringing trade unions and grassroots organisations together) is rare. But it is through such a holistic approach that *gender* differences — in a relational sense (as opposed to a focus on *women*) — in migrant worker organising can be teased out. This chapter, thus, attempts to take the first step towards the analysis of political organising of migrant labour from a holistic institutional set-up to assess the gender differences in terms of the type, form, and influence migrant workers' political activism takes. Empirical examples are taken from the context of intra-regional migration flows in Southeast and East Asia.

The analytical link between migration and the politicisation of migrants' concerns through non-governmental institutions is established here via the concept of 'the network'. Within migration studies, networks theory have mostly been approached from socio-cultural and/or spatial perspectives, whereby the political sphere has not yet received sufficient attention (Piper 2006a; as also noted by Faist 2004). Social movement scholars and political scientists working on advocacy networks, on the other hand, have investigated the transnational sphere of such network activities and the transnational nature of the issues advocated for, as well as the transnational form of such activism[2], but hardly beyond the context of NGOs neglecting trade unionism and thus collective political action. Migrant worker organising has, therefore, not been looked at from a transnational nor trans-institutional perspective. Furthermore, it is precisely this perspective which allows us to assess gender differences.

PATTERNS OF LABOUR MIGRATION IN ASIA — BACKGROUND

The scale, scope and complexity of international migration have grown considerably — so much so that states and other stakeholders have become more aware of the challenges and opportunities presented by human movements (GCIM 2005). This can also be observed in the Asian context. Of the world-wide estimated 185 to 192 million international migrants, nearly 50 million (or 29%) were in Asia as of 2000 (UN 2004 cited in IOM 2005:1). The ILO estimates that about 22.1 million were economically active in Asia from among the 86 million migrant workers globally (excluding refugees) (ILO 2004:7). In Southeast and East Asian countries that admit migrants exclusively for temporary labour purposes, the share of independent women in the labour migration flows has increased sharply since the late 1970s (ILO 2003: 9). By 2000, 50.1 percent of all migrants in Southeast and East Asia were women (UN 2002), and in some cases women clearly dominate over their male counterparts, reflecting the decrease of traditional male jobs and the increase in female dominated jobs. This has led commentators to refer to this as the 'feminisation of migration'.

Asia is comprised of origin, transit and destination countries. It hosts the world's largest labour exporting country, the Philippines, which has recently surpassed Mexico to take top position. In addition, its overseas migrant population is the most widely dispersed — in almost 200 countries. It has the most diversified migrant population in terms of skill levels, type of migrants, and destination countries. The feminisation of migration is also clearly pronounced: Of all newly deployed and land-based overseas migrant workers, women represent between 61 percent and 72 percent for 1998 to 2002 and between 69 percent and 72 percent for 2000–2002.[3]

Indonesia, the largest Muslim country in the world, has also become a significant exporter of labour, female and male. Since about 1993, two-thirds of all legal migrants have been women, working mainly as domestic workers in West Asia, Hong Kong and Singapore (Yamanaka and Piper 2003). Thailand has been described as a country that is not purely a labour exporter any longer, but that which has also become attractive for foreign workers from its neighbours (Cambodia, Laos, and mostly Burma). Until the 1980s, Southeast (and also South) Asian migrants mainly went to work in West Asia, but since then the newly industrialized countries (NICs) in Southeast and East Asia have also become a major magnet. Singapore constitutes the destination country with the highest percentage of migrant workers (30 percent of its population). In terms of absolute numbers, Malaysia has the largest foreign worker population in this part of the world. Hong Kong constitutes another important destination. In East Asia, it is only Taiwan which has implemented an official scheme for the 'import' of temporary labour. Korea and Japan stand out in that their migration policies prohibit the entry of unskilled migrant workers, with the result that most unskilled migrants are undocumented. Today, Bangladeshi, Nepalese, Sri Lankans, Thai, Filipinos and Vietnamese are among the diversifying foreign workforce in the higher developed destination countries in Southeast and East Asia.

The vast majority of migrants in Asia are low- or semi-skilled workers who are participating in migratory systems with specific characteristics: labour migration is largely contracted and mediated by employment agencies with the effect of increasing the overall costs of migration; legal cross-border flows are of strictly temporary nature; partly as a result of being tied to one employer, migrants are subject to widespread incidences of abuse and rights violations; upon return, they are faced with uncertain reintegration (ILO 1999).

Similarly to other parts of this world, migrant workers in Asia are highly represented in the construction sector, in the manufacturing sectors for small firms or for sub-contracting companies, in services, in agriculture (esp. on plantations), rice mills and fisheries. They are typically provided low salaries with little or no benefits. Migrant women are largely confined to traditional roles in the labour market, mostly in the health, entertainment and domestic service sectors; in addition they can also be found working in factories, especially in the garment sector. As entertainers and domestic workers, they are inadequately addressed by labour legislation, and so are the so-called 'trainees' (mostly male), a system commonly used in Japan and Korea to get around official policy of not allowing the employment of unskilled foreign workers (see Piper and Yamanaka, this volume).[4] But it has to be said that even in those sectors covered by labour laws in theory, unskilled migrant workers often have their employment and associational rights violated in practice (see below).

The characteristics of labour migration in Asia (temporary contract work in informal or sub-contracting sectors), thus, pose specific problems to the issue of protection and political representation of migrants' rights by non-governmental organisations — which have an additionally difficult stance in many Southeast Asian countries because of the lack of democratic space.

POLITICAL AGENCY, PARTICIPATION AND EMPOWERMENT

Some conceptual thoughts

Participation is the opposite of passivity and social exclusion. Agency is the opportunity to make choices on life events — to define one's goals and act upon them. One might be free to act or participate but not do so, due to lack of capability or lack of knowledge — a situation which can result in indifference. The notion of empowerment derives from the standpoint of the disempowered and the marginalized. It is a means of providing agency, that is, an opportunity to make choices and a means of achieving better welfare (ILO 2004: 8–9). Agency can be exercised by individuals individually or collectively in form of group representation. The former is sometimes seen as related to rights, although it is not clear that having agency directly leads to having rights (as argued by Briones 2006). The latter — in its most effective way — involves the setting up of a formal body that can act on behalf of a group (ILO 2004). In the context of migrant workers and women in specific, it is often the NGO environment which starts their empowerment process (Courville & Piper 2004). As a result, the process of empowerment is not only an individual, but also a collective experience (Lisboa 2003).

By bringing participation, agency and empowerment together under one conceptual framework, a link or continuum is established between the social and political spheres of life. Political scientists and development scholars have promoted another concept to address the neglect of the 'social' in the theorising of participation — 'social capital'. However, the literature on social capital does not usually give much attention to the issue of power, inequality, and social differentiation which is of importance when investigating change from the perspective of marginalised people. Elsewhere, I have argued (Courville & Piper 2004: 50) that power is explicitly recognised in the notion of empowerment. Presser and Sen define empowerment as the "process of changing power relations in favour of those at the lower levels of a hierarchy" (2001: 17). In this sense, the notion of empowerment refers to the expansion of choice and agency for those who have less power in society. Empowerment is a complex process that involves altering power relations in multiple spheres through a range of means and has been subject to much critical analysis also (e.g. Cornwall & Brock 2005; Mohan & Stokke 2000). In this chapter I confine the application of the notion of 'empowerment' to the public sphere and organised struggles. NGO run empowerment programs can constitute an important attempt to bring marginalized groups into the political arena, such as by way of education and information campaigns (Courville & Piper 2004). One aspect of educating migrant workers is to raise their awareness of their rights — vis-à-vis their country of origin as well as destination.

Explicitly feminist thinking on agency and empowerment takes as its starting point the recognition that in all societies, women have been denied choices to a far greater extent than men and as a result women have had less influence on strategic areas of their lives. Thus, "(w)omen's empowerment involves gaining a voice, having mobility and establishing a public presence." (Johnson 1994: 148, quoted in Kabeer 1999: 12). Moreover, feminists' approaches to agency and empowerment put a lot of emphasis on the importance of intangible cognitive and resource-related elements that are largely unrecognised in mainstream social scientific literature. Such understanding results in empowerment taking on a 'fuzzy definition' which is not easily measurable. One element of criticism vis-à-vis the notion of empowerment is that it is commonly understood as a social process in which men's role as 'agents of change' often goes unrecognized (Kabeer 1999; Piper 2005d). This can result in obstructing the level (and speed) of change of norms, social behaviour, mentalities and advances in terms of women's rights.

International migration constitutes another social process — one that is characterised by contradictory outcomes with regard to empowerment (Chow 2002b: 22). On the one hand, migration exposes foreign workers to various degrees of vulnerability and marginalisation on the basis of nationality, ethnicity and class, as well as sex and gender. On the other hand, migration has the potential to liberate foreign workers from many constraints that have subjected them to poverty, exploitation and oppression in their home countries. The type of empowerment or abuse that female and male migrants experience is not always identical. There are important differences and nuances related to gender socio-cultural conditions and positions within the labour markets in the countries of origin and destination (Piper 2005b).

Without access to an organisation that can represent their interests, most people are — and remain — likely to be vulnerable to economic and social insecurity (ILO Socio-Economic Security Programme 2004). Having a meaningful organisational set-up through which influence on policy and the normative/legal framework can be channelled at all stages of the migration process (pre-migration, stay abroad, return migration) helps the promotion and implementation of migrants' rights. The creation of an enabling environment can be achieved through institutions that empower workers through education, knowledge provision and so on. Awareness is only the first step, however. What is really significant is direct participation in 'voice institutions' (ILO Socio-Economic Security Programme 2004: 339) and thus, self-organising. In the context of migration this means organising by migrants themselves (or by former migrants). This, however, often proves to be difficult based on foreign workers' legal and visa status as well as type of job — and the democratic space given to such self-organising by destination countries (Piper 2005a). In addition, there are important gender differences in terms of the extent to which organising is possible and the form such organising takes. I return to these issues below.

Studies on migrants' political agency and participation

Research on political participation by migrants has mostly been conducted from the viewpoint of immigration and, thus, in the context of countries of destination where settlement is an option. Migrants' political participation is, therefore, typically approached from the perspective of integration and, thus, citizenship. The notion of political participation is defined and measured in terms of rates of naturalisation, levels of voter registration and turnout. Research has found that the difference in political participation between foreign-born and native-born citizens is better explained by differences in mobilisation than by other factors (Minnite et al. 1999). In a similar vein, it has been argued that membership in specifically political organisations constitutes a key factor (Fuchs et al. 1999, in Minnite).

From the viewpoint of foreign workers who are on temporary contracts and not permanent residents, let alone citizens, political participation takes on a different meaning and form. The crucial vehicles for their political organisation are pre-existing trade unions and NGOs since self-organising in the destination country is often difficult. As part of the global reconfiguration of economies, however, trade unions' capacity to influence policies has been eroded in recent decades in countries where it was historically strong (such as Europe), and has been prevented from growing in many places where it was already weak (in much of Asia). The widespread de-unionisation in recent years and erosion of the strength of freedom of association has pushed collective bodies such as unions to a more marginal role in social policy making. Unions are losing their appeal as labour markets become more flexible and informal, making it more important that trade unions represent workers in a more holistic manner, i.e. as citizens (ILO Socio-Economic Security Programme 2004).

There is a great deal of academic writing on the subject of trade union reforms and summarising these goes beyond the scope of this article.[5] Trade unions' ambivalent stance on migrant labour has also been subject to some analysis (Kahmann 2002; Briggs 2001). Theoretically, the most interesting and relevant contributions as far as this chapter is concerned, has been the work by Waterman (2001) on social movement unionism and Johnston (2001) on 'labour as citizenship movement'. The latter makes direct reference to immigrant labour, documented and undocumented. Johnston highlights the increasingly *transnational* workforce and *transnational* overlapping of societies which requires, according to him, a re-conceptualisation of conventional perspectives on citizenship (as also argued by Piper and Ball 2002). New approaches and strategies are needed to address critical problems faced by migrant workers in their role as foreigners as well as labourers in certain sectors that are associated with the "three Ds" (dangerous, difficult, dirty), epitomised by construction, agriculture, and domestic work. There is growing realisation that 'coalitions of organisations' can exert far more influence than single organisations by themselves.

Waterman (2001, 2003) has developed the notion of 'social movement unionism' as a synthesis of trade-union theory with that of 'new social movement' theory[6], arguing that the crisis of trade unionism is rooted in the fact that the labour movement is still understood in organisational/institutional terms when it needs to be understood in networking/communicational ones (as new social movements have done). Both he and Johnston argue that although labour is not the only source for social change, it constitutes an important ally and would achieve its full potential if aligned with other democratic social movements. With traditional workers and unions no longer being the norm of political struggle for social justice, labour movements have to rethink their way of operating. Recent studies on migrant worker NGOs in the Southeast Asian context have argued on a similar line: that regular collaboration with trade unions would enhance NGOs' advocacy efforts (Piper and Ford 2006).

The specific situation of many migrant workers highlights the importance of organisational representation and the formation of alliances as well as networks across space, institutions and issue-specificism (human rights, women's rights, workers' rights) to address the complexity of migrants' rights.[7]

Studies on gender and migrant politics

With immigrants and their children forming an ever-growing proportion of the electorate in many cities and regions of the United States and Europe, scholarly interest in their political orientations and behaviour has increased, with a number of studies and volumes focusing on particular ethnic groups or on comparisons among groups or countries. The focus continues to be primarily on electoral politics, but within this frame, gender has come to be a more regular part of the analysis (Sawer 2004). For example, in the U.S. context, Lien's work (2001) explores the issue of political participation through the lens of Asian Americans and includes a discussion of gender differences. A smaller body of work (for example Wong 2003) addresses the gender question more directly.

Until recently, few studies by political scientists considered non-electoral participation or employed qualitative analysis that might offer explanations for gendered differences in participation. But the exceptions demonstrate the potential for further research in this area. Hardy-Fanta's work on 'Latina Politics' (1993) provides an alternative view on politics precisely because it is based on a clear gender analysis. Exploring the nature of politics for Latina women and Latino men in the United States, she analyses the interaction of gender, culture and political participation. Her data (derived from participant observation and in-depth interviews) shows that women's visions of politics include a stronger sense of community, cooperation and collective processes of organisation, leading her to argue that "there is more to politics than just voting" (1993: 23) and the holding of elective office. In analyzing her findings, she makes reference to Ferguson's argument about empowerment as "the ability to act with others to do together what one could not have done alone" (1987: 221). In other words, power is about affecting "change rather than the power over others" (Hardy-Fanta 1993: 30).

Building on arguments made by Hardy-Fanta and others[8], Jones-Correa (1998a, 1998b) pursues the investigation of a gendered understanding of immigrant political organising and socialisation in the context of Latinos in New York. He argues that immigrant Latinas are more likely to concentrate in their political activities on their new country of residence (in this case the United States), whereas immigrant Latino men tend to engage in the politics of their countries of origin. He explains this by the differing (real or perceived) status and class positions between immigrant men and women (with women tending to be upwardly mobile post-immigration and men losing status), as well as by the fact that women's social contacts in their capacity as mothers and homemakers is with American governmental institutions. These experiential differences offer an alternative route to mobilisation than immigrant organisations that tend to be formed by men with men occupying organisational or leadership positions, pushing women into alternative forms of political activism.

Gendered analyses of trade union politics and their organising, or non-organising, of migrants in the context of settlement countries do not seem to exist. The issue of women workers and (historically male dominated) trade unionism has been subject to some scholarly inquiry (see Fonow 2003), but not from the specific perspective of *migrant* workers. A gender perspective to labour organising, however, introduces an additional element to the problematic stance experienced by foreign labour. The few existing studies on civil society organisations' engagement with foreign labour have argued that it is not trade unions but NGOs which have taken on a vital role in supporting migrant workers in general and migrant women in specific (Ford and Piper in press). Political self-organising has also been mainly in the form of grassroots organisations or associations rather than trade unions[9] (Schwenken 2003; Piper 2006a).

In the Asian context, as pointed out by Yamanaka and Piper (2006), female labour's responses to oppressive conditions have been subject to much scholarly debate. As the result of rapid economic development under the tight control of development-oriented states and their industrial allies which have suppressed organised labour activities, factory workers (especially in export-oriented industries where women constitute the majority of workers) have found it extremely difficult to escape exploitative or abusive practices, let alone address them politically. Consequently, large scale labour disputes have rarely occurred in factories of multinational corporations in E/SE Asia (Chow 2002a). Instead, it has been argued that the typically female labour force uses a variety of forms of resistance referred to as "weapons of the weak" (Scott 1986) or "cultural struggles" (Ong 1991, 1996).

Female workers in general, and more so migrant workers such as foreign domestic workers, are thus often portrayed as having little or no agency in the world economy. They are either viewed as passive victims of global power structures (emphasising macro economic 'demand and supply' dynamics) or as isolated actors exerting micro agency through acts of 'everyday resistance' (Ford and Piper in press). Research on domestic worker activism in Asia tends to confine their attention to one country (typically the destination) which often results in the interpretation of such phenomenon as "local" with little influence on politics or policies (e.g. Abdul Rahman 2005). However, when the transnational nature of their activism and the increasing incidences of transnational networking is taken into account,[10] collective activism takes on a new dimension and force that can, and has, influenced national, regional and global policymaking to some extent (Piper 2005c). Such networking takes place via organisations and requires the possibility to establish such organisations — and thus is related to the issue of 'freedom of association'.

ASSOCIATIONAL RIGHTS

Legal and normative framework

The right to organise or join trade unions or form other organisations is firmly established in international human rights law. The ILO's latest Plan of Action on migrant workers — the outcome of the International Labour Congress in 2004 and its tripartite negotiation structure which includes trade unions — has revived a rights-based approach to migration. The freedom of association and collective bargaining is among the fundamental principles and rights at work championed by the ILO which are universal and applicable to all people in all States, regardless of the level of economic development. They, therefore, also apply to all migrant workers without distinction. Representation and having a voice at work are described as "important means through which migrant workers can secure other labour rights and improve their working conditions" (ILO 2004: 72–73). In addition to the ILO norms and standards, the right to form and join trade unions is also enshrined in the International Covenant on Economic, Social and Cultural Rights (ICESCR) as well as in the 1990 UN Convention on the Rights of All Migrant Workers and Their Families (CRMW).

However, there are crucial differences and nuances with regard to the scope and extent to which migrants can organise themselves politically as set out by relevant covenants. The migrant worker specific ILO conventions, and the CRMW Article 26 of the latter stipulates that all migrant workers (regardless of legal status) have the right "to take part in meetings and activities of trade unions and of any other associations established in accordance with the law" and "to join freely any trade unions and any such association as aforesaid". The explicit right to *form* an organisation, however, is confined to *documented* migrants, as stipulated in Article 40:

> Migrant workers and members of their families shall have the right to form associations and trade unions in the State of employment for the promotion and protection of their economic, social, cultural and other interests. [11]

The ICESCR in its Article 8 refers to the "right of everyone to form trade unions and join the trade unions of his (*sic*) choice, subject only to the rules of the organisation concerned". Unlike the CRMW, this Covenant, however, only refers to trade unions and not to 'other associations' which include civil society organisations.

Based on its tripartite structure including trade unions, the clauses on 'freedom of association' championed by the ILO relate to trade unions only. Unlike the CRMW, the two migrant worker specific ILO conventions (no. 97 and 143) restrict the equality of treatment and opportunity in respect to trade union rights of those migrant workers *lawfully* within the territory of the destination country. This means the CRMW goes the furthest with regard to 'rights to institutional representation' in terms of *types* of organisations, but the ICESCR takes associational rights one step further by extending this to all workers regardless of legal status, even though this right to self-organising remains restricted to trade unions. This reflects two major issues: the dominant recognition of trade unions as *the* institution to represent workers as far as international law is concerned and the widespread reluctance to allow *all* foreign workers the right to organise regardless of migration status. This confirms general comments made on migrant worker specific instruments as well as other UN conventions about their reflecting the situation and concern of *western* countries more than of countries in the global South (Piper & Iredale 2003; see Davies 2004 on the 1951 Refugee Convention) as well as the priority of controlling migration rather than the protection of all migrants in their capacity as workers.[12] Moreover, this has serious gender implications: problems specific to women migrants are more addressed by NGOs than trade unions. It is the latter, however, who have more clout in defining who is a legitimate worker which is largely related to the fact that the concept of 'work' derived from nineteenth-century definitions based on the experience of male industrial workers in the factories of Great Britain (Ford & Piper in press).

On the issue of protecting *undocumented* migrants, there has been a gradual shift in recent years (coming mainly from trade unions and NGOs) to treat migrants first and foremost as workers once they have entered the territory and are working at the destination, regardless of their legal status. More and more national trade unions take steps to offer some kind of protection to 'sans papiers' (Piper 2005a). This development has become evident on the international level also, in the revival of a rights-based approach to migration by the ILO which includes irregular migrants. The most recent and ground breaking development in this regard, however, is the ruling by the Inter-American Court of Human Rights that clarifies that all migrants — documented and undocumented — are covered by the principles of non-discrimination, equality and equal protection in the host states where they live and work and must not be excluded from the protection of labour laws on the basis of their migration status. This, however, still leaves the issue of political organising and impediments to associational rights.

Associational rights in practice

Legally, temporary migrant workers often have the right to join trade unions which is, however, more often a theoretical right in practice. Even legal migrant workers face various tactics of employers and contractors to keep them out of trade union membership despite their legal entitlement to do so (of which they are often not aware). Migrant workers are typically concentrated in the informal sectors of the labour market doing unskilled jobs and working extremely long hours without much time off; they often have a high level of mobility by moving between jobs or even sectors; they work in great isolation as in the case of domestic workers or other women factory workers whose mobility outside of the workplace is highly restricted due to cultural restrictions, such as in the case of South Asian factory workers (Dannecker 2005). Domestic workers face the additional problem that their remunerative activity is not even socio-legally recognized as 'work': most labour standards laws in Asia explicitly exclude domestic work from their coverage. Hence, established unions have never included domestic workers in their labour activism (with the rare exception of Hong Kong). The controversial issue of work in the sex industries is yet another matter entirely — this line of work is completely invisible. A related issue is that despite the legal right to join trade unions, unions rarely actively seek membership by migrants which leaves the latter often unaware of this option (and migrant workers are often not unionised in their country of origin either).

As a result of these factors, in many destination countries, organising of foreign workers is very difficult. In the Malaysian case, e.g., migrants' contracts typically contain clauses prohibiting (legal!) foreign workers to join an existing union or be politically active.[13] This actually violates the national employment law. The Industrial Relations Act and Trade Unions Act govern the formal industrial relations system in the country and the law allows migrant workers to become members of trade unions (but not hold office), although in practice, migrants are prevented from joining unions as stipulated in their contracts. The moment a migrant joins a union, the employer can sack this worker without being held accountable. Thus, the formal labour/employment system is weakened by the existence of an informal system. Even for 'willing' trade unions, this poses extraordinary obstacles.

In addition, in Southeast Asian countries, migrant workers are legally not allowed to set up their own organisations, with the notable exception of Hong Kong. In Singapore, e.g., any organisation engaging in 'political activity' is strictly scrutinised. Intentions to advocate issues of rights have to go through a lengthy registration process and it is presumed that citizenship would be an issue. An entirely non-citizen group attempting to register a rights-based organisation is unheard of. Malaysia has a more vibrant NGO sector than Singapore, even in the area of human and workers rights, but there are no NGOs set up by migrants themselves which is partly a reflection of the fairly large number of undocumented migrants. In such circumstances, migrants depend on concerned local citizens to extend support to foreign workers through existing NGOs.

GENDERING ADVOCACY AND ORGANISING OF MIGRANTS

The actors

Civil society organisations have for a long time filled an important gap by addressing labour issues (Gallin 2000). Empirical evidence from the developing South acknowledges even more the importance and influence of non-traditional, non-union labour organising (Ford 2004; Hutchison & Brown 2001). Not all of these NGOs concern themselves primarily with labour issues but all contribute to a complex web of activism supportive of marginalised workers who often are female and/or migrant (Ford 2004). Along with broader human rights organisations, women's organisations have emerged as particularly active in advocating for migrants' rights in general and migrant women's rights in specific. It is human rights and women NGOs that have been at the forefront of advocacy for migrant workers in Asian destination countries. As far as countries of origin are concerned, the Philippines stands out with regard to the breadth of associations set up by former migrants and/or 'left behind' family members of migrants which have been politically active for many years. Such organisations are beginning to appear also in Indonesia. Trade unions, by contrast, have not given much attention to neither migrants nor gender issues.

Existing NGOs can be divided into two broad categories, 'migrant labour organisations (understood as those run by migrant workers themselves) and NGOs involved in migrant labour (i.e. organisations which do not focus on foreign workers *per se* and which are run by concerned citizens, not the migrants themselves). The second type can be further classified into the following types of NGOs: (1) faith-based organisations, (2) worker/labour NGOs, (3) women's rights organisations; and (4) human rights organisations. Destination countries in Southeast Asia and the region at large have at least one group of each type.

Unlike trade unions, NGOs engaged in migrant worker advocacy usually do not take a sector specific approach (although there are NGOs catering specifically to domestic workers) and often conceptualise migration as part of broader globalisation processes establishing links to other issue areas such as trade, poverty, governance — and the sexual division of labour. In places where domestic workers constitute the dominant job category for foreign women, it is not surprising to find quite a few NGOs set up to exclusively assist foreign domestic workers (hereafter FDWs). This is the case in Hong Kong and Singapore. In Malaysia, interestingly enough, the most active and outspoken NGO, Tenaganita, started off as a women's NGO but having been mostly called upon by a great number of male migrants, it could not refuse assistance and has gradually become a migrant worker NGO in practice. This is a reflection of the huge problems the large number of male migrants encounters in Malaysia: breach of contracts (non-payment or under-payment of wages) and hassle by security forces (police and immigration). But this is also a reflection of the fact that domestic workers in Malaysia seem to be more invisible than in city states like Singapore and Hong Kong. Furthermore, this reflects the general apathy of the local and national trade unions to reach out to migrant workers.

On the international level, the trade union movement has identified three types of migrant workers as particularly vulnerable: agricultural, construction workers (most of whom are male) and domestic workers. The latter, however, has never been unionized in Asia (again, with the notable exception of Hong Kong). Local unions are mainly concerned with the rights of the workers occupied in a particular sector that is mostly part of the formal economy, of whom only a small percentage are women. With union advocacy for workers' rights being sector specific, this also has gender implications as the incorporation of migrant workers into the labour force is sex-segregated.[14] However, it has to be said that even within a specific sector, there are nevertheless differences according to skill and hiring/working practices. Frost (2005) has shown that in the case of Nepalese construction workers in Hong Kong, most of them are day labourers and suffer from high levels of job insecurity and informal practices. They do not enjoy any assistance by trade unions.

Apart from sector-related problems, the availability or lack of political space for the setting up of institutions offers another explanation for the different types of organisations involved in migrant labour advocacy. Recent country studies of four major countries[15] involved in labour migration in Southeast Asia — Singapore, Malaysia, Indonesia and the Philippines — have provided a detailed mapping of existing organisations and their strategies to promote and protect migrants. These studies have made a clear distinction between migrant worker associations (run by migrants or former migrants) and NGOs involved in assisting foreign workers. Self-organising has been identified as particularly effective and this underpins not only the importance of 'freedom of association', but also 'freedom to form political organisations' of any kind — and the addressing of widespread direct and indirect violation thereof.

ISSUE AREAS

Broadly, the main issues fought for by migrant worker associations and NGOs in Southeast and East Asia revolve around employment-related rights and improved working conditions. In the specific case of domestic workers who are locked into informal interactions within the home, much of the activism has appealed to the "morals" of employers as reflected in campaigns such as "Dignity is Overdue" (Singapore, Malaysia). NGOs have called for standard contracts as a minimum protection and are also demanding the inclusion of domestic work in the coverage of national labour laws (more vocally in Malaysia; in Singapore there is disagreement among NGOs whether a uniform contract is to the benefit of all FDWs). In Malaysia, the trade union council and NGOs have begun to jointly call for the right of all workers to seek redress to put an end to under- or non-payment of wages and to create a 'culture of payment of wages'. This includes a call for the right to stay by issuing foreign workers not just social pass visas but work permit visas to allow them to earn money while waiting for labour disputes to be resolved.

In the Philippines, activism for migrants' rights has become particularly broad to include, e.g., the rights of family members left behind, rights to economic security 'at home', as well as absentee voting rights — a campaign which resulted in the passing of the Overseas Voting Bill in 2004. To assist returned migrants with reintegration has also become part of their advocacy agenda. Filipinos have emerged as the most widely and best organised group of migrants, to the extent that they are even engaged in 'training' other groups of migrants to become good activists (as it happens in Hong Kong) (Piper 2005c). They have the most extensive networks 'at home' and 'abroad' — a reflection also of their being the most dispersed workforce in the world.

The International Confederation of Free Trade Unions' (ICFTU)[16] Regional Organisation for Asia and the Pacific (ICFTU-APRO) has recently organised a few regional consultations on the role of trade unions in protection migrant workers (ICFTU-APRO 2003). ICFTU-APRO's Action Plan from 2003 includes two major recommendations: (1) establishing a migrant workers' desk or committee; (2) recruiting migrant workers as union members. The first has been realized by some national centres, such as Singapore's National Trades Union Congress (NTUC).[17] Malaysia's

Trades Union Congress (MTUC) has a sub-committee/section on foreign workers but they do not have the funding for full time staff to work on migrant labour related issues, let alone for legal assistance (interview, July 2005, Kuala Lumpur). The second recommendation by ICFTU-APRO constitutes still an underdeveloped aspect of trade union work in Southeast Asia (as elsewhere). But more recently, the MTUC has reaffirmed its commitment to assist and organise migrant workers, including domestic workers.[18] In Thailand, trade union leaders have formulated the so-called Phuket Declaration resulting from an ILO workshop on migrant labour in August 2005 in which they declare (amongst other items) that "Thai Trade Unions should be committed to organise and recruit migrant workers".[19] Domestic workers, or any women specific job categories for that matter, are not highlighted in this declaration as especially vulnerable and thus in need of trade union action.

POLITICAL ALLIANCES AND NETWORKS

The Activism — Transnational and trans-institutional networks

Within the existing literature on social movements and other civil society groups operating across state borders, there has been a tendency to deal exclusively with one kind of transnational group (such as transnational advocacy networks, transnational social movements, INGOs) and to treat the two major forms of 'collective activism' (social movements and NGOs) as different phenomena. Elsewhere, I (Piper and Uhlin 2004,) have argued in favour of a focus on transnational *activism* by any type of actor to move beyond this divide and bridge research on social movements and studies of NGOs. Political activities that are referred to by 'activism' are: (1) based on a conflict of interests, (2) challenging or supporting certain power structures (i.e. public goals), and (3) involving non-state actors (2004: 4). The focus on the actual activism links up to the network argument and allows us to link the trade union movement and other civil society organisations.

An interesting argument which has been emerging is that the labour movement can only achieve its full potential today in alignment, or merger, with other democratic social movements ('social movement unionism' or 'citizenship unionism'). Participants need to be enabled to express themselves and act not only as workers but as members of a community (Johnston, 2001). In other words, struggles for labour rights are feeding into the larger citizenship movement that is a movement of women, the future of children and family relationships which cross borders. This links up with another argument made in addressing the root cause of trade unions' loss of power in recent years: unions are urged to reflect upon their form of operating which is said to be still primarily organisational/institutional during times when both capitalism and the global NGO solidarity movement are adopting the network form (Waterman 2003).

What has to be stressed in this regard is the need for national and transnational activist networks to achieve their full potential. "The key to successful campaigning abroad is a strong movement 'at home'" is the statement by a Filipino activist[20] which shows that the success of transnational activism is linked to, or rooted in, a strong national movement. This is one of the major reasons why Filipinos are the most active and most successful in mobilising migrant workers. The 'list' of their achievements 'at home' includes the ratification of the CRMW in 1995, the passing of the Overseas Voting Rights Bill in 2004 and the anti-trafficking law in the same year (which is the most gender-sensitive in the world). Partly in response to activist pressure, embassy services have hugely improved over the years also. Abroad, activists who have raised awareness with regard to domestic worker issues, had successfully fought for the maintenance of the minimum wage in Hong Kong (but lost the battle finally in 2003). Indonesians have also become very active during the last few years in Indonesia itself as well as in certain key destinations in Asia, such as Hong Kong (Ford 2004).

Impediments to alliance formation — Gender and class

The extent to which migrant worker associations are able to form alliances, in destination as well as origin countries, and assert sufficient pressure on governments to achieve change depends on many issues, gender roles being one of the more important. In countries such as Bangladesh, coalition forming between male and female migrant worker specific organisations or networks seems largely based on a strict understanding of gender roles. As Dannecker has shown (2005), gender norms and relations based on an ideal gender order of *purdah* severely restrict women's mobility. Because there is a low level of "social legitimacy" with regard to women's migration (Oishi 2005), male Bangladeshi workers commonly stigmatise Bangladeshi women working and living abroad by claiming these women have a 'loose lifestyle' (Dannecker 2005). They therefore exclude women from their support systems by establishing male-dominated networks.

With regard to women-to-women alliances, domestic work emerges again as a particularly vulnerable job category where forming alliances with other women's organisation is hampered by the contradictory processes of alliance formation between local women's organisations and FDW groups (see Wee and Sim 2005 for Hong Kong; and Lyons 2005 for Singapore). In Hong Kong, middle-class women have largely failed to support FDWs' successful campaigns (Wee 2003), perhaps because opposition to the government's proposal to lower the minimum wage is seen as an economic threat to working families who seek to minimise the costs of hiring a live-in maid.

This tension is clear in countries of origin such as Indonesia, where middle-class women engaged in activism on behalf of FDWs do not generally raise issues faced by domestic workers employed locally by women like themselves with the same vigour as they promote the interests of Indonesian nationals employed as domestic workers overseas.

In destination countries such as Hong Kong, Malaysia and Singapore, where middle-class women almost always employ foreign workers, class thus intersects with ethnicity or non-citizen status. Even in Japan and Korea, where advocacy is conducted by concerned citizens, and thus on behalf of migrants rather than by the migrants themselves[21], the majority of citizens and women's NGOs in these countries have remained aloof and indifferent to issues regarding the welfare and rights of migrant workers.

Yet despite these contradictions it would be wrong to depict all middle-class women as uninterested in the plight of *all* migrant women. Their active engagement in organisations that have included the plight of migrant workers and migrant women into their portfolio of activities have played an important role in both sending and receiving countries. A 2001 study of migrant education programs in six countries (Philippines, Indonesia, India, Hong Kong, South Korea and Japan) identified 248 groups which are directly involved or supporting migrants' issues (AMC 2001). Women make up a large part of the activists and founders of these NGOs.

Class and ethnicity can also be issues hampering trade union organising and collaborating with working class unions and middle-class NGOs. In the Malaysian context, it has also been argued that its ethnic composition has resulted in ethnic identity out-weighing class identity (Sing 2002). Class identity (or the lack thereof) and gender issues, therefore, add another layer to the complex obstacles to the political organising of migrant workers.

Opportunities: Transnational, trans-ethnic and trans-institutional networking

The forming of national NGO networks on migrant workers is quite rare. What seems more often the case is that NGOs gather on an ad hoc basis on a specific issue or the result of a specific event. Interestingly, they are often more active in regional networks rather than in national networks for which there are a variety of possible explanations (competition for funding and publicity locally, clashing of personalities and/or agendas etc.).

Among the migrant NGOs involved in transnational networking, there are two main types: networks set up in support of one nationality group or in support of migrant workers at large, regardless of nationality. The arguably most successful of the first category, in terms of its widespread grassroots support as well as overseas networking, is MIGRANTE International, a global alliance of overseas Filipino organisations. Membership based, staffed by activists who were formerly migrants themselves, and supported from the grassroots level, MIGRANTE has been vital in organising Filipino migrants on a large scale. Among its objectives are to strengthen unity and organisations of overseas Filipinos and their families in the Philippines and to defend the rights and welfare of overseas Filipinos. It has 95 member organisations in 22 countries globally. By trying to address the root causes of migration in the Philippines, the NGO and its networks are addressing migrant workers' rights "at home". Although also Philippine-based, another important network is the Migrant Forum in Asia (MFA) which is non-Filipino focused and thus clearly more regionally oriented. It is a 260+ membership organisation covering the whole of Asia (West, South, Southeast, Northeast, and East), including NGOs from sending and receiving countries.[22] Its member-NGOs support any migrant workers, female and male, of any nationality in Asia. They hold regular regional meetings and exchange information (and also engage in lobbying) via email.

Another important regional network whose secretariat is located in Kuala Lumpur is CARAM Asia (a sub-network part of MFA), which stands for Coordination of Action Research on AIDS and Mobility. It is not only concerned with domestic worker issues, but with larger health and other migration issues. Yet its work has been particularly influential with regard to FDWs. As a follow up to a regional summit on domestic workers in 2002, CARAM Asia launched a campaign to make FDW issues visible and expose the violations of their rights. It also seeks to bring about legal and extra legal protection of FDWs and lobbies for the recognition of domestic work as 'proper' work. To do so, it organised two consultative meetings with the UN Special Rapporteur for the Human Rights of Migrants. In addition, the network also produced a declaration called the *Colombo Declaration* in 2002 at the conclusion of a regional summit on FDWs which was attended not only by NGOs but also by trade unions.[23] This network has thus included trade unions in their activist endeavours. Whether trade unions attended these meeting purely to get information or in view of addressing FDW-related issues as part of their programmes and services remains to be seen.

Within trade unionism, the international structure of labour organisations has lent itself to 'global solidarity networks' whereby local workers have been politically active in support of workers in different countries (Herod 1995). These types of solidarity networks have, however, not been analysed by political scientists working on transnational political activism or by social movement scholars. This does not necessarily mean that transnationalism is not part of the unions' way of operating. When looking at the various statements made by international unions or federations, one can observe a trend towards greater awareness of the need for collaboration between migrant sending and receiving countries' unions since the late 1990s.[24] At the level of national or local unions, however, a recent ILO survey has shown that hardly any union has ever sent a delegation to countries of migrant origin to discuss protection issues with local unions (Johansson,

2005). This might have to do to some extent with lack in resources. The NTUC in Singapore has recently begun to have meetings with the MTUC in Malaysia and migrant worker organisations in Indonesia. Philippine based trade unions have sent organisers to Hong Kong to assist with the setting up of domestic worker unions there. For this type of transnational cooperation, however, there is often not enough funding available and many unions find it difficult to justify the spending of national workers' membership fees on such transnational issues.[25]

New initiatives are nevertheless on the horizon: Two recent declarations by the MTUC and Thai trade unions (see also below) include in their 'action plan' the promotion of close cooperation with unions in sending and receiving countries. The MTUC document recommends that sending countries should "develop a system for networking and information exchange between sending and receiving countries". As laudable as these rhetoric statements are, it is yet to be seen whether resources will be made available to turn rhetoric into transnational action.

Another element of transnational networking involves trans-*institutional* networking, i.e. alliances or coalitions formed between trade unions and civil society organisations domestically as well as across borders. Global policy statements by international unions have mentioned the need to collaborate with civil society organisations (but to a lesser degree than collaboration with unions across borders), and the above mentioned ILO survey confirms that some unions do collaborate with migrant worker organisations nationally. There is, however, far less evidence of trade unions networking transnationally with organisations other than trade unions. A notable exception is Hong Kong where a Philippine trade union has been involved in local organising of domestic workers into a union with support by the Hong Kong Confederation of Trade Unions (HKCTU). Interesting to note is that in specific context, transnational networking with NGOs can actually be preferred by trade unions to working with local NGOs. This is the case with the NTUC in Singapore. A recent study has shown that there is very little trust between the national union centre and local NGOs based on different styles and the fact that the NTUC (being close to the government) cannot be seen cooperating with explicit human rights organisations (see footnote 5). However, the Singapore NTUC has a good working relationship with the MFA, a regional NGO network based in Manila, and through this network, initial meetings have taken place in Indonesia and Malaysia between trade unions and NGOs.

GENDERING MIGRANT POLITICS — CONCLUDING REMARKS

Generally speaking, migrant workers suffer from greater levels of socio-economic and legal insecurities than national workers due to their status as non-citizens, and often as undocumented workers, and their relegation to unskilled and/or informal sector jobs. As a result, foreign workers on the whole are politically under-represented and relatively voice-less. The gender-segregated nature of labour markets means that migrant women dominate certain 'sectors' which have traditionally been outside of the purview of conventional trade unionism and also excluded from labour laws. In theory, freedom of association and legal protection is, thus, more available to male than to female migrant workers. In practice, however, the violation of freedom of association is widespread in most South-East Asian countries where labour activism generally has historically had a tougher stance than in the industrialized North. In East Asian destination countries, one major obstacle to trade union engagement is the undocumented status of many migrant workers.

Trade unions' political weakness means that the active organising of any workers, let alone migrants, has been poorly developed. NGOs have, therefore, been vital players in the struggle for workers' rights. The extent and effect to which woman migrants' issues have been the focus of NGO (and union) activism depends largely on the opportunity for self-organising of the migrants. In Asian destination countries, this is a very rare phenomenon. On the political/activist level, broader coalition building and extensive networking between human rights, women and worker organisations extending to lawyers and consumer associations across origin and destination countries is needed. Academically, more in-depth studies could explore the obstacles and opportunities to do so.

I have argued elsewhere (2006a) that the increasing levels of international labour migration and the political activism surrounding foreign workers — especially when seen from a transnational perspective — have the potential to reinvigorate labour activism in general by highlighting the global connections between local and foreign workers. Apart from transnational networking, however, it is equally as important for the various organisations involved in worker advocacy to form alliances trans-institutionally and trans-ethnically. Freedom of association and the right to self-organise for *all* workers could be the common political framework to "make labour a whole".[26]

The starting point of this chapter was to provide an integrated analytical framework on political activism on behalf of and by migrant workers from a gender perspective by investigating trade union and NGOs' political and legal positioning against the backdrop of the dominant migration patterns in Asia. This was supported by a snap-shot of empirical examples. I argued that the concept of the network is the most useful tool to bridge migration studies with studies on political activism The academic literature on gender and migration has begun to engage with migrant worker activism from a social movement perspective, but more detailed studies on the gender and sector dynamics from a holistic viewpoint (i.e. engagement by civil society organisations and the trade union movement) are needed. As it stands now, the focus in the existing literature has been on one type of job category (e.g.

domestic work) and often in the context of one specific (usually the destination) country. There are no in-depth studies on the political dynamics within a specific sector, let alone cross-sectoral studies conducted from a multi-country and trans-institutional perspective which would help to further explore gender differences. There are many context specific differences and particularities requiring detailed studies on the specific dynamics in, and across, countries of origin and destination to fully explore the linkages between institutional politics and empowerment of migrant workers.

Despite the many structural and legal constraints that many migrants are facing, the few existing gender analyses of political participation and behaviour of migrants have highlighted migrants' role as political agents when politics is understood in a broad sense. Transnational citizenship and human rights activism are important components of 'alternative' politics. Migrants' role in transformative politics and linkages to global networking, alliance-building across the boundaries of nation-states, class, and gender, and the empowerment of migrants in general and migrant women in particular, however, is not yet fully understood. Such a comprehensive research agenda would inform, and lead to, a workable policy agenda.

NOTES

1. I would like to thank the following colleagues for reading earlier drafts and giving me invaluable comments: Dr. Tanya Basok and Professor Eleonore Kofman.
2. For a full literature review, see Piper and Uhlin (2004).
3. If seafarers and rehires were included, the gender distribution would be about balanced.
4. Domestic workers and trainees are explicitly excluded from national labour laws in most of the Asian destination countries where this type of migrant worker occurs. Entertainment is completely invisible in legislation — not even mentioned as a type of work to excluded.
5. Useful references can be found on http://www.crimt.org/2eSite_renouveau/Samedi_PDF/Cradden_Hall_Jones.pdf
6. To be precise, Waterman (2003) argues that social movement unionism should be reconceptualised in "Class+New Social Movement' terms.
7. See Piper (2006) for a detailed discussion of the transnationalisation of rights.
8. E.g. Grasmuck and Pessar (1991), Hondagneu-Sotelo (1994).
9. In Asia, there is however one notable exception and this is Hong Kong where foreign domestic workers have been successful in setting up a union.
10. For full text of the entire Convention, see http://www.ohchr.org/english/law/cmw.htm.
11. The concern with the 'control of migration' has recently experienced a discursive shift to the 'management of migration' (see Piper 2006c).
12. The exact wording in one contract for a Nepalese worker is "The Employee shall not marry with any Malaysian and shall not participate in any political activities of those connected with Trade Unions" (copy shown to the author during interview, June 2005, Kuala Lumpur).

13. This has also been observed by Basok (2006) in the context of Latin America.
14. See footnote 5, page 7.
15. The ICFTU is a global confederation of national trade union centres, each of which links together the trade unions of that particular country. Membership is open to independent trade union organisations which have a democratic structure. The ICFTU cooperates closely with the ILO and has consultative status with the UN's Economic and Social Council. It has three regional offices in Africa, the Americas and Asia.
16. According to a recent questionnaire by the ILO sent out to trade unions around the world (to which 42 trade unions responded, among them NTUC Singapore), 16 unions replied affirmatively to the question whether they have a designated migration officer, two of which in Southeast Asia: Hong Kong and NTUC Singapore. The main responsibilities of such migration officers were mostly (1) training and information, followed by (2) policy advocacy, (3) individual assistance and lastly (4) recruiting members. NTUC Singapore's designated migration officer is part of the 'Migrant Workers Forum' (MWF) which was set up in 2002, chaired by Mr. Yeo Guat Kwang.
17. Concluding Resolution, MTUC Conference on Migrant Workers, April 18-19, 2005, Petaling Jaya Malaysia. I thank Mr. Ragwhan, ILO Bangkok, for sharing this information with me.
18. I am grateful to Mr. Ragwhan at the ILO Bangkok office for sharing this document with me.
19. Piper, interview, November 2003, Manila.
20. This is largely because most labour migrants are undocumented (and foreign women work as entertainers rather than FDWs).
21. For more details, see http://www.mfasia.org.
22. For wording and more details, *see* http://www.caramasia.gn.apc.org/page.php?page=regional_summit/.
23. See Public Services International (1996), Going out to Work – Trade Unions and Migrant Workers; final statement by ILO Asia-Pacific Regional Symposium for Trade Union Organisations on Migrant Workers, December 1999, in Petaling Jaya/Malaysia.
24. Personal interview, Kuala Lumpur, April 2005.
25. Expression by Dr. Thomas Palley, Assistant Director of Public Policy, American Federation of Labour and Congress of Industrial Organizations (AFL-CIO), Panel Discussion Transcript, 30 November 2001, retrieved May 11, 2006, from http://www.cis.org/articles/2001/unionpanel.html.

REFERENCES

Abdul Rahman, N. (2005) 'Shaping the migrant institution: the agency of Indonesian Domestic Workers in Singapore", in L. Parker (ed.), *The Agency of Women in Asia*, Singapore: Marshall Cavendish.

Basok, T. (2006) 'Gendered Advocacy for Nicaraguan Migrants in Costa Rica', unpublished *conference paper* presented at the Canadian Sociology and Anthropology Association Annual Conference, York University, Toronto, June 1.

Basok, T. (2005) 'Migrant Workers, Grassroots Organizations, Citizenship rights: the Lingering Power of Nation-States', unpublished *conference paper* presented at the Human Rights in a Globalizing Era? Conference, Centre for Studies in Social Justice, University of Windsor, August 4–6.

AMC (Asian Migration Centre) (2001) *Clearing a Hurried Path: A Study on Education Programs for Migrant Workers in Six Asian Countries*. AMC: Hong Kong.
Briggs, V. M. (2001) *Immigration and American Unionism*, ILR Press.
Briones, L. (2006) 'Beyond agency and rights: capability, migration and livelihood in Filipina experiences of domestic work in Paris and Hong Kong', *Unpublished PhD Thesis*, Centre for Development Studies, Flinders University of South Australia.
Chow, E. N. (ed.) (2002a) *Transforming Gender and Development in East Asia*. Routledge, New York.
Chow, E. N. (2002b) 'Globalisation, East Asian development, and gender: A historical view', in E. Ngan-ling Chow (ed.), *Transforming Gender and Development in East Asia*. Routledge, New York.
Cornwall, A. and K. Brock (2005) 'What do buzzword do for development policy? A critical look at 'participation', 'empowerment' and 'poverty reduction', in: *Third World Quarterly*, vol. 26(7): 1043–1060.
Courville, S. and N. Piper (2004) 'Harnessing Hope through NGO Activism', in: *The American Academy of Political and Social Science*, special issue edited by V. Braithwaite, vol. 592, pp. 39–61.
Dannecker, P. (2005) 'Transnational Migration and the Transformation of Gender Relations: the Case of Bangladeshi Labour Migrants', in: *Current Sociology*, vol. 53(4): 655–674.
Davies, S. (2004) 'International Refugee Law – Can New Problems be Met with Old Solutions?, in: *International Journal of Human Rights*, vol. 8(3), autumn.
Faist, T. (2004) 'Towards a Political Sociology of Transnationalization', in: *Archives Européennes de Sociologie* vol. 45(3): 331–366.
Ferguson, K. E. (1987) 'Male-Ordered Politics: Feminism and Political Science', in: T. Ball (ed.), *Idioms of Inquiry – Critique and Renewal in Political Science*, New York: State University of New York Press, pp. 209-226.
Fonow, M. M. (2003) *Union Women: Forging Feminism in the United Steelworkers of America*, Minneapolis: University of Minnesota Press.
Ford, M. (2004) 'Organizing the Unorganizable: Unions, NGOs and Indonesian Migrant Labour', in: *International Migration*, vol. 42(5): 99–119.
Ford, M. and N. Piper (in press) 'The Construction of Informal Regimes as Sites of Female Agency: Foreign Domestic Worker-Related Activism in East and Southeast Asia', in: J. Dobson and L. Seabrooke (eds.), *Everyday Politics of the World Economy*, Basingstoke: Macmillan.
Frost, S. (2005) 'Building Hong Kong: Nepalese labour in the construction sector', in: K. Hewison and K. Young (eds.), *Transnational Migration and Work in Asia*, London: Routledge, pp. 110–125.
Gallin, D. (2000). 'Trade Unions and NGOs: A Necessary Partnership for Social Development', *Civil Society and Social Movements Programme Paper Number 1*, Geneva: United Nations Research Institute for Social Development.
Global Commission for International Migration (GCIM) (2005) *Migration in an interconnected world: New directions for action*', Geneva: GCIM.
Grasmuck, S. and P. Pessar (1991) *Between Two Islands – Dominican International Migration*. Berkeley: University of California Press.
Hardy-Fanta, C. (1993) *Latina Politics – Latino Politics*. Philadelphia: Temple University Press.
Herold, A. (1995) 'The Practice of International Labor Solidarity and the Geography of the Global Economy', in: *Economic Geography*, vol. 11(4): 341–363.
Hondagneu-Sotelo, P. (1994) *Gendered Transitions: Mexican Experiences of Immigration*. Berkeley: University of California Press.

Hutchinson, J. and A. Brown (eds.) (2001) *Organising Labour in Globalising Asia*, London: Routledge.
International Confederation of Free Trade Unions-Asian and Pacific Regional Organisation (ICFTU-APRO) (2003) *Migration Issues Concern Trade Unions*, Singapore: ICFTU-APRO.
ILO (2003) *Preventing Discrimination, Exploitation and Abuse of Women Migrant Workers: An Information Guide – Booklet 1: Why the Focus on Women International Migrant Workers*. Geneva: ILO.
ILO (2004) *Towards a Fair Deal for Migrant Workers in the Global Economy*, Geneva: ILO.
ILO Socio-Economic Security Programme (2004) *Economic Security for a Better World*, Geneva: ILO.
ILO (1999) 'Conclusions and Recommendations', Asia-Pacific Regional Symposium for Trade Union Organisations on Migrant Workes, 6–8 December 1999, Petaling Jaya, Malaysia. Retreived June 2005, from http://www.ilo.org/public/english/dialogue/actrav/genact/socprot/migrant/migrant1.htm.
IOM (2005) *World Migration Report*, Geneva: IOM.
Johansson, R. (2005) 'Role of TU in Respect to Migrant Workers: Summary of Responses', unpublished background paper, Geneva: ILO.
Johnston, P. (2001) 'Organize for What? The Resurgence of Labor as Citizenship Movement', in H. Katz and L. Turner (eds.), *Rekindling the Movement: Labor's Quest for Relevance in the 20th Century*, Ithaca, NY: Cornell University Press.
Jones-Correa, M. (1998a) 'Different Paths: Gender, Immigration and Political Participation', in: *International Migration Review*, 32(2): 326–349.
Jones-Correa, M.(1998b) *Between Two Nations – The Political Predicament of Latinos in New York City*. Ithaca, NY: Cornell University Press.
Kabeer, N. (1999) 'The Conditions and Consequences of Choice: Reflections on the Measurement of Women's Empowerment', *UNRISD Discussion Paper No. 108*, Geneva: UNRISD.
Kahmann, M. (2002) 'Trade Unions and Migrant Workers: Examples from the United States, South Africa and Spain', Discussion and Working Paper 2002.02.03, ICFTU, Brussels.
Lien, P. (2001) *The Making of Asian America through Political Participation*. Philadelphia: Temple University Press.
Lisboa, T. K. (2003) 'Migration and female empowerment in Brazil', in: M. Morokvasic-Mueller, U. Erel, and K. Shonozaki (eds.), *Crossing Borders and Shifting Boundaries*, Opladen: Leske + Budrich, pp. 299–308.
Lyons, L. (2005) 'Transient Workers Count Too? The intersection of citizenship and gender in Singapore's civil society', in: *Sojourn*, vol. 20(2): 208–248.
Minnite, L. C., J. Holdaway and R. Hayduk (1999) 'The Political Incorporation of Immigrants in New York', Paper presented at the *Annual Meeting of the American Political Science Association*. Atlanta. September 2–5.
Mohan, G. and K. Stokke (2000) 'Participatory development and empowerment: the dangers of localism', in: *Third World Quarterly*, vol. 21(2): 247–268.
Oishi, N. (2005) *Women in Motion – Globalization, State Policies, and Labor Migration in Asia*, Stanford, CA: Stanford University Press.
Ong, A. (1991) 'The gender and labour politics of postmodernity', in: *Annual Review of Anthropology*, vol. 20, pp. 279–309.
Ong, A. (1996) 'Strategic sisterhood or sisters in solidarity? Questions of communitarianism and citizenship in Asia', in: *Indiana Journal of Global Legal Studies*, vol. 4, no. 4, pp. 107–136.

Piper, N. (2006a) 'Economic Migration and the Transnationalisation of the Rights of Foreign Workers – A Concept Note', *ARI Working Paper Series No. 58*, February 2006, ARI: Singapore (http://www.nus.ari.edu.sg/pub/wps.htm).

Piper, N. (2006b) 'Gendering the Politics of Migration', in: *International Migration Review*, vol. 40(1): 133–164.

Piper, N. (2006c) 'The Management of Migration — An Issue of Controlling or Protecting? Normative and institutional developments and their relevance to Asia', *ARI Working Paper Series No. 69*, Singapore: ARI (www.ari.nus.edu.sg/docs/wps/wps06-069.pdf).

Piper, N. (2005a) 'Rights of Foreign Domestic Workers – Emergence of Transnational and Transregional Solidarity?', in: *Asian and Pacific Migration Journal*, vol. 14(1-2): 97–120.

Piper, N. (2005b) 'Gender and Migration', *Background Paper*, Geneva: GCIM (http://www.gcim.org).

Piper, N. (2005c) 'Transnational Politics and Organizing of Migrant labour in South-East Asia – NGO and Trade Union Perspectives', in: *Asia-Pacific Population Journal*, vol. 20(3): 87–110.

Piper, N (2003) 'Bridging Gender, Migration and Governance: Theoretical Possibilities in the Asian Context', in: *Asian and Pacific Migration Journal*, vol. 12 (1-2): 21–48.

Piper, N. (2005d) 'A Problem by a Different? A Review of Research on Trafficking in Southeast Asia and Oceania', in: *International Migration*, vol. 43(1/2): 203–233.

Piper, N. and R.E. Ball (2002) 'Globalisation and Regulation of Citizenship – Filipino Migrant Workers in Japan', in: *Political Geography*, vol. 21(8): 1013–1034.

Piper, N. and M. Ford (eds.) (2006) 'Migrant Labor NGOs and Trade Unions: A Partnership in Progress?', Special Issue, in: *Asian and Pacific Migration Journal*, vol. 15(3) (whole issue).

Piper, N. and R. Iredale (2003) *Identification of the Obstacles to the Signing and Ratification of the UN Convention on the Protection of the Rights of All Migrant Workers: The Asia Pacific Perspective*, Asia Pacific Migration Research Network (APMRN) Working Paper 14, Wollongong: University of Wollongong.

Piper, N. and A. Uhlin (2004) 'New Perspectives on Tarnsnational Activism', in: Piper, N. and A. Uhlin (eds.), *Transational Activism in Asia – problems of power and democracy*, London: Routledge, pp. 1–25.

Presser, H. B. and G. Sen (2001) *Women's empowerment and demographic processes: Moving beyond Cairo*, Oxford: Oxford University Press.

Sawer, M. (2004) 'The Impact of Feminist Scholarship on Australian Political Science', in: *Australian Journal of Political Science*, 39(3): 553–566.

Schwenken, H. (2003) 'Respect for All: The Political Self-Organization of Female Migrant Domestic Workers in the European Union', in: *Refuge: Canada's Periodical on Refugees*, vol. 21(3): 45–52.

Scott, J. (1986) *Weapons of the Weak*. New Haven, CT: Yale University Press.

Sing, Ming (2002) 'Civil Society in Southeast Asia: Cases of Singapore and Malaysia', in: R.K.H. Chan, K.K. Leung and R.M.H. Ngan (eds.), *Development in Southeast Asia*, Aldershot: Ashgate, pp. 17–35.

United Nations (2002) *International Migration Report: 2002*, New York: United Nations.

Waterman, P. (2001) *Globalization, Social Movements and the New Internationalism*, London and Washington: Mansell (second edition).

Waterman, P. (2003) 'Adventures of Emancipatory Labour Strategy as the New Global Movement Challenges International Unionism', http://groups.yahoo.com/group/GloSoDia/files/LABOUR%20INTERNATIONALISM/
Wee, V. (2003) 'Whose problem is it any way and why does it matter? Structured vulnerabilities and innovative alliances among migrant women workers in East and Southeast Asia,' *Paper presented* at the *Third International Convention of Asia Scholars*, Singapore, August 19–2.
Wee, V. and A. Sim (2005) 'Hong Kong as a destination for migrant domestic workers', in: S. Huang, B.S.A. Yeoh and N. Abdul Rahman (eds.), *Asian Women as Transnational Domestic Workers*, Singapore: Marshall Cavendish.
Wong, J. (2003) "Gender and Political Participation among Asian Americans", in: J. Lai and D. Nakanishi (eds.) *Asian American Politics*, Rowman and Littlefield, pp. 211–230.
Yamanaka, K. and N. Piper (2003) 'An Introductory Overview', in: *Asian and Pacific Migration Journal*, vol. 12(1-2): 1–20.
Yamanaka, K. and N. Piper (2006) 'Feminised Migration in East and Southeast Asia: Policies, Actions and Empowerment', UNRISD Occasional Paper No. 11.

9 Using Human Rights Law to Empower Migrant Domestic Workers in the Inter-American System[1]

Margaret L. Satterthwaite

BEYOND NANNYGATE: EMPOWERING MIGRANT DOMESTIC WORKERS THROUGH HUMAN RIGHTS LAW

The Nannygate phenomenon

For many years in the United States, the only significant power that migrant domestic workers seemed to possess was the ability to bring down high-level political appointees. Ironically, this power has come through their vulnerable position in the legal order of the United States: through their relative rightslessness. Starting with the sequential nominations of Zoë Baird and Kimba Wood by then-President Clinton for the position of Attorney General in 1993, the foreign nanny who was employed illegally has halted the ascension of those nearing the heights of the social and political system; this ability has come, ironically, through their status as underpaid, unprotected, and undocumented workers (*The Financial Times*, Dec 2004). Because recent nominees for the offices of Secretary of Labor and Secretary of the Department of Homeland Security have not paid taxes, arranged for visas, or ensured that their domestic workers were authorized to work, they too were forced to withdraw their candidacies from prized positions in Presidential Cabinets (Fournier 2001; Scheer 2004).[2]

The unasked questions in these debates concern the treatment and rights of the "nannies" themselves. Powerful economic and legal forces ensure that such women remain exploited yet ubiquitously present in the intimate spaces of the well-to-do in the United States, as well as in other industrialized countries in the Global North. U.S. law defines migrant domestic workers out of many of the protections available for other workers under U.S. labor and employment law. For example, domestic workers are explicitly excluded from certain legal protections available to other workers under U.S. law in part because of the status of their workplace: private homes that are not easily conceptualized as workplaces. Migrant domestic workers are also vulnerable to abuses based on their migration status: while even undocumented workers are entitled to the most basic worker's rights — including the right to be paid minimum wage for their labor — they are often unable to access those rights due to threats of deportation or reprisal should they seek remedies. Because many domestic workers are undocumented, they are rendered vulnerable to abuses on the basis of their status as migrants *and* as workers in the home.

In addition to these formal exclusions, migrant domestic workers often suffer racial and ethnic discrimination, which takes the form of assumptions about their documentation status and discrimination on that basis, lower pay scales, inferior working conditions and lack of opportunities for certain "unpopular" nationalities, and verbal and sexual harassment on the job. These forms of discrimination are often not remediable by U.S. non-discrimination law because the discrimination takes place in workplaces — "homes" — that are not covered by federal non-discrimination statutes.

These abuses are the very types of discrimination and exploitation that human rights law was created to prevent and remedy. So why have advocates not focused on using human rights law, institutions, and language to advance the rights of migrant domestic workers in the United States? Certainly, it is in part because human rights norms have not been systematically incorporated into U.S. domestic law, and the United States actively works to insulate itself from human rights norms and oversight bodies. This insulation is accomplished through selective treaty ratification, imposition of substantive reservations to the covenants that it does ratify, and the non-recognition of the jurisdiction of key human rights bodies over disputes arising within the United States (Koh 2003). Another reason is that advocates for migrants' rights have focused much of their attention on convincing states to ratify the International Convention on the Protection of the Rights of Migrant Workers and Members of Their Families, a treaty the United States is nowhere near ratifying (Satterthwaite 2005). Finally, as many advocates for migrant domestic workers have emphasized through campaigning and legal actions, domestic workers are already protected by some labor laws in the United States: a major part of the problem for such workers is lax enforcement rather than a lack of standards, making recourse to international norms seem irrelevant.

Compelling reasons remain, however, to use human rights law in campaigns to advance migrant domestic workers' rights in the United States. First, U.S. actions and inactions *can* be scrutinized in certain international institutions charged with monitoring compliance with human rights law. Second, human rights law allows advocates to clearly articulate the obligations of the state to halt abuses that occur in the "private" realm. Finally, human rights law already binding on the United States can provide robust norms for migrant domestic workers fighting overlapping forms of discrimination that may not be easily challenged under U.S. law. Through its expansive norms, progressive interpretive practices, and venues for complaint and investigation with jurisdiction over the United States, the Inter-American system can provide useful norms and procedures for U.S.-based advocates fighting the interlocking forms of vulnerability and discrimination that migrant domestic workers face. This chapter will evaluate the potential role for this human rights system in empowering migrant domestic workers.

MAP OF THE CHAPTER

This chapter begins by setting out some of the forces that contribute to the exploitation of migrant domestic workers in the United States, and moves on to consider the potential role of regional human rights standards and institutions in improving the lives of migrant domestic workers in the United States. Because the chapter examines the Inter-American human rights treaties and conventions that could be brought to bear on the actions of the U.S., it does not discuss the International Convention on the Protection of the Rights of All Migrant Workers and their Families and the other U.N. treaties, except insofar as they could be examined by the Inter-American human rights bodies. The Inter-American human rights norms, most prominently embodied in the American Convention on Human Rights and the American Declaration on the Rights and Duties of Man, address many of the forces of vulnerability relevant to migrant domestic workers, seeking to protect such women from the abuses they widely suffer. After uncovering a significant gap between the protective standards applicable to migrant domestic workers and the reality on the ground, the chapter will consider the possibilities for bridging that gap through human rights advocacy and litigation. Against a backdrop of hegemonic American power and official disdain for the work of regional human rights bodies, advocates have achieved some small successes by using legal norms and bodies indirectly — through media coverage, work actions, and the integration of human rights language and rules into private contracts and local legislation. Litigation efforts have been successful in some cases, allowing women to access wages and contract damages; in such instances, there may be a role for increased use of human rights law, perhaps through the filing of amicus briefs.

There are several troublesome obstacles for those seeking vindication through U.S. courts, however. These include the sense of vulnerability to retaliation or deportation that many domestic workers feel when pressing their individual claims through private legal actions. Immunity is also a significant problem in the United States, where diplomats and employees of international institutions may hire migrant domestic workers through a special visa program, but also enjoy immunities within the legal system that can block enforcement of judgments. These obstacles also create impediments for litigation within the Inter-American system, where petitioners must demonstrate that they have "exhausted" available domestic remedies before seeking international remedies. While litigation is not always possible, a number of options remain to vindicate the rights of migrant domestic workers through the Inter-American system. In the final section of the chapter, potential avenues for human rights-related action are considered.

Although the chapter does not examine the norms and institutions in other regional systems, it may be helpful to advocates considering engagement with the Council of Europe system (encompassing the European Court of Human Rights and the European Convention for the Protection of Human Rights and Fundamental Freedoms) or the African Union system of human rights protection (encompassing the African Court on Human and Peoples' Rights, the African Commission on Human and Peoples' Rights and the African Charter on Human and Peoples' Rights). These systems are significantly different from the Inter-American human rights system —and from each other — so the discussion here will not be easily mapped onto those regions. It may, however, raise useful points for discussion and research.

PROFESSIONAL WOMEN, NANNIES AND EXPLOITATIVE TERMS OF WORK

The global division of reproductive labor

The International Labor Organization estimates that there are between 80 and 100 million migrant workers in the world today, 18 million of whom live in North America (ILO). Women account for about half of these workers reflecting what many analysts — most notably the ILO — have called the increasing feminization of migration (ILO 2003a: 9; Taran & Geronimi 2002). This feminization results from a number of worldwide forces in which gender roles and sex discrimination are intertwined with globalization. Trends contributing to this include: the growing demand for labor in fields dominated by women (especially the service sector); the lower cost of production when labor-intensive tasks are shifted to women migrant workers (Sassen 1984); and the sex-stereotyping of large business enterprises and governments that may see women as cheap, temporary, or supplemental laborers whose "docile" nature makes them easily exploitable (ILO 2003a: 19).

In the Americas, women's widespread participation in the wage labor market in the North has combined with global income disparities in the global South and persisting demands for Northern women to retain responsibility for household and childrearing tasks. This combination creates a dynamic in which Northern women's reproductive labor is transferred to women migrants working as domestics, whose reproductive labor is in turn shifted to family members or poor women in home countries, as exemplified in works on the "international transfer of caretaking" (Parrenas 2001; Young 2001; Hondagneu-Sotelo 2001). The United States is the largest receiving country for migrants in the Americas, with an estimated 35 million migrants residing in the United States (Lyon & Paoletti 2003/4). It is impossible to know the exact proportion of migrants who are undocumented; reputable estimates vary from 7.8 to 8.5 million (Lyon 2003). Of the undocumented workers, it has been estimated that 80 percent are from Latin American countries (IACHR 2004). For many of the women within these groups, domestic work will be the first job obtained in the United States.

Most job opportunities for women migrants are in unregulated (or under-regulated) sectors, including domestic work, informal/"off the books" industries or services, and criminalized sectors, including the sex industry (Taran & Geronimi 2002: 10). This means that even women who cross borders legally may find themselves in unregulated — and often irregular — work situations (ILO 2003b: 18). In addition, the majority of opportunities that offer legal channels of migration are in male-dominated sectors such as agriculture and construction work, putting women at a great disadvantage (Taran & Geronimi 2002: 10). In the United States, a significant exception to this general state of affairs exists for migrant domestic workers working for diplomatic officials; such officials can obtain special visas for their domestic workers. The ILO explains that "the demand for foreign labor reflects the long term trend of informalization of low skilled and poorly paid jobs, where irregular migrants are preferred as they are willing to work for inferior salaries, for short periods in production peaks, or to take physically demanding and dirty jobs" (Taran & Geronimi 2002: 5).

In sum, globalization has ushered in increasing "pull" and "push" factors for women's migration for labor at the same time as it has resulted in decreasing regulation of the labor market, growth in the informal sector, and the emergence of new forms of exploitation, many of which are gendered. In the midst of these trends, many governments are tightening migration controls while simultaneously allowing private employers and recruiting agencies to operate unchecked by regulation or inspection. This interplay of competing incentives sets the scene for abuse of those already disadvantaged through systems of discrimination and marginalization that operate along axes of gender, race, poverty and position within the global economic order. For women in many parts of the world, these trends spell increased vulnerability to exploitation and abuse, while simultaneously presenting opportunities for empowerment.

In the United States, these forces in combination produce both new opportunities for women who find positions as domestic workers, as well as setting the scene for interlocking forms of abuse and discrimination in which migrant domestic workers are often left largely without remedy.

CREATING THE RIGHTSLESS NANNY: EXPLOITATIVE TERMS OF WORK

A number of forces combine to render migrant domestic workers vulnerable to exploitative terms of work in the United States, especially in relation to pay, hours of work, and contracts. Restrictions on the right to enter the United States for work, for example, create incentives for legal and illegal agents alike to take advantage of migrant domestic workers. Immigration laws in the United States are widely recognized as extremely strict, and the large number of undocumented workers in the U.S. attests to the gap between U.S. immigration law and the economic demand for cheap labor.

Two categories of special visas are available to women entering the United States to work temporarily as live-in domestic workers for foreign business persons, employees of international organizations, and foreign diplomats (U.S. Embassy Domestic Employees).[3] U.S. citizens seeking domestic help may also sometimes sponsor migrant women for employment visas (ibid.), though it is generally easier to locate a domestic worker through an agency or the informal job market. In practice, the proportion of domestic workers on special visas is probably rather small. Though statistics are hard to come by in this under-studied sector, the United States Bureau of Labor Statistics reported that in 2004, 92.2 percent of all persons employed in services within "private households" were women (*Women in the Labor Force*), and a recent survey of domestic workers in New York found that 99 percent were born outside the United States, with only 1 percent identifying as white (Domestic Workers United & Data Center 2006).

In theory, all migrant domestic workers with special visas are given contracts, since a contract is a requirement for those entering on such visas (USDS Foreign Affairs Manual). The U.S. Department of State (USDS) requires that certain elements be included in these contracts as a condition for issuance of a domestic worker visa. These elements include: an undertaking that the domestic worker will be paid at the applicable minimum wage; a promise to the employee that her passport will not be confiscated by the employer; and a statement that both parties understand that the domestic worker may not be required to be on the premises of the employee without being paid for her time (ibid.). In practice, even when they are validly concluded, contracts are often taken from workers or considered irrelevant by employers once they arrive in the United States. Human Rights Watch reports that many migrant domestic workers are told by their employers that their contracts are not binding:

> [D]omestic workers explained to Human Rights Watch that their employers explicitly told them that their employment contracts were signed to satisfy U.S. consular offices' requirements, were not binding, and were not intended to govern their employment relationships in the United States. (Human Rights Watch 2001: 24)

U.S. government officials have told human rights workers that they do not have the capacity to monitor these contracts; nor do they maintain files of such legal documents (Human Rights Watch 2001: 23–24). Further, the requirement that employers conclude a contract with their domestic workers is a condition of obtaining a visa, meaning that the only federal "remedy" that exists for breach of this rule is the non-issuance of the visa in the first place. Domestic workers do not have the right to file a civil complaint against their employer for non-compliance with the State Department policy (though they may sometimes be able to file a traditional contract claim in court).

Regardless of their means of entry, women migrants face myriad forms of exploitation in the United States, including extreme forms of abuse such as trafficking, forced labor, and enslavement. Contract problems abound for those who enter on special visas as well as those who do not. Women who actually receive a contract may not understand the language in which it is written. They may find that the contract they sign is later replaced by an inferior version stripped of worker protections, or they may be refused a copy entirely (ILO 2003c: 22–23). Sometimes, contracts are concluded between the employer and the recruitment agency alone, leaving the worker without any protection. As may be expected, undocumented women are rarely given contracts.

While there are no specific remedies or procedures for domestic workers seeking to vindicate their rights, women who have signed contracts do have the right — like anyone else harmed by breach of contract — to file a claim in court seeking contract remedies. A number of organizations take such cases on behalf of migrant domestic workers, and some have seen results, including significant payments for workers who did not receive adequate payment from their employers.[4] Even domestic workers who did not have a contract may recover lost wages: recently, a jury awarded $226,000 to a domestic worker from Nepal who sued in Federal Court to recover the reasonable value of her services (Mayra Peters-Quintero, interview, New York 29 June 2006).

Recruitment agencies in home countries — even when working legally — often charge steep fees for placement and travel. When working irregularly or without government oversight, such agencies often charge fees that are close to impossible to repay, trapping women migrants into conditions akin to debt bondage (ILO 2003a: 18, ILO 2003c: 22–23). Others house migrant workers in "collection" centers in the sending country for as long as several months before the receiving country processes the needed papers; conditions in such centers are sometimes horrendous, with women held incommunicado and given inadequate or rotten food (ILO 2003c: 24). Finally, agents who are working in direct contravention of U.S. and sending countries' national laws by facilitating women's crossing of borders illegally, may use coercion, force, or false promises, placing women in clandestine domestic settings, illegal sex work, or exploitative sweatshops

— practices that amount to trafficking. The ILO reports that "[w]omen tend to be more likely than men to make use of these illegal recruitment and migration channels because of their limited access to information, lack of time to search for legal channels and lack of financial resources to pay the fees. The nature of the work and the forms of migration open to women often force them to rely on fraudulent recruiters and dubious agents" (ILO 2003a: 18).

Migrant domestic workers in the United States face a range of abuses connected with compensation (ILO 2003d: 23). Even when paid on time and according to the law and the terms of any contract they may have been given, they are often paid substandard wages. Under national law, domestic workers are entitled to the federal minimum wage and employment record-keeping requirements, though live-in domestic workers are explicitly excluded from the requirement that employers pay workers one and a half their usual hourly rate for hours worked in excess of forty hours per week. Human Rights Watch reports that the migrant domestic workers in a study conducted in the United States received an average of $2.14 per hour — less than half the required minimum wage (Human Rights Watch 2001:17). A study conducted by Domestic Workers United and DataCenter found that only 13 percent of domestic workers in New York City receive living wages (defined as wages more than 1.5 times above the federal poverty line), and that 67 percent do not receive overtime pay for hours they work overtime (Domestic Workers United & Data Center 2006: 4–5).

In addition to failing to pay fair wages, employers have been found to deduct dubious or blatantly unfair charges, including fees for health services that are never received, or fees for rent in situations of squalor (ILO 2003d: 25). While the law allows employers to deduct the "reasonable cost" of room and board for live-in domestic workers, federal regulations place limits on these deductions (Code of Federal Regulations, V. 29). Workers on certain sets of special visas are entitled to free room and board (U.S. Department of State 2000).

Despite these protections, payments are often delayed, improperly calculated, or withheld arbitrarily. In one exemplary case, an employer placed her domestic worker's wages into a joint bank account that she opened for the domestic worker, but then withdrew the money for her own use. In another case, wages were paid directly to the husband of a domestic worker from Bangladesh, with none of the payments going into the hands of the worker herself (Human Rights Watch 2001: 10). A similar case was reported recently in Los Angeles, where an Indonesian woman worked for a couple for seven years without receiving any pay directly; her family in Indonesia was being paid less than two dollars per day for her labor (Micek 2006).[5] At the extreme end of the spectrum, women who are in conditions of debt bondage or slavery may not receive wages at all (Break the Chain Campaign, n.d.). Although there has been less attention to the issue in the

United States than in Asia, anecdotal evidence shows that domestic workers are often paid salaries that are based more on their nationality, ethnicity, or race, than their actual experience or skills (Poo, interview, New York 9 May 2005). This kind of race and ethnicity discrimination is exemplary of other forms of discrimination on multiple bases within the labor market in the United States.

Another major obstacle to full equality and rights for migrant domestic workers in the United States is the way in which their work may define them out of certain workers' rights protections under domestic law. Domestic workers as a category are specifically excluded from the protections of the National Labor Relations Act ("NLRA"), which protects workers' rights to bargain collectively, organize, and strike:

> The term "employee" shall include any employee . . . but shall not include any individual employed as an agricultural laborer, or in the domestic service of any family or person at his home. . . (*National Labor Relations Act*, U.S. Code, title 29, sec. 152(3))

In practice, this means that domestic workers do not have legal remedies under federal law if they are fired or otherwise sanctioned by their employers for organizing a union or striking.[6] Live-in domestic workers are also excluded from the health and safety protections of the federal Occupational Safety and Health Act through the regulations that implement the legislation (OSHA, title 29; Code of Federal Regulations, title 29). Domestic workers are also functionally excluded from coverage by Title VII of the Civil Rights Act, the federal anti-discrimination statute, which applies only to individuals working for employers with fifteen or more employees (Code of Federal Regulations, title 29). This exclusion is especially unfortunate for migrant women who work as domestic workers, since the kind of sex- and race-based discrimination and abuse they face is that which is normally outlawed by Title VII. Although domestic workers are covered by the minimum wage and employment record keeping requirements, live-in domestic workers are explicitly excluded from the overtime provisions, as noted above (Parreñas 2001: 179–195).

In such circumstances, many employers take advantage of the vulnerability of migrant domestic workers by coercing them to work long hours, often without breaks or leisure time (Human Rights Watch 2001: 16–17; Anderson 2003). Indeed, "unscheduled availability at all times" is a characteristic of unpaid household work for women, an expectation modeled on gendered assumptions about women's roles in the home. Filipina live-in workers in Los Angeles and Rome have complained of the "absence of set parameters between their work and rest hours" (Parreñas 2001:164). Further, women working as domestics in the United States are often denied days off, including sick days (Human Rights Watch 2003: 16–17,19–22;

Domestic Workers United & Data Center 2006:9). While the families who employ domestics may explain the long hours by saying that such women are "part of the family," (Parreñas 2001: 165) this feeling often is not shared by the employees themselves. One researcher in the United States found that many migrant domestic workers were asked to use a separate set of utensils and told when and how much to eat (Parreñas 2001: 165).

Although some laws exist to protect the rights of migrant domestic workers, these laws are subject to lax enforcement and widespread disregard. The U.S. Department of Labor's Wage and Hour Division is the federal agency charged with monitoring compliance with the Fair Labor Standards Act, the law that provides standards for hourly wages, overtime pay, recordkeeping and allowable deductions for room and board. Human Rights Watch reports that the Wage and Hour Division has developed initiatives to enforce labor laws in industries where abuses are common but complaints are not; these initiatives have targeted the following industries: agriculture, garment, security guard, janitorial services, restaurant, hotel, day-haul, and health care (Human Rights Watch 2001: 31). Domestic workers' advocates report that the Wage and Hour Division has never developed or implemented such an initiative to enforce labor laws in the domestic work sector (Human Rights Watch 2001:31; Poo, interview, New York 9 May 2005). HRW reports that the Wage and Hour Division has historically initiated investigations into labor law violations in relation to domestic workers in only 0.006 percent of the known domestic work relationships (Human Rights Watch 2001: 31).

Like other categories of workers covered by federal labor law, domestic workers may file individual lawsuits to enforce their rights. These individual claims are meant to function as incentives for employers to follow the law even when government enforcement is lacking. Unlike other workers, however, domestic workers are frequently unaware of the laws protecting them, and are especially vulnerable to reprisal by employers and other collateral consequences of pressing a claim. The immigration status of domestic workers with special visas depends on their continued employment by their sponsor, making them especially vulnerable if they complain. Undocumented workers may fear exposing their migration status should they pursue legal claims. While there are some protections against the forced disclosure of this information for migrants seeking labor remedies in the United States, they are not widely known and are often flouted. Human Rights Watch reports the following in relation to domestic workers who the organization interviewed:

> There were a variety of reasons mentioned by domestic workers for their failure to file complaints, including: lack of knowledge of the U.S. legal system, exacerbated by social and cultural isolation; fear that employers would report them to the [immigration authorities] and that

they would subsequently be removed from the United States; and fear of retaliation by politically powerful employers against their families in their countries of origin. (Human Rights Watch 2001: 32)

Many of these fears have proven to be well-founded. Organizations report that some domestic workers pursuing lawsuits have had their families targeted in their home countries, and have been deported during the pendancy of their claims (Human Rights Watch 2001: 33–35). The ILO explains that

> a major incentive for exploitation of migrants and ultimately forced labor is the lack of application and enforcement of labor standards in countries of destination as well as origin. These include respect for minimum working conditions and consent to working conditions. Tolerance of restrictions on freedom of movement, long working hours, poor or non-existent health and safety protections, non-payment of wages, substandard housing, etc. all contribute to expanding a market for trafficked migrants who have no choice but to labor in conditions simply intolerable and unacceptable for legal employment. Worse still is the absence of worksite monitoring, particularly in such already marginal sectors as agriculture, domestic service, sex-work, which would contribute to identifying whether workers may be in situations of forced or compulsory labor. (Taran & Geronimi 2002: 11)

In addition to these problems, a special issue arises for those employed by diplomats and employees of international institutions: the problem of immunity from suit. Those entitled to full immunity from the criminal, civil, and administrative jurisdiction of the United States include diplomats and their families, as well as officials of the United Nations, the Organization of American States, and country missions and observer offices. In addition, the technical and administrative staff of diplomatic missions and observer offices enjoy limited immunity in the form of absolute immunity from criminal sanction combined with immunity from civil and administrative proceedings for acts performed "in the course of their duties" (Human Rights Watch 2001:34). These immunities may be waived at the discretion of the official's home government, and the U.S. Department of State is entitled to request such waivers. The Department's policy is to request waivers in most criminal cases, and in some civil matters (Human Rights Watch 2001: 34–35). In many cases, however, the Department of State affirmatively supports the immunity extended to diplomatic staff through letters submitted to courts or enforcement agencies (Human Rights Watch 2001: 34–35). Even when immunities are waived and enforcement is possible, employers may escape penalties by leaving the United States or insulating their assets by holding them abroad.

USING HUMAN RIGHTS LAW TO EMPOWER MIGRANT DOMESTIC WORKERS

When used creatively, the norms and procedures encompassed by the Inter-American human rights system can be used by advocates as one method among many to respond to the myriad forms of abuse that migrant domestic workers experience in the United States. Before examining the ways in which the system could be used, it is important to examine two common concerns that women's rights advocates have often voiced about the human rights framework. First, some have argued that human rights discussions can be disempowering, since they present women as "victims" of human rights violations instead of empowered subjects, agents of their own lives. I will address this concern below. The second concern is that human rights law may not be a good instrument to reach conduct that happens in the "private" sphere — among non-state actors such as individual workers and her domestic employers. As I will explain below, human rights law has evolved significantly in the last several decades, and obligations in the "private" sphere have been sufficiently developed to make the framework a useful one for advocates fighting abuses that take place in private homes.

ON WOMEN'S "VULNERABILITY"

Although necessary, rooting an analysis of human rights violations in women's lived experiences is fraught with danger. As Ratna Kapur has explained, this kind of focus can lead to "victimization rhetoric," in which women — usually from the global South — are presented as nothing other than the sum of their vulnerability, abuse, and victimhood (Kapur 2002: 5–6).

I attempt to avoid this problem by rejecting the common narrow focus on migrants' experience of violence against women and trafficking. Many scholars have critiqued the seemingly exclusive focus on the "vulnerability" of women migrants — which often manifests itself through the emphasis on ending (usually sexual) violence against women migrants (Maeda 2002:317, 326) and trafficking in women (Lewis 2001:222). I do not mean to dispute the existence, pervasiveness, or perniciousness of these violations. I simply mean to shift the focus to the human rights entitlements that women migrant workers should enjoy — civil and political, social and economic — in this chapter, most specifically, exploitative conditions of work. Finally, it is important to note that women's "vulnerability" is not a quality that inheres in them, but is instead the product of political, economic, and cultural forces acting along a variety of identity axes, including gender, race, and nationality, that disempower specific sets of women in particular ways. Focusing exclusively on women's vulnerability effectively shifts the focus away from the forces of global inequality, the gendered divisions of labor, and the forms of racism and xenophobia that work together to ensure that women migrant workers remain marginalized. Emphasizing that women are rightsholders as workers and as migrants, on the other hand, may assist in efforts to empower domestic workers.

REACHING "PRIVATE" CONDUCT THROUGH HUMAN RIGHTS LAW

Women migrant workers face abuses at the hands of government officials, as well as private individuals, companies, and other "non-state actors." This is true all along a migrant's trajectory of movement, as well as in her chosen place of work. In fact, most of the abuses that migrant domestic workers face are committed by "private" actors in the sense that they are not carried out directly by government personnel, but are instead perpetrated by employers and recruitment agencies. For this reason, it is important to acknowledge the ways in which the human rights framework has evolved to respond to abuses that are carried out by agents other than the state. These advances have been especially well articulated in the Inter-American system.

Against a general backdrop in which human rights obligations were assumed to function as a check on state actions, a number of developments have emerged in the last several decades that can be said to have dramatically altered that orientation forever (Shelton 2002). First, as scholars of economic and social rights are quick to point out, human rights law was never really designed to halt only the abuses of the state: it was also written to include affirmative duties on states to ensure that those within their jurisdiction enjoyed a set of basic subsistence rights, such as the right to food, adequate housing, education, and health (International Covenant on Economic, Social and Cultural Rights Dec. 16, 1966). Through the development of the economic, social and cultural rights regime, it has become clear that the state is not necessarily required to *provide* the goods needed to fulfill rights (Craven 1995). Private individuals and groups — including families, communities, companies, or other groupings — may be the most well situated providers of food, water, shelter and work to people in various settings. The state, however, is recognized as obligated to ensure that (a) conditions are such that even the most marginalized and poor can access their subsistence rights in some way — whether through access to private schemes or through direct provision of goods by the state (Craven 1995:140–142), and (b) when entrusting basic rights protections to the private sector, the state must regulate and monitor actions that could impinge on the rights of its people — through both action and inaction (United Nations Committee on Economic, Social, and Cultural Rights 2002).

In truth, civil and political rights have always involved similar obligations on the state to protect human rights even when rights violations take place among non-state actors. The Inter-American Court of Human Rights famously described the duties inherent in the requirement that states "ensure" human rights to all within their jurisdiction in the *Velasquez-Rodriguez Case*, which concerned forced disappearances:

> This obligation implies the duty of States Parties to organize the governmental apparatus and, in general, all the structures through which public power is exercised, so that they are capable of juridically ensuring the free and full enjoyment of human rights. As a consequence of this obligation, the States must prevent, investigate and punish any violation of the rights recognized by the Convention and, moreover, if possible attempt to restore the right violated and provide compensation as warranted for damages resulting from the violation. (Velasquez-Rodriguez Case 1988)

These obligations were amplified in a later case decided by the Inter-American Court. In the *Garrido and Baigorria Case*, the Court explained that the measures taken to ensure human rights can be considered effective only once "the community, in general, adapts its conduct to conform to the principles of the Convention" and when there are violations, "the penalties provided... are effectively applied" (Garrido and Baigorria Case Reparations 1998).

The second major development that clarified the affirmative duties of the state in the "private" sphere was the achievement, through the work of feminists in many parts of the world, of acceptance that abuses such as domestic violence, even when carried out in the most sacrosanct of spaces, constitute human rights violations (UNIFEM 2003). This means that the state is required to take steps to prevent such abuses, to punish them when they occur, and to provide remedies to those who have been injured (United Nations Committee on the Elimination of Discrimination Against Women 1989). In the Inter-American system, the Inter-American Convention on the Prevention, Punishment and Eradication of Violence Against Women sets out a very detailed set of obligations for states — from training and education to protective measures for victims seeking redress and punishments for abusers (Inter-American Convention on the Elimination of All Forms of Discrimination Against Persons with Disabilities 1999). Having established that violence in the most intimate of spaces amounts to a human rights violation, this principle is now available for use with other forms of violation, including, for instance, discrimination that happens inside of companies, clubs, or recruitment agencies.

This broad set of positive and negative obligations for both private and public conduct has been abbreviated in the human rights field into the three-part requirement that states must respect, protect, and fulfill rights. States must *respect* rights by ensuring that the state and its instrumentalities do not violate rights; *protect* rights by preventing violations at the hands of non-state actors and investigating, punishing, and redressing violations when they do occur; and *fulfill* rights by creating enabling conditions for all individuals to enjoy their full rights. In sum, then, in relation to both civil and political rights and economic, social and cultural rights, the state must ensure that conditions are such that all people enjoy all of their rights. Though the state actions required in relation to each set of rights — and indeed each individual right — may differ, this common framework is a helpful way of conceptualizing state obligations. The focus of human rights law is on the obligations of states, even when the abuses are occurring in private at the hands of non-state actors, since the state is ultimately responsible for setting up regulatory systems and monitoring schemes to halt such abuses.

THE UNITED STATES IN THE AMERICAS: THE WORK OF THE INTER-AMERICAN HUMAN RIGHTS SYSTEM CONCERNING VIOLATIONS IN THE UNITED STATES

Having set out some of the more conceptual reasons why human rights law could be useful for migrant domestic workers, the next question that requires some answers is what use can human rights be when dealing with the United States? There are different answers to this question in different settings, and in relation to different human rights issues. This section will engage with the problem of American exceptionalism, and then look at how the U.S. has treated — and has been treated by — the Inter-American Court of Human Rights ("the Court" or "the Inter-American Court") and the Inter-American Commission on Human Rights ("the Commission" or "the Inter-American Commission") (collectively "the Inter-American human rights system").

AMERICAN EXCEPTIONALISM

American exceptionalism concerning international law — the view that the actions of the U.S. government should not be scrutinized under international law, and that adherence to that law is not in line with "American interests" — has been prominently noted in the last few years in relation to the "war on terror." This exceptionalism has historical antecedents that are all too familiar to human rights advocates. The U.S. has long been regarded as a strong promoter of human rights institutions, but has demonstrated itself to be an at-best reluctant participant in international human rights systems that might be used to redress abuses that take place under its jurisdiction. The U.S. has interposed reservations altering the substantive effect of the key human rights treaties that it has ratified (often pledging to uphold human rights law only insofar as it is in line with U.S. constitutional law) and has refused to ratify others, including such widely ratified treaties as the Convention on the Elimination of All Forms of Discrimination Against Women, and the Convention on the Rights of the Child, the latter of which has been ratified by all states in the world except Somalia and the United States (Convention on the Rights of the Child 1989).

The United States has also been unwilling to participate in human rights bodies with jurisdiction over individual complaints. Although it has ratified these treaties, the United States has refused to consent to the individual complaints procedures under the International Covenant on Civil and Political Rights, the Convention Against Torture and Other Cruel, Inhuman or Degrading Treatment or Punishment, or the Convention on the Elimination of All Forms of Racial Discrimination. This reluctance extends to — and is perhaps exemplified by — the nature of U.S. participation in the Inter-American human rights system. As Richard Wilson (2002: 1164) notes:

> In the Inter-American system, while the Untied States has always been a strong political supporter of its human rights enforcement mechanisms, it has blanched at assuming treaty obligations or in complying with the decisions against it by those same mechanisms.

The United States has signed but not ratified the American Convention on Human Rights (1969), and has not signed or ratified either of its protocols[7] or any of the other major Inter-American human rights conventions.[8]

Despite this dismissive attitude, the United States cannot escape the scrutiny of the Inter-American human rights bodies. Unlike the committees that monitor United Nations conventions, the major investigatory human rights institution within the Inter-American system, the Inter-American Commission on Human Rights, has jurisdiction over individual complaints concerning the United States by virtue of U.S. membership in the Organization of American States. Further, unlike the U.N. bodies, which are limited to interpreting the provisions of the single treaty under their purview, the Inter-American Commission, following the lead of the Inter-American Court, has developed and used interpretive strategies (explored below) to incorporate and draw upon human rights norms from other systems, thus indirectly opening enforcement opportunities for norms that are binding on the United States but not opposable to it in other venues, such as the substantive norms encompassed in the International Covenant on Civil and Political Rights and the Convention on the Elimination of All Forms of Racial Discrimination.

The Inter-American Court of Human Rights has also been willing to interpret human rights treaties that are binding on the United States in its advisory capacity, handing down key rulings on the rights of aliens that provide significant opportunities for migrants' rights advocates. The open-textured nature of the human rights corpus in the Inter-American system makes it an especially promising venue for complaints by migrant domestic workers seeking redress for multiple forms of discrimination and exploitation within the United States.

THE UNITED STATES BEFORE THE INTER-AMERICAN COMMISSION AND COURT

The United States is a member of the Organization of American States, a regional organization whose members include all 35 states in the Americas.[9] As a member, the United States is subject to the investigatory and adjudicatory reach of the Inter-American Commission on Human Rights, as well as the advisory jurisdiction of the Inter-American Court of Human Rights, the two main human rights organs of the Organization of American States (OAS). Briefly, the Commission began working in 1960 and is charged with a number of activities in relation to all member states of the OAS — regardless of whether they have ratified the Inter-American Convention on Human Rights or not. These activities are: (a) considering individual petitions alleging human rights violations by specific member states; (b) human rights monitoring in OAS member states, including through site visits; and (c) promotional and educational activities concerning human rights law.

With respect to states that have not ratified the Convention, the Commission applies the American Declaration of the Rights and Duties of Man ("the Declaration" or "the American Declaration"), using it as a rule of decision in individual cases as an authoritative interpretation of the human rights obligations imposed on all member states by the OAS Charter (IACHR 1987). This approach is based on the reasoning set out by the Inter-American Court in its advisory opinion on the *Interpretation of the American Declaration of the Rights and Duties of Man Within the Framework of Article 64 of the American Convention on Human Rights* (1989). In that case, the Court determined that the Declaration has indirect legal effect on members of the OAS as an embodiment of the states' legal obligations under the OAS Charter (ibid. paras. 33–34, 47).

The Inter-American Court of Human Rights is an autonomous judicial institution charged with determining whether a state has violated an individual's human rights (in contentious cases), interpreting the Convention as well as any other treaties concerning human rights in the Americas (in advisory cases); and, at the request of a state party, determining the compatibility of that state's legislation with human rights norms (American Convention, art. 64(2)). Contentious cases may be referred to the Court by a State party or by the Inter-American Commission. In contentious cases, the Court's primary role is to determine the merits of complaints alleging that a state has violated the rights of an individual as set out in the American Convention (ibid.). States that have not ratified the Convention are not subject to the contentious jurisdiction of the Court. The Court's advisory jurisdiction empowers it to issue legal interpretations of the American Convention or any other treaty concerning human rights applicable to member states of the OAS; advisory opinions may be requested by the Commission, a member state of the OAS, or an OAS organ (ibid.). The phrase extending the Court's advisory jurisdiction to treaties other than the Convention — "other treaties concerning the protection of human rights in the American states" — has been liberally interpreted by the Inter-American Court to include, for example, treaties that may not have human rights as their primary subject matter, but which include individual rights protections nonetheless. This strand of advisory jurisdiction has proven, in practice, to be a back door method of obtaining decisions from the Court on the legal obligations of states that have not ratified the Convention, most prominently the United States.

Over the years, many complaints have been filed against the United States with the Inter-American Commission, most notably in the context of the death penalty, but also covering such issues as the rights of American Indians, the detention of foreign nationals at Guantánamo Bay, and injuries caused by the United States when it invaded Panama (Wilson 2002:1174–75). The U.S. government has defended itself vigorously before the Commission in recent years — a change from early non-engagement, even in contentious cases against the United States (ibid. p.1184). This engagement with the body does not, however, signal an acceptance of the authority of the Commission's decisions. As Richard Wilson explains:

> It seems incongruous, at least, and arrogant, at worst, to respect the forum enough to accept its procedures and engage in debate about the appropriate application of its norms, but not to respect the outcome when it is not favorable to the government. When the Commission, or even the I[nternational] C[ourt of] J[ustice], issues a decision, report or order, the U.S. government simply ignores, declines, or refuses to comply with it. In short, the U.S. legal position in international capital litigation can be summarized as follows: resist new obligations, vigorously contest everything and comply with nothing. (ibid. p.1163)

Although a significant portion of the cases filed never proceed to their resolution (especially with respect to death penalty cases, where the individual complainants are often executed before their cases are dealt with on the merits (ibid. p.1174–76), those that have resulted in decisions against the United States have not produced compliance by the U.S. government. Indeed, the United States rejects any findings of the Commission that are based on the premise that the American Declaration is binding on the United States through the OAS Charter (ibid. p.1159–60, 1172–73). In addition to this fundamental disregard for the authority of the Commission, the U.S. government has also argued forcefully against the unique interpretive practices of the Inter-American Commission. In one case against the United States, the Commission explained that:

> In interpreting and applying the Declaration, it is necessary to consider its provisions in the context of the international and inter-American human rights systems more broadly, in the light of developments in the field of human rights law since the Declaration was first composed and with due regard to other relevant rule[s] of international law applicable to member states against which complaints of violations of the Declaration are properly lodged. (*Garza v. United States* 2001)

It is this kind of expansive interpretive practice that the United States especially dislikes.

OPEN-TEXTURED NORMS: THE INTERPRETIVE PRACTICE OF THE INTER-AMERICAN COMMISSION AND COURT OF HUMAN RIGHTS

The Inter-American Commission has used two interpretive techniques that allow it to import progressive norms into individual cases alleging abuse under Inter-American standards. First, it has looked to its sibling commissions and courts in other regional contexts as persuasive authority in interpreting Inter-American norms. This technique is commonly used by human rights bodies around the world, and is unremarkable since it does not alter the standard approach to interpreting norms. The second methodology, however, is more unusual. Beyond looking for persuasive guidance in analogous legal norms and interpretations from other systems, the Commission will directly call upon provisions from treaties binding on the respondent state to determine whether that state has complied with its obligations under the American Declaration (or Convention, as appropriate). This second technique — the incorporation of a norm into an Inter-American provision — has been used in relation to cases brought to the Commission against the United States many times, and it may be a promising practice for migrants' rights advocates.

The approach is exemplified in the 2002 *Villareal case*. There, an alien petitioner alleged that U.S. authorities breached his due process rights when he was detained for a criminal matter and not informed of his right to consular access, a right explicitly laid out for foreign nationals in Article 36 of the Vienna Convention on Consular Relations (which the United States has ratified), but which was nowhere mentioned in the American Declaration on Human Rights. In discussing this allegation, the Commission recalled that its role, as affirmed by the Inter-American Court, was to determine the merits of claims concerning rights set out in one of the instruments within its Charter-based competence: the American Convention or Declaration.

Accordingly, the Commission conceded that it could not directly interpret the Vienna Convention (Inter-American Court of Human Rights 2000). With this caveat, the Commission proceeded to determine that:

> compliance with the rights of a foreign national under the Vienna Convention on Consular Relations is particularly relevant to determining whether a state has complied with the provisions of the American Declaration pertaining to the right to due process and to a fair trial as they apply to a foreign national who has been arrested, committed to prison or to custody pending trial, or is detained in any other manner by that state. (IACHR 2002, para. 61)

The Commission then found that the U.S. had violated the American Declaration's right to due process.

With this finding, the Commission functionally inserted the right of consular access embodied in Article 36 of the Vienna Convention into the American Declaration by considering the substantive norm to be an element of the Declaration's provisions on due process. This kind of interpretive move is the only functional way for the Commission to preserve its jurisdiction over human rights issues that are not addressed directly by the Inter-American Declaration or Convention, since the Commission is limited by its statute to directly applying only these instruments (Statute of the IACHR art. 1). This interpretive approach is significant in cases dealing with the United States, since it essentially provides a forum of complaint for individuals seeking to press claims against the U.S. using a variety of substantive norms articulated in treaties outside the jurisdiction of the Commission, so long as they can be successfully incorporated into a provision of the Declaration. Because the Commission is one of very few international fora where individuals may press claims against the United States, this normative flexibility provides a potentially very valuable entry point for advocates seeking determinations on human rights claims.

This interpretive approach had been used by the Commission for some time, and was generally approved by the Inter-American Court in a 1982 advisory opinion concerning the scope of the Court's jurisdiction to interpret treaties concerning human rights. Examining the interpretive practice of the Commission, the Court held that:

> The need of the regional system to be complemented by the universal finds expression in the practice of the Inter-American Commission on Human Rights and is entirely consistent with the object and purpose of the Convention, the American Declaration and the Statute of the Commission. The Commission has properly invoked in some of its reports and resolutions "other treaties concerning the protection of human rights in the American states," regardless of their bilateral or multilateral character, or whether they have been adopted within the

framework or under the auspices of the Inter-American system. (Inter-American Court of Human Rights 1982)

Over the years since the 1982 *"Other Treaties"* Advisory Opinion, the Court has had the opportunity to develop its own approach to interpreting and incorporating norms from outside the inter-American system. While the Commission is restricted by its statute to interpreting relevant norms by incorporating them into the American Declaration (or Convention, for states parties), the Court has the ability to directly interpret other treaties under its advisory jurisdiction (but not its contentious jurisdiction), so long as they "concern the protection of human rights" (*American Convention* Article 64).

The Court's distinct approach may be illustrated through an examination of an advisory opinion case from 1999 that preceded and concerned the same underlying issue as that decided by the Commission in the *Villareal* case: the alleged violation of the right to consular access of a number of Mexican nationals who were then under sentence of death in the United States. Mexico asked the Court for clarification of meaning and significance of the right to consular access that is accorded to individuals under the Vienna Convention on Consular Relations, asking the Court to interpret the right's application (a) directly by examining Article 36 of the Vienna Convention on Consular Relations; (b) indirectly, by determining whether the right to consular access in the Vienna Convention could be considered an element of or an antecedent to the due process guarantees set out in Article 14 of the International Covenant on Civil and Political Rights; and (c) indirectly, by deciding whether the failure to inform detainees of their right to consular access would amount to an act of discrimination on the grounds of nationality under the American Declaration (Inter-American Court of Human Rights 1999).

The Court held that the Vienna Convention did indeed "concern human rights" because it sets out specific rights whose benefit runs directly to the individuals themselves (ibid. paras. 68–87). This finding could be useful for advocates seeking relief in other fora, since a finding that the provision concerns human rights could provide access to the remedies available for violations of human rights, instead of the remedies available for breaches of the rights of states. This distinction was clearly of the utmost importance for the individuals whose cases had prompted Mexico's request for an advisory opinion, since they were facing death sentences and were obviously in need of individual — not state-centered — remedies.

Interpreting the International Covenant on Civil and Political Rights (ICCPR)'s Article 14 due process of law guarantees, the Court also determined that respect for the substantive right embodied in Article 36(1)(b) of the Vienna Convention was a necessary antecedent to the full enjoyment of Article 14 of the ICCPR: the Court held that consular access "makes it possible for the right to due process of law upheld in Article 14 of the International Covenant on Civil and Political Rights, to have practical effects in tangible cases" (ibid. para. 124). Finally, the Court folded its discussion of the due process guarantees contained in the American Declaration into its discussion of the ICCPR, indicating — without explicitly finding — that the standards were identical for the purpose of understanding the right to consular access as an antecedent or element of the right to due process. This determination paved the way for the Commission's 2002 *Villareal* holding incorporating the right to consular access into the Declaration's due process provisions.

These interpretive techniques applicable in the Inter-American system may be fruitfully applied to norms relevant to the abuses that migrant domestic workers face in the United States. The next section of the article will examine current efforts to promote the rights of migrants and domestic workers through the Inter-American system, consider the significant obstacles to such efforts, and point to potential ways to overcome some of these obstacles and engage with the Inter-American system more directly to advance the rights of migrant domestic workers.

WOMEN AND MIGRANTS: THE WORK OF THE SPECIAL RAPPORTEURS OF THE INTER-AMERICAN COMMISSION ON HUMAN RIGHTS

The Special Rapporteurs of the Inter-American Commission on Human Rights

In addition to litigation, the Inter-American system also has mechanisms for investigation and promotion of human rights in the Americas. One of the most flexible mechanisms is that of rapporteurships — mandates filled by individuals who are designated to investigate and report on specific thematic human rights concerns. Rapporteurs have a significant amount of discretion to define their area of focus, to undertake investigations, and to report on their findings.

Special Rapporteurships may be created by the Inter-American Commission on Human Rights and staffed through appointments of the Commission. Currently, there are Special Rapporeturs on seven issues within the Commission: the rights of indigenous peoples; the rights of children; the rights of persons deprived of their liberty; the rights of Afro descendants and against racial discrimination; the rights of women; the rights of migrant workers and their families; and the right to freedom of expression. The quality and depth of the work of the rapporteurs varies over time and across mandates. Much depends on the individual rapporteur's creativity, commitment, and ability to leverage resources, since these positions are often severely constrained by lack of human and financial resources. This section summarizes the work of the two relevant rapporteurs and considers their potential for advancing the rights of migrant domestic workers in the United States.

SPECIAL RAPPORTEUR ON WOMEN'S RIGHTS

In 1995, the Inter-American Commission appointed Claudio Grossman to serve as Special Rapporteur on Women's Rights, asking him

> to assist the member states of the OAS by identifying instances of discrimination which are inconsistent with inter-American human rights guarantees and issuing recommendations designed to remedy such inconsistencies and advance the ability of women to fully and equally enjoy their rights and freedoms. (IACHR 1996, Chapter VI)

The Special Rapporteur designed and carried out a study on the rights of women in the Americas, focusing especially on the issue of violence against women (Inter-American Commission on Human Rights 1997). The Report, based in part on responses by member states to a questionnaire developed by the Rapporteur, presents an analysis of the compliance of states with their obligations concerning the rights of women. In sum:

> The information received showed an encouraging movement within states to place women's rights on the social agenda and to institute reforms aimed at advancing the legal, social, political, and economic status of women. This process reflects the strength of women's organizations and human rights groups, the strength and depth of the democratic movements of the region, and the conviction that democracy and its triumph in the region ultimately require full compliance with the rights to which women are entitled. Notwithstanding the advances taking place in the region, however, the Commission reported that serious problems remain. *De jure* discrimination continues to exist in a number of countries, especially with respect to family matters, administration of property, and the penal system. Even when no *de jure* discrimination is present, actual practices in many parts of the region reveal that the ability of women to freely and fully exercise their rights is often denied. Poverty and armed conflict have a disproportionate negative effect on women, and women belonging to indigenous groups and racial and ethnic minorities are the subject of further grave violations resulting from their specific situation. (Inter-American Commission on Human Rights 1998: 1)

Significantly, the Report recommended that states accept the definition of "discrimination against women" set out in the Convention on the Elimination of All Forms of Discrimination Against Women:

"discrimination against women" shall mean any distinction, exclusion or restriction made on the basis of sex which has the effect or purpose of impairing or nullifying the recognition, enjoyment or exercise by women... of human rights and fundamental freedoms. (ibid.)

As discussed below, this definition supports the use of the substantive equality model within the Inter-American system. Among the other recommendations are several directly relevant to women migrant workers. The report notes that women suffer widespread discrimination in the workplace, and recommends that states: (a) take steps to ensure equal pay for equal work; (b) ensure equal employment opportunities; (c) ensure that women's reproductive functions are not used as a justification for discrimination by employers; and (d) "prevent, punish and eradicate sexual harassment in the workplace" (ibid.)

In 2000, the Commission appointed Marta Altoguirre as Special Rapporteur on the Rights of Women (IACHR 2001). Much of the Special Rapporteur's work has since focused on women's access to justice, as well as violence against women, including the application of the standard of due diligence as the relevant test for evaluating the efforts of a state in preventing, punishing and eradicating violence against women. Although the discrimination and exploitation that migrant domestic workers face fits within her mandate, the Rapporteur has not focused directly on these concerns.

SPECIAL RAPPORTEUR ON MIGRANT WORKERS AND THEIR FAMILIES

In 1996, the Inter-American Commission created a Special Rapporteurship for Migrant Workers and Their Families and a supporting Working Group to Study the Situation of Migrant Workers and their Families in the Hemisphere (IACHR 1996). Commissioner Alvaro Tirado Mejía was named Rapporteur. The Working Group was tasked with conducting a study, and began by examining the various definitions of "migrant worker," as well as the migration patterns within the Americas. The Working Group focused its first several years of work on developing a questionnaire for states, consulting with experts, and conducting on-site visits. The Working Group made an on-site visit to the U.S. state of California in 1998, collecting information for its study; no evaluation of this information was published by the Rapporteur. A similar visit was made by the Special Rapporteur to Texas in 1999.

The 1999 report of the Special Rapporteur provides a very helpful set of "principles applicable to migrant workers and their families developed on the basis of the case law of the Inter-American System" (IACHR 1999). The principles are: the prohibition of the collective expulsion of aliens; the right to a fair trial and judicial protection; the right to nationality; and the right to protection of the family (ibid.). While the right to non-discrimination and equality is mentioned, no guidance is given concerning the application of this principle to migrants. The Special Rapporteur presents summary information drawn from the questionnaire sent to states by the Working Group; these summaries are not accompanied by any analysis.

While not terribly helpful from an evaluative point of view, the resulting summaries provide some very useful factual information concerning the treatment of migrant workers in the various countries in the Americas, and could be used by researchers. They also provide a shapshot of the unwillingness of some governments to engage seriously with the Commission on migrants' rights issues (IACHR 1999). The U.S. answered all of the questions carefully, submitting useful information about the legal and administrative rules governing migrants in the United States, as well as factual information about instances of trafficking, worker exploitation, and benefits available to migrants. In an interesting misstatement, however, the U.S. reported that "those working in irregular sectors, such as domestic service, may often fail to report, and pay taxes on, their earnings"(ibid). This inclusion of all "domestic service" work in the "irregular" category may be seen as a reflection of the U.S. government's misapprehension of this sector in which many migrant women labor, a sector that is in fact subject to many of the general labor laws in place in the United States.

In 2000, Juan Méndez was appointed as Special Rapporteur. The Rapporteur's annual report for that year focuses on migration and human rights. The report is commendable for placing migratory trends and policies into a human rights framework. It also examines the efforts of the international community to respond to human rights violations against migrants, pointing to the International Convention on the Protection of the Rights of All Migrant Workers and Members of their Families and the U.N. Special Rapporteur on the Human Rights of Migrant Workers as important institutional responses to violations. The report then provides an overview of some of the most pressing human rights concerns for migrants in the Americas, finding that discrimination, xenophobia and racism are on the rise against migrants in the hemisphere; that due process guarantees need to be more carefully protected in relation to migrants in many countries in the region; and that "conditions faced by detained migrant workers in Central America, North America, and the Dominican Republic give rise to concern."(ibid. para 118) Finally, the 2000 report includes a brief analysis of the country responses to the questionnaire sent by the Working Group, which concludes that:

> the countries of the Americas coincide on the need to attack trafficking in migrant workers and the actions of unscrupulous employers. They also agree that the large and growing number of migrants, from the Americas and elsewhere, in transit poses a problem. The Office of the Special Rapporteur notes with grave concern that the legislation

in place in most countries is not effective in extending real protection to migrant workers and members of their families, a group that faces structural vulnerability and needs government to contribute to preventing abuses against them. We are especially concerned by the fact that many governments do not recognize that violations of due process and alarming incidents of discrimination, racism and xenophobia against migrant workers and members of their family are occurring throughout the region. (ibid. para 128)

Most relevant here, the report emphasizes that countries must work much harder to enforce labor laws, since widespread trends of exploitation of migrant workers were discovered in many countries in the Americas.

The 2001 report of the Special Rapporteur provides a very useful analysis of developments in case law concerning migrants' right to a nationality, the right to a fair trial and to judicial protection, and the right to liberty and protection from arbitrary arrest. The 2002 report includes a section on the "labor market and conditions of discrimination against migrant workers" (IACHR 2002: 1233). This section of the report is a summarized version of a report submitted by the Special Rapporteur to the Inter-American Court of Human Rights in connection with a request filed by Mexico for an advisory opinion on the rights of migrant workers in 2002 (discussed below). In many ways, the report serves as a precursor to the Advisory Opinion issued in that case; much of the legal framework relied upon there is set out in the Special Rapporteur's 2002 report.

In 2003, the Special Rapporteur reported on his on-site visit to Mexico. This report is remarkably in-depth, considering the reasons and purposes of migration to and from Mexico; the government's actions in the field of migration; efforts by civil society to improve the lives of Mexican migrants; the legal framework governing migration; and the human rights obligations on the state to protect and ensure the rights of migrants. The report provides a careful analysis of Mexico's shortcomings under human rights law, and includes reasoned recommendations.

In 2004, the Commission appointed Freddy Gutiérrez Trejos as Special Rapporteur for Migrant Workers and their Families. In the report summarizing his first year of work, a chapter is devoted to the human rights situation of migrant farmworkers in the Americas. This chapter discusses the systematic violations that farmworkers face, including widespread violations of labor rights; violations of economic and social rights (including the right to education); the right to be free from trafficking; and abuses of the right to due process, in both criminal and civil matters. Concerning labor rights, the report explains that farmworkers are often paid below the legal minimum wage; suffer illnesses relating to pesticides and heavy labor without adequate rest; may not have access to employment-related entitlements such as paid holidays, rest days, health insurance and disability schemes; and are often prevented from organizing to vindicate their rights. While the section of the report describing the situation facing migrant farmworkers is useful, it is rather cursory in comparison to the work of the Special Rapporteur in 2002 and 2003.

SPECIAL RAPPORTEURS AND THE RIGHTS OF MIGRANT DOMESTIC WORKERS

The rights of migrant domestic workers fit squarely within the mandates of both the Special Rapporteur on Women's Rights and the Special Rapporteur on Migrant Workers and their Families. Neither rapporteur has focused on this group, however. Given the resource constraints on the Inter-American Commission and its rapporteurs, advocates should consider approaching these individuals about work that could be feasibly achieved within their resource limits.

USING THE INTER-AMERICAN SYSTEM TO PROMOTE THE RIGHTS OF MIGRANT DOMESTIC WORKERS IN THE UNITED STATES

The rights of migrants and women under international human rights law

Migrant domestic workers suffer specific forms of abuse and deserve full protection from these abuses under human rights law. While the international human rights framework provides a wide range of standards and mechanisms that are relevant to this group, it has been a challenge to build an analytical approach to women migrant workers' rights that will encompass *all* aspects of their experience. Migrant domestic workers are situated at the crossroads of three major sets of norms: the human rights standards pertaining to women — mostly strong, protective standards; the human rights of workers — again, clearly articulated and robust; and the human rights rules concerning aliens or migrants — rules that remain in development, but which generally offer less protection than the rules relating to women and to workers. The situation within the Inter-American system is more promising, however. Indeed, the normative developments in the Inter-American system are almost the reverse of the state of affairs under international treaty law: clear rights protections have been articulated for migrants, while in many respects, women's rights jurisprudence is still under development.

The primary principles of non-discrimination, equality and equal protection of the law are essential to any human rights analysis, since they embody the general rule that human rights must be extended to all equally, and that avenues for redress should be made available to all on an equal footing. Over the years, these guarantees have been very strongly articulated at the international level with respect to certain groups that tend to face discrimination — including women. Unlike women, however, aliens and migrants, though they often face discrimination on the basis of their status as aliens or migrants, are not always protected *as a category*. Indeed, in the state-centered world of international law, some exceptions to the standards of equal protection and non-discrimination have been carved out in relation to these groups, allowing states to impose certain limitations on the rights of aliens under international human rights law. This does not mean that states can violate the rights of aliens and migrants with impunity. Instead, it means that with respect to a small number of rights associated with citizenship, states may limit their application to nationals or to regular, documented migrants. This subset of rights *never* includes the most fundamental guarantees — so-called "non-derogable rights" such as the right to be free from torture — and even permissible restrictions may not be imposed discriminatorily as between men and women. Further, since they are only permissible in specific circumstances, distinctions between citizens and non-citizens, and between documented and undocumented aliens should be scrutinized very closely.

Despite these obstacles, in recent years, both the Inter-American Court and the Inter-American Commission for Human Rights have broken new ground in international human rights law by clarifying that migrants must fully enjoy the right to non-discrimination, equality and equal protection in the host states where they live and work. This seemingly simple rule has enormously positive potential for migrant domestic workers. This section will focus on potential uses of the various Inter-American human rights institutions in the struggle to advance migrant domestic workers' rights.

THE INTER-AMERICAN COURT OF HUMAN RIGHTS

The Inter-American Court of Human Rights has already proven to be a very useful forum for advancing migrants' rights in the United States. This is true despite the unwillingness of the U.S. to subject itself to the contentious jurisdiction of the Court. In a groundbreaking advisory opinion concerning the rights of migrants, the Court determined that equality before the law, equal protection and non-discrimination constitute *jus cogens* norms. *Jus cogens* norms are norms "accepted and recognized by the international community of States as a whole as a norm from which no derogation is permitted" (Art. 53, Vienna Convention on the Law of Treaties 1969). The Court held that:

> the principle of equality before the law, equal protection before the law and non-discrimination belongs to *jus cogens*, because the whole legal structure of national and international public order rests on it and it is

a fundamental principle that permeates all laws. Nowadays, no legal act that is in conflict with this fundamental principle is acceptable, and discriminatory treatment of any person, owing to gender, race, color, language, religion or belief, political or other opinion, national, ethnic or social origin, nationality, age, economic situation, property, civil status, birth or any other status is unacceptable. This principle (equality and non-discrimination) forms part of general international law. At the existing stage of the development of international law, the fundamental principle of equality and non-discrimination has entered the realm of *jus cogens*. (Inter-American Court of Human Rights 2003: para. 101)

Significantly, the Court made this determination in a watershed case for the rights of migrants in the Americas, its 2003 opinion concerning the *Juridical Condition and Rights of the Undocumented Migrants* OC-18/03 (ibid.). The request for this opinion was filed by Mexico, which was concerned about the impact of a recent U.S. Supreme Court ruling on its nationals working without documentation in the United States. In 2002, the United States Supreme Court determined that undocumented workers could not recover back pay when they were illegally fired in retaliation for organizing efforts. In *Hoffman Plastics Compounds, Inc. v. National Labour Relations Board (NLRB)*, 535 U.S. 137 (2002), the Court determined that the usual remedy in labor rights violations cases was not available to undocumented workers, since those workers never had the right to work and earn wages in the first place. Concerned that this decision would lead to widespread abuse of Mexican nationals working without authorization in the United States, the Mexican government filed its request seeking an opinion from the Inter-American Court concerning the human rights protections available to undocumented workers.

The Inter-American Court's finding that principles of equality have achieved *jus cogens* status is significant for several reasons. First, such peremptory norms apply to all states as a matter of customary international law. So long as the Inter-American Court is correct in its holding, the United States is bound by those principles. Second, *jus cogens* norms trump other norms of customary or treaty law, meaning that state practices that violate the norm are invalid, regardless of the ratification status of the state in question, or even its attempts to object to the norm during its development. The importance of this finding becomes clear in relation to the Court's holding that all migrants — undocumented and documented alike — are covered by the principles of equality and equal protection (ibid. para. 110, 118). The Court does not, of course, go so far as to say that any distinction on the basis of migration status is illegal; such a finding would have immediately rendered suspect all immigration and citizenship laws. Instead, the Court reminds states that they must adhere to the regular rules concerning non-discrimination when differentiating between migrants and non-migrants, or documented and undocumented individuals, by testing the use of the categories "documented/undocumented" or "migrant/national" against the principles of reasonableness, objectivity and proportionality:

> the State may grant a distinct treatment to documented migrants with respect to undocumented migrants, or between migrants and nationals, provided that this differential treatment is reasonable, objective, proportionate and does not harm human rights. For example, distinctions may be made between migrants and nationals regarding ownership of some political rights. States may also establish mechanisms to control the entry into and departure from their territory of undocumented migrants, which must always be applied with strict regard for the guarantees of due process and respect for human dignity. (ibid. para. 119)

In other words, the Court leaves undisturbed the sovereign right of states to limit certain political rights (such as voting) to nationals, and to fairly regulate the movement of individuals across its borders. The categories "migrant" and "undocumented" may not, however, be used to deprive individuals of their basic human rights. Among those basic rights is the right to equal protection of the law. This right translates into a requirement that migrants not be excluded from the protection of labor laws on the basis of their migration status. The Court explains that regardless of the source of the substantive rights of workers (such as the right to organize, to a minimum wage, or to back pay as a remedy for retaliatory firing), those rights inhere immediately upon hiring and may not be denied on the basis of migration status, even if an individual was not authorized to work under the domestic law of the state in question.

> Labor rights necessarily arise from the circumstance of being a worker, understood in the broadest sense. A person who is to be engaged, is engaged or has been engaged in a remunerated activity, immediately becomes a worker and, consequently, acquires the rights inherent in that condition. The right to work, whether regulated at the national or international level, is a protective system for workers; that is, it regulates the rights and obligations of the employee and the employer, regardless of any other consideration of an economic and social nature. A person who enters a State and assumes an employment relationship, acquires his labor human rights in the State of employment, irrespective of his migratory status, because respect and guarantee of the enjoyment and exercise of those rights must be made without any discrimination... In this way, the migratory status of a person can never be a justification for depriving him of the enjoyment and exercise of his human rights, including those related to employment. On assuming an employment relationship, the migrant acquires rights as a worker, which must be

recognized and guaranteed, irrespective of his regular or irregular status in the State of employment. These rights are a consequence of the employment relationship. (ibid. paras. 133–134)

Armed with this robust principle, the Court next makes clear that labor rights must be upheld without discrimination not only as between individuals and the state (as with government employees), but must be protected by the state as between workers and private employers. Indeed, the Court explains that the state will accrue international responsibility for violations of the rights of migrant workers if it supports systems of discrimination against them, including through laws or rules that exclude undocumented workers from protections as workers (ibid. paras. 145–160).

In the course of its discussion of the norm of non-discrimination under international law, the Inter-American Court makes clear that it is adopting a substantive approach to equality, moving beyond the formal equality model. The difference between the two models is of crucial importance for advocates considering the Inter-American norms and procedures as options for the redress of discrimination against migrant domestic workers. Briefly, formal equality is an approach to anti-discrimination doctrine that limits itself to an examination of the use by a state of impermissible distinctions or protected categories and their legitimacy. Without more, the Inter-American Court's test for the permissible use of categorization as set out above in relation to the categories "migrant" and "undocumented" would constitute formal equality, applicable only when a category describing a protected group is used by the state. Situations of indirect discrimination, in which no protected category is used, but in which the law or program has a disproportionate impact on groups covered by non-discrimination standards, would not be reachable by this formal approach to equality. The Inter-American Court goes further, however, when describing the breadth of the obligations placed on the state by the principle of non-discrimination. There, the Court explains that states must:

> abstain from carrying out any action that, in any way, directly or indirectly, is aimed at creating situations of *de facto* or *de jure* discrimination. This translates, for example, into the prohibition to enact laws, in the broadest sense, formulate civil, administrative or any other measures, or encourage acts or practices of their officials, in implementation or interpretation of the law that discriminate against a specific group of persons because of their race, gender, color or other reasons. In addition, States are obliged to take affirmative action to reverse or change discriminatory situations that exist in their societies to the detriment of a specific group of persons. This implies the special obligation to protect that the State must exercise with regard to acts and practices of third parties who, with its tolerance or acquiescence, create, maintain or promote discriminatory situations. (ibid. paras. 103–104)

This understanding of discrimination — when paired with the guarantee of equality that accompanies it — should be interpreted as embodying the substantive equality model. This means that women's rights are violated not only when, for example, laws formally treat them differently from men, but also when any law, policy, or action has the practical effect of disadvantaging them without adequate justification. The same would be true for migrants in the Inter-American system, since the Court has determined that migration status is a protected category.

This standard has important protective implications for migrant domestic workers, who often suffer harm from facially neutral laws that have a disproportionate impact on their rights to fair conditions of work, including laws concerning pay and safety standards. In effect, whenever a pattern can be found in which a certain law or policy has a disproportionately negative impact on the rights of women, the state will be required to prove that its policy has an objective and reasonable justification, and that the means employed are reasonably proportional to the ends being sought. In cases where the state cannot do so, discrimination will be present, and it will have an obligation to take active steps to ensure women their equal rights. A wide variety of laws and practices concerning migrant domestic workers, some of which are described in the next section, would fit into this pattern and should be open to challenge under the substantive equality model.

The Inter-American Court's Advisory Opinion OC-18/03 is an incredibly powerful tool, and carries with it significant potential for advancing the rights of migrant domestic workers in the United States. Advocates need not focus their efforts on the Inter-American Court, but should instead look to other mechanisms within the Inter-American system to enforce the norms the Court has so eloquently set out.

The Inter-American Commission on Human Rights

As discussed above, the Inter-American Commission on Human Rights has had occasion to examine the rights of migrants through the work of its migrants' rights rapporteur, as well as through individual petitions, which have included cases concerning the rights of aliens to due process and consular access in the context of the death penalty in the United States. In a separate line of cases, the Commission has developed an extensive non-discrimination and equal protection jurisprudence that largely tracks the approach of the Inter-American Court. Also relevant for advocates of migrant domestic workers are suggestions by the Commission, in two cases concerning the United States, that it may be possible to make out a claim of indirect discrimination through the use of statistics. In the 1989 *Celestine case*, the petitioner introduced statistical evidence of racial bias in an attempt to demonstrate that he had suffered discrimination at the hands of the jury that had sentenced him to death (IACHR 1989). The Commission found that Celestine's statistical evidence was insufficient to prove the allegations of discrimination. Similarly, in the 2003 *Statehood Solidarity Committee case*, the Commission entertained, but found insufficient, statistical evidence introduced by the petitioners to demonstrate racial bias on the part of the U.S. Congress in failing to amend the voting arrangements applicable to residents of the District of Columbia (IACHR 2003). There, the Commission held that the U.S. government had violated equal protection on the basis of Washingtonians' place of residence, but did not find discrimination on the basis of race. While the Commission rejected the claims made using statistics in both the *Celestine* and *Statehood* cases, it did—by characterizing these rejections as issues of insufficiency—indicate that statistical evidence, if strong enough, could play a significant role in making out a claim of indirect discrimination.

Given the existence of supportive norms, there are a number of specific strategies that could be used to promote the rights of migrant domestic workers before the Inter-American Commission on Human Rights: general interest hearings, petitions alleging human rights violations, and on-site visits. Domestic workers' advocates have already held one general interest hearing focusing on the issue of diplomatic immunity, and advocates for migrants have also held a general interest hearing examining the rights of agricultural and undocumented migrants. Some significant obstacles would present themselves were a petition to be lodged on behalf of migrant domestic workers, though that possibility is currently under discussion. On-site visits to meet with domestic workers' organizations may be an alternative way to follow up a general interest hearing; since the Commission has its headquarters in Washington, D.C., such visits may be possible even within the difficult financial constraints of the Commission.

GENERAL INTEREST HEARINGS

Groups and individuals who are "interested in presenting testimony or information to the Commission on the human rights situation in one or more States, or on matters of general interest" may request a hearing before the Commission (Rules of Procedure IACHR). Such hearings can be especially useful in educating the Commission about a particular concern or set of rights, or when individual cases are not strategically wise or legally possible. They can also be productive in helping frame an issue as a human rights concern. Hearings on the rights of migrant workers have already been fruitful in several of these ways.

For example, in early 2005, a coalition of organizations requested a hearing on the status of undocumented workers in the United States, and another coalition requested a hearing on the rights of migrant farmworkers in the United States. These requests were jointly granted, and a hearing was held on March 3, 2005. Farmworkers, human rights advocates, and lawyers for undocumented workers presented evidence about human rights violations before the Commission and submitted written documentation concerning those abuses.

While the hearings did not directly produce results on the ground, farmworkers' advocates point to several concrete outcomes. The Coalition of Immokalee Workers had been engaged in protracted negotiations with Taco Bell Corporation and its parent company, Yum! Brands over dire living and working conditions of farmworkers in the U.S. state of Florida. The organizations involved in the hearing credit the hearing as crucial in the struggle to frame the farmworkers' concerns as human rights issues rather than a narrow dispute over wages — a struggle they won only days later, when Yum! Brands agreed to improve working conditions, increase wages, and fight slavery in its supply chain, affirming that "human rights are universal" in its press release concerning the agreement.[10]

Advocates for undocumented workers — who came to the hearing armed with stories of such migrants' lives and struggles — felt that a general hearing would be a safe way to raise human rights concerns facing undocumented workers without making them vulnerable to potential deportation or other repercussions.[11] The message — that the United States is in contravention of the rule set out in the Inter-American Court of Human Right's Advisory Opinion OC-18 — was driven home through life stories. As one lawyer for undocumented workers explained, "talking about fundamental human rights puts a value on the individual in a way that talking about wages does not" (Paoletti, interview).

In October 2005, human rights organization Global Rights paired with domestic workers' advocates from CASA de Maryland and the Center for Human Rights and Global Justice at New York University (NYU) School of Law to present a general interest hearing on the issue of diplomatic immunity and its impact on the human rights of migrant domestic workers in the United States. The issue of diplomatic immunity was chosen because its effects were so dramatic (by barring women from obtaining even a day in court to assert their claims), and because the issue is one that advocates felt the Commissioners might relate to easily as beneficiaries of such immunities themselves. Testifying at the hearing were two domestic workers, a U.S.-based attorney who represents domestic workers in U.S. courts, and an international human rights expert.[12] The workers testified that they had suffered violations at the hands of diplomatic staff, including breach of contract, underpayment of wages, overwork, and degrading treatment (Velasco, testimony). The legal arguments then focused on the barriers to justice for workers like these, who have valid claims under U.S. law but are barred from pressing those claims due to diplomatic immunity (Keyes, testimony). Reframing the issue as a human rights violation, the hearing called on the Inter-American Commission to take action to ensure that migrant domestic workers can enjoy the "right to a remedy" when their labor rights are violated (Satterthwaite, testimony). Specifically, Global Rights called on the Commission to monitor the situation of migrant domestic workers employed by OAS Member States and OAS staff, report on the situation of migrant domestic workers in the Americas region, and make recommendations to countries that are members of the OAS, emphasizing the practical steps they should take to ensure that domestic workers employed by diplomats are protected against human rights abuses (Global Rights Hearing Recommendations). The Commissioners present at the hearing were engaged and expressed serious concern about the violations discussed. While no formal action has been taken by the Commission in response to the recommendations, the hearing was mentioned in the Commission's annual report (IACHR 2006). Advocates are hopeful that the hearing has contributed to greater sensitivity on the part of the Commission that could augur well should an individual petition be brought challenging the issues discussed.

INDIVIDUAL PETITIONS

As discussed earlier, individuals and groups may lodge petitions alleging violations of their human rights by member states of the Organization of American States. Given the strong non-discrimination, equality, and equal protection standards explicated in recent jurisprudence of the Inter-American Court of Human Rights, it may seem that individual petitions on behalf of migrant domestic workers who have suffered human rights violations in the United States would be easy to craft. Normatively, this may well be true.

Migrant domestic workers may have a variety of strong claims using the interlocking norms of non-discrimination, equality and equal protection. These claims would be based on creative use of the substantive approach to equality, discussed above. This model of equality would make certain claims cognizable within the Inter-American system that would not be meritorious under U.S. law, which uses — for the most part — the formal equality model.

Expansive non-discrimination norms could be brought to bear through interpretations of the American Declaration, especially Article 2's guarantee of equality before the law and Article 18's right to a judicial remedy. The Inter-American Commission is likely to be open to this approach, which could explicitly call upon non-discrimination norms in treaties that the United States has ratified, including the ICCPR and the Committee on the Elimination of Racial Discrimination (CERD). Both treaties have been authoritatively interpreted to use the substantive equality model. Drawing on these treaties in conjunction with the Inter-American Court's holding concerning discrimination against migrant workers would allow advocates to directly address the effects of intersecting forms of discrimination on migrant domestic workers.

The ICCPR contains strong general non-discrimination and equal protection guarantees that extend to women, migrants, and ethnic minorities. Article 3 requires states parties to "ensure the equal right of men and women to the enjoyment of all civil and political rights set forth in the present Convention." The Human Rights Committee, the body mandated to review state compliance with the ICCPR, has noted that the Covenant does not define discrimination. In the absence of an explicit definition, the Committee has determined that the definitions of discrimination set out in CERD and CEDAW should guide the interpretation of the ICCPR such that "the term 'discrimination' as used in the Covenant should be understood to imply any distinction, exclusion, restriction or preference which is based on any ground... and which has the purpose or effect of nullifying or impairing the recognition, enjoyment or exercise by all persons, on an equal footing, of all rights and freedoms" (UNHRC 1989). This "purpose or effect" standard has been recognized as essential to international efforts to combat discrimination, since it looks beyond the intent of the legislation's drafters to the impact of the deployment of the category of distinction under examination. Article 26 holds that all people are entitled to equal protection of the law. "The law shall prohibit any discrimination and guarantee to all persons equal and effective protection against discrimination on any ground..." This article is crucial because it extends equal protection of the law to all persons subject to the state party's jurisdiction, including women and aliens. One of the most important ways to enforce nondiscrimination standards is to ensure that all individuals — here, women migrant workers — are able to vindicate their rights equally under the law. Violations of the right to equal protection are among the most critical violations that women migrant workers face, since such infringements compound the underlying violation for which a remedy is sought. Finally, the Human Rights Committee has explained that the treaty's provisions on gender equality include positive obligations on the state to "take all necessary steps to enable every person to enjoy" human rights equally (UNHRC 2000). This includes removing obstacles to equal enjoyment, as well as "positive measures in all areas so as to achieve the effective and equal empowerment of women" (ibid.).

The CERD Committee, charged with interpreting the International Convention for the Elimination of All Forms of Racial Discrimination, has made a number of normative advances that could be relevant to the crafting of claims in the Inter-American system. The CERD Committee has interpreted the Convention to require that otherwise permissible distinctions between citizens and non-citizens may not be applied in a racially discriminatory manner (UNCERD 2004). Even more potentially far-reaching is the principle CERD set out in *Zaid Ben Ahmed Habassi v. Denmark*.[13] In that case, the Committee found that when circumstances suggest that alien status may be used as a proxy for racial discrimination, "a proper investigation into the real reasons" for the distinction is required by the state party (ibid.). Failure to conduct such an investigation may amount to a violation of the convention. Under that rule, states may have an obligation to investigate distinctions on the basis of alien status — even by private actors — whenever such distinctions are suspected of being used as a proxy for impermissible discrimination. In a more straightforward manner, the discrimination that migrant domestic workers face often has little to do with their actual alien status, but is instead an overt function of racism, ethnic discrimination, and xenophobia; these forms of discrimination are clearly covered by the Convention.[14] Finally, although CERD is silent with respect to sex discrimination, it has been interpreted to include prohibitions on gender-specific and gender-differential forms of racial discrimination, making it a very useful tool for women migrant workers (UNCERD 2000).

Armed with these robust standards against discrimination on the basis of gender, race, ethnicity, and nationality, advocates could then make out a number of potential claims concerning practices that have overlapping discriminatory impacts on migrant domestic workers, and which would not be cognizable under U.S. law. For example, migrant domestic workers could challenge the explicit exclusion of domestic workers from certain U.S. terms of employment laws by demonstrating that those laws disproportionately impact women in general, and especially women of racial or ethnic minorities. Women workers of nationalities considered "unpopular" for nannies could allege that their right to equal protection and a remedy under the law is violated by their inability to bring anti-discrimination claims based on their race or nationality and gender under U.S. law. Undocumented domestic workers could challenge their ineligibility for back pay under the Supreme Court's *Hoffman Plastics* decision, arguing that it constitutes an obstacle on their equal rights that impacts them especially harshly as women of protected racial and ethnic categories. Domestic workers present in the U.S. on special visas could challenge the absence of remedy for their contract claims by arguing that the Department of State's failure to enforce such contracts is discriminatory. These potential claims are a small subset of the claims that advocates could craft concerning the interlocking forms of discrimination that migrant domestic workers face in the United States.

There are a number of significant obstacles facing such petitions, however. Issues of exhaustion of domestic remedies and the vulnerability of undocumented individuals may stand in the way of filings. To be considered by the Commission, a petitioner must show that she has "pursued and exhausted" all remedies for the violation being presented to the Commission that are available under the municipal law of the United States (American Convention, art. 46a). This means that domestic workers claiming violations that could be cognizable under U.S. law, such as non-payment of wages, breach of employment contract, and even debt bondage or trafficking will be required to demonstrate that they have used (or made diligent efforts to use) all possible avenues of redress, including the filing of lawsuits, seeking the assistance of government agencies with enforcement power, or asking for the help of police and investigative bodies. For undocumented workers, these avenues of redress often heighten vulnerability to deportation or retaliation. U.S. law does provide some protection from disclosure of documentation status for individuals pursuing their labor rights, but these protections are not widely known and may not be certain enough to assuage the fears of potential petitioners. For claims that are not cognizable under U.S. law — such as the claim for back pay or reinstatement that was rejected in the *Hoffman Plastics* case, the basis of which has been attacked by the Inter-American Court — domestic remedies are arguably "unavailable" for the purpose of satisfying the exhaustion requirement. Individuals lodging petitions on the basis of such claims, however, are by definition vulnerable to enforcement actions by U.S. immigration authorities and therefore may be hesitant to agree to the filing of a petition on their behalf with the Commission.

In cases stemming from claims that are technically cognizable under U.S. law but practically unchallengeable because of fears about documentation status, individual petitions may be cognizable despite the failure to exhaust domestic remedies. Recognizing the intersecting forms of discrimination that migrant domestic workers face, advocates could recast their complaints as discrimination claims using other protected categories — especially gender, race, and ethnicity (Satterthwaite 2005: 11–12). In other words, advocates could reconceptualize the human rights violation being challenged: instead of presenting a petition focusing on the underlying labor rights claim (to unpaid wages or the minimum wage), advocates would craft petitions focusing on claims about ethnic, race, and gender discrimination. For example, a claim could be constructed challenging the discriminatory failure to enforce labor laws in settings where either women or immigrants predominate. Such claims may be constructed by examining the enforcement practices, budgets, and plans of agencies charged with ensuring workers' rights are upheld. Since the relevant agencies have not designed any enforcement actions aimed primarily at reaching domestic workers (Poo, interview; Human Rights Watch 2001, 31–33), such a claim would be colorable as having a discriminatory impact on migrants, on women, and on certain races and ethnicities.

Another set of claims may be admissible before the Commission without problems of exhaustion: the problem of immunities to criminal and civil enforcement enjoyed by members of the diplomatic corps and officials of some international institutions. These immunities have been used as defenses to claims filed under U.S. law by domestic workers seeking payment of wages, breach of contract damages, and other valid claims (American Civil Liberties Union & Global Rights, n.d.). A significant challenge will greet such petitions, however, since the United States would be likely to argue that it is required by international law to protect the immunity of foreign diplomats and officials. This obligation, based on the Vienna Convention on Diplomatic Relations, may in fact conflict with the rights of individual domestic workers to claim remedies (Rules of Procedures IACHR). A case has recently been filed by the American University School of Law Human Rights Clinic in federal court on behalf of Lucia Mabel Gonzalez Paredes seeking damages for violations she alleges she suffered while she was employed as a domestic worker by Argentine diplomats. If the case is dismissed by the court on the basis of diplomatic immunity, the case could be taken to the Inter-American Commission as an individual petition.

ON-SITE VISITS

The Inter-American Commission is empowered to make on-site visits to "observe" human rights situations. Migrant domestic workers' organizations could request such a visit and arrange for domestic workers to give testimony to Commission investigators. On-site observations are especially useful in situations where widespread or structural human rights violations are occurring, since the findings of visits are published in free-standing reports where recommendations are presented to the government in question. The problem of non-enforcement of labor laws in the domestic worker industry, as well as the problematic issue of diplomatic immunity, could lend themselves to on-site investigations. Such visits would be cost effective as well, since interviews could be arranged in the immediate vicinity of the Commission in Washington, D.C.

Advocacy using inter-American norms

Potentially more effective than direct engagement with the Inter-American human rights system are efforts that enlist human rights norms through organizing, consumer pressure, direct action, and the filing of "friend of the court" legal briefs. A wide variety of such activities supporting the rights of migrant domestic workers are already underway in the United States, and many more are possible with creative strategizing and organizing. The use of the human rights framework and the norms of the Inter-American system could be strengthened through cooperative efforts uniting human rights organizations and domestic workers' organizations.

Consumer pressure was essential in the successes achieved by the Coalition of Immokalee Workers (CIW), who were able to negotiate a higher wage for farmworkers after long-term organizing, public campaigning, hunger striking, and media work. As mentioned above, the opportunity to frame the CIW message as a *human rights* message by testifying before the Inter-American Commission was credited as essential to the final breakthrough with Yum! Brand officials. Similar efforts at framing migrant workers' struggles as a fight for human rights have been undertaken without initiating litigation before human rights bodies. In addition to the general interest hearing in October 2005, other efforts are underway in relation to domestic workers. For example, as part of a large coalition of organizations contributing "shadow" reports critiquing U.S. performance under the International Covenant on Civil and Political Rights, Global Rights paired with the University of North Carolina Human Rights Policy Clinic to produce a report examining domestic workers' rights in the United States (Global Rights 2006). This 18-page document identifies abuses against domestic workers in the United States as violations of the rights guaranteed under the convention, and sets out specific changes in law and practice that the U.N. Human Rights Committee, which monitors compliance with the treaty, could recommend to the U.S. government.

As Jennifer Gordon has documented, organizing campaigns are sometimes more challenging with respect to domestic workers than with (even immigrant) workers in other industries, since women are dispersed in private households and don't always benefit from days off (Gordon 2005). Women who are undocumented may be especially reluctant to join with other workers for fear of becoming even more vulnerable through their efforts. Some groups of documented workers, such as those working on special visas that tie their documentation status to a specific employer, may also fear repercussions should they become involved in forwarding their rights.

Despite these obstacles, a number of very successful organizing campaigns have been launched by domestic workers' organizations. In New York City, Domestic Workers United (DWU), with the support of the NYU School of Law's Immigrants' Rights Clinic, has brought together community-based organizations and domestic workers to campaign for city-wide and now state-wide legislation protecting the rights of domestic workers. Building on groundbreaking work done on Long Island years earlier by the Workplace Project, organizers created a "Bill of Rights" for domestic workers, using the language of human rights to back demands for a living wage, health insurance, paid vacation days and holidays, notice of termination and severance pay, and protection from discrimination (ibid.). DWU was founded in 2000 by Committee Against Anti-Asian Violence (CAAAV): Organizing Asian Communities and Andolan Organizing South Asian Workers, and also includes Damayan and Haitian Women for Haitian Refugees. The coalition has been extremely successful: in June 2003, the organization convinced the New York City Council to pass legislation requiring employment agencies to inform workers about their labor rights.[15] DWU is now working to pass similar legislation at the state level, which would circumvent the exclusions of domestic workers written into labor laws by requiring the payment of a living wage, the provision of family leave, paid holidays, and severance pay, among other basic protections. The bill is making its way through the legislative process now, and has garnered endorsements by a number of prominent lawmakers and organizations

(Poo, interview & personal communication, 21 June 2006). In addition to lobbying for legislative change, some of DWU's constitutive organizations, notably Andolan, have spearheaded a campaign to end the use of diplomatic immunity for employers of exploited domestic workers in New York. This work parallels efforts by CASA de Maryland, Global Rights, and the Break the Chain Campaign in the Washington, D.C., area, which have also focused advocacy efforts on the problem of diplomatic immunity.

The language and framework of human rights has been a common reference point for organizers, and could be amplified even more with the additional efforts of human rights organizations. Several human rights organizations have used their traditional "name and shame" methodology to call attention to abuses against domestic workers in the U.S. Human Rights Watch has contributed a great deal through its groundbreaking report, *Human Right Watch, 2001: Abuses of Domestic Workers with Special Visas in the United States*, published in 2001. This report, based on interviews with domestic workers, carefully documents and analyzes the human rights violations domestic workers experience under both U.S. and international law. More recently, Washington D.C.-based Free the Slaves paired with the Human Rights Center of the University of California at Berkeley to investigate and report on forced labor in the United States. Entitled *Hidden Slaves: Forced Labor in the United States*, the report found that domestic service accounted for 27 percent of the cases the researchers documented (Free the Slaves 2005: 48). The report highlights several case studies of domestic workers who were victims of trafficking and forced labor. The work of Global Rights, already mentioned above, has been exemplary, combining organizing, advocacy before human rights bodies, and public awareness activities. In October 2005, Global Rights joined with Domestic Workers United to hold a "Domestic Workers Human Rights Tribunal" in New York City. The purpose of the tribunal was to "hold the U.S. and New York State governments accountable for the systematic exploitation of over 200,000 domestic workers in the greater New York metropolitan area," by "bring[ing] the voices and experiences of domestic workers forward, in a call for justice" (Global Rights & DWU 2005: 1). During the half-day event, women spoke about their own experience and efforts to find redress; a panel of "judges" — heads of human rights, workers' rights, and migrants' rights organizations — listened and then provided closing comments that functioned as a call to renewed action.

Finally, groups already engaged in domestic litigation on behalf of domestic workers could seek out the help of human rights organizations willing to file *amicus curiae* briefs. Such efforts would fit well with the strategies adopted by some litigators, who in addition to making claims for breach of contract and violations of wage and hour laws are also bringing international law claims in extreme cases, alleging slavery, servitude, forced labor, and trafficking. "Friend of the court" briefs would set out the human rights obligations binding on the United States that support the claims of the worker. U.S. courts have proven more open to international law arguments of late; this openness could be used by advocates to introduce more wide-ranging and expansive protections relevant to domestic workers.

CONCLUSION

This chapter has argued that there are compelling reasons to use human rights law — and the Inter-American system more specifically — to advance migrant domestic workers' rights. Perhaps most importantly, the failures of the U.S. government to advance the rights of migrant domestic workers are subject to review by the human rights bodies of the Inter-American system. Also crucial is the power of human rights law to capture and conceptualize the obligations of the state vis-à-vis abuses that occur in the "private" realm. Finally, human rights law includes expansive norms that cover overlapping forms of discrimination that may not be easily challenged under U.S. law; such intersectional discrimination is at the heart of the exploitation that migrant domestic workers experience in the United States.

It is too soon to say whether the next "nannygate" will provide an opportunity for advocates to reframe the debate to emphasize the human rights of domestic workers. Domestic workers are organizing in many cities in the United States: coalitions exist in New York City, on Long Island, in Los Angeles, in Washington, D.C., and in other cities. Despite the enormous obstacles they face, the groups have had remarkable successes and are beginning to organize at the regional and national levels. Some groups are now turning to international human rights law and human rights organizations like Global Rights to support their local and national efforts. As demonstrated in this chapter, there are many ways to enlist human rights norms and institutions in the fight against exploitation and discrimination. Of course, as with any legal strategy, these institutions should be used only as part of a broader organizing strategy lest they lead to backlash or increased vulnerability of domestic workers. Now that advocates have determined that it makes sense to "internationalize" the struggle,[16] the Inter-American system may be the ideal place to start.

ACKNOWLEDGMENTS

The author expresses gratitude to Nicola Piper for inviting her to take part in this project, for fruitful suggestions, and for being a fantastic colleague-from-afar. Gratitude is also due to Arlen Benjamin-Gomez (J.D., NYU School of Law, 2006) Ellen VanScoyoc (J.D., NYU School of Law, 2006), for invaluable research assistance, and to Margaret Huang, Sarah Paoletti, Mayra Peters-Quintero, Ai-Jen Poo, and Amanda Shanor for sharing their ideas, suggestions, strategies, and success stories.

NOTES

1. A version of this chapter with detailed citations is available at: http://www.nyuhr.org/docs/WPS_NYU_CHRGJ_Satterthwaite_Final.pdf.
2. Linda Chavez was nominated for the position of Secretary of Labor by President George W. Bush in 2001, and was forced to step down when it was alleged that she employed an undocumented Guatemalan woman as a domestic helper. Chavez denied that the woman had been her employee, explaining that the woman has done "chores" for Chavez, but that the money Chavez gave her was charity, not money in exchange for work performed (see James and Dorning, 2001). Bernard Kerik was nominated by President Bush to the post of Secretary of Homeland Security in 2004, but was forced to withdraw when it was disclosed that he had employed a likely undocumented domestic worker. Mr. Kerik's nomination was subsequently marred by numerous other allegations of wrongdoing (see Scheer, 2004).
3. Live-in domestic workers may enter and work legally under two different special visa programs: they may work for diplomats through the A-3 visa program or officials of international organizations using a G-5 visa. Migrant domestic workers may also be eligible to work legally for other foreigners or U.S. citizens with a B-1 visa. *See* U.S. Embassy, *Domestic Employees* ("Personal or domestic servants who are accompanying or following to join an employer in the United States are eligible for B-1 visas; those accompanying or following to join an employer who is a foreign diplomat or official are eligible for A-3, G-5 or [North Atlantic Treaty Organization] NATO-7 visas, depending on the visa status of their employer. This category of persons includes, but is not limited to, cooks, butlers, chauffeurs, housemaids, parlormaids, valets, footmen, nannies, au pairs, mothers' helpers, gardeners, and paid companions. Please refer to the appropriate section for further information."). Available at www.usembassy.org.uk/cons_web/visa/niv/apply.htm.
4. Ai-Jen Poo (Organizer, CAAAV: Organizing Asian Communities), interview by author, New York, New York, 9 May 2005; Mayra Peters-Quintero (Immigrant Rights Clinic, NYU), interview by author, New York, New York, 29 June 2006; and Claudia Flores (Staff Attorney, Women's Rights Project, American Civil Liberties Union), personal communication, 11 July 2006. Successes include a recent settlement for $60,000 for breach of contract for a domestic worker in New York who was summarily fired after a dispute with her employers. The settlement also included a letter of reference from the employers, something that can be as valuable as years of wages in some instances, since prospective employers insist on such letters from previous employers before hiring domestic workers.
5. The worker subsequently filed suit against the couple, prevailing with a jury award of $832,000 for overtime wages and back pay, plus $5,000 in emotional damages (see Micek, 2006).
6. An additional hurdle for domestic workers is that even if they were covered by the National Labor Relations Act, those who were undocumented would not be eligible for the standard remedy of back pay for non-compliance with the Act. In a 2002 case, the U.S. Supreme Court determined that workers who were not authorized to work legally in the United States may not recover pay lost when an employer illegally firing them in retaliation for organizing efforts. *Hoffman Plastics Compound, Inc. v. NLRB*, 535 U.S. 137 (2002).
7. There are two protocols to the *American Convention*: the *Additional Protocol to the American Convention on Human Rights in the Matter of Economic, Social and Cultural Rights*, Nov. 17, 1988, O.A.S.T.S. No. 69 (1988);

and the *Protocol to the American Convention on Human Rights Relative to the Abolition of the Death Penalty*, June 8, 1990, O.A.S.T.S. No. 73 (1990).
8. These conventions include the *Inter-American Convention to Prevent and Punish Torture*, Dec. 9, 1985, O.A.S.T.S. No. 67 (1987); the *Inter-American Convention on Forced Disappearance of Persons*, June 9, 1994; the *Inter-American Convention to Prevent, Sanction and Eradicate Violence Against Women*, June 9, 1994; and the *Inter-American Convention on the Elimination of All Forms of Discrimination Against Persons with Disabilities*, June 7, 1999.
9. For general information about the OAS, see http://www.oas.org/main/main.asp?sLang=E&sLink=http://www.oas.org/documents/eng/aboutoas.asp.
10. Amanda Shanor (Program Officer, Robert F. Kennedy Memorial Center for Human Rights), interview, Washington D.C., 5 May 2005.
11. Sarah Paoletti (Clinical Supervisor and Lecturer, University of Pennsylvania School of Law), interview, Washington, D.C., 6 May 2005.
12. The author was the international expert who testified at the hearing.
13. Committee on the Elimination of Racial Discrimination, *Communication 10/1997* (1999) (holding that an alien who was denied a bank loan on the basis that only citizens could be granted loans was denied his right to an effective remedy when the state failed to investigate the "real reasons" for the use of alien status for loan eligibility).
14. As the Special Rapporteur on Migrant Workers explains: "People whose color, physical appearance, dress, accent or religion are different from those of the majority in the host country are often subjected to physical violence and other violations of their rights, independently of their legal status. The choice of victim and the nature of the abuse do not depend on whether the persons are refugees, legal immigrants, members of national minorities or undocumented migrants." *Report of the Special Rapporteur, Ms. Gabriella Rodriguez Pizarro, submitted pursuant to Commission on Human Rights Resolution 1999/44* (U.N. Doc. E/CN.4/2000/82, at para. 32 (6 Jan. 2000).
15. For information about DWU, visit their website at: http://www.domesticworkersunited.org/, as well as the CAAAV website: http://www.caaav.org/coalitions/dwu.php.
16. In 1964, African-American leader Malcolm X counseled civil rights activists in the United States to "internationalize" their struggle in order to allow for broader solidarity, collective action, and United Nations action concerning racial discrimination in the United States.

BIBLIOGRAPHY

Abdul Rahman, N., B. S.A. Yeoh & S. Huang (2004) "'Dignity Over Due': Transnational Domestic Workers in Singapore." Paper presented at the International Workshop on Contemporary Perspectives on Asian Transnational Domestic Workers, Singapore, 23–25 February 2004.

Abdul Rahman, N. (2003) "Negotiating Power: A Case Study of Foreign Domestic Workers in Singapore", unpublished Ph.D. dissertation, Curtin University of Technology.

American Convention on Human Rights. (1969) O.A.S.T.S. No. 36, 22 November.

Anderson, B. (2003). "Just Another Job? The Commodification of Domestic Labor." In B. Ehrenreich and A. Russell Hochschild (eds.), *Global Woman: Nannies, Maids and Sex Workers in the New Economy*, New York: Metropolitan Books.

Break the Chain Campaign, "Assisting the Enslaved in the Land of the Free," (website with various pages devoted to information about domestic workers). Retrieved June 25, 2006, from http://www.ips-dc.org/campaign/index.htm; hereafter cited in text as *Break the Chain*. Cleveland, S., B. Lyon, and R. Smith. (2003) "Inter-American Court of Human Rights Amicus Curiae Brief: The United States Violates International Law When Labor Law Remedies are Restricted Based on Workers' Migrant Status", *Seattle Journal for Social Justice* 1: 795–851.

Code of Federal Regulations (2006), vol. 29, sec. 552.100(b).

Convention on the Rights of the Child (1989) G.A. Res. 44/25, 61st plen. mtg., U.N. Doc. A / RES / 44 / 25. 20 November. Available at http://www.ohchr.org/english/countries/ratification/11.htm.

Craven, M. (1995) *The International Covenant on Economic, Social and Cultural Rights: A Perspective on Its Development*. Oxford: Clarendon Press.

Department of Labor Regulations (2006) *Code of Federal Regulations*, title 29, sec. 1975.6, 1604.11

Domestic Workers United (2006) "Bill of Rights for Domestic Workers", N.D. (on file with author).

Domestic Workers United & DataCenter (2006) *Domestic Workers United & DataCenter, 2006: Inside New York's Domestic Work Industry*, executive summary and powerpoint presentation. Available at: http://www.domesticworkersunited.org/. Retrieved July 10, 2006 from

Fair Labor Standards Act. (2006) U.S. Code, title 29, sec. 206(f); 207(l); 213(b)(21)

Financial Times, The (2004) "A Spoonful of Sugar: Watch Out for Problems with Mary Poppins' Visa", 18 December, p. 10.

Free the Slaves & The Human Rights Center of the University of California, Berkeley. (2005). "Hidden Slaves: Forced Labor in the United States", *Berkeley Journal of International Law* 23: 47–111.

Global Rights/Partners in Justice & Domestic Workers United (2005) "Domestic Workers Human Rights Tribunal." New York: DWU.

Global Rights/Partners in Justice & University of North Carolina Law School, Human Rights Policy Clinic (2006) "Domestic Workers' Rights in the United States: A Report Prepared for the U.N. Human Rights Committee in Response to the Second and Third Periodic Report of the United States", Atlanta: U.S. Human Rights Network.

Global Rights/Partners in Justice (2005) "Hearing on the Situation of Domestic Employees of Diplomatic and International Officials and Staff." 14 October.

Gordon, J. (2005) *Suburban Sweatshops: The Fight for Immigrant Rights*. Cambridge, Mass.: Belknap Press of Harvard University Press.

Hondagneu-Sotelo, P. (2001) *Doméstica: Immigrant Workers Cleaning and Caring in the Shadows of Affluence*, Berkeley: University of California Press.

Human Rights Watch (2001) *Hidden in the Home: Abuse of Domestic Workers with Special Visas in the United States*, New York: Human Rights Watch.

Inter-American Commission on Human Rights (2006) *Annual Report of the Inter-American Commission on Human Rights 2005*, Washington, D.C: OAS.

Inter-American Commission on Human Rights (2004) *Annual Report*.

Inter-American Commission on Human Rights (2002) *Annual Report*, Chapter VI.

Inter-American Commission on Human Rights (2001) *Annual Report*, Chapter VI(c).

Inter-American Commission on Human Rights (1999) *Annual Report*, Chapter VI(c).

Inter-American Commission on Human Rights (1998) *Annual Report*, Chapter VI(c).

Inter-American Commission on Human Rights (1997) "Report of the Inter-American Commission on Human Rights on the Status of Women in the Americas", *in Annual Report 1997*, Chapter VI.
Inter-American Commission on Human Rights (1996) *Annual Report*, Chapter VI.
Inter-American Convention on the Elimination of All Forms of Discrimination Against Persons with Disabilities (1999) 7 June.
Inter-American Court of Human Rights (2003) *Juridical Condition and Rights of the Undocumented Migrants*, Advisory Opinion OC-18/03 (2003).
Inter-American Court of Human Rights (1999) *The Right of Information on Consular Assistance in the Framework of the Guarantees of the Due Process of the Law*, Advisory Opinion OC-16/99 of October 1, 1999.
Inter-American Court of Human Rights (1989) *Interpretation of the American Declaration of the Rights and Duties of Man Within the Framework of Article 64 of the American Convention on Human Rights*, Advisory Opinion OC-10/89 of July 14, 1989.
International Labor Organization, *About MIGRANT*. Retrieved June 26, from http://www.ilo.org/public/english/protection/migrant/about/index.htm .
International Labor Organization (2003a). *Preventing Discrimination, Exploitation and Abuse of Women Migrant Workers: An Information Guide — Booklet 1: Why the Focus on Women International Migrant Workers*, Geneva: ILO.
International Labor Organization (2003b). *Preventing Discrimination, Exploitation and Abuse of Women Migrant Workers: An Information Guide — Booklet 2: Decision-Making and Preparing for Employment Abroad*, Geneva: ILO.
International Labor Organization (2003c). *Preventing Discrimination, Exploitation and Abuse of Women Migrant Workers: An Information Guide — Booklet 3: Recruitment and the Journey for Employment Abroad*, Geneva: ILO.
International Labor Organization (2003d). *Preventing Discrimination, Exploitation and Abuse of Women Migrant Workers: An Information Guide — Booklet 4: Working and Living Abroad*, Geneva: ILO.
James, F. & M. Dorning (2001) "Under Fire, Chavez Withdraws", *Chicago Tribune*, 10 January. Page 1.
Kapur, R. (2002) "The Tragedy of Victimization Rhetoric: Resurrecting the 'Native' Subject in International/Post-Colonial Feminist Legal Politics", *Harvard Human Rights Journal* 15: 1–37.
Keyes, E. (2005) "Testimony Before the Inter-American Human Rights Commission", 14 Oct. 2005.
Koh, H. H. (2003) "On American Exceptionalism", *Stanford Law Review* 55: 1479–1527.
Lewis, H. (2001) "Universal Mother: Transnational Migration and the Human Rights of Black Women in the Americas." *Journal of Gender, Race & Justice* 5: 197–231.
Lyon, R. S. (2003) "Inter-American Court of Human Rights Amicus Curiae Brief: The United States Violates International Law When Labor Law Remedies are Restricted Based on Workers' Migrant Status", *Seattle Journal for Social Justice* 1: 803–804.
Lyon, B. and S. Paoletti (2003/4). "Inter-American Developments on Globalization's Refugees: New Rights for Migrant Workers and their Families", *European Yearbook of Minority Issues* 3: 63–87.

Micek, P. (2006) "Indonesian Trafficking Victim Wins Settlement." Retrieved June 27, 2006, from http://news.newamericamedia.org/news/view_article.html?article_id=610a56fa6feb55b166125e7c5543dc4d.

Maeda, D. (2002) "Inter/National Migration of Labor: LatCrit Perspectives on Addressing Issues Arising With the Movement of Workers: Agencies of Filipina Migrants in Globalized Economies: Transforming International Human Rights Legal Discourse", *La Raza Law Journal* 13: 317–342.

National Labor Relations Act (2006), U.S. Code, title 29, sec. 152(3).

Occupational Safety and Health Act (OSHA) (2006) U.S. Code, title 29, sec. 651(b).

Parreñas, R. S. (2001) *Servants of Globalization: Women, Migration and Domestic Work*. Stanford, Calif.: Stanford University Press.

Sassen, S. (1984) "Notes on the Incorporation of Third World Women into Wage Labor Through Immigration and Offshore Production," *International Migration Review* 18: 1144.

Sassen, S. (1998) "Notes on the Incorporation of Third World Women into Wage Labor Through Immigration and Offshore Production", in Saskia Sassen (ed.), *Globalization and its Discontents*, New York: The New Press, pp. 111–172.

Satterthwaite, M. (2005) "Crossing Borders, Claiming Rights: Using Human Rights Law to Empower Women Migrant Workers," *Yale Human Rights and Development Law Journal*, 8. Retrieved July 12, 2006, from http://papers.ssrn.com/sol3/papers.cfm?abstract_id=680181.

Satterthwaite, M. (2005) "Testimony Before the Inter-American Commission on Human Rights." 14 October.

Scheer, R. (2004) "Kerik's 'Nannygate' Was the Least of It," *Los Angeles Times*, 14 December, p. 13.

Scholte, J. A. (2000) *Globalization: A Critical Introduction*, New York: St. Martin's Press.

Shelton, D. (2002) "Globalization and the Erosion of Sovereignty: Protecting Human Rights in a Globalized World", *Boston College International and Comparative Law Review* 25: 273–322.

Sim, A. and V. Wee (2002) "Labour Migration by Filipina Domestic Workers to Hong Kong: Conditions, Process and Implications", Paper presented at the International Workshop on Contemporary Perspectives on Asian Transnational Domestic Workers, Singapore, 23–25 February 2004.

Steiner, H. J. and P. Alston (2000) *International Human Rights in Context: Law, Politics, Morals*, (2nd ed.) New York: Oxford University Press.

Taran, P. A. and E. Geronimi (2002) *Globalization, Labor and Migration: Protection is Paramount*. Geneva: ILO.

United Nations Development Fund for Women (2003) *Not a Minute More: Ending Violence Against Women*. New York: UNIFEM.

United Nations Committee on Economic, Social, and Cultural Rights (2002) *General Comment No. 15 on the Right to water*, paras. 23–24. Retrived June 28, 2006, from http://www.unhchr.ch/tbs/doc.nsf/(Symbol)/a5458d1d1bbd713fc1256cc400389e94?Opendocument.

United Nations Committee on the Elimination of Discrimination Against Women (1989) *General Recommendation No. 12 on Violence Against Women*. Retrieved June 26, 2006, from http://www.un.org/womenwatch/daw/cedaw/recommendations/recomm.htm#recom12. United Nations Human Rights Committee (2000) *General Comment No. 28 on Equality of Rights between Men and Women*. Retrieved July 1, 2006, from http://www.unhchr.ch/tbs/doc.nsf/(Symbol)/13b02776122d4838802568b900360e80?Opendocument.

United Nations Human Rights Committee (1989) *General Comment No. 18 on Non-discrimination.* Retreived June 28, 2006, from http://www.unhchr.ch/tbs/doc.nsf/(Symbol)/3888b0541f8501c9c12563ed004b8d0e?Opendocument.

United Nations Committee on the Elimination of Racial Discrimination (2004) *General Recommendation No. 30 on Discrimination Against Non-Citizens.* Retrieved June 28, 2006, from http://www.unhchr.ch/tbs/doc.nsf/(Symbol)/e3980a673769e229c1256f8d0057cd3d?Opendocument. United Nations Committee on the Elimination of Racial Discrimination. (2000) *General Recommendation No. 25 on Gender-Related Dimensions of Racial Discrimination.* Available at http://www.unhchr.ch/tbs/doc.nsf/(Symbol)/76a293e49a88bd23802568bd00538d83?Opendocument (Accessed June 28, 2006.)

U.S. Department of State (2000) *Foreign Affairs Manual*, vol. 9, sec. 41.21 N6.2(A)(1), 9 February, 2000.

U.S. Department of State, *Foreign Affairs Manual*, vol. 9, secs. 41.31, note 6; 41.21, note 6.2. Available at http://foia.state.gov/regs/fams.asp?level=2&id=10&fam=0. (Accessed June 28, 2006.)

United States Department of Labor Bureau of Labor Statistics (2005) *Women in the Labor Force: A Databook.* Washington, D.C: BLS.

Wilson, R. J. (2002) "The United States' Position on the Death Penalty in the Inter-American Human Rights System." *Santa Clara Law Review* 42: 1159–1190.

Young, D. E. (2001) "Working Across Borders: Global Restructuring and Women's Work." *Utah Law Review*: 1–73.

Velasco, G. (2005) "Testimony Before the Inter-American Commission on Human Rights." 14 October.

Contributors

Monica Boyd, F.R.S.C., joined the University of Toronto in 2001 as Canada Research Chair in Equity and Health and as professor of sociology. Previously, she was the Mildred and Claude Pepper Distinguished Professor of Sociology at Florida State University, arriving from Carleton University in Ottawa, Canada. Trained as a demographer and sociologist, Dr. Boyd has written numerous articles, books, and monographs on the changing family, gender inequality, international migration (with foci on policy, on immigrant integration and on immigrant women) and ethnic stratification. Social inequality is a core theme in her research. Her current research projects are on immigrant inequalities in the labour force, and the migration of high skilled labor and related re-accreditation difficulties, with particular emphasis on women. She also is the recipient of a research grant from the (Canadian) Social Science and Humanities Research Council in regard to the socioeconomic achievements, intermarriage and acculturation of the children of immigrants in Canada (the 1.5 and 2nd generations). She has written papers and made presentations about migrant women for various UN agencies.

Hugo Ángeles Cruz is a full-time researcher in the academic area Society, Culture and Health of El Colegio de la Frontera Sur (ECOSUR), in the city of Tapachula, Chiapas, Mexico, where he has been working on subjects related to international migration in the southern border of Mexico. He has a masters degree in demographics from, and is now a PhD candidate in population studies at El Colegio de México. His previous publications include the edited book *La población en el sureste de México* (2005, El Colegio de la Frontera Sur, and Sociedad Mexicana de Demografía, Tapachula, Chiapas) and the article "Las migraciones internacionales en el Soconusco: un fenómeno cada vez más complejo" (in *Comercio Exterior*, Vol. 54, No. 4).

Belinda Dodson is a social geographer with a regional specialization in Southern Africa. She has an honours degree from the University of Kwazulu-Natal in South Africa and a PhD in geography from Cambridge

University. Her research interests fall within two broad areas: gender, migration and development; and historical and contemporary human-environment relations in South Africa. She was a lecturer at the University of Cape Town from 1990 to 1997 and a research associate of the Southern African Migration Project (SAMP) from 1997 to 2002, serving as a gender advisor. Since then she has been a faculty member at the University of Western Ontario, where she is an associate professor in the Department of Geography. In addition to writing policy papers for SAMP, she has published articles on Southern African migration issues in *Feminist Review*, *Africa Today*, *Canadian Journal of African Studies* and the *South African Geographical Journal*.

Elsie Ho is senior research fellow in the Migration Research Group of the University of Waikato, New Zealand. She has previously held teaching appointment at the Hong Kong Polytechnic University, and obtained her PhD in psychology from University of Waikato in 1995. Dr. Ho is an active researcher in the areas of cross-cultural adaptation of immigrants, refugees and international students, and has published several book chapters and numerous journal articles on the topics of Asian transnational communities, acculturation, migrant settlement, identity development and mental health, as well as diversity issues in the workplace and in the classrooms. She is a consulting editor of the *Journal of Immigrant and Refugee Studies*, an Honorary Visiting Research Fellow in the School of Social Science of the University of Adelaide, and an Honorary Research Fellow in the Centre of Asian Studies of the University of Hong Kong.

Siew-Ean Khoo is senior fellow in the Demography and Sociology Program in the Research School of Social Sciences at the Australian National University. A graduate of Harvard University, she has worked with the East-West Population Institute at the East-West Center, the Bureau of Immigration, Multicultural and Population Research and the Australian Government's Department of Immigration and Multicultural Affairs. She has published widely on international migration and immigrant settlement issues and is joint editor and contributing author of two recent books, *The Transformation of Australia's Population, 1970–2030* (Sydney: University of New South Wales Press, 2003) and *Public Policy and Immigrant Settlement* (Cheltenham, UK: Edward Elgar, 2006).

Eleonore Kofman is professor of gender, migration and citizenship at Middlesex University, UK. She has published widely on gendered migrations in Europe and is particularly interested in family and skilled migrations. She has co-authored the book *Gender and International Migration in Europe: employment, welfare and politics* (Routledge 2000) and co-edited books on *Globalization: theory and practice* (Continuum, 2003) and *Mapping Women, Making Politics: feminist perspectives on political geography* (Routledge, 2004).

Contributors

Deanna Pikkov is a PhD candidate at the University of Toronto in the Department of Sociology. Her main interests are in inter-group relations and immigrant integration. Previous research includes studies of educational and income attainments of immigrants and minorities. Her current research is on the political integration of newcomers, including a study of electoral participation among immigrants to Canada. The explanatory value of language proficiency and differing political cultures, conceived as a product of levels of democratization in source countries, are estimated, and found to be key predictors of voting. The positive obligations of the state with regard to civics education and democratic inclusion, and the various attempts of liberal democratic states in this regard, are a related focus of her work.

Nicola Piper was senior research fellow at the Asia Research Institute, National University of Singapore and has recently taken up a senior lectureship in geography at Swansea Univeristy in the UK. She holds a PhD in sociology from the University of Sheffield in the UK and had previous appointments with the Nordic Institute of Asian Studies in Copenhagen and the Australian National University in Canberra. Her research interests revolve around international economic migration, governance and policy networks, gender, non-governmental organisations and transnational political activism, the rights of migrants, with empirical focus of Southeast and East Asia as well as Europe. She is the author of the book *Racism, Nationalism and Citizenship* (1998), the co-editor of the volumes *Women and Work in Globalising Asia* (2002), *Wife or Worker? Asians Marriage and Migration* (Rowman & Littlefield, 2003), *Transnational Activism in Asia — Problems of Power and Democracy* (Routledge, 2004), as well as the author of numerous journal articles and background papers for various international organizations such as IOM, UNESCAP, UNRISD, and the Global Commission on International Migration (the paper entitled *Gender and Migration*).

Martha Luz Rojas Wiesner is a full-time researcher in the academic area Society, Culture and Health of El Colegio de la Frontera Sur (ECOSUR), in the city of Tapachula, Chiapas, Mexico, where she conducts studies related to international women migration in the southern border of Mexico. She is a PhD candidate in sociology at El Colegio de Mexico. Her previous publications include the article "La frontera de Chiapas con Guatemala como región de destino de migrantes internacionales" (in *Ecofronteras*, No. 19, 2003, with Hugo Angeles Cruz) and the chapter "Mujeres migrantes en la frontera sur de México" (2002), in *Migración: México entre sus dos fronteras, 2000–2001*, Foro Migraciones, Mexico, D. F.

Margaret L. Satterthwaite is assistant professor of clinical law at New York University (NYU) School of Law, where she co-directs the International Human Rights Clinic and is one of the faculty directors of the Center for

Human Rights and Global Justice (CHRGJ). Prof. Satterthwaite became a lawyer after many years in the human rights field, having worked for Amnesty International, Street Law, and the Haitian Truth Commission before attending law school. She clerked for Judge Betty Fletcher of the Ninth Circuit Court of Appeals in 1999–2000 and the International Court of Justice in 2001–2002. She came to NYU after working for Human Rights First and the U.N. Development Fund for Women. Her research focuses on human rights abuses in the "war on terror," the law of transfer and migration, and feminist approaches to international human rights law. Prof. Satterthwaite frequently consults with U.N. agencies, serves on the Board of Directors of Amnesty International USA, co-directs the Human Rights Interest Group of the American Society of International Law, and is a member of the International Law Committee of the New York City Bar Association.

Carmen Voigt-Graf worked as postdoctoral fellow at the Australian National University, after completing her PhD in geography at the University of Sydney in 2002. She joined the University of the South Pacific in Fiji in early 2004 as a lecturer. Her research focuses on the link between labour markets and migration, development and migration, highly skilled migration, skills development, and migrant transnationalism. Regionally, her research is focused on the Pacific Island region, Australia and the Indian diaspora. She has published several book chapters and articles in international journals, and has been involved in commissioned work by the Commonwealth Secretariat and the Asian Development Bank among others. Carmen is Assistant Coordinator of the Asia and Pacific Migration Research Network (APMRN) for the Pacific Island Region, and a Steering Committee member of the IGU Commission on Population and Vulnerability.

Keiko Yamanaka is a sociologist who is a lecturer in the Department of Ethnic Studies, and International and Area Studies, University of California, Berkeley. Since 1993, she has studied transnational migration and social transformation in Japan, focusing on two contrasting immigrant populations: authorized resident Brazilians of Japanese ancestry, and unauthorized Nepalese. In recent years she has investigated feminized migration, civil actions and emerging multiculturalism in East Asia. She has published articles and chapters on these topics in both English and Japanese. Her recent publications include: "Changing family structures of Nepalese transmigrants in Japan: Split-households and dual-wage earners" (*Global Networks*, 2005), and "Immigrant incorporation and women's community activities in Japan: Local NGOs and public education for immigrant children" (*Local Citizenship in Recent countries of Immigration*, Lexington Books, 2006). She has co-edited "Gender, migration and governance in Asia" (Special Issue, *Asian and Pacific Migration Journal*, 2003), and co-authored *Feminized Migration in East and Southeast Asia: Policies, Actions and Empowerment* (Occasional Paper 11, the United Nations Research Institute for Social Development, 2006).

Index

A
Abolitionist feminists, 161
Abusive practices
 against Central American transiting migrants in Mexico, 229–230
 difficulty of factory workers' escape from, 255
 for domestic workers, 6
 due to single-employer contracts, 250
 gendered differences in, 252
 name and shame methodology to expose, 315
 recognition of, 178
 towards immigrants at southern border of Mexico, 228–229
Accreditation, for intercultural specialists, 70
Activism, transnational and trans-institutional, 262–263
Adult worker model, 83
Advocacy networks, 249
Affiliation, 93
Affirmative action
 limited site of employment coverage for, 43
 poor enforcement in North America, 21
Africa, paucity of statistical data, 3
African Union system of human rights protection, 278
Agency
 lack of female worker, 256
 political, 251–253
 studies on migrants' political, 253–254
Agricultural labour
 in Asia, 161, 250
 below-minimum wage payments to, 300

Chiapas entry point for, 219
coffee harvesting in Mexico, 214
employer prevention of labor organisations, 300
in Guatemala, 217–221
by Guatemalans in Mexico, 218
and human rights for migrant farmworkers in U.S., 300
Mexican workers in Canada by sex, 208
from Mexico, 194
in Southern Africa, 147, 148
and three Ds, 254
American Convention on Human Rights, 290
American exceptionalism, and human rights law, 289–291
Amicus curiae briefs, 315
Ángeles Cruz, Hugo, 323
Apartheid, 137, 145
Asia. *See also* East Asia; Southeast Asia
 as contributor of migration flows to Australia and New Zealand, 103–104
 international students in Australia, 109
 number of unskilled female migrant workers by sending country, 164
 outflow of women from, 162–164
 patterns of labour migration in, 249–250
 policy differences from Europe, 168
 three source countries of female migrants, 160
Assertiveness
 discrimination against female workers', 175
 national, 183

Associational rights, 256
  impediments to, 258
  legal and normative framework, 256–258
  in practice, 258–259
Astronaut families, in New Zealand, 118
Asylum seekers, 2, 8
  disentitlements affecting, 80
  in Europe, 60, 78–80
  female labour outcomes in Oceania, 115
  in Germany, 82
  political activities issues for women, 79
  reduced openness in Europe, 65
  in South Africa, 144
Au pairs, 69–70
Australia
  categories of entry, 104 (*See also* Oceania)
  diversification of Asians in, 5
  emigration from, 111–113
  emigration of nurses and teachers, 111
  employment rates by duration of residence, 117
  female labour market outcomes, 115–119
  gendered migration in, 101–103
  health care coverage for settlers, 125
  humanitarian immigrant category, 104
  international migration as significant policy issue, 102
  language proficiency and employment outcomes in, 116
  migrant hairdressers in, 120
  overstayers in, 113, 123
  percentage of female settler arrivals by migration category, 107
  percentage of female settler arrivals by visa category, 107
  percentage of female temporary migrants and family members, 109
  settler arrivals by migration category, 105
  settler migration in, 103–107
  as source and destination country, 101
  temporary visa extensions in, 129
  Women at Risk subcategory, 104
  working holiday visas, 109
Australian diaspora, 5, 14
Australian National University, 324, 326
Austria
  female immigrants in hospitality sector, 66
  maintenance of citizenship restrictions in, 92
Autonomous decision-making
  among female migrant workers in Pacific Islands, 121
  by female Mexican migrants, 202
Awareness
  as first step to empowerment, 252
  raising for migrant workers' rights, 251

B
Baird, Zoe, 33, 275
Bali Process, 114
Bangladesh, 8
  restrictions on women's mobility in, 263
Benefits, absence for nonunionized women, 38
Bifurcation, between skilled and less skilled migration, 5, 9
Bodily integrity, 93
Botswana, 139
Boyd, Monica, 323
Bracero Program, 195, 234
  female migration to U.S. predating, 200
Brain drain, 4
Breadwinner model, 94
  replacement by adult worker model, 83
Brideprice, as motivation for male migration in Southern Africa, 139
Brokers, 6
Business, collusion with governments in Asia, 168

C
California Proposition 187, 47–48
Canada
  categories of admission for immigrants, 24
  gender stratification of immigrants, 19
  Immigration and Refugee Protection Act (IRPA), 28

Irregular immigrants in, 35
Live-In Caregiver Program (LCP), 45
migration of Mexican women to, 206–209
point system for immigration, 32
Temporary Agricultural Workers Program, 206
temporary worker category, 32
Woman at Risk program, 30
Canadian Live-In Caregiver program, 26
CARAM Asia, 265
Care deficit
    in Europe, 83
    in industrial countries, 37
Care services, marketisation in Europe, 67, 84–85
Caregivers
    in Asia, 161
    in Canada, 32
    Canadian programs, 45
    in European countries, 73
Caretaking, international transfer of, 279
Celestine case, 306–307
Central America
    Mexico as country of transit for, 191
    migrations to Mexico due to political violence, 215–216
CERD Committee, 310–311
Chavez, Linda, 317
Chiapas
    armed Zapatista movement in, 213
    asylum seekers in, 210
    detention by principal country of origin, 226
    detention of foreign women by region of origin, 225
    intensification of migration into, 227
    as major recipient of Central American workers, 216
Child care
    for children of female Mexican migrants, 225–226
    in France, 87
    in Germany, 87–88
    marketization in Europe, 85
    in Spain, 87–88
    in Sweden, 85–87
    in UK, 87
Chilling effect, 48
Circular migration, 7
    shift toward, 4

Citizen women
    increased labour force participation of, 83
    opportunities for work and family care through migrant women, 83
Citizenship, 11, 15, 22
    stratification of, 46
    U.S. path to, 34, 35
Civil Rights Act, domestic workers' exclusion from Title VII coverage, 283
Civil society organizations, 262, 267
    role in migrant political advocacy, 259
Class
    as impediment to alliance formation, 263–264
    and local citizen support for migrant rights, 264
Coalition of Immokalee Workers, 308, 313
Cohabiting partners, polities in Europe, 75
Collective activism, 262
Collectivism, in Canadian values, 21
Colonialism
    effects on migration patterns in Europe, 59
    effects on sources of skilled labour, 90
    effects on UK migration, 82
    and regional migration in Southern Africa, 137
Community work, in Europe, 70–71
Congo, 144
Construction sector
    in Asia, 250
    and three Ds, 254
Contract workers
    in Asian countries, 168
    in domestic work in Asia, 169
    prohibitions for unskilled workers in Japan and Korea, 170
    and violations of domestic workers' human rights, 280–281
Control over environment, 93
Convention Against Torture and Other Cruel, Inhuman or Degrading Treatment of Punishment, 290
Convention on the Elimination of All Forms of Discrimination Against Women, 290

Convention on the Elimination of All
    Forms of Racial Discrimination,
    290
Council of Europe system, 278
Coyotes, 195
Credentialing problems
    among migrants in Europe, 73
    for family-linked migrant women in
        Europe, 77
Cross-border movements, 1
    as means of securing livelihoods in
        Asia, 159
    of skilled women in Asia, 174
    South African permits for, 151
    in Southern Africa, 146, 148, 155
Cross-border passes, in South Africa,
    151–152, 154

D
Dangerous, difficult, dirty (3Ds),
    253–254
De-skilling, 8
    of immigrant female labour in
        Germany, 69
    of immigrant women in Europe, 68
Debt bondage, 281, 282
Decommodification, of social benefits,
    81
Demand structure, and source
    countries of female migration,
    160
Democratic space, absence in Asian
    countries, 250, 252
Demographics
    of male/female migrants in Southern
        Africa, 145–146
    of Mexican-born workers in U.S.,
        196
Dependency, through family-linked
    female migration, 76
Deportations
    avoiding via general interest hearing,
        308
    increases in North America, 48
    in South Africa, 145
    threats for domestic workers, 276
Destination countries. *See also*
    Receiver countries
    class interactions with ethnicity/non-
        citizen status in, 264
    Hong Kong, 250
    Malaysia, 250
    Mexico, 209–212

Singapore, 250
Detention centers
    and domestic workers, 281
    in Mexico, 223, 236
    in Oceania, 128–129
Development issues
    in East/Southeast Asia, 176–177
    linking migration to, 179
    and rights, 160
Diasporas, 14
    in Australia, 5
Diplomatic immunity, 285, 308, 312,
    315
    as issue for abuses of domestic
        workers, 277
    and special visas for domestic
        workers, 280, 282
Discrimination
    by devaluation of educational
        credentials, 42
    against lack of education/language
        skills, 24
    against rights-conscious women and
        nationalities, 175–176
    in South African Immigration Acts,
        151–154
    Southern African women's escape
        from, 139
Diversification, of intra-group
    differences, 5
Doctors
    emigration from Pacific Islands, 121
    foreign-born in Europe, 72
Dodson, Belinda, 323–324
Domestic violence, 77, 125
    exploitative terms of work, 280–285
    as human rights violation, 288
    and independent migration of
        Mexican women, 226
Domestic workers, 8, 14
    and ability to change employers, 93
    abuses connected with
        compensation, 282
    abuses of Guatemalan women in
        Mexico, 222
    advocacy for inclusion in national
        labour laws, 261
    by au pairs, 69–70
    back pay issues, 317
    ban on migrant womens' marriages
        to permanent citizens, 170
    conflicts with diplomatic immunity
        provisions, 313

at crossroads of three human rights norms, 301
delayed payments to, 282
demand in Asia, 161
denial of days off/sick days, 283
differences in official recognition as employment sector, 169–170
difficulty of obtaining work permits for, 77
dishonoring of contracts by employers, 280–281
in East/Southeast Asia, 169–170, 250
employment of women by nationality in Europe, 89
empowering through Inter-American System of human rights law, 275–277
in European countries, 66, 67–70
exclusion from labour legislation in Asia, 169–170, 267, 268
exclusion from NLRA provisions in U.S., 283, 311
exclusion from U.S. labour law protection, 275
failure to be protected as category, 302
fear of retaliation for legal claims, 285
female dominance in, 8
female migrants to South Africa, 139
Fijian women, 112
Guatemalan women in Mexico, 231
and immigration requirements in Canada, 32
Indonesian migrants, 249
and invisible/informal economy, 45
lack of rights to file civil complaints against employers, 281
legal and extra legal protection for, 265
live-in, 317
need for Special Rapporteurs for, 301
NGO assistance to migrant workers in, 260
nonrecognition as legal work, 258
on-site visits for human rights abuses, 313–316
partial protection under U.S. labour laws, 276
political repercussions for political appointees, 275
recasting claims as protected categories, 312
rightless nanny phenomenon, 280–285
in South Africa, 143, 147
in Southern Africa, 148
in Sweden vs. other European countries, 88–89
in Taiwan, 167
and three Ds, 254
unawareness of protective laws, 284
undercutting of wages and long working hours in, 68, 170
union organisation in Hong Kong, 266
unpaid overtime in, 68
vulnerability of, 6, 148
as vulnerable job category, 263
for women in migration, 2
as work of low social esteem, 68
Domestic Workers United, 314
Doubly disadvantaged, 37
Dual citizenship, increase in, 11

E
East Asia. *See also* Asia; Southeast Asia
changes in female migration, 175–176
control vs. protection in migration management, 177–179
domestic workers in, 169–170
entertainers in, 170–171
feminised migration in, 159–160
gendered advocacy and migrant labour organising in, 247–249
global policy discourse, rights, and development issues, 176–177
immigrant wives in, 172–173
Japanese-Brazilian and Korean-Chinese workers in, 173–174
linking migration and development in, 179
major categories of migrant female workers, 169
migration policies in, 168–169
skilled workers in, 174–175
statistics of feminised migration, 162–169
stock of resident migrant women in, 165–167
temporary labour in, 3
unauthorized workers in, 171–172
Eastern European women, as domestic workers in Europe, 69

Index

Economic development
  impact of migration on, 5
  and unstable economic conditions for women, 36
Economic migration, 2, 24
  in North America, 23–24
  percentage of female immigrants in U.S. and Canada, 27
Educated women, blocks to career paths in Europe, 76
Education
  female employment by nationality in Europe, 89
  of female/male Mexican migrants to U.S., 203–204
  and female unemployment in Oceania, 118
  as feminised sector, 6
  and gender stratification of female immigrants, 29
  of immigrants to Mexico, 211
  male bias in South African work permit structure, 152
  Scandinavian and UK employment of women in, 91
Educational credentials, devaluation for foreign-born workers, 41–43
El Colegio de la Frontera Sur (ECOSUR), 323, 325
Elder care
  in France, 87
  in Germany, 69, 87–88
  links to work permits in Germany and Italy, 69
  marketization in Europe, 85
  needs in Australia, 110
  in Spain, 87–88
  in Sweden, 85–87
  in UK, 87
Elderly immigrants, risks in North America, 46–47
Emigration
  from Australia, New Zealand, Pacific Islands, 111–113
  and loss of skills from Pacific Island countries, 121–123
  from South Africa, 144
  from Zimbabwe, 144
Employment agencies, in Asia, 250
Empowerment
  conceptual basis of, 251–253
  of foreign workers, 247–249
  gendered differences in experiences of, 252
  limited chances for socio-economic, 180
  links to rights and socio-economic development, 159
  through application of human rights law, 275–277
Entertainment workers, 182
  demand in Asia, 161
  in East/Southeast Asia, 162, 170–171, 250
  female dominance among, 8
Entitlements, 9–11
  changes in North America, 43
  decline in, 47–48
  for detainees in Oceania, 128–129
  difficulty of transferring within Europe, 60
  distinguishing from rights, 9
  and entry status, 45–47
  erosion for native residents, 22
  in Europe, 59–62
  and immigration status in Europe, 73–75
  increasing stratification in Europe, 64
  in Oceania, 123–131
  partial, 45–47
  problems for irregular immigrants in Europe, 75
  and return migration, 130–131
  stratification of, 11
  tying to linguistic knowledge, 78
Entry criteria, 49
Entry status, and partial entitlements, 45–47
Equal protection of law, 301, 304, 310
Equality, as principle of human rights law, 301
Ethnic discrimination, of domestic workers, 276
Europe
  asylum seekers and refugees in, 78–80
  caregiving work in, 73
  community and intercultural work for migrants, 70–71
  diversification of migration patterns, 60
  domestic work in, 67–70
  employment of foreign-born women by sector, 90
  employment of women by

nationality, 89
entitlements in, 59–62
family-linked migration in, 75–78
female employment by sector and birth status, 65
female employment for homestate women, 84
French services for immigrants, 87
gender and immigration categories, 63–65
gendered migration in, 59–62
German services for immigrants, 87–88
immigration status and entitlements in, 73–75
international migration by category of entry, 63
labour migration in, 65–78
livelihoods in, 59–62
migrant labor in, 88–91
percentage of women in highly skilled occupations, 71
percentage of women in immigrant population, 64
policy differences from Asia, 168
skilled labour in feminised sectors, 71–73
Spanish services for immigrants, 87–88
Swedish services for migrants, 85–87
UK services for immigrants, 87
welfare regimes and migration in, 81–85
European Union, benefits of mobility within, 60
Exceptional skills permit, in South Africa, 151

F
Faith-based organizations, 259
Family disintegration, as cost of migration, 232
Family reunification, 7, 24
absence of policies in Asia, 162
in Australia, 104
as criterion for migration in North America, 23–24
difficulties with South African permit structure, 153
European limitations on, 74
European policies on, 75–78
in France, 82
increased restrictions in European policies, 64–65
as main route of legal entry into EU, 63
and marriage relationship requirements in Australia, 125
as minor rationale for female Mexican workers in U.S., 226
as motivation for Mexican migrant women, 189
in New Zealand, 126
patterns in Europe, 59
percentage of female immigrants in U.S. and Canada, 27
predominance of women in Australia, 106
restrictions in Europe and Asia, 181
Family separations, 48
Female migrants
changes in East/Southeast Asia, 175–176
changes in head-of-household status among Mexican, 204
confinement to traditional roles in Asia, 250
domination of sectors outside of conventional trade unionism, 267
drivers of, 146
from Mexico to Canada, 209
official neglect of needs in Southern Africa, 137
and quest for alternative livelihoods in South Africa, 142
rise in share of, 3
wage comparisons with men from Mexico, 205
Feminisation
of contemporary migration, 2, 178, 249
of health care, 6
and male shift in occupations, 14
of migration in East/Southeast Asia, 159–160, 160–162
of migration patterns in Southern Africa, 138–139
of migration to South Africa, 141
and obstacles to worker organisation, 248
quantitative for Mexican workers in U.S., 199
and skilled labor in Europe, 71–73
Feminisation of survival, 19, 36
in Europe, 75

Feminised jobs, growing demand for, 3
Feminism, approaches to agency and empowerment, 252
Fiji
  Chinese temporary garment workers in, 121, 127, 128, 132
  emigration from, 132
  occupational categories of emigrants by gender, 122
  as source and destination country, 103
  view of emigrants as traitors, 112–113
Filipinas
  as domestic workers in Europe, 69
  nursing presence in Europe, 72
Fish farm workers, in Asia, 161
Forced labour, in U.S., 315
Formal equality model, 305
Fortress South Africa, 149
France, 62
  family-linked migration in, 76
  service provision for immigrants, 82, 87
  withdrawal of spousal right to work, 94
Fraudulent documentation, 33
Freedom of association, 256, 257. *See also* Associational rights
Front door policies, in Asia, 168

G
Garment workers
  in Asia, 161
  in Fiji, 121
Gender
  and contradictory outcomes of empowerment, 252
  as impediment to migrant alliance formation, 263–264
  and migrant politics, 247, 254–256
  role in stratified/polarized modes of entry, 6–9
  statistical neglect in sources of migration data, 163
  vs. sex in effects on political alliances, 248
Gender stratification, in North American female immigrants, 19
Gendered advocacy, 259–261, 266–268
  in East/Southeast Asia, 247–249
Gendered migration, xi
  in East/Southeast Asia, 159–160
  in European welfare regimes, 59–62
  in North America, 189–191
  in Oceania, 101–103
  in Southern Africa, 137–138
Gendered stratification, in international migration, 1–2
Geneva Convention refugees, 15, 80
German Immigration Law, 74
Germany, 62
  guest worker regime in, 59
  legal forms of domestic work, 68–69
  restrictions on spousal labour in, 77
  service provisions for immigrants, 87–88
  social provisions for immigrants in, 81–82
Global Commission on International Migration (GCIM), 176
Global hypergamy phenomenon, 172
Global migration flows, shifts in, 2–5
Global policy discourse, in East/Southeast Asia, 176–177
Global solidarity networks, 265
Globalisation
  links to gender roles/sex discrimination, 278–279
  and marketization of care services, 67
  of social reproduction, 83
Gold widows, 138, 139
Guatemala
  agricultural workers and women's role, 217–221, 236
  asylum seekers to Mexico, 210
  counterinsurgency movement, 215
  labour flows at Chiapas border with, 216–217
  Mexico border as focus of migratory intensity, 214–216
  refugees to Mexico from, 191
  as transit country for migrants to U.S., 236
  women in domestic service in Mexico, 221–222
Guest workers, 7
  de facto in U.S., 34, 35
  in Germany, 59
  unskilled labor and, 74

H
H-1B visa, for temporary high skill workers, 33
H-1C visa, for nurses, 33
Habilitadores, 218, 219

Hairdressers, in Australia, 120
Health care coverage
  lack among Mexican workers in U.S., 196
  as motivation for female migration in Southern Africa, 147
  for settler arrivals in Australia, 124
  in U.S. and Canada, 21, 47
Health sector
  as employer of foreign women in Singapore, 165
  European immigrant labor in, 66
  female employment in Europe, 89
  and female migrant workers in Asia, 250
  migrant employment in Sweden, 88
  reduction in effectiveness in Pacific Islands, 121
Health workers
  out-migration of, 4
  Sub-Saharan African women as, 3–4
Healthcare as feminised sector, 6
High-skilled women. *See also* Skilled workers
  in Europe, 71
  noncorrespondence with high-skill employment, 40
HIV/AIDS, in Southern Africa, 149
Ho, Elsie, 324
Hoffman Plastics Compounds, Inc. v. National Labour Relations Board, 303, 312
Home language instruction, in Europe, 72
Honduras, emigration to Mexico from, 215–216
Hong Kong, 166
  contract migration policies in, 168
  lack of middle-class support for FDWs, 263
  organisation of migrant domestic workers in, 266, 268
  as receiver country, 165, 250
Hotel industry
  female employment in Europe, 89
  and female immigrant labour in Europe, 65
  increasing dependence on female labour in Europe, 66
Human rights law. *See also* Rights
  advocacy using Inter-American norms, 313–316
  and American exceptionalism, 289–291
  empowering migrant workers in Inter-American system using, 275–277, 286
  and interpretive practices of Court of Human Rights, 293–296
  reaching private conduct through, 287–289
  rights of migrants and women under, 301–302
  state obligations under, 288–289
  and women's vulnerability, 286–287
Human Rights Watch, 280, 282, 284
Human security, deterioration of, 5
Humanitarian modes of entry, 24, 28
  gender composition of, 106
  and percentage of female immigrants in North America, 29
  under-representation of women in, 9

I
Immigrant wives, in East/Southeast Asia, 172–173
Immigration categories
  and entitlements in Europe, 73–75
  in Europe, 63–65
  prohibition of employment in South Africa, 151
Immigration policies
  Canada and U.S., 19
  in East/Southeast Asia, 168–169
  high fees in Canada and U.S., 26
  reform in South Africa, 149–154
Individualism, in U.S. values, 21
Indonesia, 161
  number of unskilled female migrant workers, 164
  as significant exporter of labour, 249
  as source country for female migrants in Asia, 160
Inequalities, regulating in North America, 40–43
Informal economy, 266
  domestic workers and, 45
  failure of trade unions to consider, 248
  and migrant women in Europe, 92
  as obstacle to worker organization, 247, 258
  in South Africa, 139
Information technology, female employment by nationality in Europe, 89

Integration
  as indicator of successful settlement, 115
  mandatory for European immigrants, 78
Inter-American Commission on Human Rights, 306–307
  Celestine case, 306
  general interest hearings, 307–309
  indirect jurisdiction over U.S. via OAS, 291
  individual petitions through, 309–313
  interpretive practices of, 293
  Special Rapporteurs of, 296–297, 297–298
  Statehood Solidarity Committee case, 307
  U.S. dealings with, 281–283
Inter-American Court of Human Rights, 291, 302–306
  advisory jurisdiction, 292, 295
  appeal to *Jus cogens* norms, 302–303
  Garrido and Baigorria Case, 288
  interpretive practices by, 291, 293–296
  substantive equality model, 305–306, 309
  Velasquez-Rodriguez case, 288
  Villareal case, 293, 296
Inter-American Human Rights System, 13
  empowering migrant domestic workers through, 275–277
  promoting rights of U.S. migrant domestic workers using, 301–312
  work to counter U.S. violations, 289
Inter-American norms, advocacy using, 313–316
Intercultural work, in Europe, 70–71
International Confederation of Free Trade Unions (ICFTU), 261, 269
International Convention on the Protection of the Rights of Migrant Workers and Members of Their Families, 276
International Covenant on Civil and Political Rights, 290
International human rights, 12
  lack of attention in Asia, 159
  neglect in Asian government migration policies, 168

International Labour Organization (ILO), 160, 176
  on associational rights, 256
  cooperation with ICFTU, 269
  migrant specific instruments, 13
  rights-based approach to migration, 258
International matchmaking services, 172, 176
International migration, xi
  contradictory gender outcomes of empowerment, 252
  and gendered stratification, 1–2
  potential to reinvigorate labour activism, 267
Internet, and dissemination of statistical information, 234
Intra-company transfer permit, in South Africa, 151
Intra-European migration, gendered nature of, 60
Invisibility, of sex trade, 258
Irregular workers, 7. *See also* Undocumented migrants
  comparison of Oceania and US, 113
  converting into temporary workers, 22
  in Europe, 62
  females in Europe as, 75
  livelihood and protection in North America, 39–40
  in North America, 33–36
  in Oceania, 113–114, 123, 128–130
  and skill levels in Europe, 73–74
  and U.S. de facto guest-worker regime, 34
  work permits in Thailand, 181
Islamophobia, in European countries, 80

J
Japan, 166
  aloofness of citizen support for rights of migrant workers, 264
  back door migration policies in, 168–169
  entertainment workers in, 167
  marriages between Japanese women and Asian immigrant men, 182
  Nikkeijin in, 173
  prohibitions against unskilled migrant workers, 250
  sex trade in, 162
  short-term visas for unauthorised workers, 171
  spousal visa rules, 173

trainee system for unskilled workers in, 167, 250
Japanese-Brazilian workers, 173–174
numbers in Japan, 167
Jus cogens norms, 302

K
Kerik, Bernard, 317
Khoo, Siew-Ean, 324
Kofman, Eleonore, 324
Korea, 166
  back door migration policies in, 168–169
  female migrant worker population in, 167
  historical intermarriage policies, 172–173
  prohibitions against unskilled migrant workers, 250
  sex trade in, 162
  sex workers from, 162
  short-term visas for unauthorised workers, 171
  trainee system in, 171–172, 250
Korean-Chinese workers, 173–174
Kraal, 155

L
Labour force
  deregulation in North America, 49
  percent by sex, 38
Labour market inequalities, in North America, 37–38
Labour migration
  in Europe, 64, 65–67
  halting in Europe, 63
  increasing formalisation and stratification in Europe, 64
  to mines in South Africa, 140
  patterns in Asia, 249–250
  rights-based approach to, 160
  in Southern Africa, 139
Labour protections
  decline in U.S., 39
  limits of coverage for, 40
  neglect of in Asian government policies, 168, 169–170
Language proficiency
  and barriers to North American immigration, 44
  and employment outcomes in Australia, 116, 119
  shifting of burden for, 45
  tying entitlements to, 78

Language teaching, as employment opportunity in Europe, 72
Latin America, paucity of statistical data, 3
Law, gendered nature of, 248
Legal migration, male-dominated sectors of, 279
Liberal professions, rights in EU countries, 90
Liberal welfare states, 21
Live-in domestic workers, 317. *See also* Domestic workers
Livelihoods, 10
  in Europe, 59–62, 81–85
  gendered, 36–43
  for irregular migrants in North America, 39–40
  migration strategy in South Africa, 144
  securing in East/Southeast Asia, 159–160
  in Southern Africa, 137–138
  strategies for securing, 9–11
Lobbying system, in U.S. politics, 20
Long-term care, and migrant work, 69

M
Malaysia, 166
  ban against male Bangladeshi workers in, 181–182
  contract migration policies in, 168
  as largest importer of labour in Asia, 165, 250
  prohibition against union organizing by legal migrants, 258, 268
  undocumented workers in, 172
Malcolm X, 318
Male unemployment, 6
  in Asia, 162
  as motivation for female migration, 3
Manufacturing industries
  in Asia, 250
  decline in male-dominated, 37
Marital conflict, due to split households, 162
Marriage relationship requirements
  in Australia, 125
  ban on marriage to permanent citizens in Asia, 170
  and informal domestic relations with host country men, 181
  in Korea and Japan, 172–173
Means-testing, in UK immigration policies, 82

338 Index

Memoranda of Understanding (MoUs), use in Asia, 178
Mexico
   age composition of immigrants to, 211
   age of migrants to U.S., 201–202
   classification of states into migration-based regions, 235
   consequences of restructuring of economy, 193–194
   as country of origin, transit, and destination, 13, 189–191, 192–193
   as country of refuge, 191
   as destination country, 192, 209–212
   detention of foreigners, 223, 225, 226, 230
   diversification of migrants' place of origin, 197
   documented Guatemalan agricultural workers in, 219
   emerging human rights issues, 228–233
   emigrants from urban areas, 194
   five phases of emigration to U.S., 234
   foreign female domestic workers in, 231
   growing unemployment and underemployment, 194
   Guatemala border as focus of migratory intensity, 214–216
   Guatemalan women in domestic service in, 221–222
   historical role as receiving country, 191
   independent migration of women, 189
   index and degree of migratory intensity by state, 198
   international migrants' region of origin, 227–228
   labour flows at Chiapas-Guatemala border, 216–217
   marital status of temporary migrants, 202
   migrants' places of origin, 204
   migration of women to Canada, 206–209
   migration to U.S., 5
   Oaxaca and Veracruz roles in transit corridor from Central America, 224
   percentage distribution of temporary migrant women returning to, 203
   percentage of foreign-born residents in, 210
   previous migration experience of migrants to U.S., 205
   role of Quintana Roo in migration, 214
   socioeconomic gaps between states, 194
   southern border as site of international migration, 190, 191, 212–214
   systematic loss of population, 196
   temporary labour migrants in, by sex, 200, 201
   as transit country, 192, 212–214, 222–227
   triple role in migratory process, 191–192
   vs. Philippines as labour exporting country, 249
   women migrating domestically to border towns, 190
   women remaining in place of origin, 190, 233
Mexico-Belize border area, 213–214
Mexico-Guatemala border, 214–216
Mexico-U.S. migration, 193–199
   females in, 199–206
   return of migrants with U.S.-born children, 235
Middlesex University, 324
Migrant Forum in Asia (MFA), 265
Migrant labour
   advocacy for recruiting into trade unions, 261
   in Europe, 88–91
   as resource for poverty reduction and sustainable development, 179
   Special Rapporteur on, 298–301
Migrant labour organising, 259–261. *See also* Trade unions
   in East/Southeast Asia, 247–249
   gendered differences in opportunities for, 252–253
Migrant politics, and gender, 254–256
Migrant rights, 11–13
Migrant women
   in Europe, 60
   and labor market in Oceania, 114–123
   in North America, 19–22

MIGRANTE International, 264–265
Migrants
  association with crime in U.S., 231–232
  failure to be protected as category, 302
  percentage in Asia, 249
  rights under international human rights law, 301–302
  and work of Special Rapporteurs of Inter-American Commission, 296–297
Migrating wives, 7
Migration, Remittances, Aid and Bureaucracy (MIRAB) states, 112
Migration criteria, in North America, 23–24
Migration management, control vs. protection in Asia, 177–179
Migration research, 1
Minimum wage levels
  and abuses of domestic workers, 275
  initiatives to establish, 178
  U.S. violations for domestic workers, 282
Mobility
  Bangladeshi restrictions on women's, 263
  domestic workers' restricted, 285
  in European Union countries, 60
  as regional characteristic of Southern Africa, 137
  restrictions for females in Asia, 161
Modes of entry
  in Australia, 104
  humanitarian-based, 9
  in New Zealand, 106–107
  in Oceania, 103–114
  role of gender in stratified/polarized, 6–9
  for women in North America, 25–28
Motives, for migration in Southern Africa, 147–149
Muslim countries
  suspicions of in Europe, 80
  targeting by European immigration policies, 65
Muslim women, perceived oppression of, 80

N
Name and shame methodology, against abuses, 315
Nannygate phenomenon, 33, 275–277
National identity, threats to, 78
National Labor Relations Act (NLRA), 317
  domestic workers' exclusion from, 283
National University of Singapore, 325
Neo-liberal discourse, 49
  and absence of resources for immigrants, 28
  effects on migrants in North America, 23
  impacts on gendered livelihoods, 36
  and lack of funding for anti-discrimination laws, 42
Networks, 248, 263
  among migrant workers, 262–266
  regional vs. national, 264
  transnational and trans-institutional, 264–266, 266
Networks theory, 248
New York University School of Law, 325
New Zealand. See also Oceania
  astronaut families in, 118
  emigration from, 111–113
  employment rates by duration of residence, 117
  female labour market outcomes, 115–119
  gendered migration in, 101–103
  modes of entry in, 106
  occupational classifications by gender, 120
  settler migration in, 103–107
  as source and destination country, 101
Nikkeijin, 173–174
Non-discrimination, as principle of human rights law, 301
Non-status workers, U.S. illegality of, 39
Nongovernmental organizations (NGOs), 267
  as advocates for empowerment, 251
  in Malaysia and Singapore, 259
  need to collaborate with trade unions, 254
  and problems specific to women migrants, 257
  protection of migrants' rights by, 250
  role in worker advocacy, 248
  as vehicles for political organization, 253
  women's organisations and migrant rights, 259

North America. *See also* Canada; Mexico; United States
  changed migration rules in, 22–31
  declining settlement assistance in, 43–45
  decreased entitlements in, 43, 47–48
  elimination of country-origin criteria, 23
  entry status and partial entitlements in, 45–47
  family *vs.* economic migration in, 23–25
  gendered livelihoods in, 36–37
  gendered migrations in, 189–191
  gendering of refugees in, 28–31
  irregular migrants in, 33–36
  labour market inequalities in, 37–38
  livelihood and protection of irregular migrants in, 39–40
  migrant women in, 19–22
  modes of entry for women in, 25–28
  percent distribution of immigrants by source area, 23
  regulating inequalities in, 40–43
  temporary workers in, 31–36
North American Free Trade Agreement (NAFTA), 31
Nurses, 8, 127
  demands in Australia, 110
  demotion to care assistants, 93
  emigration from Fiji, 121
  emigration from Pacific Islands, 121
  encouragement of migration to U.S. and Canada, 40–42
  European recruitment of foreign-born, 72
  H-1C visa for, 33
  from Korea and Philippines, 174, 182
  reduction in UK recruitment, 93

O

Oceania
  detainee conditions in, 128
  emigration from, 103
  entitlements waiting period for new migrants, 124
  gendered migration in, 101–103
  illegal work in, 128–130
  irregular migration in, 113–114
  migrant entitlements in, 123–131
  migration policies in, 103–114
  policy shifts in, 123–131
  return migration and entitlements in, 130–131
  temporary migration of workers and foreign students, 108–111
  temporary residence and employment in, 119–121
Organization of American States, U.S. membership in, 290, 291
Origin countries, 10
Out-migration
  banning of female, 8
  of native citizens from settler countries, 5
Outcomes, in Oceania, 103–114

P

Pacific Islands. *See also* Oceania
  emigration and loss of skills from, 121–123
  emigration from, 111–113
  female labour force participation rates, 116
  gendered migration in, 101–103
  MIRAB system in, 112
Pensions
  international portability in Oceania, 130, 131
  transferring within EU, 60
Permanent residence
  and backdoor immigration in U.S., 31
  decline in South Africa, 140
  eligibility in U.S., 22
  higher education as pathway in Australia, 110
  lack of opportunities for family members in South Africa, 153
  of Mexican workers in U.S., 195–196
  for migrant spouses in Australia, 125
  percentage female in Canada and U.S., 26
  unreachability for migrants in Asian countries, 168
Permit categories, in South Africa, 151
Persecution, and refugee status, 31
Personal Responsiblity and Work Opportunity Reconciliation Act (PRWORA), 48
Petty traders, in South Africa, 143, 147
Philippines, 161
  absentee voting rights, 261
  activism in mobilising migrant workers, 263
  as best organized group of migrants, 261

entertainer visas for migrating women, 8
international dispersal of workforce, 163, 249
as largest labour exporting country, 3, 163, 249
number of unskilled female migrant workers, 164
rights of family members left behind, 261
self-organising by migrant workers from, 259
sex workers from, 162
as source country of female migrants in Asia, 160
Phuket Declaration, 262
Pikkov, Deanna, 325
Piper, Nicola, 325
Polarization, 5
in modes of entry, 6–9
Political alliances, 262–266
gender and class impediments to formation of, 263–264
Political participation
conceptual basis of, 251–253
differences between foreign- and native-born, 253
by foreign workers, 247–249
gendered differences among Latinos/as in New York, 255
issue areas, 261–262
as opposite of passivity and social exclusion, 251
studies on migrants', 253–254
Political rights, 11
need to address in Asia, 159
Pregnancy, and domestic workers' deportation in Asia, 170
Private sphere
accessing through human rights law, 287–289
association of women with, 183
difficulty of conceptualizing as workplaces, 275
exclusion from federal non-discrimination statutes, 276
human rights obligations in, 386
obligation of states to halt abuses in, 276
vs. obligations of states, 288–289
women's employment in, 280
Privatization
of care services in Europe, 85
of social service provision, 21

Professional women, and exploitation of nannies, 278–279
Protection issues, for North American migrants, 39–40
Provisional spouse visa, in Australia, 125
Public assistance, barring of legal non-citizens from, 48
Public education, challenges to rights in California, 48
Public sphere, 183

Q
Quintana Roo, 214
Quota work permit, 152
in Asian countries, 168
in South Africa, 151

R
Racial discrimination, of domestic workers, 276
Receiver countries
in Asia, 165
meaninglessness of, 5
Mexico, 189–191
occupation, immigration status, country of origin in Asia, 166
Recruiters, 6
of domestic workers, 281
from Guatemala to Mexico, 218
of Mexican labourers in U.S., 195
Refoulement, 29
Refugees
androcentric definition of, 30
disentitlements affecting, 80
in Europe, 78–80
gendering in North America, 28–31
from Latin American countries to Mexico, 209
in Mexico, 235
to Mexico, 191
in South Africa, 144
Regional movements, 1, 2, 265
driving factors in Southern Africa, 142–145
post-apartheid changes in Southern Africa, 140–142
Remittances, 133
importance in Fiji, 122
by Mexican labourers in U.S., 196
to Pacific Island countries, 112
role in Southern African migration, 146

342 Index

Reproductive labor, global division of, 278–279
Resettlement criteria, in North America, 28–31
Residence permits, in domestic violence cases, 77
Resources, as criterion of family migration in Europe, 77
Restaurants, and female immigrant labour in Europe, 65
Return migration, and entitlements in Oceania, 130–131
Reversed gender roles, and marital conflict in Asia, 162
Rights, 9–11, 175, 177. See also Human rights law
  associational, 256–259
  and development, 160
  distinguishing from entitlements, 9
  of domestic workers, 280–285
  emerging issues in Mexico, 228–233
  formal exclusion of migrants from, 61
  increasing stratification in Europe, 64
  issues in East/Southeast Asia, 176–177, 261–262
  lack of attention in Asia, 159
  legal withholding in Europe, 61
  of migrant women in transit to U.S., 225, 232
  of migrants, 11–13
  poor access by migrants, 12
  precariousness for unskilled workers in Europe, 74
  raising workers' awareness of, 251
  recognition of *vs.* demand for, 12
  stratification of, 11, 90
Rights-Based Approach (RBA), 176, 177, 258
  to labor migration, 160
Rojas Wiesner, Martha Luz, 325
Rotational labour migration
  from Eastern Europe, 73
  in Europe, 63
Rwanda, 144

S
Safety nets, fraying of, 49
Same-sex couples
  European policies on, 75
  recognition in Australia, 104
Satterthwaite, Margaret L., 325
Self-organising, 252, 261
  of migrant workers, 259–261

Sender countries
  East/Southeast Asia, 164
  meaninglessness of, 5
  Mexico, 189–191
Service economy, and labour market inequalities, 37
Service provision
  exclusion of entertainment workers from, 171
  in Sweden, 85–87
Settlement, privatization of responsibility for, 43–44
Settlement assistance, limits in North America, 44
Settler countries, 22
  Australia and New Zealand, 103–107
Settler migration, 103
  in Australia and New Zealand, 103–107
Sex trade
  in Asia, 161
  in Australia, 123
  globalization of, 66
  invisibility from trade union standpoint, 258
  in Japan and Korea, 162
  lack of alternatives for women in, 148
  in South Africa, 145
  as violation of human rights, 171
Sex workers, 36. See also Trafficked women
  female dominance among, 8
Sex workers' rights, controversy over, 171
Sexual harassment, of domestic workers, 276
Short-term contract work, for Asian women, 162
Singapore, 166
  contract migration policies in, 168
  as destination country for migrant workers, 250
  highest ratio of foreign migrants to locals in, 165
Skill improvement issues, 179
Skilled/unskilled migration, increasing bifurcation, 5
Skilled workers
  and changes in South African immigration policy, 149–151
  as current emphasis in Australia, 105, 110

as current emphasis in New Zealand, 106
as current emphasis in Oceania, 104
disincentives in South African immigration policy, 153
in East/Southeast Asia, 168, 174–175
in Europe, 62
in feminised European sectors, 71–73
intensified hunt for, 14
male dominance among, 8
non-guarantee of permanent residency, 7
occupational groups in Oceania, 119
problems for women in Europe, 77
settlement and family reunification rights for, 74
in South Africa, 143, 154
unemployment and underemployment of female, 175
vs. unskilled in Europe, 73
welcoming in Europe, 74
Skills drain, 4
Social capital, 251
Social movement unionism, 254
Social reproduction, 67
in European countries, 72
globalisation of, 62, 83
role of migrant women in Europe, 60
Social rights, need to address in Asia, 159
Social services provision. *See also* Entitlements
and care deficit, 37
devolution in North America, 44
differences between Canada and U.S., 21
increasing inequalities for immigrants, 50
privatization of, 21
reductions in, 37
for temporary migrants in Oceania, 126
South Africa
bias toward women in cross-border passes, 154
diamond and gold mining industries, 138
discrimination in 2002 and 2004 Immigration Acts, 151–154
downsizing of male mine workforce, 142
emigration of skilled workers from, 144
fortress mentality, 149
Immigration Acts of 2002/2004, 138, 149
immigration policy reform, 149
male bias in skilled migration, 143
permit categories in, 151
relative regional economic strength, 137
salami approach to immigration, 151, 153
shift from alien control to skills import emphasis, 149–151
treatment of deportees in, 145
South African Human Sciences Research Council (HSRC), 141
South Asia, as labour-exporting subregion, 180
Southeast Asia. *See also* Asia; East Asia
changes in female migration, 175–176
control *vs.* protection in migration management, 177–179
domestic workers in, 169–170
entertainers in, 170–171
feminised migration in, 159–160
gendered advocacy and migrant labour organising in, 247–249
global policy discourse, rights, and development issues, 176–177
immigrant wives in, 172–173
linking migration and development in, 179
major categories of migrant women workers, 169
migration policies, 168–169
prohibition against migrant self-organising, 259
skilled workers in, 174–175
statistics of feminised migration, 162–169
stock of resident migrant women in, 165–167
temporary labour in, 3
unauthorised workers in, 171–172
Southern Africa. *See also* South Africa
contemporary gender differences/dynamics in migration, 145–149
divided families in, 139
factors driving new migrant flows, 142–145
gendered migration in, 137–138
historical migration patterns, 138–139

Southeast Asia (*continued*)
  immigration policy reform in, 149–154
  male/female demographics of migration, 145–146
  motives, patterns and experiences of male/female migration, 147–149
  petty traders in, 143
  post-apartheid changes in regional migration flows, 140–142
  rural-urban migration research, 138
Southern African Development Community (SADC) countries, 141, 155
Southern African Migration Project (SAMP), 145, 155
Southern Europe
  demand for female labour in, 63
  domestic work as dominant migrant labor form in, 67, 68, 92
  emphasis on domestic work in, 62
  employment rates for homestate women, 84
  family-linked migration in, 76
Spain, 62
  female immigrants in hospitality sector, 66
  historical migrations to Mexico, 209–210
  service provisions for immigrants, 87–88
Special Rapporteurs
  of Inter-American Commission on Human Rights, 296–297
  on migrant workers and their families, 298–301, 318
  on rights of migrant domestic workers, 301
  on women's rights, 297–298
Sponsorship obligations
  in Australia and New Zealand, 126
  disadvantaging of women by, 27
Spousal dependency, 94
  in Europe, 77
Sri Lanka, 161
  number of unskilled female migrant workers, 164
  as source country for female migrants in Asia, 160
State regulation, 7
  gendered dimensions of, 6
Statistical invisibility, 4
  in Oceania, 132

Statistical visibility, of migrant women, 2
Statistics, of feminised migration in East/Southeast Asia, 162–169
Stratification, 5
  in modes of entry, 6–9
Students
  in Australia, 109–110
  temporary migration in Oceania, 108–111
Substantive equality model, 305–306, 309
Swansea University, 325
Swaziland, 130
Sweatshop work, female dominance in, 8
Sweden, 62
  decommodification in, 81
  family-linked migration in, 76
  opening of labour migration in, 81
  service provision for immigrants, 85–87
Switzerland
  inclusion in EU migratory space, 92
  restrictions on spousal labour in, 77

T
Taiwan, 166
  contract migration policies in, 168
  official scheme for temporary labour import, 250
Teachers, emigration from Fiji, 121
Temporary labour, 5, 7, 21, 50
  and entitlements in Oceania, 126–128
  exploitation in Oceania, 127–128
  increased length of stay in U.S., 195
  in North America, 31–36
  as obstacle to organisation, 247
  in Oceania, 101, 119–121
  as sole means of migration in Asia, 168
  in Southeast/East Asia, 3
  vs. irregular workers, 114
  work rights in Australia, 114
Temporary migration
  shift toward, 4
  in South Africa, 140
  of workers and foreign students in Oceania, 108–111
Temporary protection visa (TPV), 128, 129
Thailand, 166

number of unskilled female migrant workers, 164
Phuket Declaration, 262
as receiver country, 165
sex workers form, 162
trafficking of women from, 161
undocumented workers in, 172
Third country women, overrepresentation in Europe, 61
Tourism management, by immigrant women in Europe, 70
Trade unions, 253, 257, 267
  ambivalent stance on migrant labour, 253
  employers' tactics to keep migrants from, 258
  gendered analysis of politics, 255
  historical anti-immigration stance, 248
  legal migrants' right to form and joint, 256
  limits of transnationlism within, 265–266
  for migrant workers, 247–249
  need to collaborate with NGOs, 254
  power over defining legitimate workers, 257
  root cause of recent loss of power, 262
  sector specificity of, 260
Trading, as motivation for female migration in Africa, 147
Trafficked women, 7, 132
  in Australia, 130
  domestic workers, 282
  in Europe, 66
  in Mexico, 231
  in North America, 35–36
  in Oceania, 113
  in South Africa, 145
  from Thailand, 161
Trainee system, 182
  in Japan, 167, 250
  in Korea, 171–172
Trans-Tasman Travel Agreement, 101, 102, 104
Transit countries, Mexico, 189–191, 212–214, 222–227
Transnationalism
  acvitism in context of, 262
  in family structures in South Africa, 153
  limits of union-related, 266
  in networking, 264–266
  in political activism, 262–263
  in Southern Africa, 137
  and split households in Asia, 162
  in union labour consciousness, 253

U
UK, 62
  Highly Skilled Migrants Programme, 74
  means-testing in, 82
  regulation of domestic work in, 69
  service provision for immigrants, 87
UN Convention on the Elimination of All Forms of Discrimination Against Women (CEDAW), 15
UN Convention on the Rights of All Migrant Workers and Their Families (CRMW), 12
UN Convention on the Rights of the Child (CRC), 15
UN High Commissioner for Refugees (UNHCR), 30
UN Human Rights Council (UNHRC), 28
UN International Convention on the Protection of the Rights of All Migrant Workers and Members of Their Families (CRMW), 126, 127
UN Office for the High Commissioner on Human Rights (OHCHR), 177
UN Research Institute for Social Development (UNRISD), xiii
UN Special Rapporteur on Human Rights of Migrants, 237
Undocumented migrants, 4. *See also* Irregular workers
  and abuse in domestic work situations, 170
  conditional amnesty for, 34
  in East/Southeast Asia, 171–172
  equating with drug traffickers and criminals in U.S., 231–232
  in EU, 63, 73
  fear of exposing migration status in legal claims, 284
  fear of vulnerability, 314
  general interest hearing on status of U.S., 307–308
  and inability to participate in amnesty, 35

Undocumented migrants (*continued*)
  international crackdowns on, 14
  obstacles to trade union organising, 248
  in Southern Africa, 148
  trade union issues, 257–258
  U.S. Supreme Court decision on back pay for, 303
Unemployment
  among recent immigrants to Oceania, 118
  benefits policies in Oceania, 123–124
United States
  attempts to insulate self from human rights norms and oversight bodies, 276
  categories of admission for immigrants, 25
  conditional amnesty for illegal immigrants, 34
  consequences of membership in OAS, 290, 291
  de-facto guest-worker regime based on irregular migrants, 34
  dealings with Inter-American Commission and Court, 281–283
  as destination for 98 percent of Mexican emigrants, 192
  disdain for work of regional human rights bodies, 277
  disregard for authority of Inter-American Commission, 292
  exceptionalism towards international law, 289–291
  forced labour in, 315
  forced returns of Mexican immigrants to, 305
  gap between immigration law and demand for cheap labour, 280
  gender stratification of immigrants in, 19
  Immigration Act of 1990, 32
  Immigration Reform and Control Act (1986), 194–195
  Inter-American Human Rights System and violations in, 289
  Inter-American Human Rights System jurisdiction over, 276
  lengthening of migrants' stay in, 195
  permanently settled workers from Mexico in, 195
  promoting migrant domestic workers' rights through Inter-American system, 301–312
  strict immigration laws of, 280
  temporary workers from Mexico in, 195
  tightening of border controls, 195
  view of migrants as associated with criminal groups, 231–232
  wage asymmetry with Mexico, 193
University of California at Berkeley, 326
University of Toronto, 323, 325
University of Waikato (New Zealand), 324
University of Western Ontario, 324
Unskilled work, 6, 266
  in Asia, 168
  attempts by South Africa to limit, 150
  in Europe, 62
  and family reunion visa categories in Oceania, 119
  in Japan and Korea, 169
  by Mexican labourers in U.S., 196
  number of female workers by sending country, 164
  prohibitions in Japan and Korea, 250
  in South Africa, 154
  and trainee system in Japan, 167
  in U.S. for Mexican workers, 193
  by women in Oceania, 115
Upward mobility
  barriers for immigrant women, 40
  by migrant women *vs.* men, 255

V
Victimization stance, 286–287
Vienna Convention on Consular Relations, 293
  applicability to U.S. violations of human rights, 295–296
Vietnam, as source country for factory workers, 161
Violence Against Women Act (VAWA), 36
Visitors' visas, violation of terms, 33
Voice institutions, 252
Voigt-Graf, Carmen, 326
Vulnerability
  as obstacle to court filings in U.S., 311
  as product of political-economic forces, 286–287

W

Wal-Mart, arrest of undocumented workers at, 34
War on terror, 289
Weapons of the weak, 256
Welfare benefits, 81
  reduced use due to chilling effect, 48
  restrictions in North America, 47
Welfare regimes
  in Europe, 81–85
  typology of European, 86
White Australia policy, 103
Women
  denial of life choices to, 252
  as dependants of expatriate men in Asia, 174–175
  economic migrations from Mexico to U.S., 226
  entry into male-dominated streams, 4
  increased burden of household survival on, 10
  labour force participation rate in Australia, 115
  as majority of European immigrants, 64
  migration from Mexico to Canada, 206–209
  migration from Mexico to U.S., 199–206
  participation in Oceania labour market, 114
  percentage in European immigrant population, 64
  as petty traders in South Africa, 143
  as preferred agricultural workers in Mexican coffee harvest, 220–221
  prohibition against employment in South Africa, 153
  ranking by nationality, ethnicity, class, and education in Asia, 176
  relative neglect in Southern Africa migration studies, 138
  as reliable remitters in Fiji, 122
  rights under international human rights law, 301–302
  state-imposed bans on outflow of, 163
  underrepresentation in official statistics, 163
  visions of politics, 254–255
  and weapons of the weak, 256
  and work of Special Rapporteurs of Inter-American Commission, 296–297, 297–298
Women's rights organizations, 260
Women's vulnerability, and human rights law, 286–287
Women's work, 19
  devaluing in Europe, 66
  failure to acknowledge economic and social value of, 91
  undervaluing in Europe, 60
Wood, Kimba, 275
Work ethic, and reduced entitlements, 47
Work permits, 91
  difficulties for non-principal asylum applicants, 79
  problems with domestic and unskilled work, 74
  for spouses of skilled temporary migrants in Australia, 126, 127
Worker/labour NGOs, 259–260
Workers, human rights of, 301
Worker's compensation, rights to, 39
Working conditions
  advocacy for, 261
  of rightless nannies, 280–285
Working holiday visas, 119
  in Australia, 109
Workplace abuses
  of domestic workers, 278–279
  limited ability to denounce, 38

X

Xenophobia, 4
  against migrants in U.S., 299
  in South Africa, 148, 149
  towards foreign nurses in Europe, 72

Y

Yamanaka, Keiko, 326

Z

Zimbabwe
  diaspora from, 144
  economic crisis in, 141
  migration to South Africa from, 141

Lightning Source UK Ltd.
Milton Keynes UK
UKOW020152311211

184573UK00014B/56/P